DATE DUE			

A Da Capo Press Reprint Series

FRANKLIN D. ROOSEVELT AND THE ERA OF THE NEW DEAL
GENERAL EDITOR : FRANK FREIDEL
Harvard University

———————

PART-TIME FARMING IN THE SOUTHEAST

Division of Research
Work Projects Administration

Research Monographs

Works Progress Administration
Division of Social Research
Research Monograph IX

PART-TIME FARMING
IN THE SOUTHEAST

By
R.H. Allen
L.S. Cottrell, Jr.
W.W. Troxell
Harriet L. Herring
A.D. Edwards

DA CAPO PRESS • NEW YORK • 1971

A Da Capo Press Reprint Edition

This Da Capo Press edition of *Part-Time Farming in the Southeast*
is an unabridged republication of the first edition published in Washington, D.C., in 1937. It is reprinted by permission from a copy of the
original edition owned by the Harvard College Library.

Library of Congress Catalog Card Number 74-165677
ISBN 0-306-70341-6

Published by Da Capo Press, Inc.
A Subsidiary of Plenum Publishing Corporation
227 West 17th Street, New York, N.Y. 10011

Manufactured in the United States of America

PART-TIME FARMING
IN THE SOUTHEAST

WORKS PROGRESS ADMINISTRATION

Harry L. Hopkins, *Administrator*

Corrington Gill, *Assistant Administrator*

DIVISION OF SOCIAL RESEARCH

Howard B. Myers, *Director*

PART-TIME FARMING
IN THE SOUTHEAST

By

R. H. Allen · L. S. Cottrell, Jr. · W. W. Troxell
Harriet L. Herring · A. D. Edwards

•

RESEARCH MONOGRAPH IX

1937

UNITED STATES GOVERNMENT PRINTING OFFICE, WASHINGTON

Works Progress Administration,
Washington, D. C., March 1, 1937.

Sir: I have the honor to transmit the results of a study of combined farming-industrial employment conducted in the Southeast by the Federal Emergency Relief Administration. Comparative social and economic data for part-time farmers and for nonfarming industrial workers form the basis for this report. The findings are fundamental to any proposal for the public encouragement of part-time farming, both in the Eastern Cotton Belt and in other areas.

The report emphasizes the fact that while part-time farming has proved beneficial to families engaged in it, such farming activity can be expanded only where industry has sufficiently recovered from the depression to offer satisfactory wages and hours to its workers, or where future prospects for an industry's development are promising. It is unlikely that industries will resume the long hours of predepression days. Workers today are in the process of adjusting their habits to the additional leisure that shorter hours have given them, and the encouragement of part-time farming activities at this time, under proper safeguards, will help to absorb this margin of leisure time and will increase income.

Instruction in improved farming methods and in every phase of farm operation from planting to preservation of the product was found to be needed throughout the Southeast. It is believed that assistance by educational agencies will make existing part-time farms more consistent producers of food and of a varied diet.

The study was made by the Division of Social Research, under the direction of Howard B. Myers, Director of the Division. The data were collected under the general supervision of T. C. McCormick. Analysis of the data was made under the supervision of T. J. Woofter, Jr., Coordinator of Rural Research. The report was edited by Ellen Winston and Frances Mason.

The work of setting up the study and of collecting and analyzing the material was the joint responsibility of R. H. Allen, whose services were made available by the Land Policy Section, Division of Program Planning of the Agricultural Adjustment Administration, L. S. Cottrell, Jr., and W. W. Troxell. Mr. Allen was mainly responsible for the material on farming operations, Mr. Cottrell and A. D. Edwards for the social aspects of the problem, and Mr. Troxell for the industrial analyses. Harriet L. Herring prepared the present summary volume.

Respectfully submitted.

Corrington Gill,
Assistant Administrator.

Hon. Harry L. Hopkins,
Works Progress Administrator.

Contents

PART I

PART II

FIGURES

Part I

Part-Time Farming in the Southeast

INTRODUCTION

BACKGROUND AND REASON FOR STUDY
Part-Time Farming an Old Practice

ONE OF the conspicuous changes wrought by the industrial revolution was the concentration of working people in cities. No longer, the critics of its ruthless march complained, could the journeyman, with his few apprentices, live in his cottage, and tend his small plot of land in odd moments taken from the craft he followed as his main occupation. Not only did the coming of the factory bring monotony into his work and increase the uncertainty of his employment, but at the same time it took away from him the healthful activity on his garden plot, his little bulwark against the ups and downs of the market. Division of labor, it appeared, had arrived, not only within the work place, but within society. Men tended machines and lived in towns and cities or tended farms and lived in the country.

The clear-cut distinction that came to be made between rural and urban activities has perhaps blinded many students of socio-economic life to the fact that there always have been some workers who managed to combine the two. Such combinations have existed in New England from the beginning of the nineteenth century, for the soil was stony and the opportunity for a supplementary cash wage was offered in many rural localities by small factories. As the industrial cities grew, overrunning the nearby fields, they were populated by waves of immigrants who came from rural areas. These people were accustomed to intensive cultivation of small plots of ground, and always a few of them escaped the teeming slums to tend abandoned farms.[1]

In the South, industrial development came tardily, and for a generation longer than in most other areas, the weaver, the cabinet-maker, the wheelwright, and the cooper plied their trades in sparsely settled areas. With limited markets for their services, they made part of their living from the land. When industrial development did

---

[1] Davis, I. G. and Salter, L. A., Jr., *Part-Time Farming in Connecticut*, Bulletins 201 and 204, Department of Agricultural Economics, Connecticut State College, March and July, 1935; Rozman, David, *Part-Time Farming in Massachusetts*, Bulletin 266, Massachusetts Agricultural Experiment Station, 1930.

come, it brought the industrial village to isolated locations. These villages were laid out where land was cheap on the premise that a rural people out of reach of stores, both financially and physically, could tend gardens.

With the coming of the automobile and improved roads, the rural dweller was placed within reach of industrial employment in the city and the urban industrial worker was placed within reach of land on a scale that had not existed since the rise of the factory system. City-weary people with city jobs could and did move to the country for esthetic reasons, for the creative pleasure of growing things, for space for their children, and for the economy and freedom of country life. The farmer went to the nearby village, town, or city for a cash wage that would help to stabilize an income based on gambling with both the weather and the market.

Extent of Part-Time Farming

So common had the custom of combining farming with other employment become that the United States Census of Agriculture took cognizance of it in 1930 by counting and classifying the farm operators who worked part-time off their farms. Granting the inaccuracy and incompleteness of any census of farmers and farming, the numbers discovered were impressive—approximately 1,903,000 persons, or 30.3 percent of all farm operators of the United States, reported some time worked off their farms. More than a million of them worked 50 days or more off the farm, and half of these (540,000) worked 150 days or more, thus enabling them to be classified as part-time farmers, according to the 1930 Census definition.[2] A quarter of a million (267,000) worked 250 days, or had what amounted to practically full-time jobs off the farm.[3]

During the depression the general movement of people from country to city was retarded, and on January 1, 1935, the farm population was over a million and a third larger than in 1930.[4] Almost

---

[2] Those farms were classified as part-time farms whose operators spent 150 days or more at work in 1929 for pay at jobs not connected with their farms or reported an occupation other than farming, provided the value of products of the farm did not exceed $750. This presupposes the census definition of a farm as comprising at least 3 acres or more unless it produced $250 worth of farm products or more in 1929. Under the 2 definitions there were 339,207 persons classified as part-time farmers in 1929 (*Fifteenth Census of the United States: 1930*, Agriculture Vol. III, pp. 1 and 12). Census figures in this introduction include the total number of persons reporting time off the farm rather than the more limited group of part-time farmers as determined by these definitions.

[3] *Fifteenth Census of the United States: 1930*, Agriculture Vol. IV, p. 430.

[4] *United States Census of Agriculture: 1935*. It is generally agreed among agricultural economists and students of population, however, that census procedure was so changed in 1935 as to result in a much more complete enumeration of small farms than in any earlier census.

2 million of the total farm population in 1935, or 1 out of every 16 persons on farms, had been living in a nonfarm residence 5 years earlier. Many of them were unemployed, having returned to farms owned by themselves or relatives, or having become squatters on other people's land. They had moved from urban areas to secure the benefits of low living costs, or to carry on subsistence farming, or for both reasons. A large number of them, however, had retained or found employment in villages, towns, or cities.

The number of operators employed 50 days or more off the farm was higher in 1934 than in 1929, despite the unemployment and part-time work prevalent in 1934.[5] Over one-half of the 1,121,000 farm operators with 50 days or more of off-the-farm employment in 1934 fulfilled one phase of the census definition of part-time farmers by working at least 150 days off the farm.

Surveys in different States and areas have shown that there are many individuals combining farming with other employment who have farms smaller than 3 acres and hence are not included in the census count. A study published in 1930 in Massachusetts estimated that there were at least 60,000 farming enterprises in that State on a part-time basis.[6] The Census of Agriculture of 1930 reported only 25,600 farms in Massachusetts and only 9,900 farm operators reporting any time worked off the farm. A study of part-time farming in Connecticut, published in 1935, concluded that 60 percent of the farms in that State were operated on a part-time basis.[7] The 1930 Census listed 37.3 percent of the operators as reporting time worked off the farm.

According to a study of rural nonfarm workers in Ohio in 1934, there were an estimated 100,000 rural nonfarm families (and, therefore, not counted as farm operators in the census) who obtained some of their living from the land.[8] The supervisors of the Civil Works Administration survey of part-time farmers in 1933 made general community surveys in addition to securing full schedules from households that combined farming and other employment. An estimate of the number of farmers making such combinations in six Piedmont and foothill counties of North Carolina ranged from 50 to 90 percent of all farmers.[9]

---

[5] 1,121,000 in 1934 as compared with 1,059,000 in 1929.

[6] Rozman, David, *Part-Time Farming in Massachusetts, op. cit.*, p. 146.

[7] Davis, I. G. and Salter, L. A., Jr., *Part-Time Farming in Connecticut, op. cit.*, p. 4.

[8] Morison, F. L. and Sitterley, J. H., *Rural Homes and Non-agricultural Workers, A Survey of Their Agricultural Activities*, Bulletin 547, Agricultural Experiment Station, Wooster, Ohio, February 1935.

[9] Woofter, T. J., Jr., Herring, Harriet L., and Vance, Rupert B., *A Study of the Catawba Valley*, unpublished manuscript in the Institute for Research in Social Science, University of North Carolina.

All of these data refer to families in which the head divided his time between farming and some other occupation. In addition, there are, of course, families in which the head is a full-time farmer while one or more other members work at another occupation and bring in a cash wage, or vice versa.

Partly because the Census of 1930 indicated the extensiveness of the practice, partly because of recent pronouncements and policies of large manufacturers concerning decentralization of industry with just such combinations in mind, and partly because the depression focused attention on the many individual efforts to bridge the gap between earnings and living costs, the various types of part-time farming have roused much interest.

Reasons for Present Study of Part-Time Farming

A great deal of the recent interest in part-time farming has centered around proposals that the various combinations of farming with industry be given public encouragement as a means of improving the living conditions and increasing the security of many more families, of keeping needy families off relief, or of removing them from the relief rolls. Proposals for the advancement of part-time farming fall into three major groups:

Provision of garden plots for industrial workers in order that produce from these plots may supplement their income from industrial employment and aid in tiding them over seasons of unemployment.

Establishment of new communities of families, each family to be provided with a small acreage on which to raise a considerable portion of its food, with the expectation that industries will locate in such communities and provide supplementary cash income.

Settlement of families on small farms near communities in which industrial establishments already exist, where they may produce a considerable portion of their food and may also obtain some employment in the industries.

In view of the scarcity of factual information available for use in formulating public policy with respect to such proposals, the Research Section, Division of Research, Statistics, and Finance of the Federal Emergency Relief Administration in cooperation with the Land Policy Section, Division of Program Planning of the Agricultural Adjustment Administration, undertook a study of this question.[10]

Such public programs as have actually been undertaken have been chiefly of the second type, but they are too new to allow an adequate appraisal of incomes and living in the resulting communities. In this investigation attention was directed toward families that had already made farming combinations of the first and third types.

---

[10] Since the study was undertaken, the former agency has become the Division of Social Research, Works Progress Administration, and the latter has become the Land Use Planning Section, Land Utilization Division, Resettlement Administration. The study was continued by these agencies.

Objectives of Present Study

The principal objectives of this study were as follows:

To describe existing types of combined farming-industrial employment.

To appraise the benefits and disadvantages of these existing types.

To determine the possibilities for further development of desirable farming-industrial combinations; in particular, to appraise the extent to which these combinations might be utilized in a rehabilitation program.

In order to reach these main objectives, answers were sought to questions concerning the part-time farm enterprise,[11] off-the-farm occupation, and living and social conditions. The questions relating to the part-time farm were:

What land, buildings, and equipment do existing part-time farming units have; in other words, what amount and kind of investment is necessary for a practicable part-time farming unit?

What do these farms produce for home use and for sale?

What are the cash expenses and labor requirements of these farms?

Questions relating to the off-the-farm occupation were:

What industrial employment is, or may become, available for combination with farming?

What are the labor requirements and wage scales of these industries?

Do his farming activities place the part-time farmer at a disadvantage in opportunities for employment or in earnings?

Questions relating to living and social conditions were:

What living conditions are associated with these farming-industrial combinations, and how do the part-time farmers compare in this respect with other groups at the same occupational levels?

What are the social characteristics of persons and families who have combined farming with industrial employment?

In the light of survey findings, the possibility and the desirability of further development of part-time farming, either by extension to more families or by the improvement of existing part-time farms, were considered.

Secondary sources of information were first explored. The Bureau of the Census cooperated in making special tabulations of data from the 1930 Census of Agriculture and the 1930 Census of Manufactures. A field study was undertaken to provide the additional factual information needed in the analysis. This field study included a schedule study of a sample of part-time farm families and, for comparative purposes, a sample of nonfarming industrial employees. It also included an inspection of the areas in which enumeration was made, an inspection of industrial establishments, and interviews with employers, public officials, and other informed persons.

---

[11] For definition of part-time farming used in the survey, see p. XXX.

Reasons for Selection of Eastern Cotton Belt

It was evident that answers to the above questions should be sought in an area where the practice of combining farming with industrial work had been of sufficient duration to furnish examples of varied experience, and in a region where relatively homogeneous conditions prevailed. Since it was believed that part-time farming might be found to have a bearing on rural rehabilitation as well as upon the entire question of relief, it was considered desirable to select an area in which the need for a soil program was widespread and urgent, and where the relief load was at least average for the country.

The region selected as fulfilling all these conditions was the Eastern Cotton Belt, which is composed of the whole or parts of eight cotton-raising States as follows: North Carolina, South Carolina, Georgia, Alabama, Arkansas, Tennessee, Louisiana, and Mississippi. This study was limited to the three States, Alabama, Georgia, and South Carolina, which comprise most of the eastern end of the Cotton Belt.

THE EASTERN COTTON BELT
Comparative Extent of Part-Time Farming

The Eastern Cotton Belt is preeminently an agricultural region and in Alabama, Georgia, and South Carolina roughly one-half of the gainfully occupied males are engaged in agriculture. According to the 1930 Census, all other occupations employ less than one-fourth of a million males in South Carolina, less than one-half of a million in Georgia, and a little over one-third of a million in Alabama. This means that opportunity for off-the-farm employment in the Eastern Cotton Belt is relatively much more limited than in States like Massachusetts, which has 1,232,000 males in other occupations and only 54,000 in agriculture, or Pennsylvania, which has 2,674,000 males in other occupations and 244,000 in agriculture.

Yet, to revert to the Census of Agriculture classification of a part-time farmer, the number of farm operators in Alabama, Georgia, and South Carolina who reported work off the farm in 1929 comprised 28.9, 24.7, and 31.3 percent, respectively, of all farm operators (table 1), which was close to the national average of 30.3 percent.[12] The percentages of farm operators reporting work off the farm in Connecticut, Massachusetts, and Pennsylvania were higher than those for the three southern States. When the number of farm operators working off the farm is taken as a percent of males in non-farm occupations, the three southern States show higher percentages than do the three northern States: 19.4 percent for Alabama, 14.4 percent for Georgia, and 22.0 percent for South Carolina [13] as compared with 1.3 percent for Connecticut, 0.7 percent for Massachusetts, and 2.6 percent for Pennsylvania.

[12] *Fifteenth Census of the United States: 1930*, Agriculture Vol. IV, p. 432.
[13] For location of part-time farms, see fig. 1.

Table 1.—Number of Farm Operators Working Part-Time off the Farm in 1929[1]
Compared With Number in Occupations Other Than Agriculture

State	Males 10 years of age and over gainfully occupied	Males 10 years of age and over in agriculture		Males 10 years of age and over in all occupations other than agriculture		Farm operators reporting work off the farm		
		Number	Percent	Number	Percent	Number	Percent of all farm operators	Percent of males in non-farm occupations
Massachusetts	1,285,316	53,720	4.2	1,231,596	95.8	9,852	38.5	0.8
Connecticut	499,201	35,311	7.1	463,890	92.9	6,420	37.3	1.4
Pennsylvania	2,918,211	243,850	8.4	2,674,361	91.6	69,717	40.4	2.6
South Carolina	480,976	256,039	53.2	224,937	46.8	49,484	31.3	22.0
Georgia	850,219	412,311	48.5	437,908	51.5	63,146	24.7	14.4
Alabama	772,281	388,316	50.2	383,965	49.8	74,493	28.9	19.4

[1] Figures for 1929 are used so as to have comparable figures for other employment. The Census of Agriculture of 1935 shows that the actual number reporting time worked off the farm has increased in South Carolina and decreased in Georgia and Alabama. All 3 of the above-mentioned northern States showed increases in part-time farmers. The changes, however, were not so great as to alter the general relationship.

Source: *Fifteenth Census of the United States: 1930*, Agriculture Vol. IV, p. 432; and Population Vol. IV, p. 19.

As a result of the straggling character of towns of the South, there are many out-of-the-way places where part-time farms would not be looked for. Moreover, since many heads of industries have always encouraged a large number of their employees to engage in some agricultural activity, there must be numerous plots of this type in the South that would be too small to be included by a census enumerator. Evidence of this was seen in the present survey, which showed that 61 percent of the part-time farmers included had less than 3 acres of

Fɪɢ. I- CENSUS PART-TIME FARMS, 1929

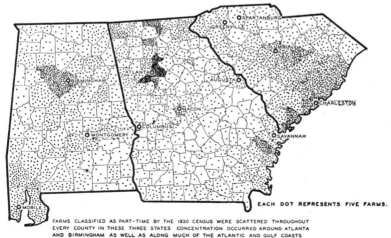

EACH DOT REPRESENTS FIVE FARMS.

FARMS CLASSIFIED AS PART-TIME BY THE 1930 CENSUS WERE SCATTERED THROUGHOUT EVERY COUNTY IN THESE THREE STATES CONCENTRATION OCCURRED AROUND ATLANTA AND BIRMINGHAM AS WELL AS ALONG MUCH OF THE ATLANTIC AND GULF COASTS

AF-2490.W P A

cropland, and 55 percent had less than 3 acres in their entire farms, and so would not have been counted as farmers by the census. It will be apparent from a consideration of the amount of products produced on the average part-time farm that not many of those having less than 3 acres would have produced $250 worth of farm products and so have been included in the census definition of a farm.

Basic Homogeneity

In spite of the variety of industries in the region, the subregions of the Eastern Cotton Belt have several common features that make for a basic homogeneity. The entire Cotton Belt has a long growing season and a good climate for raising food products. It has a fairly fertile soil although much of it has suffered from erosion and harmful farming practices. The industries of the region, while not so large and varied as in the northeastern part of the United States, are less concentrated in congested areas. Recent road improvements place much of the rural population within easier reach of existing industries than are their city cousins of their jobs.

One result of the lack of intense concentration of industry is that land values within a reasonable radius of employment are not so high as to make purchase or rental prices for farming enterprises exorbitant. Many houses for rent in small towns have lots large enough for family gardens. Suburban houses often include an acre or more of land, while plots unattached to houses frequently can be rented for as little as $5 an acre.

The Eastern Cotton Belt is an area of low wages, largely because of the great surplus of labor. Studies of income, of consumption, of living conditions as associated with housing, and of the possession of modern conveniences show the entire region to be one of low standards.[14]

The people in this area are more homogeneous than are those in any other area of similar size in the United States. Even differences between whites and Negroes are, as they relate to the problems of part-time farming, those of degree rather than kind. Both races are of native stock long subject to the same cultural and economic patterns, and a majority of both have a recent if not immediate farm background, with an elemental, although limited, knowledge of farm practices and familiarity with farm living. All have been fundamentally affected by the commercial farming habits of the South, where the growing of a single cash crop has for generations minimized the custom

---

[14] Heer, Clarence, *Income and Wages in the South*, Chapel Hill: University of North Carolina Press, 1930; Odum, Howard W., *Southern Regions of the United States*, Chapel Hill: University of North Carolina Press, 1936; Leven, Maurice, Moulton, Harold G., and Warburton, Clark, *America's Power to Consume*, The Brookings Institution, Washington, D. C., 1934.

of producing foodstuffs. As a result, unfamiliarity with a variety of vegetables, dairy products, and meats limits their production almost as much as does the lack of experience in producing them or the lack of land and capital with which to do so.

The rural background and habits also result in a minimum of participation in social and group organizations which the paucity and feebleness of these agencies in the villages and small towns have done little to counteract. In the purely rural neighborhoods, the church, almost as exclusively as in the past, is the principal center of group activity.

DIVISION OF AREA INTO SUBREGIONS

An examination of industrial employment within the three States, Alabama, Georgia, and South Carolina, to which this study was limited, indicated the necessity for dividing the area into subregions, in each of which a different type of industry predominated. For the purposes of this study, industrial employment was taken to mean any gainful pursuit other than agriculture, though exceptions had to be made in some areas to include casual or contract work in agriculture for cash wages. Industry, thus defined, was divided into two groups, for convenience called "manufacturing and allied industries" and "service industries." Manufacturing and allied industries included those classified in the 1930 Census under forestry and fishing, extraction of minerals, and manufacturing and mechanical. Service industries included transportation, communication, trade, public service, professional service, and domestic and personal service.

The 1930 Census was used as a basis for delimitation of the subregions. The first step was to rank the manufacturing, extractive, and building industries of each county according to the number of persons occupied in each industry. The important industries in each county were then marked on a map, and the boundaries of the subregions were drawn by inspection. These boundaries, shown in figure 2, do not indicate any sharp break in condition, but they roughly mark out those areas in which types of industry are sufficiently different to warrant separate study.

Named according to the predominating industry, the subregions are Cotton Textile, Coal and Iron, Lumber, and Naval Stores. In addition, there is a fringe of Atlantic Coast counties which differs rather materially from the other groups of counties and is treated as a separate subregion. Within each subregion a county was chosen which showed a distribution of employment typical of the subregion, and which reported considerable part-time farming in the 1930 Census. An effort was made to avoid the selection of any county possessing some special condition which would prevent it from being generally representative of the subregion. Figure 3 shows the counties chosen.

Fig. 2 – INDUSTRIAL SUBREGIONS* OF ALABAMA, GEORGIA, AND SOUTH CAROLINA

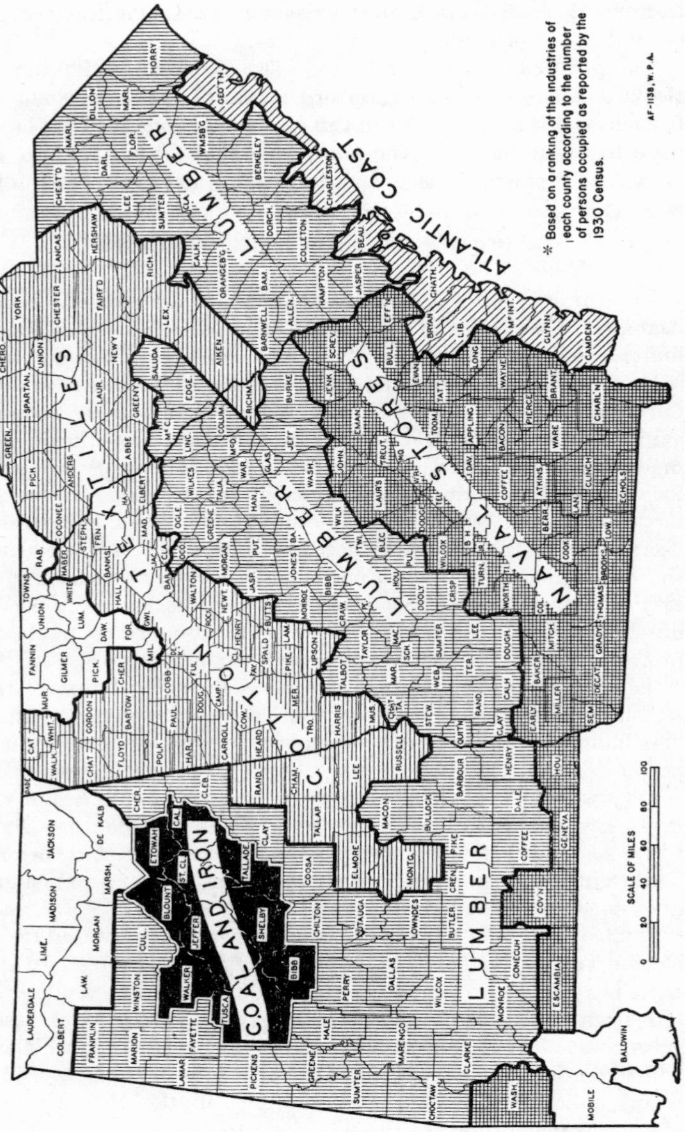

* Based on a ranking of the industries of each county according to the number of persons occupied as reported by the 1930 Census.

AF-1138, W. P. A.

SCALE OF MILES
0   20   40   60   80   100

In the separate subregion studies of part-time farming, which make up Part II of this report,[15] the areas are described in some detail. Suffice it here, therefore, to characterize each subregion very briefly.

The Cotton Textile Subregion

The most important industry in these three States of the Eastern Cotton Belt is textiles. In the 73 counties of western South Carolina, northern Georgia, and eastern Alabama, which make up what is herein designated as the Textile Subregion, textiles employs 52.5 percent of those engaged in manufacturing and allied industries (table 81, page 84). No other manufacturing or allied industry except building employs as many as 10 percent of the gainful workers.

The industry experienced rapid expansion during and immediately following the World War, but in many localities it has existed for 2 generations and in some for 100 years. Thus it has built up a definite pattern of working and living conditions, customs, and traditions, and many of these favor the carrying on of a part-time farming enterprise. The textile industry suffered from underproduction and shortened working hours before as well as during the depression. The shortened hours of the N. R. A. have, in part, been continued by the industry through voluntary agreement,[16] thus providing the leisure for farming activities. Traditionally low wages were lowered further by the depression and, although the N. R. A. raised wages considerably, incomes are still small, making any addition to the family living important. Most mill villages offer space for gardening, and many mill managements have long given encouragement to this enterprise as well as to the keeping of cows and pigs.[17] The scattered location of the mills in many towns and villages places a large number of rural people in reach of employment. After the monotonous, though relatively light, indoor work of the mill, farming is enjoyed as a healthful change and as recreation.

Some part-time farmers raise cotton, the chief crop of the subregion. The subregion is, however, an area of small family-sized farms growing

---

[15] Preliminary reports on the subregions included: Troxell, W. W., Cottrell, L. S., Jr., Edwards, A. D., and Allen, R. H., *Combined Farming-Industrial Employment in the Cotton Textile Subregion of Alabama, Georgia, and South Carolina; Combined Farming-Industrial Employment in Charleston County, South Carolina; Combined Farming-Industrial Employment in the Coal and Iron Subregion of Alabama; Combined Farming-Industrial Employment in the Naval Stores Subregion of Georgia and Alabama; Combined Farming-Industrial Employment in the Lumber Subregion of Alabama, Georgia, and South Carolina;* and Troxell, W. W., *Employment in the Cotton Textile Industry in Alabama, Georgia, and South Carolina;* Research Bulletins J–1—J–6.

[16] Bowden, Witt, "Hours and Earnings Before and After the N. R. A.," *Monthly Labor Review,* Vol. 44, No. 1, January 1937, pp. 13–36.

[17] Herring, Harriet L., *Welfare Work in Mill Villages,* Chapel Hill: University of North Carolina Press, 1929, pp. 206–209.

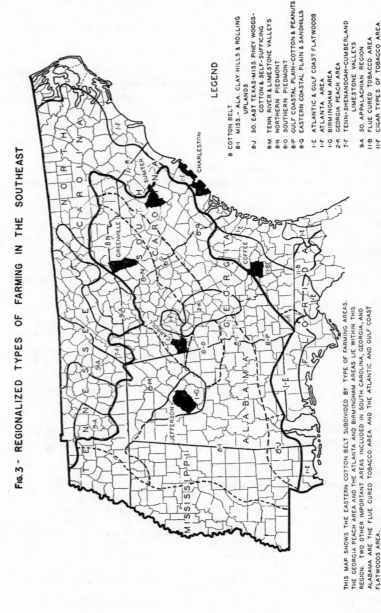

FIG. 3 - REGIONALIZED TYPES OF FARMING IN THE SOUTHEAST

LEGEND

8   COTTON BELT
8-I MISS.- ALA. CLAY HILLS & ROLLING
     UPLANDS
8-J SO. EAST TEXAS-MISS. PINEY WOODS-
     COTTON & SELF-SUFFICING
8-M TENN. RIVER & LIMESTONE VALLEYS
8-N NORTHERN PIEDMONT
8-O SOUTHERN PIEDMONT
8-P GULF COASTAL PLAIN-COTTON & PEANUTS
8-Q EASTERN COASTAL PLAIN & SANDHILLS

I-E ATLANTIC & GULF COAST FLATWOODS
I-F ATLANTA AREA
I-G BIRMINGHAM AREA
2-K GEORGIA PEACH AREA
7-F TENN-SHENANDOAH-CUMBERLAND
     LIMESTONE VALLEYS
9-A SO. APPALACHIAN REGION
11-B FLUE CURED TOBACCO AREA
11-F CIGAR TYPES OF TOBACCO AREA

AF-1124, W.P.A.

THIS MAP SHOWS THE EASTERN COTTON BELT SUBDIVIDED BY TYPE OF FARMING AREAS.
THE GEORGIA PEACH AREA AND THE ATLANTA AND BIRMINGHAM AREAS LIE WITHIN THIS
REGION. TWO OTHER IMPORTANT AREAS INCLUDED IN SOUTH CAROLINA, GEORGIA, AND
ALABAMA ARE THE FLUE CURED TOBACCO AREA AND THE ATLANTIC AND GULF COAST
FLATWOODS AREA.

Source U. S. Department of Agriculture.

a variety of crops rather than an area of larger farms with the tenant system and the concentration on cotton that characterize the lower South.

The Coal and Iron Subregion

The coal, iron, and steel industries are centered in 10 counties of north central Alabama, with a concentration in Jefferson County. There the close proximity of coking coal, iron ore, limestone, and dolomite made possible the development of a group of interdependent heavy industries. These enjoyed a rapid growth during the period following 1900, when national expansion opened markets for steel and iron. In the last quarter of a century, intensive and highly specialized industry has created in Birmingham and its vicinity a metropolitan district of dense population, the majority of the population being rural people, predominantly young, and economically and biologically productive. In 1930, 55.9 percent of the persons gainfully occupied in manufacturing and allied industries were in coal and iron industries (table 89, page 115). No other industry in this group employed as many as 10 percent of the workers.

During the depression, unemployment and underemployment cut sharply into the relatively high incomes made possible by the former large and profitable markets and a fairly vigorous trade union movement. Families who had had good wages and high standards of living felt the sharp declines in incomes more than those who had had smaller incomes. Pressed by necessity and encouraged by their employers, many coal, iron, and steel workers began gardening. Such farming enterprises were limited in size by the lack of available land and in productivity by the nature of the soil on the rough stony ridges and mountain slopes.

The Atlantic Coast Subregion

The Atlantic Coast Subregion is in an intermediate position between the regions with a single large factory industry and those with essentially rural industries. Small and varied manufacturing industries are found in the three port cities of Charleston, Savannah, and Brunswick, which also offer possibilities of employment in the service industries. In Charleston County, particularly, truck farming is a major industry. Thus, in this region, as throughout the Eastern Cotton Belt, part-time farming is combined with agriculture itself as an outside, cash income industry. A long growing season and suitable soil make gardening easy, while association with truck farming familiarizes workers with the growing of vegetables.

In Charleston County, chosen as representative of part-time farming conditions in the Atlantic Coast Subregion, several factors favorable to this enterprise are counteracted by factors just as unfavorable. Low wages on the truck farms, irregular work on the docks, and seasonal employment in the fertilizer factories result in low annual incomes and make production of food for home consumption desirable.

Charleston County is cut up by rivers that are spanned in some cases by toll bridges, while the city, with its opportunities for employment, is concentrated on the peninsula. The large-scale truck farms have taken up most of the land near transportation facilities, pushing farther away the sites that would be available in small parcels for part-time farming. Geographical features of the area thus place farming out of immediate reach of industry. The part-time farmer is placed at an unusually great disadvantage if he is dependent for employment upon industries where demand is for casual labor, and where hiring methods make it necessary for the applicant to be on hand when wanted.

A further disadvantage to part-time farmers of this region is the fact that seasonal peaks of employment are common and conflict about as often as they dovetail with activities on part-time farms. In many of the industries, the hours are long and the work is heavy; and workers who might undertake part-time farming are still further discouraged by the fact that truck products, at reasonable prices, are abundant.

The Lumber Subregion

The Lumber Subregion includes the southeastern half of South Carolina, the lower Piedmont Area of Georgia, and most of the Coastal Plain and Piedmont Region of Alabama. It is predominantly an agricultural area with 68 percent of the gainfully occupied persons engaged in agriculture as compared with 37 percent in the Textile Subregion and only 19 percent in the Coal and Iron Subregion. Manufacturing and allied industries employ only 11 percent of the gainfully occupied persons, who are distributed among a fairly varied group of industries (table 112, page 170). The only concentration worthy of note is in the group exploiting the forests or processing their products. Saw and planing mills, furniture, and other wood manufacturing employ 43 percent of the persons in manufacturing and allied industries.

The group of lumber and woodworking industries is affected by the demand for lumber, and is subject both to local market variations and to the long national trend. Lumber consumption has been gradually falling off in the United States since 1906, due to the substitution of material other than wood in building construction, and in vehicles, furniture, and other former wood-using manufactures. The depression especially decreased building activities on farms, which are large users of lumber.

The lumber industry in the South is limited by the amount of sawtimber drain the forests can stand. Destructive cutting and uncontrolled fires in the past have so depleted the growing stock that production will not be able to reach former high levels for many years to come. The future of the industry will depend largely on the forest management policies adopted.

Within these limits, the lumber industry is suited to combination with farming because it is widely scattered, the sawmills, planing mills, and woodworking plants being located in small towns easily accessible to farm lands. The work in the sawmills is heavy and the hours are long, thus discouraging the additional exertion of part-time farming; but wages are very low and so encourage enterprises that supplement the family food supply. In this area, as in the Atlantic Coast Subregion, agriculture itself constitutes a form of employment to be combined with part-time farming, especially among Negroes. The basis is somewhat different, however, the laborer being under contract to work for the landlord, and furnished with a house and a little land on which to grow food products. Sometimes he even grows a little cotton as a cash crop.

The Naval Stores Subregion

The area designated as the Naval Stores Subregion consists of southeastern Georgia, northern Florida, and southern Alabama. The division between this subregion and the Lumber Subregion (figure 2) is somewhat arbitrary, since there is some overlapping both in territory and in the nature of the industries.

The Naval Stores Subregion is another distinctly rural area in which the chief opportunities for employment center around the forests and their products. Here, however, forest industries mainly include the collecting and distilling of turpentine from pine forests, and employ nearly two-fifths of the persons engaged in manufacturing and allied industries (table 123, page 199). Saw and planing mills and wood-working factories employ another fifth. In the turpentine industry, activity is greatest during the farming season, the hours are long and the work fairly strenuous, all of which factors tend to discourage part-time farming. On the other hand, gum collecting in the forests in which the majority of workers are engaged makes possible the arrangement of working days to permit the part-time farming enterprise.

Both the forest activities and the stilling are scattered over a sparsely settled area, and land for farming is easily available. Wages are so low that additions to the family food supply are necessary for maintenance of anything beyond a bare subsistence standard of living.

The agriculture of the subregion centers around the growing of cotton, although in some of the Georgia counties in the area tobacco forms a second cash crop. During the early years of the depression the low prices received for these products forced many families to seek a supplementary wage in off-the-farm employment. Many became gum producers, working in the turpentine woods part of the time, either on their own or on someone else's land, and continuing their farming much as before. Thus, in this area most part-time farmers are really commercial farmers who work part-time in industry.

SELECTION OF CASES FOR SURVEY

The part-time farmers were selected without regard to the industry in which they worked, and included workers not only in the chief industry of each area, but in the minor manufacturing and extractive industries of each region and in the service industries. This made possible an examination of every possible industrial combination with part-time farming, and showed, in particular, how part-time farming is best carried on under conditions which offer the most opportunities for employment. It is believed that the 1,113 part-time farmers surveyed in the Eastern Cotton Belt represent a fair cross section of those who throughout the region are combining farming with some other occupation.

In order to include a wider range of farming-industrial combinations than would have resulted from selection of families according to the census definition of a part-time farmer, rather low limits were set upon the amount of each type of employment necessary to qualify a family for inclusion in the field survey. These limits were that in 1934 the family should have operated at least three-quarters of an acre of tillable land and/or have produced farm products valued at $50 or more;[18] and the head of the household should have worked at least 50 days off the home farm. Only families which had operated the same farm during both 1933 and 1934 were included. The purpose of this limitation was to exclude part-time farmers who were just getting established. All professional and proprietary workers, except small storekeepers, were excluded, since it was considered that a different set of considerations was involved in the case of white collar workers with small farms, and of "gentleman" farmers.

Following popular usage, the heads of the families surveyed will be referred to in this report as part-time farmers, meaning that they spend part of their time operating a farm and part at some employment away from this farm. Their farms will be referred to as part-time farms and their activities on them will be called part-time farming. Part-time farmers with small enterprises which would not normally be expected to produce beyond the needs of a single family will be designated as noncommercial farmers, while those with larger acreages and at least

---

[18] Objection may be raised to calling a home which included only a 1-acre garden plot a farm, especially when its owner is a full-time industrial worker. The same criticism applies to the dweller in an industrial village whose only farming enterprise is the keeping of a cow. For the purpose of this study, however, it was desirable that the term farm be used to refer to any holding upon which farming activities were carried on. For further details regarding methodology, see appendix C.

one crop produced primarily for market will be referred to as commercial part-time farmers.

For comparative purposes, a sample of nonfarming industrial workers in each subregion was included in the study. Only those families were enumerated which had raised less than $50 worth of farm or garden products in 1934; which had a male head physically capable of working at a full-time job during 1934; and whose head was employed at least 50 days each during 1933 and 1934 in certain clerical and kindred occupations or in skilled, semiskilled, and unskilled occupations.

The number of cases included in the field enumeration, by areas, is given in table 2.

Table 2.—Part-Time Farm and Nonfarming Industrial Households Enumerated, by Color and by Subregion, 1934

Subregion and color	Part-time farm households	Nonfarming industrial households
Total	1, 113	1, 334
Textile:		
White	293	314
Coal and Iron:		
White	204	222
Negro	124	346
Atlantic Coast:		
White	71	103
Negro	142	105
Lumber:		
White	76	92
Negro	132	103
Naval Stores:		
White	71	49

SUMMARY

THE COMBINATION of farming with a job that brings a cash wage has long existed in the United States—particularly in rural areas where the presence of natural resources has led to the growth of industries and of industrial communities. The widespread ownership of automobiles and the extension of improved roads have contributed to the development of combined farming-industrial employment in the Southeast by placing residents of outlying rural districts in touch with industrial centers.

The long depression in agriculture and, more recently, the depression in industry have had an important influence on the growth of part-time farming in the Southeast. In recent years industrial workers have sought to supplement their reduced wages in industry with part-time farming, farmers have been induced to supplement their reduced farm incomes with off-the-farm employment, and many persons already engaged in combined farming-industrial employment have extended their farming activities. One-half of the families surveyed had been carrying on part-time farming for 6 continuous years prior to 1935, however, indicating that part-time farming enterprises were not undertaken purely as a result of the depression.

Part-time farming in Alabama, Georgia, and South Carolina is at present carried on by workers in all of the major industries of the region—cotton textile manufacturing, lumber, naval stores, and coal and iron mining—as well as by workers in other manufacturing and mechanical industries, in transportation and communication industries, in trade, and in public service. In none of the industries, with the possible exception of coal and iron mining, is the labor involved so heavy as to discourage the additional work required by a farm enterprise, although the nature of available employment and the lack of available transportation facilities in some urban areas, such as in Charleston, discourage daily commutation of farm operators from remote rural areas.

The survey of combined farming-industrial employment in five major subregions of the Southeast showed that economically the part-time farm is an advantage. It requires in investment in house and land little more than ordinarily would be spent in housing; it requires only a small amount of capital for equipment or livestock; and the expenditure for seed, fertilizer, or hired labor is negligible.

A part-time farm enterprise undertaken on as small a scale as those found in the Eastern Cotton Belt, however, does not give the operator and his family economic self-sufficiency. At best, it only supplements a cash wage from employment in industry, and the possibility of carrying on part-time farming activities successfully is contingent upon possession of off-the-farm employment.

In all of the subregions, the part-time farms surveyed were small, and the enterprises were conducted mainly to produce food for home consumption. Most of the farms surveyed had less than 5 acres of cropland, and almost half of them had less than 2 acres. The small acreage was sufficient, however, for the farm to produce a definite contribution to the family living—not only fresher and more abundant products for the diet, but also a monetary saving in grocery bills during the summer months that ranged from a few dollars to as much as $20 per month.

The value of products consumed by typical part-time farmers during the year ranged from about $70 by part-time farmers who had only a garden to about $400 by those with a garden, a cow, several hogs, and a small flock of poultry. Since the majority of the part-time farmers surveyed made less than $500 a year at their principal off-the-farm employment, the farm's contribution to family living was an important one.

Although most of the part-time farmers kept a cow, a hog or two, and a flock of chickens, a vegetable garden was the activity that was most general. On half of the farms, gardens produced three or more summer vegetables for 3, 4, and 5 months. Many of the gardens were only ¼ acre in size. Few of the farmers reported three or more vegetables for as long as 8 months, in spite of the long growing season throughout the Eastern Cotton Belt and the small expense attached to garden production. Most part-time farm families were obviously unfamiliar with winter vegetables, but some garden products, such as sweet and Irish potatoes and corn, were stored by two-thirds of the families, while vegetables were canned by three-fifths of the households, thereby prolonging the period of the garden's usefulness through the winter months.

In view of the actual saving in dollars and cents that was made possible by the part-time farm's contribution of vegetables, pork, dairy products, and livestock products, the operators on the whole did not feel that their farm enterprises took a burdensome amount of time. From 3 to 5½ hours a day were required in farm work from April through August on the white noncommercial part-time farms. Although in some cases the head of the family did all of the work alone, the farm tasks were usually shared by members of the family.

Few of the part-time farmers spent as much as $15 for hired labor in 1934.

The part-time farmers' investment in farm buildings and land was small, amounting to less than $2,000 in over one-half of the cases surveyed. Only a few of the farmers had holdings valued at more than $5,000, and these were commercial farmers, for the most part, who produced some cash crop for the market or carried on some distinctly commercial livestock enterprise.

Investment in implements and machinery was practically negligible, most of the farmers owning only a few simple hand tools, such as hoes and rakes. In most cases, only the part-time farmers operating 10 acres of land or more owned horses or mules. The limited cropland on most enterprises prevented the growing of sufficient feed for work animals, and besides, the small enterprises common to the majority of part-time farmers did not warrant ownership of a mule.

In order to carry on farming activities, part-time farmers on the average were forced to live slightly farther from their places of work than were the nonfarming industrial workers. But residence at a greater distance from an employment center placed the workers in only one subregion at a disadvantage in securing work, as was shown by a comparison of part-time farmers and nonfarming industrial workers with respect to rates of pay, total earnings, and number of days employed. Further evidence that part-time farmers on the whole were not at a disadvantage with respect to employment opportunities was given by the fact that part-time farmers and nonfarming industrial workers were closely parallel in distribution in the industries of each subregion, as well as in the proportions of their numbers who were skilled and unskilled workers.

The suburban or open country residence that was involved in a part-time farming enterprise in some subregions carried with it some definite advantages. Housing cost part-time farm families who lived in the suburbs or open country less than it would have in town. Since families of part-time farmers were larger than those of nonfarming industrial workers, the lower rents, especially for large families, were one of the advantages that accompanied part-time farming. Nearly one-fourth of the part-time farm families consisted of seven or more persons. Part-time farmers' homes were larger than those of nonfarming industrial workers, but because of the larger families, there was slightly more overcrowding in the farm group.

Lack of modern conveniences was one of the disadvantages that frequently accompanied part-time farming, because power lines and water mains were not generally extended into sparsely settled rural areas. Electric lights, running water, and bathrooms were often lacking.

Home ownership was more common among part-time farmers than among the nonfarming industrial workers, but a large proportion of tenancy existed even among part-time farmers, and especially among Negro part-time farmers.

From the social viewpoint, too, the part-time farmer's life had its advantages and disadvantages. In general, more part-time farm than nonfarming industrial families participated in organized social and community life. Also, the extent of participation of part-time farmers was greater than that of nonfarmers in almost every type of activity available to them, which was surprising in view of the greater distances many of them had to go to attend meetings. More members of part-time farm than nonfarm families were in positions of leadership as represented by officeholding, and enumerators in more than one area remarked that the part-time farmers enjoyed a higher social status than that of the nonfarming industrial workers.

Fewer social organizations, however, were available to part-time farmers. Inasmuch as such groups stimulate social intercourse and interest in community affairs, the lack of social organizations was particularly disadvantageous to young people in part-time farm families.

The present survey shows that while part-time farming can be a decided financial aid, in the sense that it supplements wages from industrial employment, no blanket endorsement for developing or extending present part-time farming or for encouraging new part-time farming enterprises may be given. Because a fairly small part-time farm enterprise alone is not enough to give self-sufficiency to the operator, part-time farming cannot be considered as an economic "way out" for unemployed persons or for families on relief, although a part-time farm, coupled with even a small cash wage, would alleviate the acute distress of many families now on relief. Part-time farming cannot be a solution for unemployment in the Eastern Cotton Belt, because possibilities of increased industrial activities, which would provide the necessary cash wage, are slight. Consequently, part-time farming as an activity can be encouraged only where industry has sufficiently recovered from the depression to offer satisfactory wages and hours to its workers, or where future prospects for an industry's development are promising.

From the point of view of available land in the Eastern Cotton Belt, there is a possibility of increasing the number of part-time farms, and many nonfarmers expressed a wish to become part-time farmers. Whether or not they should be helped to attain this objective depends on many factors other than existence of a cash wage. The possession of such qualities as industry, energy, and initiative is an essential pre-requisite to the undertaking of a farming enterprise, and the willingness to follow farm supervision is equally important. Possession of the above characteristics was found to be more essential to the success of a part-time farming venture than actual previous farm experience.

Although about one-fifth of the farmers surveyed had had no farm experience since they were 16 years of age, the garden production of those without such farm experience did not differ greatly from that of part-time farmers with previous experience.

While the extension of part-time farming to households not at present engaged in this activity is not recommended as generally desirable or possible, the improvement of existing part-time farming is strongly advocated. Assistance by existing educational agencies would be valuable in improving some of the present farming practices, and with this aid part-time farms could be made more consistent producers of food and of a more varied diet.

Because people are familiar with a variety of governmental activities, the present would be an auspicious time in which to launch an educational part-time farm program, especially since many Federal agencies now in existence—such as the Farm Credit Administration, the Federal Housing Administration, and the Resettlement Administration—have facilities for putting such a program into effect.

Another argument for the introduction of a part-time farm program at the present is the unlikelihood of industries resuming the long hours of predepression days. Workers today are in the process of adjusting their habits to the additional leisure that shorter hours have given them, and if part-time farming activities are encouraged now, they will absorb this margin of leisure time.

Some industries in the Southeast were found to be better adapted to a combination with part-time farming than others, although, as it has been stated, none of them gives any promise of a marked increase in employment.

The textile industry offers particular advantages to workers who wish to engage in part-time farming. Farming land in the Textile Subregion is conveniently situated in relation to the textile industry, which is widely distributed in the area. Even the mill villages, such as those surveyed in South Carolina and Georgia, afford space for small farm enterprises. Employment in the textile industry involves no heavy manual work and the hours in the industry allow the worker time for carrying on a farming enterprise. The variety of work within the industry normally offers employment to employable members of all ages in a single family, thus increasing the family cash income, essential to the success of part-time farming. A special advantage accrues to part-time farmers in the Textile Subregion through the provision by mill villages of group activities usually denied to part-time farmers who live in the open country or on the outskirts of a town.

Coal mining and the steel and iron industries are less well adapted to part-time farming under normal conditions. The mines and mills are located in thickly settled metropolitan areas, where farm land is poor and scarce. The labor involved, when operations approximate full time, is too heavy to make anything more than a small enterprise physically desirable. Part-time farming, however, has been remarkably successful in the Coal and Iron Subregion in spite of the handicaps of poor and limited farm land, and as long as the mines continue to operate so few days per year, such farming would seem to be both feasible and desirable for those workers who have access to the necessary land. Normal full-time wages in these industries will suffice to insure a standard of living equal to, or better than, that of the average industrial worker in the South. Any future approximation of normal work schedules and wages, by reducing the need for incomes to be supplemented, may result in a decrease in part-time farming.

Charleston County, in the Atlantic Coast Subregion, offers opportunities for combined farming-industrial employment to workers in rural areas engaged in the truck farming industry. Truck farming pays such low wages that an additional income in the form of home-grown products is highly desirable, and those wishing to undertake part-time farming activities have plenty of good farming land at their disposal. The fact that the rush season on truck farms coincides with the necessity for work on the part-time farm is one disadvantage to such a combination. The manufacturing, service, and port industries of the city of Charleston do not offer reasonable chances fof combined farming-industrial employment, due to the isolation or Charleston from the mainland and the scarcity of farming land within commuting distances. In the port industries, in particular, only workers whose residences are accessible to places of employment can avail themselves of the irregular work offered.

With respect to location, the lumber industry is well adapted to part-time farming. Saw and planing mills are located in rural areas and woodworking industries are scattered in many small towns and cities. Hours are not now, nor likely to be, so long as to make small farming enterprises burdensome. Wages are low enough to make food production desirable. The cash-crop tenant system provides some part-time farmers with a cash income, and at the same time, it insures land and equipment for farm production for home consumption.

The naval stores industry is almost entirely a rural industry, and land is easily available for part-time farming. In the Naval Stores Subregion, wages are so low that a bare subsistence level of living is common. The chief disadvantages to combining farm work with employment in turpentining are the rather strenuous work and the coincidence of its rush season with the growing season on the farm. The outlook for increased employment in the industry is particularly unsatisfactory, depending upon development of new uses and markets for naval stores products and upon the development of an enlightened forest policy which will preserve the natural resources of the subregion.

Chapter I

THE PART-TIME FARMER

AND HIS FARM

IT IS the operation of some sort of farming enterprise in addition to his regular job which distinguishes the part-time farmer from the usual worker in manufacturing, mechanical, and service occupations. The first objective of this study, therefore, was an examination of the farming enterprise: its requirements and its operation.

CHARACTERISTICS OF THE PART-TIME FARMER

Though most of the data on the social aspects of part-time farming has its place in later discussions, a few facts about the characteristics of the part-time farmers studied in this survey are appropriate here.

Age

In age, the part-time farmers enumerated ranged from 20 to 65 years (tables 3 and 4). Few were in the extremely young age brackets. The median ages varied somewhat in the different areas, with 43 years the highest average age occurring among whites or Negroes in any of the five areas studied. This average age was found among Negro part-time farmers in the Coal and Iron Subregion, white and Negro part-time farmers in the Atlantic Coast Subregion, and white part-time farmers in the Lumber Subregion. The lowest median was 34 years, the average for white part-time farmers in the Naval Stores Subregion.

The average age of the nonfarming industrial group ranged from 41 years among the whites in the Coal and Iron Subregion to 29 years among the whites in the Naval Stores Subregion.

Table 3.—Age of Heads of Part-Time Farm and Nonfarming Industrial Households,[1] 1934

Age of head	Part-time farm households		Nonfarming industrial households	
	Number	Percent	Number	Percent
Total	1,113	100	1,334	100
Under 20 years	5	*	11	1
20 to 24.9 years	67	6	130	10
25 to 29.9 years	126	11	238	18
30 to 34.9 years	143	13	228	17
35 to 39.9 years	186	17	228	17
40 to 44.9 years	172	16	160	12
45 to 49.9 years	159	14	132	10
50 to 54.9 years	115	10	109	8
55 to 59.9 years	72	7	57	4
60 to 64.9 years	68	6	41	3

* Less than 0.5 percent.
[1] For data by subregions, see appendix table 1.

Table 4.—Average Age of Heads of Part-Time Farm and Nonfarming Industrial Households, by Color and by Subregion, 1934

Subregion and color	Median age of head	
	Part-time farm households	Nonfarming industrial households
Total	41	36
Textile:		
White	39	35
Coal and Iron:		
White	42	41
Negro	43	39
Atlantic Coast:		
White	43	36
Negro	43	35
Lumber:		
White	43	33
Negro	36	30
Naval Stores:		
White	34	29

Size of Household

The difference in the median ages of the heads of part-time farm and nonfarming industrial households partially accounts for the difference in size of households of the two groups, the average [1] for the former being 5.2 persons and for the latter 4.2 persons (table 6). Nearly a fourth (24 percent) of the part-time farm households consisted of seven or more persons, while only one-eighth (12 percent) of the nonfarming industrial households consisted of seven or more persons (table 5). The average size of part-time farm households varied only slightly by subregions while the size of nonfarming industrial households ranged from 4.8 persons among whites in the Atlantic Coast Subregion to 3.8 persons among Negroes in the Lumber Subregion.

[1] Unless otherwise specified, the averages used in this report are arithmetic means.

Table 5.—Size of Part-Time Farm and Nonfarming Industrial Households,[1] 1934

Size of household	Part-time farm households		Nonfarming industrial households	
	Number	Percent	Number	Percent
Total	1,113	100	1,334	100
1 person	6	1	4	*
2 persons	101	9	235	18
3 persons	161	14	328	25
4 persons	203	18	273	20
5 persons	213	19	192	14
6 persons	157	14	137	10
7 persons	105	9	79	6
8 persons	66	6	41	3
9 persons	37	3	25	2
10 persons	32	3	11	1
11 persons or more	32	3	9	1

*Less than 0.5 percent.
[1] For data by subregions, see appendix table 2.

Table 6.—Average Size of Part-Time Farm and Nonfarming Industrial Households, by Color and by Subregion, 1934

Subregion and color	Average number of persons	
	Part-time farm households	Nonfarming industrial households
Total	5.2	4.2
Textile:		
White	5.3	4.1
Coal and Iron:		
White	5.1	4.5
Negro	5.0	4.2
Atlantic Coast:		
White	5.2	4.8
Negro	5.2	4.0
Lumber:		
White	5.3	4.5
Negro	5.3	3.8
Naval Stores:		
White	5.0	3.9

Whether the needs of a larger household caused the families to engage in part-time farming or whether the presence of family labor to carry on the enterprises made part-time farming appear practicable is not clear. It was found, however, that part-time farming was particularly advantageous to large families.[2]

Farm Experience

The common assumption that the industrial workers in the Southeast have farm backgrounds was strikingly supported by the results of this survey. Eighty-two percent of the part-time farmers had had some regular farm experience since they were 16 years of age (table 7). Over 75 percent reported 3 years or more of farming, which was enough to give them considerable familiarity with farming routine, even if

[2] See p. 15.

that experience had not been preceded by a childhood on the farm, as was so often the case.

The average length of time that had been spent on a farm varied greatly from subregion to subregion (table 8). The average was as high as 22 years among white commercial part-time farmers of the

Table 7.—Farm [1] Experience of Heads of Part-Time Farm and Nonfarming Industrial Households,[2] 1934

Number of years head had lived on farm since 16 years of age	Part-time farm households		Nonfarming industrial households	
	Number	Percent	Number	Percent
Total	1,113	100	1,334	100
None	200	18	683	51
1 year	19	2	57	4
2 years	47	4	88	7
3 to 4 years	130	12	162	12
5 to 9 years	208	19	190	14
10 to 14 years	155	14	70	5
15 to 19 years	101	9	36	3
20 to 29 years	128	11	34	3
30 to 39 years	79	7	12	1
40 to 49 years	39	3	—	—
Unknown	7	1	2	*

* Less than 0.5 percent.
[1] Following the census definition, a farm was defined as a tract of land of at least 3 acres unless its agricultural products were valued at $250 or more. Hence, those who had had farm experience on small acreages only appear in this table as having had no experience.
[2] For data by subregions, see appendix table 3.

Table 8.—Average Length of Farm [1] Experience of Heads of Part-Time Farm and Nonfarming Industrial Households, by Type of Farm, by Color, and by Subregion, 1934

Subregion, color, and type of farm	Average number of years on farm since 16 years of age [2]	
	Part-time farm households	Nonfarming industrial households
Total	12	4
Textile:		
White	11	4
Commercial	20	
Noncommercial	9	
Coal and Iron:		
White	5	2
Negro	7	4
Atlantic Coast:		
White	12	2
Commercial	14	
Noncommercial	11	
Negro	20	2
Lumber:		
White	15	5
Commercial	19	
Noncommercial	11	
Negro	18	6
Naval Stores:		
White	13	6
Commercial	22	
Noncommercial	3	

[1] Following the census definition, a farm was defined as a tract of land of at least 3 acres unless its agricultural products were valued at $250 or more. Hence, those who had had farm experience on small acreages only appear in this table as having had no experience.
[2] Averages based on total number of households.

Naval Stores Subregion,[3] where regular farmers had recently become part-time turpentine workers. The lowest average length of farm experience (3 years) was found among the noncommercial part-time farmers in the Naval Stores Subregion.

When the previous farming experience of part-time farmers was compared with that of the nonfarming industrial workers, it became obvious that an agricultural background played an important part in the decision to undertake part-time farming. Over half of the heads of the nonfarming households had had no regular farming experience since they were 16 years of age, and an additional 11 percent had spent only 1 or 2 years on a farm. For the 49 percent of industrial workers who had had some experience on a farm, the average number of years for each color and subregion was considerably less than that spent by part-time farmers (appendix table 3), though their younger average age somewhat reduced this apparent difference.

Years Engaged in Part-Time Farming

The undertaking of a part-time farming enterprise was not entirely a result of the depression with all of the households studied though it apparently was with many of them. Over half of the part-time farmers in the sample had been farming for 6 continuous years prior to 1935. The schedules did not ask for data earlier than 1929, and the field workers were instructed to omit households which had been engaged in part-time farming for only 1 year, so that the study might cover a group that had had at least a reasonable amount of experience with farming. Since the farmers reported the number of years and not the specific calendar years that they had been farming, it was impossible to find how many of those who had done part-time farming less than 6 years (48 percent) had done so intermittently. However, the additions to the group by the number of years the head had been

Table 9.—Number of Years Head of Household Had Been a Part-Time Farmer Since December 31, 1928 [1]

Number of years head had been a part-time farmer	Heads of part-time farm households	
	Number	Percent
Total	1,113	100
1 year [2]	4	*
2 years	165	15
3 years	183	16
4 years	120	11
5 years	68	6
6 years	573	52

*Less than 0.5 percent.
[1] For data by subregions, see appendix table 4.
[2] Practically all of these cases were eliminated by definition. See pp. XXX–XXXI.

[3] Regular farmers who had undertaken part-time work in the turpentine forests. Part-time turpentine workers would be a more exact term.

a part-time farmer were such as to suggest that, for the majority at least, the 6 years could be numbered serially from 1929 to 1934. Thus, with 5 years of part-time farming representing those beginning in 1930, the addition was only 6 percent of the total. As the depression deepened, the additions to the number of part-time farmers increased (table 9).

This is even more apparent in the figures for the subregions (appendix table 4). In the Textile Subregion, for example, where the depression had been of longer standing than in the other areas, the number who had been part-time farmers for at least 6 years prior to 1935 was comparatively large (56 percent of all cases), and the additions were gradual. Among the Negroes of the Coal and Iron Subregion, on the other hand, where wages had been good, the facilities even for gardening were limited, and the number farming for 6 years was small (28 percent). The additions to the number of part-time farmers were small until 1932 and 1933, when the increasing force of the depression and encouragement of the employers caused large numbers to undertake some food-producing enterprises.

Enterprises in 1929 and 1934

Of the 1,113 part-time farmers surveyed, there were 573 who were known to have been part-time farmers in 1929. A comparison of a few indices of their activities in that year with those in 1934 shows that a few part-time farmers were carrying on more extensive enterprises in 1934 than in 1929 (tables 10 and 11). The comparison indicates, however, that the majority of part-time farmers had reached what they considered an optimum general size of operations in 1929. In 1934, 97 percent of the part-time farmers had gardens as compared with 88 percent in 1929, but the gardens averaged only 0.2 of an acre larger. Fifty-three percent had cows in 1934 as compared with forty-three percent in 1929, but the average number of cows owned had not

Table 10.—Size of Garden on 573 Part-Time Farms,[1] 1929 and 1934

Acres in garden	Part-time farms			
	1929		1934	
	Number	Percent	Number	Percent
Total	573	100	573	100
None	67	12	16	3
¼ acre	202	35	176	31
½ acre	110	19	105	18
¾ acre	40	7	66	12
1 acre	85	15	89	15
1½ acres	18	3	52	9
2 acres	23	4	34	6
3 acres or more	28	5	35	6
Average for those having a garden	0.9		1.1	

[1] For data by subregions, see appendix table 5.

changed. A few more farmers had hogs, but the average number of hogs was slightly less than in 1929. The proportion having poultry had increased from 67 percent to 72 percent. The number of those having large flocks had decreased, however, and the average size of all flocks had decreased by four birds.

Table 11.—Number of Livestock on 573 Part-Time Farms,[1] 1929 and 1934

Number of livestock	Part-time farms			
	1929		1934	
	Number	Percent	Number	Percent
Total_____	573	100	573	100
Cows:				
None_____	326	57	269	47
1_____	205	36	251	44
2 or more_____	42	7	53	9
Average for those owning cows_____	1.2		1.2	
Hogs:				
None_____	336	59	298	52
1_____	109	19	136	24
2_____	62	11	61	11
3 or more_____	66	11	78	13
Average for those owning hogs_____	3.3		2.8	
Poultry:				
None_____	187	33	159	28
1 to 9_____	59	10	90	16
10 to 19_____	142	25	152	27
20 to 29_____	86	15	78	13
30 to 49_____	53	9	53	9
50 or more_____	46	8	41	7
Average for those owning poultry_____	30		26	

[1] For data by subregions, see appendix table 5.

THE FARM

Location

Forty-four percent of the part-time farms were located in what was designated as open country, though the relatively short distances to work (table 50, page 35) indicate that many must have been in what were really the outskirts of small towns. Forty-one percent were in villages and the remaining fifteen percent in cities (table 62, page 51). Four-fifths of those in cities and almost two-fifths of those in villages were in the Coal and Iron Subregion. Nearly one-half of those in villages were in the Textile Subregion.

Type and Size

The part-time farmers included a small group (2 percent) that only kept a cow, a large group (14 percent) that only grew vegetables (table 21, page 14), and a group (13 percent) that carried on what might be termed commercial farming. The commercial part-time farmers grew for market whatever was the local cash crop, such as cotton in the Lumber and Textile Subregions, cotton or tobacco in the Naval Stores Subregion, and truck produce in the Atlantic Coast Subregion.[4] The commercial farms were usually in the open country and were larger than the noncommercial ones. The commercial farmers had more livestock and machinery than the noncommercial farmers, and often hired considerable labor. Since it was the production of food for home use with which this study was primarily concerned, no analysis of commercial part-time farming, as a whole, was attempted, except as it bore upon production for home consumption.

In spite of a wide range in size and variety, nearly all of the part-time farms studied were small. Only 1 percent contained 75 acres or more of cropland and only 3 percent contained 50 acres or more (table 12). The majority of those with 10 acres or more belonged to

Table 12.—Acres of Cropland on Part-Time Farms,[1] 1934

Acres of cropland	Part-time farms	
	Number	Percent
Total	1,113	100
None	24	2
1 acre	528	47
2 acres	137	12
3 to 4 acres	152	14
5 to 9 acres	82	7
10 to 19 acres	71	6
20 to 29 acres	54	5
30 to 49 acres	39	4
50 to 74 acres	18	2
75 acres or more	7	1
Unknown	1	*

*Less than 0.5 percent.
[1] For data by subregions, see appendix table 6.

the group described as commercial part-time farms. Three-fourths of all part-time farms surveyed had less than 5 acres and almost one-half had less than 2 acres. Part-time farms containing only an acre of cropland or less were found among four-fifths of the noncommercial part-time farmers of the Textile Subregion, among three-fifths of the whites in the Coal and Iron Subregion, and among four-fifths of the Negroes in that subregion (appendix table 6). For the white non-commercial farmers the average amount of cropland was not more than 3 acres in any of the areas studied (table 13).

The size of these part-time farms does not seem so small when it is remembered that all farms throughout the South are small in comparison with farms in other parts of the United States. In 1929 the

[4] Due to the limited amount of land available, there was practically no commercial part-time farming in the Coal and Iron Subregion. In the other four subregions, the part-time farmers who had the larger acreages and who produced at least one crop primarily for sale were classified as commercial part-time farmers.

Table 13.—Average Acres of Cropland on Part-Time Farms, by Type of Farm, by Color of Operator, and by Subregion, 1934

Subregion, color, and type of farm	Average acres of cropland
Total	6. 9
Textile:	
White:	
Commercial	20. 4
Noncommercial	1. 5
Coal and Iron:	
White	2. 9
Negro	1. 5
Atlantic Coast:	
White:	
Commercial	26. 4
Noncommercial	3. 0
Negro	4. 1
Lumber:	
White:	
Commercial	40. 4
Noncommercial	2. 9
Negro	7. 4
Naval Stores:	
White:	
Commercial	41. 3
Noncommercial	1. 5

average amount of cropland harvested per farm for the South as a whole was 34 acres.[5]

The number of Negroes who carried on commercial enterprises was so small that no separate classification of Negro commercial part-time farmers was made. Hence their inclusion in the group of non-commercial farmers served in some areas to raise the average acreage above that of the noncommercial whites. In the Atlantic Coast Subregion, for instance, a few Negroes had what amounted to fairly sizable truck farms, and in the Lumber Subregion some worked as contract agricultural laborers for landlords who allowed them some acreage for cotton or corn.

Tenure

Over half (58 percent) of the part-time farmers not living in mill villages were tenants (table 14). The amount of tenancy was much greater among Negroes than among whites. Forty-eight percent of the whites as compared with seventy percent of the Negroes were tenants.

There was considerable variation among the subregions with respect to the tenure of operators of commercial and noncommercial part-time farms (appendix table 7). Data on part-time farmers, however, were considered primarily by color and by production for market versus home use (i. e., commercial and noncommercial) and a detailed analysis of tenancy or trends of tenancy was not properly within the limits of this survey.

---

[5] *Abstract of the Fifteenth Census of the United States*, p. 547.

Table 14.—Value of 610 Part-Time Farms,[1] by Color and Tenure of Operator,[2] 1934

Value of farm	Part-time farms					
	Total		White		Negro	
	Number	Percent	Owner	Tenant	Owner	Tenant
Total	610	100	175	161	81	193
Less than $500	59	10	—	8	5	46
$500 to $999	121	20	1	18	24	78
$1,000 to $1,999	158	26	15	55	34	54
$2,000 to $2,999	122	20	58	43	13	8
$3,000 to $3,999	70	11	44	20	3	3
$4,000 to $4,999	37	6	29	6	1	1
$5,000 or more	43	7	28	11	1	3

[1] Exclusive of 328 white and Negro cases in the Coal and Iron Subregion, 162 white cases in the Textile Subregion (59 mill-village cases in Greenville County and 103 cases in Carroll County), and 13 white share-croppers in the Naval Stores Subregion.
[2] For data by subregions, see appendix table 7.

Value and Indebtedness

Estimates of the value of the properties represented in this study are necessarily of uncertain accuracy because of housing conditions peculiar to the Eastern Cotton Belt. Company housing by industries at nominal rents in the Textile and Coal and Iron Subregions precludes the capitalization of the rental rate to secure approximate values. In the Coal and Iron Subregion the garden plots were often located on company land, unattached to the house and used by the employee free of charge or at a nominal rent. If rental values had been used, the resulting calculation would not have included the actual farming enterprise. Property estimates could not be obtained for share-croppers of the Naval Stores Subregion, whose houses and land were part of their crop contracts with the landlord, and for agricultural contract laborers in the Lumber Subregion, whose houses and land were likewise perquisites of the working arrangement with the landlord.

The chief fact of importance that emerges from any estimate of the value of the farms of the remaining part-time farmers is that the investment was small. In 56 percent of the cases, it amounted to less than $2,000. Only 7 percent of the farms were valued at more than $5,000 and these were mostly the holdings of commercial part-time farmers (table 14).

As was to be expected, the holdings of owners were considerably more valuable than those of tenants: 31 percent of the owners' holdings, as compared with 73 percent of those of tenants, were valued at less than $2,000. A considerable portion of this advantage of owners over tenants, however, was counterbalanced by more frequent and larger debts (table 15). Among the white owners, commercial part-time farmers having mortgage indebtedness reported consistently higher debts than did noncommercial farmers (table 16). In contrast, white tenants operating noncommercial farms had larger debts than those with commercial farms except in the Naval Stores Subregion.

Table 15.—Total Debt [1] of Part-Time Farm Households, by Color and by Tenure,[2]
January 1, 1935

Total debt, January 1, 1935	Total			White			Negro		
	Total	Owner	Tenant	Total	Owner	Tenant	Total	Owner	Tenant
Number	1,113	368	745	715	264	451	398	104	294
Percent	100	100	100	100	100	100	100	100	100
None	67.8	47.3	77.9	64.8	49.3	73.6	73.1	42.4	84.4
$1 to $49	7.5	6.2	8.2	5.3	1.1	7.8	11.6	19.2	8.8
$50 to $99	4.0	4.1	3.9	4.6	3.0	5.5	2.8	6.7	1.4
$100 to $249	4.6	4.9	4.4	5.0	3.8	5.8	3.8	7.7	2.4
$250 to $499	2.8	5.7	1.3	3.6	6.4	2.0	1.3	3.8	0.3
$500 to $749	2.9	7.3	0.7	3.2	7.6	0.7	2.3	6.7	0.7
$750 to $999	1.9	4.9	0.4	2.0	5.3	—	1.8	3.8	1.0
$1,000 to $1,999	5.3	12.0	2.0	7.1	14.4	2.9	2.0	5.8	0.7
$2,000 to $2,999	1.7	3.8	0.7	2.5	4.9	1.1	0.3	1.0	—
$3,000 to $3,999	0.4	0.8	0.3	0.7	1.1	0.4	—	—	—
$4,000 or more	0.7	1.9	0.1	1.1	2.7	0.2	—	—	—
Unknown	0.4	1.1	0.1	0.1	0.4	—	1.0	2.9	0.3
Average total debt for those having debts	$733	$1,019	$402	$900	$1,281	$475	$320	$408	$209

[1] Mortgage indebtedness (real estate and chattel).
[2] For data by subregions, see appendix table 8.

Table 16.—Average Total Debt [1] of Part-Time Farm Households, by Type of Farm, by
Color, by Tenure, and by Subregion, January 1, 1935

Subregion, color, and type of farm	Average total debt for households having debts	
	Owner	Tenant
Total	$1,019	$402
Textile:		
White:		
Commercial	1,602	160
Noncommercial	1,443	438
Coal and Iron:		
White	1,377	920
Negro	955	560
Atlantic Coast:		
White:		
Commercial	2,291	175
Noncommercial	466	275
Negro	99	42
Lumber:		
White:		
Commercial	1,298	105
Noncommercial	437	650
Negro	191	56
Naval Stores:		
White:		
Commercial	718	108
Noncommercial	75	87

[1] Mortgage indebtedness (real estate and chattel).

Except in the Coal and Iron Subregion, Negro part-time farmers
were in debt for only small amounts, reflecting their limited assets.

The holdings of whites were much more valuable than those of
Negroes, only 29 percent of the white holdings, as compared with
88 percent of those of Negroes, falling below $2,000. Fifty-six
percent of the holdings of Negroes were below $1,000, and nineteen
percent were below $500.

Average values are always unsatisfactory because a few cases in the higher ranges can easily distort the picture. When the data are classified by subregion, type of farm, and tenure and color of operator, however, they bear out the general statements made above, as is shown in table 17.

Table 17.—Average Value of 610 Part-Time Farms,[1] by Type of Farm, by Color and Tenure of Operator, and by Subregion, 1934

Subregion	Average value of part-time farms					
	White				Negro	
	Commercial		Noncommercial		Owner	Tenant
	Owner	Tenant	Owner	Tenant		
Textile	$4, 331	$2, 532	$3, 528	$2, 141	—	—
Atlantic Coast	7, 705	4, 584	4, 400	2, 293	$1, 242	$599
Lumber	3, 780	3, 214	2, 332	1, 500	1, 876	1, 217
Naval Stores	3, 000	2, 000	2, 500	1, 800	—	—

[1] Exclusive of 328 white and Negro cases in the Coal and Iron Subregion, 162 white cases in the Textile Subregion (59 mill-village cases in Greenville County and 103 cases in Carroll County), and 13 white share-croppers in the Naval Stores Subregion.

Buildings

When it is remembered that the average values of farm enterprises given above represented the farm dwellings as well as the plots of land, it is not surprising to find that relatively little of the farmers' modest investments went into other buildings. A lack of buildings is fairly general in the South, and really adequate farm buildings are rarely found, even among full-time farmers.

All except 6 percent of the sample part-time farmers had some sort of building other than the dwelling, and all except 9 percent had at least two farm buildings (table 18). However, less than one-half of the farms were equipped with barns.

Table 18.—Buildings Other Than Dwellings on Part-Time Farms,[1] 1934

Buildings other than dwellings	Part-time farms	
	Number	Percent
Total	1, 113	100
None	63	6
Barn only	13	1
Barn and garage	8	1
Garage only	27	2
Barn and other buildings	286	26
Garage and other buildings	141	13
Barn, garage, and other buildings	216	19
Other buildings only	359	32

[1] For data by subregions, see appendix table 9.

Implements and Machinery

The small investment in the farm enterprises was also reflected in the limited amount of working equipment. Three-fourths of the farmers had no farm implements or machinery (table 19), although most of them had a few simple hand tools, such as hoes and rakes.

Table 19.—Cost of Implements and Machinery on Part-Time Farms,[1] 1934

Cost of implements and machinery	Part-time farms	
	Number	Percent
Total	1, 113	100
None	813	74
$1 to $4	12	1
$5 to $14	65	6
$15 to $24	52	5
$25 to $49	36	3
$50 to $99	70	6
$100 to $149	23	2
$150 to $199	15	1
$200 or more	24	2
Unknown	3	*
Average cost for those having machinery	$100	

*Less than 0.5 percent.

[1] For data by subregions, see appendix table 10.

Only 5 percent of the farmers had implements costing $100 or more; most of these farmers were in the commercial group (appendix table 10). Almost one-half of the farmers who owned machinery had paid less than $25 for it.

Livestock

Work stock was chiefly found among part-time farmers with 10 or more acres of cropland, except in the Atlantic Coast Subregion where nearly one-half of the Negroes had work stock (appendix table 11). As has already been pointed out, a number of Negroes in this subregion did considerable truck farming. In individual cases even there, however, it was apparent that small enterprises did not warrant the ownership of a mule, especially since limited cropland prevented the growing of sufficient feed for the animal.

Over three-fourths of the part-time farmers owned no horses and mules. Less than one-fourth of the farmers with horses or mules owned two or more (table 20).

One-half of the part-time farmers owned at least one milk cow; almost one-half of them owned one or more hogs; and seven-tenths owned some poultry.[6]

[6] For further discussion of livestock, see following section on Farm Production.

Table 20.—Number of Livestock and Size of Garden on Part-Time Farms,[1]
January 1, 1934

Number of livestock and acres in garden	Part-time farms	
	Number	Percent
Total_____	1, 113	100
Cows:		
None_____	558	50
1_____	448	40
2_____	83	8
3 or more_____	24	2
Poultry:		
None_____	341	31
1 to 9_____	184	16
10 to 19_____	255	23
20 to 29_____	141	13
30 to 49_____	100	9
50 or more_____	92	8
Hogs:		
None_____	614	55
1_____	239	22
2_____	103	9
3 or more_____	157	14
Horses and mules:		
None_____	852	77
1_____	202	18
2 or more_____	59	5
Acres in garden:		
None_____	37	3
¼_____	320	29
½_____	225	20
¾_____	141	13
1_____	182	16
1½_____	87	8
2 or more_____	121	11

[1] For data by subregions, see appendix table 11.

FARM PRODUCTION

Part-time farmers in the Eastern Cotton Belt produced one or more of four principal types of products for home consumption: vegetables, dairy products, poultry and poultry products, and pork.

Only 16 percent of the part-time farmers produced one type only, and 27 percent produced two types (table 21). Almost one-third produced three types of products, and one-fourth produced all four types. Those reporting all four types of products included three-

Table 21.—Types of Food Produced for Home Use on Part-Time Farms,[1] 1934

Food products	Part-time farms	
	Number	Percent
Total_____	1, 113	100
Vegetables only_____	160	14
Dairy products only_____	18	2
Poultry products only_____	4	*
Vegetables and dairy products_____	64	6
Vegetables and poultry products_____	189	17
Vegetables and pork_____	41	4
Vegetables, dairy and poultry products_____	152	14
Vegetables, dairy products, and pork_____	54	5
Vegetables, poultry products, and pork_____	141	12
Vegetables, dairy and poultry products, and pork_____	272	24
Other combinations_____	18	2

*Less than 0.5 percent.   [1] For data by subregions, see appendix table 12.

fifths of the white commercial group, one-fourth of the white noncommercial group, including the Coal and Iron Subregion, and slightly over one-tenth of the Negroes (appendix table 12).   Thus, it would seem that among the whites size of farm had a direct bearing on the variety of products as well as on ownership of work stock.   With the Negroes, however, who averaged somewhat larger acreages than the noncommercial whites, capital and custom probably had more to do with the matter.   Of the 182 part-time farmers who produced only one type of product, one-half were Negroes, although Negroes constituted only 36 percent of the total families surveyed.   One-half of the Negroes with only one product were in the Atlantic Coast Subregion where these part-time farms averaged 4.1 acres of cropland.   Most of the remainder were in the Coal and Iron Subregion where they had only garden plots.

Gardens

The *sine qua non* of part-time farming in the Eastern Cotton Belt was the vegetable garden.   All except 3 percent of the part-time farmers had gardens in 1934 (table 20).   These ranged in size from ¼ acre to 2 or more acres.   Production for sale often took place when gardens were in the larger sized group.

Approximately one-half of the gardens contained ½ acre or less, and over three-fifths contained less than 1 acre.   A much larger proportion of the white commercial part-time farmers than of the noncommercial group had gardens of 1½ acres or more, while a slightly larger proportion of white noncommercial farmers [7] than Negroes had gardens of this size (appendix table 11).

The long growing season and the small expense attached to garden production was responsible for the popularity of gardens.   They supplied not only fresh vegetables to families cultivating them but vegetables in larger quantities than would have been consumed had the families bought them.   A garden is obviously of special advantage to a large family.

The gardens varied in productivity perhaps even more than in size. No attempt was made to estimate the amounts of vegetables produced because of the very doubtful accuracy of such figures.   Some rough measures that were likely to be more accurate were the number of months in which the various vegetables grown were used fresh from the garden, the number of quarts canned, the amounts stored, and the amount of reduction in the grocery bill during the 6 summer and fall months when garden vegetables were most likely to be available as compared with the rest of the year.

The results of the first of these measures form a commentary on the gardening practices in the Eastern Cotton Belt.   Fairly varied

[7] Including whites in the Coal and Iron Subregion.

summer gardens were common, but only a few families grew winter vegetables, and only a small variety was grown. Three or more vegetables were consumed fresh from the garden for 3, 4, or 5 months on about half of the part-time farms and for 3 to 7 months on almost three-fourths of the farms (table 22). Only 9 percent had three fresh vegetables for 8 months or more, and only 1 percent had them for 10 months or more.

Table 22.—Number of Months Three or More Fresh Vegetables Were Consumed on Part-Time Farms,[1] 1934

Number of months 3 or more fresh vegetables were consumed	Part-time farms	
	Number	Percent
Total	1,113	100
None	94	8
1 month	41	4
2 months	96	8
3 months	142	13
4 months	193	17
5 months	177	16
6 months	143	13
7 months	133	12
8 months	63	6
9 months	19	2
10 months or more	12	1

[1] For data by subregions, see appendix table 13.

Surprisingly enough, the number of months in which three vegetables were available varied in the several subregions in almost inverse proportion to the length of the frost-free growing season. In the Textile Subregion, where there was a frost-free period of 7 months, the families had three vegetables for an average of about 5 months (table 23), while in the Coal and Iron Subregion, with 8 frost-free months, three or more fresh vegetables were available for almost 7 months for

Table 23.—Average Number of Months Three or More Fresh Vegetables Were Consumed on Part-Time Farms, by Color of Operator and by Subregion, 1934

Subregion and color	Average number of months 3 or more fresh vegetables were consumed
Total	4.4
Textile:	
White	4.5
Coal and Iron:	
White	6.8
Negro	5.3
Atlantic Coast:	
White	3.4
Negro	1.9
Lumber:	
White	4.3
Negro	3.4
Naval Stores:	
White	4.4

the whites and for 5 months for the Negroes. In the Lumber Sub-region with an 8-month frost-free period, white families had three vegetables for an average of about 4 months, and Negroes, for a little over 3 months. In the Naval Stores and Atlantic Coast Subregions with a 9-month frost-free period, the white families had three vegetables for more than 4 and more than 3 months, respectively. Negroes in the Atlantic Coast Subregion had three vegetables for only 2 months.[8]

The average southern gardener is notoriously unfamiliar with a variety of winter vegetables. Collards and turnips are the only ones frequently grown, although cabbage can be grown throughout the Eastern Cotton Belt from early spring until late fall, and in many areas during the entire winter.

Table 24.—Number of Months Any Fresh Vegetable or Fruit Was Consumed on Part-Time Farms,[1] 1934

Number of months any fresh vegetable or fruit was consumed	Part-time farms	
	Number	Percent
Total	1,113	100
None		
1 to 2 months	33	3
3 to 4 months	22	2
5 months	65	6
6 months	64	6
7 months	121	11
8 months	147	13
9 months	160	14
10 months	185	16
11 months	154	14
12 months	77	7
	85	8

[1] For data by subregions, see appendix table 14.

Table 25.—Average Number of Months Any Fresh Vegetable or Fruit Was Consumed on Part-Time Farms, by Color of Operator and by Subregion, 1934

Subregion and color	Average number of months any fresh vegetable or fruit was consumed[1]
Total	7.8
Textile:	
White	7.4
Coal and Iron:	
White	8.8
Negro	7.6
Atlantic Coast:	
White	8.1
Negro	6.0
Lumber:	
White	8.8
Negro	8.1
Naval Stores:	
White	8.6

[1] By those consuming fresh vegetables and fruit.

[8] The table includes fruits as well, but since these obviously are available in summer months, their inclusion does not lengthen the period.

Since three fresh vegetables are a rather high standard, a count was made of the months in which any vegetable was consumed fresh from the garden (table 24). On this basis, the periods lengthened considerably. Twenty-nine percent of all families had something fresh from the garden for 10 months or more, and eight percent had some garden product for 12 months. The average was a little less than 8 months (table 25).

Moreover, the length of time when some fresh vegetable was available varied considerably among the subregions. In the Atlantic Coast, Naval Stores, and Lumber Subregions, it was customary to grow at least one of the fresh winter vegetables. In all groups in these three areas, the average number of months when one vegetable was available was at least double (and among the Negroes of the Atlantic Coast treble) the months in which three were available. In the Textile and Coal and Iron Subregions, the summer and early fall gardens were generally much more varied than were those in other regions, but many households had no late fall and winter vegetables at all and there was not as much difference between the average number of months when one vegetable was available and when three vegetables were available.

The production of fruits was far less common than that of vegetables. Three-fifths of the part-time farmers produced no fruits, berries, or nuts (table 26). Peaches were produced by 29 percent of the farmers, but only 10 percent of the farmers produced apples. Figs were grown

Table 26.—Part-Time Farms Producing Fruits, Berries, or Nuts,[1] 1934

Fruits, berries, or nuts produced	Part-time farms	
	Number	Percent
Total	1,113	100
None	660	59
1 or more	453	41
Peaches	323	29
Apples	106	10
Figs	93	8
Grapes	62	6
Pears	57	5
Plums	33	3
Cherries	10	1
Other fruit	5	*
Strawberries	50	4
Blackberries	59	5
Huckleberries	5	*
Berries unknown	43	4
Walnuts	3	*
Pecans	23	2

*Less than 0.5 percent.
[1] For data by subregions, see appendix table 15.

by only 8 percent and grapes by only 6 percent of the farmers. Only 4 percent produced strawberries. It is likely that all other berries were wild.

More commercial than noncommercial part-time farmers produced fruit, while relatively few Negroes produced any (appendix table 15). In most cases the amounts grown were small—a few bushels or even 1 bushel of fruit and sometimes only a few quarts of berries. Some canning of these products was done, however, so that the fruit added variety to the family diet over a period of time. Fifty-seven percent of the part-time farmers did some canning of fruits and vegetables (table 27), and thirty-three percent of all households canned 50 quarts or more. Both the proportion of households doing any canning and the average number of quarts canned varied greatly in the several subregions (table 28 and appendix table 16). Almost nine-tenths of the white part-time farmers and over one-half of the Negroes of the Coal and Iron Subregion did some canning, but only 21 percent of the whites and practically none of the Negroes in the Atlantic Coast Subregion did canning. The average amount canned ranged from about 110 quarts by the whites in the Atlantic Coast, Coal and Iron, and Naval Stores Subregions to 37 quarts by the Negroes in the Lumber Subregion.

Table 27.—Quantity of Fruits and Vegetables Canned on Part-Time Farms,[1] 1934

Quarts of fruits and vegetables canned	Part-time farms	
	Number	Percent
Total	1,113	100
None	470	43
1 to 19 quarts	103	9
20 to 49 quarts	166	15
50 to 99 quarts	167	15
100 to 199 quarts	147	13
200 quarts or more	60	5

[1] For data by subregions, see appendix table 16.

Table 28.—Part-Time Farm Households Canning Fruits and Vegetables and Average Quantity Canned, by Color and by Subregion, 1934

Subregion and color	Percent of total households doing canning	Average number of quarts canned by those doing canning
Total	57	88
Textile:		
White	81	91
Coal and Iron:		
White	87	110
Negro	55	47
Atlantic Coast:		
White	21	111
Negro	1	†
Lumber:		
White	74	83
Negro	36	37
Naval Stores:		
White	56	111

† Average not computed for less than 10 cases.

Storage of garden and field products was somewhat more frequent than canning, two-thirds of the part-time farmers storing some products. At least half of the whites in all areas except the Naval Stores Subregion stored vegetables, but the proportion of Negroes storing vegetables varied greatly from area to area (table 29). In the Coal and Iron Subregion all Negroes stored some products, while in the Lumber Subregion both the number that stored products and the amounts stored were small. Sweet potatoes were the most frequently stored product, being reported by 55 percent of all families. The average amount stored was 22 bushels (appendix table 17). Irish potatoes were stored by about one-third of the families, the average amount being 11 bushels. A wide assortment of products—onions, peas, peppers, beans, apples, peanuts, cane syrup, etc.—were stored by a few families.

Table 29.—Part-Time Farm Households Storing Vegetables,[1] by Type of Farm, by Color, and by Subregion, 1934

Subregion, color, and type of farm	Percent storing vegetables
Total	66
Textile:	
White:	
Commercial	98
Noncommercial	53
Coal and Iron:	
White	86
Negro	100
Atlantic Coast:	
White:	
Commercial	79
Noncommercial	51
Negro	71
Lumber:	
White:	
Commercial	92
Noncommercial	49
Negro	33
Naval Stores:	
White:	
Commercial	19
Noncommercial	26

[1] Grown in garden or truck patch.

Another measure of the contribution of the gardens and fields to the family living is the amount by which the grocery bill was reduced during the productive months, as compared with the rest of the year. The proportion of families with gardens reporting reductions varied from 88 percent among the whites in Carroll County in the Textile Subregion to 37 percent among the Negroes of the Atlantic Coast Subregion.[9] The average amounts by which grocery bills were reduced varied from $10 a month among the whites of the Coal and Iron Subregion to $3.50 among the Negroes of the Atlantic Coast Subregion. With many individual families the reductions amounted to only $2, $3, or $4 a month, but with a few families they were as high as $20.

[9] See Gardens under subregion reports in Part II.

This method of measuring production is unsatisfactory in that it makes a poorer rather than a better showing for those groups of families in which winter gardens and canned and stored products are most common. The latter had a reduction in grocery bills for all 12 months and hence reported little difference between summer and winter. For those families who raised pork the greater use of this product in winter would also conceal differences in the grocery bill made by the garden. Some heads of families noted this factor as responsible for small differences between summer and winter grocery bills.

Poultry and Poultry Products

Next to a garden, the most common type of enterprise among part-time farmers was the keeping of poultry; 69 percent had some birds.

Table 30.—Quantity of Home-Produced Eggs Consumed on Part-Time Farms,[1] 1934

Eggs consumed	Part-time farms	
	Number	Percent
Total	1,113	100
None	368	33
1 to 19 dozen	109	10
20 to 49 dozen	214	19
50 to 99 dozen	212	19
100 to 199 dozen	158	14
200 dozen or more	52	

[1] For data by subregions, see appendix table 18.

Table 31.—Average Quantity of Home-Produced Eggs Consumed on Part-Time Farms, by Type of Farm, by Color of Operator, and by Subregion, 1934

Subregion, color, and type of farm	Average number of dozens of eggs consumed [1]
Total	84
Textile:	
White:	
Commercial	92
Noncommercial	73
Coal and Iron:	
White	113
Negro	38
Atlantic Coast:	
White:	
Commercia	152
Noncommercial	84
Negro	47
Lumber:	
White:	
Commercial	160
Noncommercial	117
Negro	69
Naval Stores:	
White:	
Commercial	124
Noncommercial	†

† Average not computed for less than 10 cases.
[1] By those consuming home-produced eggs.

In general, the flocks were small. Almost three-fifths (57 percent) of those keeping poultry had fewer than 20 birds (table 20). Only 12 percent of those keeping poultry had 50 or more birds. The great majority (89 percent) of the commercial part-time farmers had some poultry (appendix table 11), and the flocks of more than half of those who had poultry consisted of 30 or more birds. Three-fifths (63 percent) of the noncommercial group, including the whites of the Coal and Iron Subregion, had poultry, but less than one-half of those with poultry (44 percent) had 20 birds or more. Almost three-fourths of the Negroes (72 percent) kept poultry, but most of the flocks were small.

Consumption of home-produced eggs was limited; 33 percent of the families had no home-produced eggs and 29 percent averaged less than 1 dozen eggs a week throughout the year (table 30). There were wide variations by type of farming, color, and subregion (table 31). White commercial part-time farm families in the Textile Subregion consumed an average of nearly 2 dozen home-produced eggs a week, while in the Atlantic Coast and Lumber Subregions their average consumption was approximately 3 dozen a week.

The average consumption of home-produced eggs for white non-commercial part-time farm families was from 1½ to 2 dozen per week in all areas except the Naval Stores Subregion. Here the average consumption was less than three eggs per week.

Consumption of home-produced eggs by Negro families was less than 1 dozen a week throughout the year, except in the Lumber Subregion.

Table 32.—Quantity of Home-Produced Poultry Consumed on Part-Time Farms,[1] 1934

Dressed poultry consumed	Part-time farms	
	Number	Percent
Total	1, 113	100
None	456	41
1 to 19 pounds	104	10
20 to 49 pounds	193	17
50 to 99 pounds	181	16
100 to 199 pounds	124	11
200 pounds or more	55	5

[1] For data by subregions, see appendix table 19.

Consumption of home-raised poultry was also limited (table 32). A few families in each subregion used 200 pounds of dressed poultry or more in 1934, which was enough to be a real contribution to the food supply. The average amounts consumed, however, were very small, ranging from 26 pounds among Negroes in the Atlantic Coast Subregion to 173 pounds among white commercial part-time farm families in the Textile Subregion or from a chicken now and then to about one a week (table 33). The amount consumed by commercial part-time farm families was about twice as large as that consumed by their noncommercial neighbors in the Atlantic Coast and Textile Subregions, while that consumed by Negroes in general was so small as to be an insignificant contribution to the food supply.

Table 33.—Average Quantity of Home-Produced Poultry Consumed on Part-Time Farms, by Type of Farm, by Color of Operator, and by Subregion, 1934

Subregion, color, and type of farm	Average number of pounds of poultry consumed [1]
Total	81
Textile:	
White:	
Commercial	173
Noncommercial	85
Coal and Iron:	
White	70
Negro	35
Atlantic Coast:	
White:	
Commercial	117
Noncommercial	67
Negro	26
Lumber:	
White:	
Commercial	156
Noncommercial	153
Negro	75
Naval Stores:	
White:	
Commercial	44
Noncommerical	†

† Average not computed for less than 10 cases.
[1] By those consuming home-produced poultry.

Dairy Products

A cow was the most important contribution to the family living of any single phase of part-time farming in food value, in continuity of contribution, and in production of surplus available for sale. One-half of the part-time farmers had one or more cows on January 1, 1934, but only 10 percent had two or more (table 20). More than four-fifths (83 percent) of all white commercial farmers and over three-fifths (61 percent) of all white noncommercial farmers, including all farmers in the Coal and Iron Subregion, had one or more cows, but only one-fifth (22 percent) of the Negroes had a cow (appendix table 11). Most of the part-time farms with two or more cows, except those in the Textile Subregion, were in the commercial groups.

Some of the cows were very poor milk producers. On 11 percent of the farms having cows, production was less than 1,000 quarts a year, or less than 3 quarts a day (table 34). There were some individual animals that produced 3 to 4 gallons a day, but the average was considerably below this. In the Textile and Coal and Iron Subregions, the average amount of milk per cow ranged from about 2,500 to 3,000 quarts during 1934 (table 35), which is well above the national average.[10] The averages for cows in the Lumber and Naval Stores Subregions, however, ranged from a little over 1,000 to less than 2,000 quarts a year. The few cows belonging to Negroes in the Atlantic Coast Subregion averaged less than 1,000 quarts. Although more commercial part-time farmers had two or more cows, the average milk production per cow was better among the noncommercial groups, except in the Atlantic Coast Subregion.

As in the case of gardens, a cow was a great advantage to the large family. Few part-time farm families would have been able to buy milk in the quantities they used.

Table 34.—Quantity of Milk Produced on Part-Time Farms,[1] 1934

Milk produced	Part-time farms	
	Number [2]	Percent
Total	1,113	100
None	537	48
1 to 499 quarts	19	2
500 to 999 quarts	47	4
1,000 to 1,499 quarts	82	7
1,500 to 1,999 quarts	39	4
2,000 to 2,499 quarts	84	8
2,500 to 2,999 quarts	87	8
3,000 to 3,499 quarts	71	6
3,500 to 3,999 quarts	45	4
4,000 to 4,999 quarts	57	5
5,000 quarts or more	45	4

[1] For data by subregions, see appendix table 20.
[2] The difference in the number of farms with milk production and the number of farms with cows (table 20) is due to the dates for which the data were taken.

Table 35.—Average Quantity of Milk Produced per Cow on Part-Time Farms, by Type of Farm, by Color of Operator, and by Subregion, 1934

Subregion, color, and type of farm	Average number of quarts per cow producing milk
Total	2,180
Textile:	
White:	
Commercial	2,440
Noncommercial	2,650
Coal and Iron:	
White	3,069
Negro	2,709
Atlantic Coast:	
White:	
Commercial	2,440
Noncommercial	1,770
Negro	920
Lumber:	
White:	
Commercial	1,375
Noncommercial	1,941
Negro	1,265
Naval Stores:	
White:	
Commercial	1,081
Noncommercial	1,283

[10] 4,030 pounds in 1934, or about 1,874 quarts. *Yearbook of Agriculture, 1935,* U. S. Department of Agriculture, p. 601.

Families keeping a cow usually consumed 2 or 3 quarts of milk fresh per day and made butter and buttermilk out of the remainder. Buttermilk is a common article in the diet of Eastern Cotton Belt families, as it is throughout the South. Any surplus buttermilk was fed to the pigs or chickens.

Nearly all of the part-time farm families with cows made butter (table 36). The amount varied widely from family to family and from region to region, from an average of less than 1½ pounds a week among the Negroes of the Lumber Subregion to 4½ pounds among the whites of the Coal and Iron Subregion (table 37).

Table 36.—Quantity of Home-Produced Butter Consumed on Part-Time Farms,[1] 1934

Butter consumed	Part-time farms	
	Number	Percent
Total_____	1, 113	100
None_____	589	53
1 to 49 pounds_____	46	4
50 to 99 pounds_____	89	8
100 to 199 pounds_____	200	18
200 to 299 pounds_____	104	9
300 pounds or more_____	83	8
Unknown_____	2	*

*Less than 0.5 percent.

[1] For data by subregions, see appendix table 21.

Table 37.—Average Quantity of Home-Produced Butter Consumed on Part-Time Farms, by Color of Operator and by Subregion, 1934

Subregion and color	Average number of pounds of butter consumed [1]
Total_____	180
Textile:	
White_____	190
Coal and Iron:	
White_____	234
Negro_____	176
Atlantic Coast:	
White_____	151
Negro_____	100
Lumber:	
White_____	124
Negro_____	73
Naval Stores:	
White_____	167

[1] By those consuming home-produced butter.

Pork

Almost one-half of the part-time farmers, including some who lived in cities or villages, had one or more hogs (table 38). One-half of those who raised pork had only one hog (table 20). Except in the Atlantic Coast Subregion, a greater proportion of commercial than non-commercial white part-time farmers raised pork, and the majority of the commercial farmers who had hogs reported two or more (appendix table 11). Negroes received about the same advantage from this phase of part-time farming as did their white neighbors, 50 percent of the Negro part-time farmers owning hogs.

Table 38.—Quantity of Home-Produced Pork Consumed or Stored on Part-Time Farms,[1]
1934

Dressed pork consumed or stored	Part-time farms	
	Number	Percent
Total	1, 113	100
None	603	54
1 to 99 pounds	30	3
100 to 199 pounds	103	9
200 to 299 pounds	95	9
300 to 399 pounds	85	8
400 to 499 pounds	59	5
500 to 599 pounds	45	4
600 to 999 pounds	57	5
1,000 pounds or more	36	3

[1] For data by subregions, see appendix table 22.

Consumption and storage of home-produced pork averaged around 400 pounds for those families which had hogs (table 39). In view of the general use of lard as a cooking fat and of pork and bacon as seasoning for vegetables in the South, this amount represented an important contribution of the part-time farm to the family living. The average amount of home-produced pork consumed or stored ranged from 217 pounds among the Negroes in the Coal and Iron

Table 39.—Average Quantity of Home-Produced Pork Consumed or Stored on Part-Time Farms, by Type of Farm, by Color of Operator, and by Subregion, 1934

Subregion, color, and type of farm	Average number of pounds of dressed pork [1] consumed or stored
Total	406
Textile:	
White:	
Commercial	460
Noncommercial	366
Coal and Iron:	
White	376
Negro	217
Atlantic Coast:	
White:	
Commercial	†
Noncommercial	306
Negro	230
Lumber:	
White:	
Commercial	583
Noncommercial	249
Negro	263
Naval Stores:	
White:	
Commercial	1, 263
Noncommercial	†

† Average not computed for less than 10 cases.
[1] By those consuming or storing home-produced pork.

Subregion to 583 pounds among the white commercial part-time farmers in the Lumber Subregion (table 39). Over 1,200 pounds were produced by the commercial part-time farmers of the Naval Stores Subregion, but many of the families who dressed and stored such quantities traded cured meat for groceries throughout the year.

Field Crops

Only a very small number (18 percent) of the part-time farmers, most of whom were commercial part-time farmers (appendix table 23), grew any roughage, and over half of these produced less than 3 tons (table 40). Therefore, most of the feed for cows had to be purchased. Commercial farmers in the Naval Stores and Atlantic Coast Subregions produced the largest average amounts of roughage, 13 and 11 tons, respectively (table 41). Noncommercial farmers produced very

*Table 40.—*Quantity of Roughage Produced on Part-Time Farms,[1] 1934

Roughage produced	Part-time farms	
	Number	Percent
Total_____	1, 113	100
None_____	913	82
1 to 2 tons_____	108	10
3 to 4 tons_____	39	3
5 to 9 tons_____	31	3
10 to 14 tons_____	11	1
15 to 19 tons_____	3	*
20 tons or more_____	7	1
Unknown_____	1	*

* Less than 0.5 percent.   [1] For data by subregions, see appendix table 23.

*Table 41.—*Average Quantity of Roughage Produced on Part-Time Farms, by Type of Farm, by Color of Operator, and by Subregion, 1934

Subregion, color, and type of farm	Average number of tons of roughage produced [1]
Total_____	5. 0
Textile:	
White:	
Commercial_____	3. 4
Noncommercial_____	1. 4
Coal and Iron:	
White_____	2. 9
Negro_____	†
Atlantic Coast:	
White:	
Commercial_____	11. 0
Noncommercial_____	3. 0
Negro_____	3. 4
Lumber:	
White:	
Commercial_____	6. 5
Noncommercial_____	†
Negro_____	2. 8
Naval Stores:	
White:	
Commercial_____	13. 1
Noncommercial_____	—

† Average not computed for less than 10 cases.   [1] By those producing roughage

little. In the Textile Subregion it was common for employers to have pastures available for workers' cows, but the pastures were often overgrazed and of little value. In all areas the farmers made a practice of tying their cows along the roadside or in vacant lots, and in the Naval Stores Subregion, the cows were allowed to roam in the woods (hence their name: "piney woods cows").

A much larger proportion (51 percent) of the part-time farmers produced some field corn, and nearly all who grew any corn at all produced enough for meal for the family and to help in the feeding of chickens or a hog (table 42). The commercial part-time farmers, most of whom had work stock to feed, produced fairly sizable amounts of corn (table 43).

Table 42.—Quantity of Field Corn Produced on Part-Time Farms,[1] 1934

Field corn produced	Part-time farms	
	Number	Percent
Total	1, 113	100
None	551	49
1 to 9 bushels	70	6
10 to 19 bushels	106	9
20 to 29 bushels	84	8
30 to 49 bushels	85	8
50 to 74 bushels	52	5
75 to 99 bushels	32	3
100 to 149 bushels	42	4
150 to 199 bushels	20	2
200 to 299 bushels	37	3
300 to 399 bushels	13	1
400 to 599 bushels	9	1
600 bushels or more	12	1

[1] For data by subregions, see appendix table 24.

Table 43.—Average Quantity of Field Corn Produced on Part-Time Farms, by Type of Farm, by Color of Operator, and by Subregion, 1934

Subregion, color, and type of farm	Average bushels of corn produced[1]
Total	81
Textile:	
White:	
Commercial	101
Noncommercial	21
Coal and Iron:	
White	68
Negro	21
Atlantic Coast:	
White:	
Commercial	310
Noncommercial	48
Negro	21
Lumber:	
White:	
Commercial	281
Noncommercial	41
Negro	49
Naval Stores:	
White:	
Commercial	228
Noncommercial	—

[1] By those producing corn.

Fuel

Part-time farms, especially in the more populous areas, were too small to provide firewood. Only a few part-time farmers in the Textile, Coal and Iron, or Atlantic Coast Subregions cut their fuel. In the Coal and Iron Subregion, the chief industrial employers made provision for the sale of fuel at wholesale rates. In the Lumber Subregion, most commercial and some noncommercial part-time farmers were able to cut their fuel from their own or their landlords' woodland, while in the sparsely settled, wooded Naval Stores Subregion practically all were able to cut their fuel.

FARM RECEIPTS AND EXPENSES

Sale of Products

Commercial part-time farmers, by definition, were those who produced some crop for market. Since no attempt was made in the study to analyze this phase of their activity, the commercial group is omitted from the discussion of the sale of products.

Of the white noncommercial and the Negro part-time farmers,[11] one-half sold no products and one-fourth sold less than $50 worth (table 44).

In the Textile Subregion and among the white part-time farmers of the Coal and Iron and Atlantic Coast Subregions (appendix table 25), the relatively large proportion selling products (59 percent, 47 percent,

Table 44.—Relation Between Cash Receipts From All Products Sold and Total Cash Farm Expenses [1] on White Noncommercial and Negro Part-Time Farms,[2] 1934

Cash receipts from all products sold	Part-time farms		Average cash receipts	Average cash expenses	Net receipts
	Number	Percent			
Total	970	100	$40	$56	$−16
None	493	51	0	37	−37
$1 to $49	244	25	25	55	−30
$50 to $99	114	12	75	66	−9
$100 to $199	84	9	150	106	44
$200 or more	34	3	384	174	210
Unknown	1	*	—	20	—

* Less than 0.5 percent.
[1] Exclusive of taxes and rent.
[2] For data by subregions, see appendix table 25.

[11] The Negro part-time farmers of the Lumber Subregion should likewise be omitted from the discussion of the sale of products because two-thirds of them cultivated from 1 to 16 acres of cotton, and very few sold any product except cotton. The proportion of Negroes in this subregion selling products (77 percent) and the average cash receipts ($96) are, therefore, not strictly comparable with the figures for the other groups. Some Negro part-time farmers in the Atlantic Coast Subregion were commercial farmers in the same sense, in that they grew several acres of vegetables for sale.

and 45 percent, respectively) was due chiefly to their production of surplus milk or butter, these two products accounting for from one-half to three-fourths of all sales. It is pertinent to recall at this point that it was these groups which had cows producing the highest average number of quarts of milk.

Expenses

If receipts of part-time farmers were small, so also were expenses. Roughly one-fourth of all who sold any products took in more than enough to meet their cash outlay for farm expenses (table 44). Those whose receipts averaged less than $50 had an average deficit of $30, while for those whose average receipts were between $50 and $100, the deficit was very small. Those whose sale of products brought them $100 or more showed a cash surplus at the end of the year. Exclusive of white commercial farmers, average cash receipts exceeded average cash expenses only among Negroes in the Atlantic Coast and Lumber Subregions, who raised truck crops and cotton, respectively, for sale (table 45).

Table 45.—Average Cash Expenses [1] and Receipts on White Noncommercial and Negro Part-Time Farms, by Subregion, 1934

Subregion, color, and type of farm	Average cash expenses	Average cash receipts
Total	$56	$40
Textile:		
White:		
Noncommercial	92	45
Coal and Iron:		
White	73	33
Negro	15	4
Atlantic Coast:		
White:		
Noncommercial	62	30
Negro	26	38
Lumber:		
White:		
Noncommercial	55	15
Negro	38	96
Naval Stores:		
White:		
Noncommercial	25	†

† Average not computed for less than 10 cases.
[1] Exclusive of taxes and rent.

Except in the Textile Subregion and among white farmers in the Coal and Iron Subregion, where feed for a cow added from $50 to $75 to the expenses, from one-fifth to two-thirds of the expenses of part-time farmers went for labor (tables 45 and 47). Since few members of these groups had work stock, they usually hired labor for plowing. On nearly half (48 percent) of all part-time farms no labor was hired, and on 40 percent the amount paid for labor was less than $25 a year (table 46). Of the remaining 12 percent, whose expenses for labor ranged from $25 to $500 or more, almost two-thirds were commercial part-time farmers (appendix table 26).

Table 46.—Amount Paid for Hired Labor on Part-Time Farms,[1] 1934

| Amount paid for hired labor | Part-time farms | |
	Number	Percent
Total	1,113	100
None	527	48
$1 to $4	216	19
$5 to $14	181	16
$15 to $24	51	5
$25 to $49	38	3
$50 to $99	44	4
$100 to $199	24	2
$200 to $499	22	2
$500 or more	9	1
Unknown	1	*

*Less than 0.5 percent.
[1] For data by subregions, see appendix table 26.

Table 47.—Amount Paid for Hired Labor per Farm and per Crop Acre on Part-Time Farms, by Type of Farm, by Color of Operator, and by Subregion, 1934

| Subregion, color, and type of farm | Average amount paid for hired labor [1] | |
	Per farm	Per crop acre
Total	$41	$4.50
Textile:		
White:		
Commercial	86	4.00
Noncommercial	11	6.40
Coal and Iron:		
White	14	5.50
Negro	5	4.40
Atlantic Coast:		
White:		
Commercial	350	11.50
Noncommercial	34	9.30
Negro	18	4.70
Lumber:		
White:		
Commercial	151	3.60
Noncommercial	17	5.10
Negro	25	2.50
Naval Stores:		
White:		
Commercial	76	1.80
Noncommercial	5	3.60

[1] On farms having hired labor.

LABOR REQUIREMENTS OF PART-TIME FARMS

The relatively small amounts spent for labor indicate that the part-time farmers and their families did most of the work. Labor requirements were greatest from April through August (table 48). On white noncommercial part-time farms, the average labor requirement ranged from a little less than 3 hours to about 5½ hours a day for these months. On commercial farms, the averages ranged from about 6 hours to about 16 hours per day.

After August the number of hours required on noncommercial farms decreased, but on the commercial farms where there was more harvesting, labor requirements were heavy until November. During the winter months, both types of farms required relatively fewer hours of labor.

Table 48.—Average Number of Hours Worked per Day on Part-Time Farms by Heads and Other Members, by Type of Farm, by Color, by Season, and by Subregion, 1934

Subregion, color, and type of farm	Season			
	April–June	July–August	September–October	November–March
AVERAGE HOURS WORKED PER DAY BY HEADS AND OTHER MEMBERS				
Textile:				
White:				
Commercial	10.3	10.9	10.5	5.5
Noncommercial	3.5	3.5	2.7	1.7
Coal and Iron:				
White	4.7	4.3	3.1	1.8
Negro	6.4	6.3	3.9	1.1
Atlantic Coast:				
White:				
Commercial	6.0	5.8	5.8	5.1
Noncommercial	3.9	3.4	3.1	2.6
Negro	6.4	5.1	5.3	3.6
Lumber:				
White:				
Commercial	10.5	10.4	10.2	7.2
Noncommercial	5.5	5.4	4.5	3.6
Negro	9.0	8.2	8.0	4.9
Naval Stores:				
White:				
Commercial	14.8	16.9	12.3	7.8
Noncommercial	2.8	2.5	1.8	1.5
AVERAGE HOURS WORKED PER DAY BY HEADS				
Textile:				
White:				
Commercial	4.5	4.6	3.8	2.1
Noncommercial	1.5	1.4	1.2	0.7
Coal and Iron:				
White	2.5	2.3	1.8	0.9
Negro	3.1	3.0	2.0	0.6
Atlantic Coast:				
White:				
Commercial	4.5	3.9	4.2	3.5
Noncommercial	2.0	1.6	1.7	1.4
Negro	2.7	2.1	2.4	1.6
Lumber:				
White:				
Commercial	3.5	3.4	3.2	2.3
Noncommercial	2.2	1.9	1.8	1.3
Negro	2.9	2.6	2.5	1.6
Naval Stores:				
White:				
Commercial	8.5	8.9	7.3	5.6
Noncommercial	1.9	1.9	1.6	1.4
AVERAGE HOURS WORKED PER DAY BY MEMBERS OTHER THAN HEADS				
Textile:				
White:				
Commercial	5.8	6.3	6.7	3.4
Noncommercial	2.0	2.1	1.5	1.0
Coal and Iron:				
White	2.2	2.0	1.3	0.9
Negro	3.3	3.3	1.9	0.5
Atlantic Coast:				
White:				
Commercial	1.5	1.9	1.6	1.6
Noncommercial	1.9	1.8	1.4	1.2
Negro	3.7	3.0	2.9	2.0
Lumber:				
White:				
Commercial	7.0	7.0	7.0	4.9
Noncommercial	3.3	3.5	2.7	2.3
Negro	6.1	5.6	5.5	3.3
Naval Stores:				
White:				
Commercial	6.3	8.0	5.0	2.2
Noncommercial	0.9	0.6	0.2	0.1

In the Coal and Iron Subregion, the Negro part-time farmers seem to have spent more time on their farms than did their white neighbors, although their farms or gardens were only about half as large. Negroes of this region spent, on an average, as much time on their farms from April through August as did the Negroes of the Atlantic Coast Subregion, and almost as much as did those of the Lumber Subregion, where the presence of some semicommercial truck farmers and cotton growers increased the need for labor. Because of the presence in the Atlantic Coast and Lumber Subregions of these semicommercial farm operations, figures for these groups do not reveal the true situation as to the labor requirements for home consumption.

In some areas and groups, the head of the family worked half or over half of the total time spent by the family on the part-time farm, but in most cases other members of the family did as much work on the farm as did the head. On 16 percent of the farms, the head of the household did all of the work. Both the head and his wife worked on almost two-fifths of the farms; on one-third of the farms work was done by the head, his wife, and one or more other members (table 49).

The work of children under 12 years of age was not included in labor calculations. While it was not uncommon for younger children to help, their work was not of great importance. In many households, there were some boys and girls, elderly parents, relatives, or friends sharing the house who did not work on the farm.

Table 49.—Number of Persons, Except Heads, 12 Years of Age or Over, Working on Part-Time Farms,[1] 1934

Number of persons, except heads, 12 years of age or over, working on farms	Part-time farms	
	Number	Percent
Total	1,113	100
No member except head	182	16
Wife only	411	37
Wife and 1 or more other members	356	32
1 other member	86	8
2 other members	47	4
3 other members	20	2
4 or more other members	11	1

[1] For data by subregions, see appendix table 27.

The relation of the time spent in working on the part-time farm, especially by the head, to the hours worked at off-the-farm occupation is of considerable importance in any estimate of the value of part-time farming. If the farming enterprise takes too much of the head's time and energy, it not only handicaps him economically in obtaining and keeping a job, but absorbs all his spare time and leaves none for recreation and normal social activities. Both of these questions are treated more fully in sections of this study dealing with off-the-farm occupation and the social features of part-time farming, and also in the more detailed discussion of the several areas in Part II.

Suffice it to say here that, in general, there was no indication that the farm enterprise took a burdensome amount of time. Hours in the chief industries were shortened by the N. R. A. in 1934 and were often shortened by market conditions to less than those allowed by the codes.

When this study was made, hours in the service industries were about what they always were, but part-time farmers engaged in service industries apparently had sufficient time for their farming enterprises. Even the part-time farmers working in rural industries, such as turpentine, or in agriculture, as truck farm laborers, made no complaint of lack of time.

Chapter II

OFF-THE-FARM EMPLOYMENT

THIS STUDY was concerned both with the off-the-farm employment of part-time farmers and with comparisons of their employment with that of their nonfarming neighbors in similar occupations.

DISTANCE TO WORK

Over half (57 percent) of the part-time farmers included in the survey lived within 1½ miles from their work, or within easy walking distance (table 50). An additional 13 percent lived between 1½ and 2½ miles away—a not unreasonable walking distance. Not all of those living at short distances walked to work, however; nor did all those who lived at even considerable distances ride. A number of the part-time farmers walked 2 miles, a few walked 3 miles, and an occasional part-time farmer, especially among the Negroes of the Atlantic Coast Subregion, walked 4 miles or more.

Automobiles were the most common form of transportation, although in the Coal and Iron Subregion trolleys and buses were used

Table 50.—Distance to Place of Employment of Heads of Part-Time Farm and Nonfarming Industrial Households,[1] 1934

Distance to place of employment	Part-time farmers		Nonfarming industrial workers	
	Number	Percent	Number	Percent
Total	1,113	100	1,334	100
None	25	2	2	*
Less than ½ mile	320	29	512	38
1 mile	291	26	394	30
2 miles	148	13	169	13
3 miles	108	10	65	5
4 to 5 miles	99	9	126	10
6 to 9 miles	85	8	46	3
10 miles or more	35	3	17	1
Unknown	2	*	3	*

* Less than 0.5 percent.
[1] For data by subregions, see appendix table 28.

35

almost as frequently. Work trains operated by employers were common in the Coal and Iron Subregion, and in other areas, though to a less extent, work trains, buses, or trucks were used. Bicycles were rare as a means of transportation.

It may be that distances of 10 miles or more, traveled by 3 percent of the part-time farmers, are uneconomical, but this would depend upon the wages earned and the mode of transportation. Part of those going long distances were in the Coal and Iron Subregion, and since they traveled by trolley, they probably paid little more to ride a longer than a shorter distance. Many others traveled in groups in an automobile, sharing expenses, so that the distance traveled was not burdensome from a financial point of view. In general, the time consumed in going to and from work, except for the few who walked more than 2 miles, did not make serious inroads into the time available for farm work.

To get to their work, the Negroes traveled considerably shorter distances on the average than did the whites—a fact which may have been the result of their lack of transportation facilities and their smaller incomes. In all subregions except the Atlantic Coast, the commercial part-time farmers traveled twice the distance the non-commercial farmers did, since they had to be farther from town to secure the larger acreages to cultivate (table 51).

The nonfarming industrial group lived a little nearer their work on the average than did the part-time farmers (table 50). Thus 68 per-

Table 51.—Average Distance to Place of Employment of Heads of Part-Time Farm and Nonfarming Industrial Households, by Type of Farm, by Color, and by Subregion, 1934

Subregion, color, and type of farm	Average number of miles to place of employment	
	Part-time farmers	Nonfarming industrial workers
Total	2.3	1.6
Textile:		
White	1.7	0.8
Commercial	3.2	
Noncommercial	1.4	
Coal and Iron:		
White	3.3	1.6
Negro	1.6	2.8
Atlantic Coast:		
White	3.9	1.1
Commercial	3.0	
Noncommercial	4.3	
Negro	1.8	1.1
Lumber:		
White	3.2	1.3
Commercial	4.5	
Noncommercial	1.9	
Negro	1.6	1.3
Naval Stores:		
White	1.9	2.7
Commercial	2.1	
Noncommercial	1.6	

cent of them, as compared with 57 percent of the part-time farmers, lived within 1½ miles from work; 81 percent, as compared with 70 percent of the part-time farmers, lived within 2½ miles. Only 4 percent of the nonfarming industrial group lived 6 miles or farther, whereas 11 percent of the part-time farmers lived that distance. An examination of figures for the various subregions shows that the greater average distances traveled by part-time farmers is largely due to the inclusion of the commercial group (appendix table 28). In the noncommercial group, with which the nonfarming industrial workers are more nearly comparable in respect to location, the actual distances traveled are not much greater in some areas than those traveled by the nonfarming industrial workers. In the Naval Stores Subregion, the nonfarming industrial workers traveled greater average distances than did the part-time farmers (table 51).

INDUSTRY AND OCCUPATION

Every main census classification of industry was represented in the off-the-farm employment of the part-time farmers in the Eastern Cotton Belt. More than half of the farmers (54.7 percent) were in the manufacturing and mechanical industries, which were representative of all the chief manufacturing industries of the three States in which surveys were made (table 52). There was a small group (8.8 percent) in transportation and communication and a similar group (7.9 percent) in trade. Sixteen percent of the farmers, chiefly Negroes in the Atlantic Coast and Lumber Subregions, found a cash wage in agriculture.

With respect to distribution in industry, the nonfarming industrial workers and the part-time farmers were in the main comparable (table 52). However, some differences were to be expected inasmuch as the sample of part-time farmers in all subregions was made without any regard to the industry in which the farmers worked, whereas the sample industrial workers were chosen to represent the major industries of each subregion[1] (appendix table 29).

In general occupational level,[2] the two groups were more closely parallel (table 53). One-fourth of each group were classified as skilled; 29 percent of the part-time farmers and 32 percent of the nonfarmers were classified as semiskilled; and 37 percent of each were classified as unskilled. In all areas, Negroes made up the bulk of the unskilled workers in both groups (appendix table 30).

Within these industries and occupational levels, part-time farmers worked at a large variety of specific jobs. The combination of farming

---

[1] See Introduction for criteria used in selecting part-time farm households and nonfarm industrial households.

[2] The occupational classification used follows Dr. Alba M. Edwards' social-economic groups. See *Journal of American Statistical Association*, December 1933, pp. 377–387.

with another type of job was limited, apparently, only by the resources of the locality and not by any lack of ingenuity on the part of the workers.

Jobs held by part-time farmers ran the gamut of the division of labor within the main industries—textiles, coal and iron mining, iron

Table 52.—Industry of Heads of Part-Time Farm and Nonfarming Industrial Households,[1] 1934

Industry in 1934	Part-time farmers		Nonfarming industrial workers	
	Number	Percent	Number	Percent
Total	1,113	100.0	1,334	100.0
Agriculture	177	15.9	—	—
Forestry	7	0.6	—	—
Fishing	1	0.1	—	—
Extraction of minerals:				
Coal mining	24	2.2	193	14.5
Iron mining	76	6.8	130	9.7
Other extraction of minerals	1	0.1	—	—
Manufacturing and mechanical industries:				
Building and construction	47	4.2	20	1.5
Food and allied	9	0.8	10	0.7
Iron, steel, machinery, and vehicles:				
Blast furnaces, steel rolling mills, and coke works	170	15.3	218	16.3
Car and railroad shops	16	1.4	—	—
Other iron, steel, machinery, and vehicles	19	1.7	43	3.2
Saw and planing mills	16	1.4	42	3.1
Furniture and other woodworking	38	3.4	153	11.5
Paper, printing, and allied	1	0.1	5	0.4
Cotton mills	113	10.2	165	12.4
Knitting mills	7	0.6	20	1.5
Other textile	74	6.7	29	2.2
Independent hand trades	3	0.3	1	0.1
Turpentine farms and distilleries	37	3.3	49	3.7
Fertilizer factories	19	1.7	18	1.3
Asbestos products	—	—	42	3.1
Other manufacturing and mechanical	40	3.6	30	2.2
Transportation and communication:				
Construction and maintenance of streets	15	1.3	1	0.1
Garages, greasing stations, etc	6	0.5	1	0.1
Postal service	3	0.3	3	0.2
Steam and street railroads	49	4.4	19	1.4
Other transportation and communication	26	2.3	36	2.7
Trade:				
Automobile agencies and filling stations	18	1.6	13	1.0
Wholesale and retail trade	64	5.9	42	3.1
Other trade	4	0.4	1	0.1
Public service (not elsewhere classified)	12	1.1	17	1.3
Professional service	6	0.5	2	0.2
Domestic and personal service	13	1.2	29	2.2
Industry not specified	2	0.1	2	0.2

[1] For data by subregions, see appendix table 29.

Table 53.—Occupation of Heads of Part-Time Farm and Nonfarming Industrial Households,[1] 1934

Occupation	Part-time farmers		Nonfarming industrial workers	
	Number	Percent	Number	Percent
Total	1,113	100	1,334	100
Proprietary	27	2	6	*
Clerical	72	7	76	6
Skilled	282	25	336	25
Semiskilled	321	29	432	32
Unskilled:				
Farm laborer	17?	16	—	—
Servant	16	1	21	2
Other unskilled	224	20	463	35

* Less than 0.5 percent.
[1] For data by subregions, see appendix table 30.

and steel manufacturing, port industries, truck farming, fertilizer factories, saw and planing mills, veneer and cooperage factories, and turpentining. Part-time farmers held a variety of jobs connected with railways and railway shops, ranging from locomotive engineer to section hand. They held many kinds of mechanical and construction jobs, such as those of machinist, garage mechanic, electric welder, steam-shovel operator, carpenter, mason, painter, plumber, and blacksmith. Among part-time farmers, there were drivers of trucks, buses, and delivery wagons. There were automobile salesmen, filling station attendants, store clerks, and peddlers. Others held public service jobs, such as policeman, constable, postman, rural mail carrier, drawbridge attendant, road construction guard, forester, and convict guard. Some held service jobs, such as janitor, caddy, barber, hostler, gardener, and caretaker. There were a number of small proprietors: cobblers, barbers, millers, and operators of markets and stores. There were bank employees and preachers.

It must be remembered also that some other members of the part-time farm households were employed. The gainfully occupied women worked at jobs within the chief industries which were almost as varied as those held by the men, thus adding to the total list many which, within certain factories, were normally women's jobs. Outside manufacturing industries, workers other than the head of the household held jobs as teachers, stenographers, telephone operators, seamstresses, beauty parlor operators, newspaper carriers, and messengers.

It may be of interest to note in passing that among the part-time farmers and the nonfarming industrial workers there was remarkable stability both in the industry in which they worked and in their occupational level since 1929. In only two areas were there notable shifts in industry. In Carroll County in the Textile Subregion, nearly all of the cases surveyed who were full-time farm operators in 1929 had become textile operatives by 1934. In Coffee County in the Naval Stores Subregion, practically all of the cases that were farm operators in 1929 had become turpentine workers (table 52 and appendix table 31). Both of these changes represented a movement from full-time farming to a combination of farming with an industrial job. There was a similar movement, involving fewer cases, in the Lumber Subregion, in Greenville County in the Textile Subregion, and among the Negroes of the Atlantic Coast Subregion. In the last-mentioned area, Negro farm operators became part-time farmers, with day labor in agriculture furnishing their cash-wage employment.

EMPLOYMENT, EARNINGS, AND INCOME

In questions relating to hours, regularity of employment, wages, and earnings, the difficulties of comparing part-time farmers with nonfarming industrial workers were multiplied by the fact that the two groups were not parallel in their off-the-farm industry. The widest differences between the two groups in employment and earnings occurred in the areas where there were the greatest differences in industrial groupings. In the Atlantic Coast Subregion, for example, two-thirds of the Negro part-time farmers found their cash-wage occupation in agriculture, which has long hours, seasonal employment, and low wages. It was not surprising, therefore, that these Negro part-time farmers reported longer working hours, an average of almost 20 percent fewer working days, and somewhat less than half the annual earnings of the Negro nonfarming industrial workers (appendix tables 32 and 34). A similar situation, though not so extreme, existed among the Negroes of the Lumber Subregion.

In the Naval Stores Subregion the situation was almost reversed. The nonfarming industrial workers surveyed were concentrated in the turpentine industry, where a very low wage placed them at a disadvantage, as compared with the neighboring noncommercial part-time farmers. Members of the commercial group in this area were at even a greater disadvantage than the nonfarming industrial workers as regards their off-the-farm occupation, since they were chiefly farmers working relatively few days at the low-paid job of turpentine collecting.[3]

Since summary figures comparing part-time farmers and nonfarming industrial workers are reliable only in a very general way, the questions of earnings and employment are discussed very briefly here.[4]

That a man's status as a part-time farmer did not affect his opportunity for regularity of employment is suggested by the fact that the commercial part-time farmers averaged almost as many days' employment as did the noncommercial farmers (appendix table 32), though the former lived farther from their jobs and spent much more time working on their farms. Only 19 percent of the part-time farmers and 27 percent of the nonfarmers had 250 or more days' work, while 57 percent of the part-time farmers and 53 percent of the nonfarmers had less than 200 days' employment (table 54). The area of greatest underemployment was the Coal and Iron Subregion, where the average for each group of whites was approximately 150 days and for each group of Negroes slightly less than 115 days (table 55).

With a somewhat smaller average number of days employed, and a large number in some areas working at low wage agricultural day labor, the heads of households in the part-time farm group as a whole had

---

[3] The effect of local labor conditions on employment and earnings was naturally reflected in this survey. In one locality, for example, a large number of the part-time farmers worked in a plant that closed down for several months in 1934, while in another subregion a large number of the nonfarming workers were employed in a plant that closed down.

[4] For data by subregions, see Part II.

Table 54.—Number of Days of Off-the-Farm Employment [1] of Heads of Part-Time Farm and Nonfarming Industrial Households,[2] 1934

Number of days employed	Part-time farmers		Nonfarming industrial workers	
	Number	Percent	Number	Percent
Total	1,113	100	1,334	100
1 to 49 days [3]	11	1	1	*
50 to 99 days	226	20	241	18
100 to 149 days	213	19	274	21
150 to 199 days	184	17	187	14
200 to 249 days	270	24	264	20
250 to 299 days	94	9	224	17
300 to 349 days	79	7	111	8
350 days or more	35	3	32	2
Unknown	1	*	—	—

* Less than 0.5 percent.
[1] At principal off-the-farm employment (job with the largest earnings).
[2] For data by subregions, see appendix table 32.
[3] A few cases working off the farm less than 50 days were enumerated.

Table 55.—Average Number of Days of Off-the-Farm Employment [1] of Heads of Part-Time Farm and Nonfarming Industrial Households, by Type of Farm, by Color, and by Subregion, 1934

Subregion, color, and type of farm	Average number of days of off-the-farm employment	
	Part-time farmers	Nonfarming industrial workers
Total	180	186
Textile:		
White	217	233
Commercial	214	
Noncommercial	218	
Coal and Iron:		
White	156	151
Negro	112	114
Atlantic Coast:		
White	226	261
Commercial	219	
Noncommercial	229	
Negro	155	189
Lumber:		
White	216	240
Commercial	211	
Noncommercial	221	
Negro	191	221
Naval Stores:		
White	159	221
Commercial	83	
Noncommercial	241	

[1] At principal off-the-farm employment (job with the largest earnings).

somewhat smaller average earnings than nonfarmers (table 56). Fifty-six percent of the part-time farmers made less than $500 in 1934 at their principal off-the-farm employment [5] as compared with fifty-one percent of the nonfarming industrial group. Only 12 percent of the part-time farmers and 14 percent of the nonfarming industrial workers made $1,000 or over.

[5] For the few cases that reported more than one type of off-the-farm employment, see appendix table 33.

Table 56.—Earnings[1] From Industrial Employment of Heads of Part-Time Farm and Nonfarming Industrial Households,[2] 1934

Earnings from industrial employment	Part-time farmers		Nonfarming industrial workers	
	Number	Percent	Number	Percent
Total	1,113	100	1,334	100
$1 to $99	100	9	9	1
$100 to $249	246	22	174	13
$250 to $499	271	25	491	37
$500 to $749	225	20	297	22
$750 to $999	128	12	180	13
$1,000 to $1,249	67	6	78	6
$1,250 to $1,499	25	2	39	3
$1,500 to $1,999	36	3	46	3
$2,000 to $2,499	9	1	13	1
$2,500 or more	2	*	7	1
Unknown[3]	4	*	—	—

* Less than 0.5 percent.
[1] At principal off-the-farm employment (job with the largest earnings).
[2] For data by subregions, see appendix table 34.
[3] 4 Negro cases in the Atlantic Coast Subregion included services of a mule.

Commercial part-time farmers not only worked almost as many days as did the noncommercial farmers, but their average annual earnings from all off-the-farm sources were at least as high in all areas except in the Naval Stores Subregion. In the Atlantic Coast and Lumber Subregions, their earnings averaged approximately the same as those of the nonfarming industrial workers [6] (table 59).

EMPLOYMENT OF OTHER MEMBERS OF HOUSEHOLD

Another indication that the farming enterprise does not handicap the part-time farm family in filling outside jobs was found in the records of employment for other members of the household (table 57).

Table 57.—Employment of Members[1] in Addition to the Head of Part-Time Farm and Nonfarming Industrial Households,[2] 1934

Number of members working in addition to the head	Part-time farm households		Nonfarming industrial households	
	Number	Percent	Number	Percent
Total	1,113	100	1,334	100
No member except head	632	57	877	65
Wife only	162	15	215	16
Wife and 1 or more other members	93	8	48	4
1 other member	139	12	145	11
2 other members	61	6	37	3
3 other members	16	1	9	1
4 or more other members	10	1	3	*

* Less than 0.5 percent.
[1] 16–64 years of age.
[2] For data by subregions, see appendix table 35.

[6] Comparison of data in table 59 and in appendix table 34 indicates the small amount earned on the average from jobs other than the principal off-the-farm job. Few heads had more than one off-the-farm job either simultaneously or through changing jobs.

In 43 percent of the part-time farm families, someone besides the head was employed in industry, as compared with 35 percent of the nonfarming households. Wives of part-time farmers had industrial employment in 23 percent of the cases, as compared with 20 percent of the nonfarming industrial cases. The distribution of households by number of members employed showed a slightly larger percentage of part-time farm than of nonfarming industrial households in each classification. It will be remembered, however, that part-time farm households were larger and their heads were older so that the members available for employment would naturally be more numerous than in nonfarming industrial households. This consideration partly counterbalances the more frequent outside employment in part-time farm families, but it is safe to conclude that the opportunities are no less for part-time farm than for nonfarming industrial households.

The proportion of households with only the head working varied considerably from area to area, but there was a close parallel between part-time farmers and nonfarming industrial workers within each area (table 58). In the case of employed wives, differences among the

Table 58.—Employment of Heads and Other Members [1] of Part-Time Farm and Nonfarming Industrial Households, by Color and by Subregion, 1934

Subregion and color	Percent of households with only the head employed		Percent of households with the wife employed		Percent of young people 16–24 employed	
	Part-time farm	Non-farming industrial	Part-time farm	Non-farming industrial	Part-time farm	Non-farming industrial
Total	57	65	23	20	35	34
Textile:						
White	46	46	24	39	54	55
Coal and Iron:						
White	75	84	2	1	20	18
Negro	83	81	6	6	9	16
Atlantic Coast:						
White	80	75	4	5	25	33
Negro	32	48	55	40	48	59
Lumber:						
White	62	65	15	13	32	48
Negro	27	42	58	50	51	40
Naval Stores:						
White	77	68	7	22	17	70

[1] 16–64 years of age.

areas were more marked than for heads. In the Coal and Iron Subregion, for example, there was not much opportunity for women to work, whereas in the Textile Subregion, there was almost as much industrial opportunity for wives as for their husbands. In the Atlantic Coast and Lumber Subregions, about half of the Negro women found employment in domestic service and in the fields of regular and truck farms.

On the average, young people in part-time farm households had opportunities for employment equal to those in nonfarming industrial families, despite their greater distance from towns. Over one-third of the youth 16–24 years of age in both part-time farm and nonfarming industrial households were employed. The employment opportunities for young people varied considerably in the different areas, however. The highest percentages of young people employed were among whites in the Textile Subregion and among Negroes of the Atlantic Coast Subregion.

The amounts earned by the employed members of part-time farm and nonfarming industrial households varied greatly from area to area, depending upon the employment opportunities for women and young people. Earnings of members other than the heads of part-time farm households ranged from 7 percent of the total off-the-farm household earnings for Negroes in the Coal and Iron Subregion to 54 percent for white commercial part-time farm families in the Naval Stores Subregion. Members other than the heads in nonfarming industrial households contributed from 8 to 25 percent of the total household income.

Table 59.—Earnings of Heads and Other Members of Part-Time Farm and Nonfarming Households at Industrial Employment, by Type of Farm, by Color, and by Subregion, 1934

Subregion, color, and type of farm	Average total nonfarm earnings			Percent earned by other members
	Total	Heads	Other members	
PART-TIME FARM HOUSEHOLDS				
Total	$723	$546	$187	26
Textile:				
White	1,097	739	358	33
Commercial	956	738	218	23
Noncommercial	1,116	740	376	34
Coal and Iron:				
White	899	739	160	18
Negro	370	345	25	7
Atlantic Coast:				
White	1,184	909	275	23
Commercial	1,440	1,055	385	27
Noncommercial	1,054	836	218	21
Negro	264	196	68	26
Lumber:				
White	802	636	166	21
Commercial	808	659	149	18
Noncommercial	796	612	184	23
Negro	339	276	63	19
Naval Stores:				
White	394	299	95	24
Commercial	191	87	104	54
Noncommercial	621	531	90	15
NONFARMING INDUSTRIAL HOUSEHOLDS				
Total	763	626	137	18
Textile:				
White	1,150	859	291	25
Coal and Iron:				
White	810	733	77	10
Negro	432	373	59	14
Atlantic Coast:				
White	1,244	1,048	196	16
Negro	503	413	90	18
Lumber:				
White	834	679	155	19
Negro	546	456	90	16
Naval Stores:				
White	290	268	22	8

Earnings by members other than the head in both part-time farm and nonfarming industrial households were relatively low in the Coal and Iron Subregion and relatively high in the Textile Subregion (table 59). Earnings of members of part-time farm households in the Coal and Iron Subregion amounted to 18 percent of the total off-the-farm earnings for the whites and 7 percent for Negroes; those of members of nonfarming industrial households averaged 10 percent of the total for the whites and 14 percent for the Negroes. In the Textile Subregion, earnings by members other than the heads of all white households studied, averaged 33 percent of the total off-the-farm income among the part-time farmers, and 25 percent of the total income among the nonfarming industrial group.

In the Atlantic Coast and Lumber Subregions, there were employment opportunities for members other than the heads of Negro households in agriculture, but the rates of pay were so low that the amounts earned were small. In all areas, the employment of other members, especially of young people, was often irregular and poorly paid.

CONTRIBUTION OF FARM ENTERPRISE TO FAMILY INCOME

Among the commercial part-time farmers, the cotton, tobacco, or truck crops constituted a considerable addition to the family income. No detailed analysis of this phase of their farming enterprise was made, but with a net cash farm income averaging $165 in the Lumber, $343 in the Naval Stores, and $324 in the Atlantic Coast Subregions,[7] the commercial group was well ahead of the nonfarming industrial workers in total income.

The average value of products sold by noncommercial part-time farmers was so little in excess of cash expenses that it would not serve to lessen the difference between part-time farm and nonfarm cash incomes. The value of products consumed by the family was not calculated for all part-time farmers. Some typical cases [8] reveal, however, that even modest enterprises, such as those of Negroes in the Atlantic Coast Subregion, yielded products worth about $70 to a typical part-time farmer, while those of typical Negroes in the Lumber and Coal and Iron Subregions yielded twice that amount. Enterprises which included a cow produced an average of from $200 to nearly $400 worth of products in all areas.

Thus, the value of the products consumed among the whites of the Lumber, Atlantic Coast, and Textile Subregions would make the incomes of the noncommercial part-time farmers equal to, and in many cases greater than, those of the nonfarming industrial workers. It is doubtful whether the small amount of produce of the Negroes in the Atlantic Coast and Lumber Subregions would make up the difference

[7] See Part II.
[8] See Appendix A, Case Studies of Part-Time Farmers.

between incomes of the farming and nonfarming groups. In these regions Negro part-time farmers were at a disadvantage in the kind of employment that was open to them. In the Coal and Iron Subregion, where the industrial earnings of part-time farmers and nonfarmers were nearly the same, the value of products used and sold constituted an advantage of some $200 or $300 for the more successful white part-time farmers and an advantage of about half that amount for the Negroes.

CHANGES IN INCOME, 1929–1934

To secure another side light on the reasons that caused part-time farmers to undertake farming enterprises, incomes for 1929, where it was possible to obtain them, were compared with those for 1934. In general, of course, incomes for 1934 were smaller than those for 1929, though reductions varied greatly from area to area. In the Coal and Iron Subregion, practically all part-time farm households had suffered large income decreases between 1929 and 1934 (table 60). Similar

Table 60.—Average Total Income From Nonfarm Sources of All Members of Part-Time Farm and Nonfarming Industrial Households, by Color and by Subregion, 1929 and 1934

Subregion and color	Part-time farm households				Nonfarming industrial households			
	Number of households whose income was known in 1929 and 1934	Average 1929 income	Average 1934 income	Number of households with less income in 1934 than in 1929	Number of households whose income was known in 1929 and 1934	Average 1929 income	Average 1934 income	Number of households with less income in 1934 than in 1929
Total_____	857	$944	$712	428	1,116	$1,108	$751	703
Textile:								
White_____	185	1,054	1,095	65	232	1,119	1,192	67
Coal and Iron:								
White_____	198	1,561	893	159	213	1,605	809	193
Negro_____	121	775	373	91	326	1,049	425	294
Atlantic Coast:								
White_____	45	1,294	1,142	19	80	1,344	1,252	34
Negro_____	119	298	258	31	83	595	504	39
Lumber:								
White_____	65	865	818	23	64	1,164	824	34
Negro_____	95	378	335	26	83	578	541	26
Naval Stores:								
White_____	29	867	639	14	35	394	325	16

income reductions, though not so extreme, were reported by part-time farmers in the Atlantic Coast and Naval Stores Subregions. In the Textile and Lumber Subregions, on the other hand, the operation of the N. R. A. codes in 1934 had resulted in some income increases since 1929. In the Textile Subregion, about two-thirds of the part-time farm families, who knew the amount of their incomes in 1929, had as much or more income in 1934. In both the Atlantic Coast and Lumber Subregions, almost three-fourths of the Negro part-time farm families had as much or more income in 1934.

RELIEF

Relatively small proportions of the part-time farm and nonfarming industrial families studied in the Eastern Cotton Belt had ever received relief.   The qualifications for part-time farmers used in this survey automatically eliminated most relief cases,[9] however.

Table 61.—Percent of Part-Time Farm and Nonfarming Industrial Households That Received Public or Private Relief During the Period 1929–35 and Public Relief in 1934, by Color and by Subregion

Subregion and color	Part-time farm households		Nonfarming industrial households	
	1929–35	1934 only	1929–35	1934 only
Textile:				
White	13	4	18	2
Coal and Iron:				
White	40	32	44	28
Negro	82	78	71	58
Atlantic Coast:				
White	27	21	15	16
Negro	34	16	22	15
Lumber:				
White	9	7	13	8
Negro	17	11	7	7
Naval Stores:				
White	10	8	29	10

Figures on the number of sample households that received public or private relief from 1929 to 1935 and public relief in 1934 (table 61) show that there was no consistent difference between part-time farmers and nonfarming industrial workers in the matter of relief.   In some areas more of one group had been on relief, and in others just the reverse was found.   The families which were on relief usually received small amounts and were aided mainly because of illness or prolonged unemployment.

The only area in which many families of either group were on relief was the Coal and Iron Subregion where employment and earnings were most sharply curtailed.   Eighty-two percent of the Negro part-time farm households and seventy-one percent of the Negro nonfarming industrial households received relief at some time during the period 1929–1934.   At some time during 1934 alone, 78 percent of the Negro part-time farm households and 58 percent of the Negro nonfarming industrial households were on relief.   While the relief figures of corresponding white groups were not so high as were the Negro figures, they were greater than those for whites in any other subregion.   Doubtless the fact that the Coal and Iron Subregion was a metropolitan area partially explains the comparatively high relief figures for this subregion, since relief standards in cities are usually

[9] To secure a sample of part-time farmers as the term is usually understood, i. e., heads of households who were employed at some cash-wage job while carrying on farming enterprises, it was necessary to place some minimum on the amount of employment at the industrial job.   The minimum was set at 50 days.

higher than those for rural areas.   The large relief load in this sub-region can also be explained by the high turnover of labor that accompanied fluctuations in employment.   In spite of the high relief load, however, part-time farm and nonfarming industrial households in the Coal and Iron Subregion had not received relief a dispropor-tionately large number of years (appendix table 36).

The relief statistics by themselves do not justify any conclusion as to whether part-time farming kept families off relief or not.   Many of the heads of part-time farm households, however, asserted emphat-ically that their gardens and other farm enterprises had kept them from the relief rolls.   Many of those who were classified as nonfarming industrial workers had become convinced of the value of part-time farming enterprises by the spring and summer of 1935, when they were interviewed, and were joining the ranks of part-time farmers.

OUTLOOK FOR EMPLOYMENT

From the survey, it would appear that the greatest need of part-time farmers and nonfarming industrial workers alike is more regular work, and more opportunity for the employment of other members of their families who would normally be contributing to the support os the household.   The outlook for employment is best considered in relation to the chief industry of each subregion.   Since the status of the service industries depends upon the activity of the leading industry of a locality, employment opportunities in those industries will improve as the main industry recovers.[10]

In the cotton textile industry, it seems probable that the general trend of employment will be downward for some time to come. Many factors point to a decreasing amount of labor per unit of out-put: new labor-saving machinery, now in the experimental stage, which eventually will replace several machines now being used; the probable retirement of obsolete plants; and the application of scientific management principles in the interest of economy and efficiency. Other factors which will adversely affect future cotton textile employ-ment are declining foreign trade and the increasing competition of cotton substitutes.

The major possibilities for stimulated employment in this industry are the increased activity of the knit goods industry and the recent develop-ment in the South of mills for the finishing and dyeing of textiles, which will probably lead to some increase in employment in this region.

In the Coal and Iron Subregion, low production of iron ore, pig iron, steel, and cast iron pipe has been general since the middle twenties.   Because of technological improvements, as well as loss of demand for the products, employment in iron and steel manufacturing has decreased steadily since 1923.   Employment in the coal mines

---

[10] For detailed discussions of major industries in the subregions, see Part II.

declined from 30,000 to 18,000 men between 1923 and 1933, and average work days were drastically reduced. Replacement of old blast furnaces by more efficient ones resulted in a 55 percent employment decrease in this industry between 1923 and 1929. In 1933, the coke plants employed less than one-half the number employed during the peak period of the middle twenties, and the cast iron pipe plants were employing barely one-third of the previous number.

A revival of general business activity to predepression levels would increase total employment in the iron and steel and allied industries of Alabama, but because of technological advances, return to predepression employment figures would be possible only with an output considerably beyond former high levels. Nevertheless, some increase in employment will come with any boom in construction activity, railroad buying, expansion of gas and water utility systems, etc.

Although no hope of any marked industrial revival is held out for the Atlantic Coast Subregion, the fact that manufacturing employment figures have remained fairly steady during the depression augurs well for those who are already engaged in part-time farming. The shipping and fertilizer business of Charleston, South Carolina, the industrial center of this subregion, and to a certain extent the trade industries of the city depend on the agricultural prosperity of the region. Any marked employment increase in those industries must await a solution of the agricultural problem.

The future of the forest products industries in the Lumber Subregion depends on the solution of many problems, such as the ownership and management of forest lands, the balancing of timber drain and growth, taxation of forest lands, and the development of new uses for forest products. Because of the widespread saw-timber drain of recent years, the lumber cut in the South must remain substantially below the 1925–1929 rate, and such a reduction will obviously be accompanied by an approximately proportionate decrease in employment. The greatest possibilities for employment in forest industries lie in the expansion of such wood-using industries as the pulp and paper industries.

Employment in the Naval Stores Subregion appears to depend almost wholly on a general world trade revival, although technological progress may bring changes in demand for the gum turpentine and gum rosin which are produced in this subregion. Improved practices within the industry itself may enable it to extend its markets, but such changes usually develop slowly.

Because of continued underemployment in the major industries of the Southeast, and the small hope of any vigorous industrial revival, the immediate future of part-time farming would seem to rest largely in the hands of industrial workers who have already had experience and success in part-time farming and of those with reasonably secure sources of income who would like to undertake such farming.

Chapter III

THE PART-TIME FARMER'S LIVING AND
SOCIAL CONDITIONS

THE THIRD group of questions with which this study concerned itself related to the living and social conditions of the part-time farmers as compared with the living and social conditions of their nonfarming neighbors.

LOCATION

As was to be expected, the great majority of part-time farmers included in the survey lived in the open country or in villages and towns, the number living in the open country being almost equal to

Table 62.—Residence of Part-Time Farm and Nonfarming Industrial Households, by Color and by Subregion, 1934

Subregion and color	Part-time farm households					Nonfarming industrial households				
	Total		Residence			Total		Residence		
	Num-ber	Per-cent	City	Village and town	Open coun-try	Num-ber	Per-cent	City	Village and town	Open coun-try
Total_____	1, 113	100	165	462	486	1, 334	100	805	485	44
Textile:										
White_____	293	26	1	212	80	314	23	79	231	4
Coal and Iron:										
White_____	204	18	47	136	21	222	17	110	112	—
Negro_____	124	11	86	38	—	346	26	290	56	—
Atlantic Coast:										
White_____	71	7	5	18	48	103	8	59	44	—
Negro_____	142	13	—	15	127	105	8	89	16	—
Lumber:										
White_____	76	7	11	1	64	92	7	83	9	—
Negro_____	132	12	15	8	109	103	8	95	8	—
Naval Stores:										
White_____	71	6	—	34	37	49	3	—	9	40

51

the number living in villages and towns. Well over one-half of the nonfarming industrial workers enumerated lived in cities [1] (table 62).

Almost one-half of the nonfarming industrial households living in villages and towns and the same proportion of part-time farm families were in the Textile Subregion.[2] One-half of the nonfarming industrial households and almost three-fourths of the part-time farm families that lived in cities were in the Coal and Iron Subregion. Practically all of the nonfarming industrial families studied who lived in the open country were in the Naval Stores Subregion.

HOUSING

In the Textile and Coal and Iron Subregions, company housing, higher town standards, and better industrial wages resulted in many neat cottages and bungalows with grass and shrubs, though there were some ramshackle farmhouses. In other areas, however, particularly in the Naval Stores Subregion and among the Negroes in the Lumber and Atlantic Coast Subregions, rough "up and down" houses and shacks were commonly found. In these regions paint is a luxury many houses have never known, and a lawn and flowers are not in the folkways. The houses of both white and Negro part-time farmers averaged larger, on the whole, than those of nonfarming industrial workers (appendix tables 37 and 38). The one exception to this was among the Negroes of the Coal and Iron Subregion, where the dwellings of part-time farmers and nonfarming industrial workers were the same, averaging 3.5 rooms per house. Houses of white part-time farmers averaged from 4.5 rooms in the Lumber Subregion to 5.6 rooms in the Atlantic Coast Subregion, with three-fifths of the houses of all white part-time farmers having 5 rooms or more.

Houses of white nonfarming industrial workers ranged from an average of 2.9 rooms in Carroll County of the Textile Subregion to an average of 4.8 rooms in the Atlantic Coast Subregion and in Greenville County of the Textile Subregion. A little over two-fifths of the houses of all nonfarming industrial workers had 5 rooms or more.

Houses of Negro part-time farmers were smaller than those of the whites in all areas. Those of Negro part-time farmers ranged from an average of 3.2 rooms in the Atlantic Coast Subregion to 3.7 rooms in the Lumber Subregion, with only 16 percent of all Negro part-time farmers having houses with 5 rooms or more (appendix tables 38 and 39).   Houses of nonfarming industrial Negroes ranged from 2.8 rooms in the Atlantic Coast Subregion to 3.5 rooms in the Iron and Coal Subregion, with 12 percent having 5 rooms or more.

[1] Open country—outside of centers with 50 or more inhabitants; villages—centers with 50 to 2,500 inhabitants; towns—centers with 2,500 to 10,000 inhabitants; cities—centers with 10,000 or more inhabitants.

[2] The distribution of the part-time farmers by residence is closely related to the sampling method used. See appendix C.

It will be remembered, however, that part-time farm households were larger than those of their nonfarming industrial neighbors (table 6, page 3), so that the apparent advantage of the part-time farmers disappears when the size of houses is considered in relation to the size of households. The commonly used standard for adequate housing allows only one person per room, while more than one person can be called crowded, more than two persons overcrowded, and more than three persons greatly overcrowded.[3]

An analysis of housing facilities of part-time farmers and non-farmers based on the number of persons per room (table 63 and appendix tables 38 and 39) makes it apparent that there tended to be slightly more crowding and overcrowding among white part-time farmers, and considerably more among Negro part-time farmers, than among their nonfarming industrial neighbors. There were only a few households in the white groups where there were more than three persons to a room, but in the case of Negroes such serious overcrowding was more frequent.

Table 63.—Number of Persons per Room [1] in Part-Time Farm and Nonfarming Industrial Households, by Color,[2] 1934

Type of household, by color	Total	1 person or less per room		2 persons or less but more than 1 per room		3 persons or less but more than 2 per room		More than 3 persons per room	
		Num-ber	Per-cent	Num-ber	Per-cent	Num-ber	Per-cent	Num-ber	Per-cent
White:									
Part-time farm households	715	411	58	265	37	36	5	3	*
Nonfarming industrial households	780	475	61	262	34	35	4	8	1
Negro:									
Part-time farm households	398	145	37	155	39	77	19	21	5
Nonfarming industrial households	554	254	46	231	41	60	11	9	2

*Less than 0.5 percent.

[1] According to accepted housing standards, 1 person or less per room is considered adequate; 2 persons or less, but more than 1 per room, crowded; 3 persons or less, but more than 2 per room, overcrowded; and more than 3 persons per room, greatly overcrowded.
[2] For data by subregions, see appendix table 39.

Among both white part-time farm and nonfarming industrial households, crowded conditions existed most frequently in the Lumber Subregion. Among Negro part-time farmers, crowding was greatest in the Atlantic Coast Subregion, but was apparent also in the Coal and Iron and Lumber Subregions. Among Negro nonfarming industrial households, crowding was greatest in the Atlantic Coast Subregion (appendix table 39).

Crowding, however, was more closely related to local housing conditions and standards than it was to the location and size of part-

[3] *Real Property Inventory, 1934*, Summary and Sixty-four Cities Combined, U. S. Department of Commerce, 1934.

time farm households as compared with those of nonfarming industrial workers. The areas with the most crowded living conditions among part-time farmers showed almost identical crowding among the nonfarming industrial groups.

The largest proportions of white part-time farm families with adequate housing were in the Coal and Iron Subregion (63 percent), in the Atlantic Coast Subregion (62 percent), and in the Naval Stores Subregion (62 percent). The largest percentage of adequacy among white nonfarming industrial families was in the Atlantic Coast Subregion (67 percent), although almost two-thirds of the nonfarm families in both the Textile (62 percent) and the Coal and Iron (64 percent) Subregions reported one person or less per room. The most adequate housing conditions among Negro part-time farm families were found in the Lumber Subregion; among Negro nonfarming industrial families, in the Coal and Iron Subregion.

It is impossible to compare the rents which the part-time farmers and nonfarming industrial workers paid. As was pointed out in the discussion of value of the part-time farm holdings, the subject is complicated by special local conditions and variations.

Some of both groups—but not necessarily the same proportion— lived in company houses and paid lower rents than would be asked for the same houses by a private landlord. In many cases tenants, especially Negroes in the Atlantic Coast, Lumber, and Naval Stores Subregions, paid little or no rent, receiving a house as part of their labor contract or upon agreement to work for the landlord whenever he needed them. Some tenants had land attached to their houses, while other tenants had to rent land for gardens. Houses of nonfarming industrial tenants usually had no land.

It seems incontestable, however, that housing costs part-time farm families, especially those living in the suburbs and open country, less than it would in town, and that lower rents, especially for large families, are another of the advantages that go with part-time farming. Many of the heads of households included in the survey told interviewers that they had moved to the country to secure lower rents.

Figures on the general condition or state of repair of houses of part-time farmers and nonfarmers are likewise unsatisfactory. They are derived either from statements of members of families or from estimates of enumerators and are colored to a certain degree by the personal standards of one or the other. Also, standards as to what constitutes a good or poor state of repair vary from community to community. In Greenville County of the Textile Subregion, for example, many of both part-time farmers and nonfarming industrial workers lived in houses of mill companies whose policy was to keep their property in good condition. In the Naval Stores Subregion, company housing consisted of barrack-like houses or rough shacks belonging to small turpentine companies that were unable to maintain them in good repair. Houses of resident owners or private landlords likewise reflected the low wages and low rentals of the area, as well as the varying community standards.

In general, the homes of part-time farmers were not very different from those of their nonfarming neighbors (table 64). About the same proportion of houses in both groups needed no repairs, though slightly more houses of part-time farm families than of nonfarming industrial families needed each type of repairs. The homes of both part-time farm and nonfarming industrial households needed more exterior and interior repairs than they did roof or structural repairs.

Table 64.—Condition of Dwellings of Part-Time Farm and Nonfarming Industrial Households,[1] 1934

Condition of dwelling	Part-time farm house-holds	Nonfarming industrial households
Total dwellings	1, 113	1, 334
Percent needing:		
No repairs	27	28
Exterior or interior repairs	67	63
Roof repairs	31	24
General structural repairs	22	17

[1] For data by subregions, see appendix table 40.

The percentage of part-time farm homes in good repair (i. e., needing no repair) was greater among the white households in the Textile, Coal and Iron, and Lumber Subregions than among the white households of the Atlantic Coast and Naval Stores Subregions (table 65). In all except the Atlantic Coast Subregion, there was a larger proportion of white farm homes than nonfarm homes in good repair. With the exception of the Coal and Iron Subregion, however, a greater percentage of white part-time farm homes than nonfarm homes needed general structural repair.

Table 65.—Condition of Dwellings of Part-Time Farm and Nonfarming Industrial Households, by Color and by Subregion, 1934

Subregion and color	Percent needing no repairs		Percent needing general structural repairs	
	Part-time farm house-holds	Nonfarming industrial households	Part-time farm house-holds	Nonfarming industrial households
Textile:				
White	32	28	10	6
Coal and Iron:				
White	45	37	13	19
Negro	19	28	41	16
Atlantic Coast:				
White	27	41	14	5
Negro	6	21	24	9
Lumber:				
White	37	25	14	1
Negro	20	15	42	3
Naval Stores:				
White	11	4	37	27

In all subregions, more Negro than white part-time farm homes were in need of general structural repairs, as high as two-fifths of the Negro farmers' houses in some areas needing this type of repairs. The proportions of the Negro nonfarmers' houses in the Atlantic Coast and Lumber Subregions needing structural repairs were extremely low.

The greater need of structural repairs by part-time farm homes can be partially explained by the fact that heads of these households were supporting larger families than were heads of nonfarming industrial households on approximately the same incomes. Other explanations are that more of the nonfarmers than farmers occupied company houses, which in general were more frequently repaired than were houses owned by low-income resident owners, or by landlords receiving low rentals; and that more part-time farmers than nonfarmers lived in the country where the upkeep of houses is neglected more, as a rule, than in the city.

CONVENIENCES AND FACILITIES

In the matter of household conveniences, differences between part-time farmers and nonfarming industrial workers were more apparent than in any other comparative phase of their living and social conditions.[4] In some areas, electric lines and water mains did not reach out into the country, and part-time farmers, located on the edges of small towns or in the open country, did not possess conveniences to as great a degree as did nonfarming industrial workers located in urban districts. A little over one-half (53 percent) of the part-time farmers had electric lights as compared with over three-fifths (63 percent) of the nonfarmers (table 66). In the Textile and Coal and Iron Subregions, where electricity was available, almost as large a proportion of the white part-time farmers as nonfarmers had electric lights. Few of the Negro part-time farmers or industrial workers in the Atlantic Coast or Lumber Subregions had electric lights.

Table 66.—Conveniences in Dwellings of Part-Time Farm and Nonfarming Industrial Households,[1] 1934

Convenience	Part-time farm households [2]	Nonfarming industrial households
Total dwellings	1,081	1,334
Percent having:		
Electric lights	53	63
Running water	41	74
Bathroom	20	34
No conveniences	42	18

[1] For data by subregions, see appendix table 41.
[2] Exclusive of all white commercial farmers and of white noncommercial farmers with off-the-farm employment in agriculture in the Atlantic Coast Subregion.

[4] The point must be kept in mind that such differences were probably due largely to differences in residence.

Only two-fifths of the part-time farmers, as compared with three-fourths of the nonfarm group, had running water. About one-half of those in each group who had running water also had bathrooms.

Forty-two percent of the part-time farmers, as compared with eighteen percent of the nonfarming group, had none of these three conveniences.

In respect to telephones, radios, and automobiles, the part-time farmers were not unlike their nonfarming neighbors. Few of either group had telephones (table 67). About the same proportion of each (38 and 40 percent, respectively) had radios. Since electricity in the house is not a prerequisite for a radio, a few more households in some areas had radios than had electric lights. A larger proportion of white part-time farmers than of white nonfarmers had radios in the Textile and Naval Stores Subregions, while the reverse was true for the other subregions, although the differences were slight except in the Lumber Subregion (appendix table 42). Very few Negroes owned radios.

Table 67.—Communication and Transportation Facilities of Part-Time Farm and Nonfarming Industrial Households,[1] 1934

Facility	Part-time farm house-holds [2]	Nonfarming industrial households
Total households	1,081	1,334
Percent having:		
Telephone	4	4
Radio	38	40
Automobile	39	25
No telephone, radio, or automobile	47	52

[1] For data by subregions, see appendix table 42.
[2] Exclusive of all white commercial farmers and of white noncommercial farmers with off-the-farm employment in agriculture in the Atlantic Coast Subregion.

Almost two-fifths of the part-time farmers, as compared with one-fourth of the nonfarming industrial workers, had automobiles (table 67). Part of this ownership of cars was, of course, associated with distance from work, but this relationship held for individual cases rather than for whole groups. For example, among white part-time farmers and nonfarmers alike in the Textile, Atlantic Coast, and Lumber Subregions, the percentage having cars was higher than the percentage who had to travel 2 miles or more to work (appendix tables 28 and 42). In all areas, the percentage of Negroes who owned cars was much smaller than the percentage of those who had to travel 2 miles or more to work.

Approximately half of all part-time farm and nonfarming industrial households were without telephones, radios, or automobiles.

STABILITY AND TENURE

It has been argued that a stake in a crop tends to make a man more stable and, therefore, less apt to leave his job; and it is also argued that a secondary source of living makes a man more independent and more apt to leave a job. Perhaps the crops of part-time farmers interviewed in 1935 were too small or jobs too scarce for either of these antipodal contentions to be borne out. At any rate, only 5 percent of both part-time farmers and nonfarming industrial workers were found to have changed jobs during 1934.

There was no striking difference between the part-time farm households and nonfarming industrial households in the number of changes in residence since 1929. A few more nonfarming industrial workers than part-time farmers had made no change in residence in the period 1929–1934 (67 percent as compared with 60 percent of the part-time farmers). Almost the same proportion had made two or more changes, 11 percent for the nonfarming industrial workers and 12 percent for the part-time farmers (table 68).

Table 68.—Changes in Residence Since October 1, 1929, of Part-Time Farm and Nonfarming Industrial Households,[1] 1934

Number of changes in residence since October 1, 1929	Part-time farm households		Nonfarming industrial households	
	Number	Percent	Number	Percent
Total	1,113	100	1,334	100
None	672	60	896	67
1	308	28	285	22
2	88	8	92	7
3	35	3	45	3
4 or more	10	1	15	1
Unknown	—	—	1	*

*Less than 0.5 percent.

[1] For data by subregions, see appendix table 43.

It will be remembered that a group of full-time farmers in the Textile and Naval Stores Subregions and a few in other areas had changed to part-time farming with an industrial job.[5] For all of these, except in the Naval Stores Subregion where they became turpentine workers in adjacent forests, this change necessitated a change of residence. There were 69 such cases, which, if added to the 672 who made no change, would make the percentage of those changing residence exactly the same for part-time farmers as for nonfarming industrial workers.

More part-time farmers than nonfarming industrial workers owned their homes. Part of this difference was due to the fact that in the Textile and Coal and Iron Subregions, and to some extent in the Naval Stores Subregion, nonfarming families surveyed were more concentrated in company villages than were part-time farmers. The amount of home ownership was largest among white part-time farmers in the Atlantic Coast and Lumber Subregions, half of them owning their own homes (table 69). Home ownership by Negro part-time farmers was highest in the Atlantic Coast Subregion.

[5] See p. 39.

Table 69.—Owners Among Part-Time Farmers and Nonfarming Industrial Workers, by Color and by Subregion, 1934

Subregion and color	Part-time farmers			Nonfarming industrial workers		
	Total	Number owning homes	Percent owning homes	Total	Number owning homes	Percent owning homes
Total_____	1,113	368	33	1,334	175	13
Textile:						
White_____	293	102	35	314	29	9
Coal and Iron:						
White_____	204	70	34	222	40	18
Negro_____	124	23	19	346	70	20
Atlantic Coast:						
White_____	71	35	50	103	16	16
Negro_____	142	55	39	105	7	7
Lumber:						
White_____	76	37	49	92	2	2
Negro_____	132	26	20	103	11	11
Naval Stores:						
White_____	71	20	28	49	—	—

There was some change in the tenure status of part-time farmers between 1929 and 1934 (table 70). Because of the small numbers involved, however, and because the records relate only to those who were farming full or part time in 1929, the data are by no means conclusive. With these limitations, it may be said that there was more movement toward ownership than away from it. Forty-one tenants

Table 70.—Tenure Status in 1929 and 1934 of Part-Time Farmers [1] Who Operated Farms in 1929

Tenure status in 1929	Tenure status in 1934			
	Owner		Tenant	
	Number	Percent	Number	Percent
Total_____	321	100	488	100
Owner_____	280	87	10	2
Tenant_____	41	13	478	98

[1] For data by subregions, see appendix table 44.

in 1929 had become owners by 1934, and only ten who were owners in 1929 had become tenants by 1934. Most of the changes were among the white part-time farmers, 36 of the 41 who had raised their status and 9 of the 10 who had lowered it being whites (appendix table 44). It is noteworthy that nearly all of the part-time farmers who were owners were able to retain their status during a period of depression when so many owners were losing their homes, and that a few part-time farmers were able to raise their status. However, a number of the owners were in debt.[6]

[6] See pp. 10–11.

HEALTH

This survey made no attempt to secure detailed data on the highly technical question of health. The only measure obtained by which this subject could be judged was the number of days the heads of part-time farm and nonfarming industrial households were incapacitated during the year 1934. On this score, no marked difference between part-time farmers and nonfarming industrial workers was found.

Thirty percent of the part-time farmers as compared with twenty-two percent of the nonfarming industrial workers were incapacitated for work at some time during the year (tables 71 and 72). However, part-time farmers were incapacitated for shorter periods than were

Table 71.—Number of Days Heads of Part-Time Farm and Nonfarming Industrial Households Were Incapacitated,[1] 1934

Number of days head was incapacitated	Part-time farm households		Nonfarming industrial households	
	Number	Percent	Number	Percent
Total	1,113	100	1,334	100
None	781	70	1,043	78
1 to 4 days	64	6	38	3
5 to 9 days	63	6	54	4
10 to 14 days	72	6	69	5
15 to 19 days	17	2	16	1
20 to 29 days	30	3	39	3
30 to 39 days	39	3	30	2
40 to 49 days	15	1	11	1
50 days or more	32	3	34	3

[1] For data by subregions, see appendix table 45.

Table 72.—Percent of Heads of Part-Time Farm and Nonfarming Industrial Households Who Were Incapacitated and Average Number of Days Incapacitated, by Color and by Subregion, 1934

Subregion and color	Percent incapacitated		Average number of days incapacitated [1]	
	Part-time farmers	Nonfarming industrial workers	Part-time farmers	Nonfarming industrial workers
Total	30	22	20	25
Textile:				
White	33	34	18	18
Coal and Iron:				
White	16	14	28	33
Negro	18	8	15	33
Atlantic Coast:				
White	17	6	24	†
Negro	50	13	26	24
Lumber:				
White	43	47	25	27
Negro	45	41	14	32
Naval Stores:				
White	7	47	†	14

† Average not computed for less than 10 cases.
[1] For those who were incapacitated.

nonfarming industrial workers, the averages being 20 days and 25 days, respectively (table 72).

By subregions, the highest percentages of those incapacitated during the year were found among both groups of whites and Negroes in the Lumber Subregion, among Negro part-time farmers in the Atlantic Coast Subregion, and among white nonfarming industrial workers in the Naval Stores Subregion (table 72).

EDUCATION

The amount of formal education received by part-time farmers was strikingly similar to that received by nonfarming industrial workers. In each group, one-tenth had had no formal education while two-thirds had had a partial or complete grammar school education. Slightly over one-fifth had been in high school, and only 2 percent had attended college (table 73).

Table 73.—Education of Heads of Part-Time Farm and Nonfarming Industrial Households,[1] 1934

Education of heads	Part-time farm households [2]		Nonfarming industrial households	
	Number	Percent	Number	Percent
Total	1,081	100.0	1,334	100.0
None	114	10.5	133	10.0
1 to 4 grades completed	333	30.8	364	27.3
Grade school not completed [3]	268	24.8	364	27.3
Grade school completed	117	10.8	174	13.0
1 to 3 years high school	169	15.6	208	15.6
High school completed	40	3.7	57	4.3
1 to 3 years college	16	1.5	22	1.7
College completed	4	0.4	6	0.4
Unknown	20	1.9	6	0.4

[1] For data by subregions, see appendix table 46.
[2] Exclusive of all white commercial farmers and of white noncommercial farmers with off-the-farm employment in agriculture in the Atlantic Coast Subregion.
[3] This category includes grades 5 to 7 for the Coal and Iron Subregion, and grades 5 to 6 for all other subregions.

Of those who had had no formal schooling, the great majority in both groups were Negroes, and the lack of education was more marked among the part-time farming Negroes than among the nonfarming Negroes. Of the 114 part-time farmers who had had no schooling, 89 (78 percent) were Negroes, while of the 133 nonfarming industrial workers who had had no schooling, 85 (64 percent) were Negroes (appendix table 46). The proportion of Negroes with no education was highest in the Atlantic Coast Subregion, where one-third of the Negro part-time farmers and one-fourth of the Negro nonfarming industrial workers had had no formal schooling. The Negro part-time farmers in this subregion were at a disadvantage because most of them lived in the rural areas of Charleston County where schools for Negroes were nonexistent or far apart, or were operated for very short terms during the years in which the heads of households were of school age.

The same situation was responsible for the lack of education among the Negroes of the Lumber Subregion. The proportion of Negroes in the Coal and Iron Subregion having had no education was about the same as that of Negroes in the Lumber Subregion due to the fact that workers in the coal and iron industries were drawn from the surrounding rural areas.

The proportion of white heads of households having had no formal education was highest in the Coal and Iron Subregion, where there had been extensive migration from rural areas with poor school facilities, and in the Naval Stores Subregion, where a sparse population had resulted in poor school facilities.

The average grade attained by white heads of households in the various subregions ranged from 5.7 to 7.0 grades among part-time farmers and from 4.3 to 6.8 grades among nonfarming industrial workers (table 74). Within each area, however, the difference between part-time farmers and their nonfarming neighbors was slight except in the Naval Stores Subregion.

Table 74.—Average Grade Completed by Heads of Part-Time Farm and Nonfarming Industrial Households, by Color and by Subregion, 1934

Subregion and color	Average grade completed by heads	
	Part-time farm households	Nonfarming industrial households
Total	5.2	5.5
Textile:		
White	6.4	6.4
Coal and Iron:		
White	7.0	6.8
Negro	3.8	4.3
Atlantic Coast:		
White [1]	6.5	6.8
Negro	2.1	4.0
Lumber:		
White	5.7	6.2
Negro	3.2	3.7
Naval Stores:		
White	6.0	4.3

[1] Exclusive of all white commercial farmers and of white noncommercial farmers with off-the-farm employment in agriculture.

There was a striking similarity between the part-time farm and nonfarm groups in regard to education of the children. Over one-fourth of the children 7–16 years of age in both groups who were not in school in 1933–34 were children 7 years of age who had not yet started to school (table 75). There were a few children who were physically unable to attend school, and an occasional child in each group who was employed.

In most areas, the children 7–16 years of age in both part-time farm and nonfarming industrial white households had made nearly

Table 75.—School Attendance of Children, 7–16 Years of Age, in Part-Time Farm and Nonfarming Industrial Households, by Color and by Subregion, 1934

Item	Total	Textile White	Coal and Iron White	Coal and Iron Negro	Atlantic Coast White	Atlantic Coast Negro	Lumber White	Lumber Negro	Naval Stores White
PART-TIME FARM HOUSEHOLDS									
Total number of households with children 7–16 years of age	716	196	144	85	²23	95	53	79	41
Total number of children 7–16 years of age	1,632	454	312	174	62	215	125	195	95
Number of children in school	1,505	416	300	166	62	174	120	177	90
Number of children not in school	127	38	12	8	—	41	5	18	5
Number employed	12	6	—	—	—	2	—	4	—
Number not employed	115	32	12	8	—	39	5	14	5
With disability	10	—	3	1	—	1	—	1	4
Without disability	105	32	9	7	—	38	5	13	1
Age, 7 years	33	4	8	6	—	8	2	5	—
Age, 8–14 years	45	14	9	7	—	27	—	3	1
Age, 15–16 years	27	14	8	6	—	3	3	5	—
NONFARMING INDUSTRIAL HOUSEHOLDS									
Total number of households with children 7–16 years of age	678	151	137	176	62	45	44	44	19
Total number of children 7–16 years of age	1,267	295	252	329	111	87	81	79	33
Number of children in school	1,181	263	240	315	108	80	76	71	28
Number of children not in school	86	32	12	14	3	7	5	8	3
Number employed ¹	13	2	1	1	—	2	1	3	3
Number not employed	73	30	11	13	3	5	4	5	2
With disability	4	1	1	—	1	1	—	—	—
Without disability	69	29	10	13	2	4	4	5	2
Age, 7 years	25	4	10	6	—	2	2	—	2
Age, 8–14 years	24	15	10	2	2	1	—	3	1
Age, 15–61 years	20	10	—	5	—	1	2	2	—

¹ All except 2 of the employed children were 15 or 16 years of age.
² Exclusive of commercial households and of noncommercial households with off-the-farm employment in agriculture.

normal [7] progress in school (table 76).   The children in white non-farming industrial households in the Naval Stores Subregion were the only ones who averaged more than 1 year retardation.

Among Negroes retardation was particularly evident in the Atlantic Coast Subregion.   There the children of Negro part-time farmers were retarded about 3 years on the average, while the children of nonfarming industrial workers were retarded 2.4 years.   This reflects the poor school facilities for Negroes outside the city of Charleston.   A similar situation existed among the Negroes in the Lumber Subregion.

It would appear that provision by the local communities rather than part-time farming *per se* was the determining factor in the question of educational facilities.

Table 76.—Retardation in School of Children, 7–16 Years of Age, in Part-Time Farm and Nonfarming Industrial Households, by Color and by Subregion, 1934

Subregion and color	Average number of years of retardation of children 7–16 years of age [1]	
	Part-time farm households	Nonfarming industrial households
Total	0. 97	0. 75
Textile:		
White	0. 33	0. 49
Coal and Iron:		
White	0. 47	0. 34
Negro	0. 79	0. 37
Atlantic Coast:		
White	0. 31	1. 01
Negro	2. 96	2. 40
Lumber:		
White	0. 72	0. 82
Negro	2. 06	1. 64
Naval Stores:		
White	0. 43	2. 21

[1] For method of determining retardation, see footnote 7.

[7] The following age-grade schedule was taken as normal in the computation of retardation.

Age	Last grade completed in school
7 years	1
8 years	2
9 years	3
10 years	4
11 years	5
12 years	6
13 years	7
14 years	8
15 years	9
16 years	10

All children 7–16 years of age were included whether in school or not.   A child who had not completed the specified number of grades for his age level was considered retarded.   For example, a child 9 years of age who had completed only the second grade was retarded 1 year.

There was no great difference between the amount of education of young people 16 through 24 years of age in part-time farm and non-farming industrial households, though such as existed was in favor of youth in part-time farm families. Thirty-six percent of the young people in part-time farm families between those ages were in school, as compared with thirty percent of the youth in nonfarming industrial

Table 77.—School Attendance and Employment of Youth, 16–24 Years of Age, in Part-Time Farm and Nonfarming Industrial Households,[1] by Sex, 1934

School attendance and employment. by sex	Youth in part-time farm households		Youth in nonfarming industrial households	
	Number	Percent	Number	Percent
Total	831	100	644	100
In school	296	36	195	30
Employed	288	35	217	34
Neither employed nor in school	247	29	232	36
Male	419	100	311	100
In school	144	34	87	28
Employed	179	43	133	43
Neither employed nor in school	96	23	91	29
Female	412	100	333	100
In school	152	37	108	32
Employed	109	26	84	25
Neither employed nor in school	151	37	141	43

[1] For data by subregions, see appendix table 47.

families (table 77). As has been previously noted, the two groups were about equal in the proportions (slightly over one-third) that were employed. Only 29 percent of the young people in part-time farm households, as compared with 36 percent of those in nonfarm families, were neither employed nor in school.

LIBRARY FACILITIES

Library facilities varied greatly from area to area. Such facilities were available to nearly all white families in Greenville County of the Textile Subregion and in the Coal and Iron Subregion. They were also available to nearly all white noncommercial families of the Atlantic Coast Subregion, but outside of Charleston there were no such facilities for Negroes in the Atlantic Coast Subregion, nor were there library facilities for whites in the Naval Stores Subregion (table 78).

Use of library facilities was not always proportionate to the number of families to whom such facilities were available. In the Atlantic Coast and Lumber Subregions, for example, libraries were available to practically all white nonfarming industrial workers, but only one-fifth of those in the former area and only one-tenth of those in the latter area made use of them.

In the Textile, Coal and Iron, Atlantic Coast, and Lumber Sub-regions, on the other hand, half or more of the white part-time farm

Table 78.—Availability and Use of Library Facilities Among Part-Time Farm and Nonfarming Industrial Households, by Color and by Subregion, 1934

Subregion and color	Percent having library facilities available		Percent having library facilities who used them	
	Part-time farm house-holds	Nonfarming industrial households	Part-time farm house-holds	Nonfarming industrial households
Textile:				
White	60	70	58	41
Greenville	83	84	61	47
Carroll	17	40	24	13
Coal and Iron:				
White	86	82	49	58
Negro	74	43	17	12
Atlantic Coast:				
White	85	100	58	22
Negro	1	78	0	21
Lumber:				
White	46	98	52	11
Negro	12	97	37	0
Naval Stores:				
White	—	—	—	—

[1] Based on 39 noncommercial part-time farm households with off-the-farm employment in nonagriculture.
[2] Based on 68 part-time farm households with off-the-farm employment in nonagriculture.

families to whom library facilities were available used them; while in the Textile and Coal and Iron Subregions, about half of the white nonfarming industrial families also used such facilities. Libraries were available to only a small percentage of Negro part-time farmers except in the Coal and Iron Subregion, but only one-sixth of these Negroes used the libraries.

PARTICIPATION IN SOCIAL ORGANIZATIONS

As in the case of library facilities, great differences existed among the areas with respect to availability of social organizations. In Greenville County of the Textile Subregion, for example, the number of organizations common to most urban, suburban, and village communities was augmented by mill community programs, thus making a wide variety of organizations available to all who lived near their places of work (appendix table 48). For those in Greenville County who lived in the open country, there were special types of rural organizations common to thickly settled farming communities.

Few social organizations, on the other hand, were available in the Naval Stores Subregion, where towns are small and the country population sparse and scattered. In this area, almost the only organizations outside of the town of Douglas were a few connected with church and school.

The extent to which members of families, whether part-time farm or nonfarming industrial, took part in available social organizations varied just as widely as did the number of organizations available.[8]

[8] The differences in social participation among the subregions were so great that much of this discussion must be reserved for the detailed reports on the subregions which make up Part II.

All members of some large families attended regularly while in other families only one or two members attended, and then only occasionally. In general, more part-time farm than nonfarming industrial families participated in organized social and community life. Also, the extent of participation of part-time farmers was greater than that of nonfarmers in almost every type of activity available to them (table 79).

Table 79.—Availability of Specified Social Organizations and Participation of Part-Time Farm and Nonfarming Industrial Households in These Organizations,[1] 1934

Organization	Part-time farm households				Nonfarming industrial households			
	Households to which organization was available		Households to whom available with one or more members participating		Households to which organization was available		Households to whom available with one or more members participating	
	Number	Percent	Number	Percent	Number	Percent	Number	Percent
Total households	[2] 1,073				1,334			
Church	1,068	99	1,013	95	1,312	99	1,242	93
Adult church organization	918	86	336	37	1,219	91	411	34
Young people's organization	887	83	350	40	1,172	88	284	24
Sunday School	1,022	95	875	86	1,244	93	971	78
School club	413	38	89	22	910	68	140	15
Athletic team	686	64	136	20	1,053	79	162	15
Fraternal order	639	59	165	25	982	74	142	14
Labor union	404	38	157	39	851	64	293	34
Parent-Teacher Association	744	69	221	30	1,190	89	218	18
Boy Scouts	304	38	19	6	655	42	28	4
Girl Scouts	201	19	14	5	531	40	19	4
Cooperatives	15	1	2	13	319	24	15	5
Women's organization	323	30	62	19	621	47	60	10
4-H Club	267	25	57	21	188	14	2	1
Special interest group	90	8	10	11	387	29	20	5
Other	166	15	61	37	259	19	17	7

[1] For data by subregions, see appendix table 48.
[2] Exclusive of all white commercial farmers and of white noncommercial farmers with off-the-farm employment in agriculture in the Atlantic Coast Subregion and of white farmers with off-the-farm employment in agriculture in the Lumber Subregion.

Since all types of organizations were not available to all part-time farmers, however, their greater rate of participation is more apparent if the participation of the two groups is compared on the basis of the number to whom each activity was actually available. Young people's organizations, for example, were available to 83 percent of the part-time farm families and to 88 percent of the nonfarming industrial families. Yet, there were 40 percent of the part-time farm and only 24 percent of the nonfarm families who had one or more members participating in such organizations. Fraternal orders were available to 74 percent of the nonfarming industrial workers but to only 59 percent of the part-time farmers. Yet, 25 percent of the part-time farm households in comparison with 14 percent of the nonfarming industrial households had participating members. The same situation was true of other organizations.

The greater participation of part-time farm families in young people's organizations, Parent-Teacher Associations, and women's organizations was surprising because of the greater distance many of them had to go in order to attend meetings. Particularly surprising was the comparatively large percentage of part-time farmers who were members of labor unions.

Individual members of white part-time farm families, on the average, participated to a greater extent in social activities than did white nonfarm members. In the Coal and Iron and Atlantic Coast Subregions, the participation of Negro nonfarming industrial workers was greater on the average than that of Negro part-time farmers while the reverse was true in the Lumber Subregion (table 80).

Table 80.—Average Attendance at Social Gatherings of Members of Part-Time Farm and Nonfarming Industrial Households, and Number of Households in Which One or More Persons Held Office, by Color and by Subregion, 1934

Subregion and color	Average attendance per person		Number of households in which one or more persons held office [1]	
	Part-time farm households	Nonfarming industrial households	Part-time farm households	Nonfarming industrial households
Total	69	69	304	245
Textile:				
White:				
Greenville	83	84	107	36
Carroll	56	29	4	1
Coal and Iron:				
White	78	70	76	54
Negro	89	92	26	102
Atlantic Coast:				
White	[2] 61	56	7	8
Negro	55	63	48	27
Lumber:				
White	[3] 69	48	6	1
Negro	76	67	27	11
Naval Stores:				
White	11	14	3	5

[1] In 1 or more social organizations, 1934. In practically all households, only 1 member held office in any given organization.
[2] Exclusive of all white commercial farmers and of white noncommercial farmers with off-the-farm employment in agriculture. The average attendance of the entire group of 71 cases was 53.
[3] Exclusive of white farmers with off-the-farm employment in agriculture. The average attendance for the entire group of 76 cases was 68.

In most areas, members of part-time farm families held office more frequently than did their nonfarming industrial neighbors (table 80 and appendix table 49). The average amount of officeholding by members of part-time farm households was so much greater in some areas than that by nonfarmers that some factor other than more frequent and more regular participation of the former group must be present. It seems likely that the higher esteem in which the farmer was held in comparison with the factory worker may have had something to do with the more frequent officeholding of members of part-time farm households.

Whatever the cause, it seems fairly evident that in leadership as well as in participation the part-time farm family takes a more active part in the organized social life of the community than does the nonfarming industrial family.

Chapter IV

CONCLUSIONS

THE PRESENT survey shows that part-time farming is economically advantageous. It requires in investment or in rent for land little more than ordinarily would be spent in housing; it requires only a small amount of capital for equipment or livestock; and the expenditure for seed, fertilizer, or hired labor is negligible.

The survey makes equally clear, however, that while part-time farming activities may be encouraged within certain limitations, they cannot advantageously be extended on a large scale to unemployed families. Part-time farms alone cannot make families self-sufficient, and possession by the head of the household of a cash income job is indispensable to any part-time farming undertaking.

A program calling for the building of new communities remote from industry, with the hope that unemployed farmers or industrial workers can be rehabilitated by part-time farming, appears to be of doubtful wisdom. Industry moves to these communities very slowly, if at all. The possibilities of increased industrial expansion in the Eastern Cotton Belt hardly warrant hope of sufficient work in the near future to take up the slack of underemployment and to set to work the unemployed previously attached to these industries.[1]

The promotion of part-time farming, therefore, except in the vicinity of established industry and for those employed or with definite prospect of employment, would not be likely to meet with success.

---

[1] For discussion of the outlook for increased industrial employment, see Part I, pp. 48–49 and Part II, pp. 90–91, 121–122, 149, 176–178, 204–205.

THE PART-TIME FARMER A HYBRID

As the cover design of this monograph suggests, the part-time farmer faces two ways. The division of his time and interest between two types of enterprise ranges from almost complete attention to the farm to almost complete absorption in the industrial job. This division has both advantages and disadvantages.

For many, the outdoor exercise involved in looking after a part-time farm is a welcome change from monotonous factory, office, or other indoor work. Some of the part-time farmers surveyed said that their gardens were a source of recreation to them. It was clear from their comments, and from those of the interviewers, that in some cases, where discouragement with economic conditions had resulted in lowered morale, the farm work had therapeutic value. For others, especially those whose industrial jobs were very fatiguing, the extra effort required by the part-time farm had no charms. If hours in the industries of these areas are lengthened, or even if full time at current hours is resumed, the labor required for anything more than a small garden may easily become burdensome. For all with livestock there is the everlastingness of daily chores. As some part-time farmers as well as nonfarming industrial workers expressed it, they would rather "just sit around after work."

Part-time farming in the Eastern Cotton Belt was not entirely a product of the depression, although the depression increased its volume, and prosperity may decrease it. For example, industrial workers living in areas where land is poor and scarce and not easily accessible, such as Jefferson County, Alabama, may discontinue their parttime farming activities as soon as wages become high enough for them to support themselves by industry alone. Better times may also decrease part-time farming among farmers who undertook it primarily as an emergency measure. In this category would be placed many part-time farmers in Coffee County, Georgia, in the Naval Stores Subregion where off-the-farm jobs are scarce, where the seasonal peak of off-the-farm employment comes at the height of the busy season on the farm, and where industrial wages are so low that a small increase in the price for staple crops would make undivided attention to the farm more profitable than part-time farming. On the other hand, there are many industrial workers who have long done some farming and will continue to farm because it is an economic asset over and above its cost in money and labor.

ADVANTAGES OF PART-TIME FARMING

The part-time farms surveyed produced a definite contribution to the family living: not only fresher and more abundant products for the diet, but also a monetary saving in grocery bills during the summer months, ranging from a few dollars to as much as $20 a month. Sometimes small amounts of additional food products were produced for sale, while may of the families canned or stored products for winter use. Typical part-time farm families which had only a garden consumed products during the year valued at $70, while those with a garden, a cow, several hogs, and a small flock of poultry consumed products with an equivalent value of about $400.

The garden's contribution represented a definite financial advantage for part-time farmers, whose earnings in industry were practically the same as those of nonfarming industrial workers. Over one-half of the part-time farmers surveyed, and almost that proportion of nonfarming industrial workers, made less than $500 a year at their industrial employment. Only a small proportion of the workers made as much as $1,000 or more yearly. That the garden's products were appreciated during periods of unemployment and underemployment was apparent from the comments of many of the part-time farmers, who declared that they "could not have made it," "would have starved to death," or "would have had to go on relief," had it not been for the farming enterprise.

From the social viewpoint, also, the part-time farmer's life has its advantages. From the rather intangible evidence of the survey, it would appear that the status of the part-time farmer, especially if he owns his home, is a degree higher than that of the nonfarming industrial worker. In spite of the longer distances from town, participation by part-time farm families in available group life in the community seemed to be more frequent than that by nonfarming industrial workers; and positions of leadership were more often held by part-time farmers and members of their families. The fact remains, however, that the part-time farmer had fewer social organizations available. To the extent that these organizations stimulate social intercourse and interest in community affairs, the lack of group life is a disadvantage, especially in the case of young people in the family.

A large number of the working people of the Eastern Cotton Belt have a farm background and are to an extent rural-minded. Many of the heads of families interviewed expressed a preference for country life and an opinion that the country is the best place in which to rear children. Since the contacts and the interests of the part-time farm family are necessarily those of the village, town, or city, the former tastes and wants of such families are modified by these quasi-urban standards and activities. This contrast of rural and urban ways of living makes adjustments difficult for some part-time farm families. For others, such as those who take pleasure in the creative activity of a farm or garden, the part-time farm affords a satisfying and even stimulating way of life.

More part-time farmers than nonfarming industrial workers owned their homes. Aside from any sentimental, social, or economic arguments for home ownership, it is a fact that under modern industrial conditions, home ownership tends to limit the mobility of the worker whether he is a part-time farmer or not, and in so doing may constitute a disadvantage. Since a garden alone, whether or not the home is owned, may deter the part-time farmer from moving to better himself in his industrial job, part-time farming may also be said to limit mobility. However, there was no striking difference between the part-time farm and nonfarming industrial households surveyed in the number of changes in residence since October 1, 1929.

If the part-time farm enterprise is conceivably a limit to mobility, it is just as conceivably a source of industrial independence and advantage for the part-time farmer who lives in a community large enough, and industrially complex enough, to contain a number of opportunities for employment. Having the resource of a part-time farm enterprise to fall back upon, the worker is less subject to control by the employer.

It might be thought that the possession of a farming enterprise could, in individual cases, threaten employment security. When industrial workers in the Eastern Cotton Belt are known to need work badly, employers might be tempted to lay off a man known to have a farm enterprise large enough to enable him to get along. In one neighborhood, there was so strong a suspicion among those interviewed that the reporting of an additional resource might affect employment security that the survey had to be abandoned. On the other hand, employers, like those in the Coal and Iron and Textile Subregions, actively encouraged part-time farming, or at least gardening, and at times of reduction in labor force, they did not penalize employees who had responded to their garden programs. The findings of this study, regarding opportunity for employment, days worked, and rates of pay and earnings, indicated that up to the present time there has been no discrimination against part-time farmers.

Many employers in the Eastern Cotton Belt expressed satisfaction and even pride that some of their workers came from nearby farms. In recent years, many textile mill managers have begun to question the necessity of the mill village. The cost of building and maintaining the type of houses and villages now common has increased in recent years at the same time that a large labor supply has been made available through the depression in agriculture. Moreover, the automobile has greatly enlarged the territory from which workers may be drawn. There is no further need to domicile all the employees within the shadow of the mill.

Part-time farmers as a whole were thought well of by their neighbors, and were spoken of as "the hardest working men in this community." Occasionally a few fellow industrial workers expressed antagonism, saying that a man with a farm "and a way to make a living" should leave his industrial job to an unemployed industrial worker. A complete "living," however, was made only by some of the commercial part-time farmers, since they were the only ones with any sizable financial returns from their farms. Moreover, many of them operated farms too small to support a family.

A number of the full-time industrial workers expressed a desire to join the ranks of the part-time farmers. Most people believed that if a man were energetic enough to use his leisure time to produce food, he was entitled to the economic advantage it gave him.

It has been objected that the part-time farmer competes with the full-time farmer by producing for his household foodstuffs that otherwise would have to be purchased. To an extent this is true, but as was pointed out above,[2] the part-time farm family probably would not buy as large a quantity of farm products as it produces for home use. A study of the possible effects of this small reduction in the demand for products of commercial farms was beyond the scope of this study.

Certainly, most of the part-time farmers surveyed offered no competition by selling products. The few who sold much truck, or poultry, or milk were really farmers with an industrial job on the side. Any competition that these offered was with industrial workers, therefore, rather than with other farmers.

POSSIBILITY OF INCREASING THE NUMBER OF PART-TIME FARMS

Land is plentiful in most parts of the Eastern Cotton Belt, except in the more congested metropolitan areas, so from this point of view, there would be no obstacle to increasing the number of part-time farmers. As long as a plot of land comes free with the rent of a suburban or country house, is made available to a tenant by a landlord, or can be rented for $5 or less per acre, part-time farming is possible. Improvement in roads is constantly increasing the radius from which industry draws its workers, and so increases the land available for the farming enterprise.

Many of the nonfarming industrial workers surveyed had a farm background. Among the heads of households, 49 percent of such workers had had some regular farm experience since they were 16 years of age, and 38 percent had had 3 years or more. Many of these, as well as others who had had no farm experience, expressed a wish to become part-time farmers.

Whether all who say they want to farm would do so if given assistance is questionable. In any event, the survey did not indicate that past experience on a regular farm is necessary for the success of a small farm enterprise or that it guarantees success. Of the 1,113 part-time farmers surveyed, 200 had had no farm experience since

---

[2] See p. 15.

they were 16 years of age, but, on the whole, the garden production of those without such farm experience did not differ greatly from that of part-time farmers with previous experience. The average number of years' experience on farms was greatest among part-time farmers in the Atlantic Coast Subregion, but in general part-time farming in that area was poor. The average amount of previous farming experience was shortest in the Coal and Iron Subregion where, considering the limited opportunities, part-time farming was most successful.

DESIRABILITY OF INCREASING PART-TIME FARMING

In spite of the obvious advantages of part-time farming, it should again be emphasized that such farming is not sufficient for the support of families engaged in it. Part-time farm families may be kept off the relief rolls only if they have some type of industrial employment which provides an income sufficient to meet necessary cash expenses.

As was pointed out elsewhere in this report, the possibilities for expansion of employment by the various industries of the region appear to be sharply limited. This fact suggests the doubtful wisdom of any plan for the wholesale extension of part-time farming to unemployed households.

The wholesale extention of part-time farming to employed households not at present engaged in farming activities is also of doubtful wisdom, even though the members have expressed a desire to cultivate gardens and keep cows, pigs, and chickens. It has been shown earlier that successful noncommercial part-time farming requires from 3½ to 5 hours work per day during the spring and summer months. This will be considered a heavy burden by many families. It is one thing, therefore, to assist households which have shown the initiative, energy, and desire to undertake such an enterprise. It is quite another to encourage part-time farming among families which would not only require assistance in establishing themselves as part-time farmers, but which would also need close supervision over an extended period. In fact, experience with relief families has shown that large numbers are unable to farm successfully even with such supervision.

That part-time farming offers a wide field for improvement, however, is clearly indicated by the survey. Any public policy for encouraging part-time farming in the Southeast might well begin with the improvement of existing enterprises carried on by those who have had the interest and the initiative to undertake farming. It is believed that part-time farming would be greatly benefited if encouragement, advice, actual guidance, and perhaps small loans were given both to present part-time farmers who want to increase their farming activities and to nonfarming industrial workers with steady employment who wish to begin farming and who appear to have the qualifications needed for success.

THE IMPROVEMENT OF EXISTING PART-TIME FARMING

Some part-time farmers need a little more land or better land. One of the most frequently expressed desires of heads of families in the more thickly settled areas was for 1 or 2 acres on which they could raise enough potatoes for the family, feed for the cow, or carry on more varied part-time farming. Many expressed the wish for a 3- or 4-acre farm, which they felt would be a safeguard against the uncertainties of industrial employment or would offer a bit of security in old age.

Some needed, and would merit, assistance in securing a cow, while others would not properly care for stock if they had it. Quite a number remarked that they could do much better if they had work stock, but sensibly recognized that the overhead would be too large for the size of their enterprise, and thought a good solution would be to own a mule with some other part-time farmer. As a matter of fact, one mule would probably be sufficient for several small-scale part-time farmers.

The survey disclosed that one of the greatest needs of part-time farmers is instruction in improved farming methods. Training is needed in every phase of farm operation, from planting to preservation of the product. A few expressed a wish to know how to farm more efficiently, and an occasional part-time farmer was trying to improve his farming methods by studying Government publications or taking extension courses.

There are today more agricultural extension workers—farm agents, home demonstration agents, and so on—in the Southeast than in any other region of the United States,[3] showing that there is already public recognition of the need for such educational work. So far, however, these agents have given their attention and services almost exclusively to commercial farmers. More recently, the relief agencies have taught gardening and canning to relief clients, in order that they may help themselves and so lighten the relief load. Few of the part-time farmers were on relief, however, so they have missed both sources of information—the one by having too small enterprises, the other by retaining economic independence.

Production of a greater variety of foodstuffs should be a major item in any program for improved farm practices in the Eastern Cotton Belt. There are numerous useful and nutritious vegetables, especially among those suitable for fall, winter, and early spring gardens, with which many part-time farmers interviewed in this survey were not familiar. Only a few grew English peas, carrots, or spinach; none grew parsnips, asparagus, broccoli, Brussels sprouts, or a variety of winter kale and greens. Only a small number of part-time farmers had fresh vegetables during 10 months of the year.

[3] Odum, Howard W., *Southern Regions of the United States*, Chapel Hill: University of North Carolina Press, 1936, p. 56.

The growing of fruits and berries is another farm activity that needs stimulating. Relatively few part-time farm households grew fruits and berries or attempted the canning of surplus garden products. This is one of the fields in which instruction is eagerly received.

Instruction in relative values of crops is also needed. For example, many part-time farmers with small plots of land planted corn; and while this crop is made into meal and is also used as feed for pigs and chickens, it takes considerable space in relation to its value. The same amount of land planted in a variety of vegetables, sweet potatoes, and Irish potatoes would yield greater food value. An extreme example of impractical use of cropland found in the survey was the planting of ½ to 1 acre in watermelons, although the growers did not report selling the melons.

This proposal to acquaint part-time farmers with new products and the methods of producing them is not as difficult as it may sound. Farm and home demonstration agents, working among full-time farmers, already have done much to stimulate diversified and year-round gardening and to overcome prejudices in favor of former farming practices.

Planting, like many other activities, is often influenced by fashion, and what one person does, his neighbor can be encouraged to do. Examination of the schedules revealed examples of some very good local farm activities in the Eastern Cotton Belt which might easily be made more general. For instance, many part-time farmers in Coffee County, Georgia, of the Naval Stores Subregion grew winter cabbage and cane for syrup, which were produced by few, if any, part-time farmers in other areas. Only in Sumter County, South Carolina, of the Lumber Subregion did part-time farmers raise rutabagas, although they are hardier than turnips, give better yields, and are good feed for stock. In some areas nearly all farmers raised collards, while in others few part-time farmers seemed to recognize the hardiness and palatability of this typical southern vegetable.

Examples of the possibilities of educating groups in better gardening practices were furnished by the Textile and Coal and Iron Subregions, where employers have long encouraged gardens by making land available, by having plowing done, and by giving prizes. It is hardly an accident that the summer gardens in these two areas were the best of any surveyed.

Need of improved practices, not only in gardening but also in other types of farming enterprises, was evident. Many families had only a half dozen chickens or so, which were too few to produce sufficient eggs or meat for family consumption, whereas the products of a larger flock, the care of which would have taken no more time, would have been a real contribution to the food supply.

Need of improvement in the quality of the livestock owned was also seen, particularly in areas where practically all of the feed for cows had to be purchased. There were as many owners of cows producing only 1,000 quarts of milk a year who spent $75 to $150 for feed as there were owners whose cows gave 3,000 or 4,000 quarts.

There is apparent need for stimulating the interest of young people in sharing the work on part-time farms. As has been pointed out earlier,[4] many young people between 16 and 24 years of age did not help in part-time farm work, although 29 percent of them were neither employed nor in school. An adaptation of 4–H Clubs for young members of part-time farm households might rouse their interest. Such a program would not have to meet the prejudice, common among some classes of southerners, against girls and women working in the field. There were some instances in all areas of girls 14 to 20 years of age helping in the gardens, and in commercial part-time farm families, they helped in the fields. It will be remembered that more than two-thirds of the wives helped with the farming enterprise.

Since the amount of interest and energy spent on part-time farms in all areas is considerable, the provision of educational direction would markedly increase the returns from the various enterprises.

A GOVERNMENTAL PART-TIME FARMING PROGRAM

The recent spread of part-time farming throughout the Southeast and the increasing interest of industrial workers in this activity as a means of supplementing their wages have prepared the way for the public encouragement of part-time farming. The fact that shorter hours than formerly prevailed now exist in all of the major industries of the country, allowing workers adequate time to tend a part-time farm, suggests the present as the psychological time in which to inaugurate a program of assistance for those who have already undertaken part-time farming and for those who have both the supplementary income and personal characteristics which are basic to successful farming.

Workers today are in the process of adjusting their habits to the additional leisure that shorter hours have given them. In a few years, they may have developed activities to absorb this margin of time. If they have not already undertaken part-time farming, they may find it as difficult then to add part-time farming to a 40- or 44-hour week as they formerly did to a 50- or 56-hour week. The majority of industries have maintained the shortened work schedules initiated by the N. R. A., and it is generally believed that most industries will not resume the long hours of predepression years.

An added argument for launching a public part-time farming program at the present time is that people throughout the country are familiar with a variety of governmental activities, and would be apt

4 See p. 33.

to receive an educational part-time farming program sponsored by the Government with more understanding and cooperation than they formerly would have given to it.

Establishment of credit that would enable industrial workers to acquire land for farming would be the first essential in any governmental program directed either toward setting up new part-time farming enterprises or toward enabling existing farmers to expand their activities. Part-time farmers in either category would need aid in order to purchase work stock and farm equipment.

Instruction of part-time farmers in modern farming practices and, in many cases, actual supervision of the enterprises would be needed to enable farmers to make the most of their farming enterprises and so justify the expenditures of time, money, and effort.

Within the limits prescribed for part-time farming by specific geographic and industrial conditions, this aid could be supplied by existent Federal agencies, which have the facilities for putting such a program into effect. The Farm Credit Administration and the Federal Housing Administration could, under certain circumstances, provide credit to individual part-time farmers. The Resettlement Administration could furnish valuable advice and experience, as well as make loans to finance the purchase of land or equipment. Agencies now concerned with families on relief could assist in the necessary field work and supervision.

Results of the survey suggest that any program for the improvement of existing part-time farms should have as its first goal the restoration of the individual families to the highest standard of living which they have enjoyed, rather than their establishment on some level recognized by scientific social work as a desirable standard. The practical common sense of this observation will be apparent to all, especially as applied to the region surveyed, and indeed to the entire South. Because of the exceptionally low standard of living in southern rural districts, it would be a temptation to establish for a few families a high standard of living which others could not attain, and which even the experimental families would not be prepared, economically or psychologically, to maintain.

Part II

Part-Time Farming in the Southeast

INTRODUCTION

THE FOLLOWING sections give somewhat detailed accounts\ of the basic industries of the subregions surveyed and analyze in detail the farming activities, industrial employment, and social activities of the part-time farmers and their nonfarming neighbors.

The major part of the income of part-time farm families is earned by work off the farm. The success of part-time farming, therefore, and the possibilities for future development of combinations of farming and industrial employment depend to a considerable extent on the probable future trends of employment in industry, as well as on the amount of industrial employment which will be available to them.

Therefore, production methods and organization, trends in production, wage rates, types of labor required, and other features of the principal industries of a region must be studied before an adequate appraisal of the possibilities of part-time farming can be made.

81

Chapter I

THE COTTON TEXTILE SUBREGION OF ALABAMA, GEORGIA, AND SOUTH CAROLINA

GENERAL FEATURES OF THE SUBREGION

THE COTTON Textile Subregion of Alabama, Georgia, and South Carolina is located generally in the Piedmont Area of these States [1] but does not coincide exactly with it (figure 2, page XXIV). It includes roughly 85 percent of the textile industry of these States, and has no other single industry approaching textiles in importance (table 81). This subregion and the 10 counties surrounding Birmingham are the 2 important industrial areas of the Southeast.

The textile industry is spread unevenly throughout the subregion, and is located mostly in the smaller towns and on the outskirts of large cities. This decentralization of the industry is made possible by the fact that most of the subregion is well supplied with railroads, roads, and electric power. There is a wide variation from county to county in amount of industry, northwestern South Carolina, particularly Spartanburg, Greenville, and Anderson Counties, being the area of greatest concentration.

The Piedmont Region of North Carolina, South Carolina, Georgia, and Alabama is, next to the Mississippi Delta, the most intensive cotton-farming area in the country. But whereas the latter area developed large plantations based first on slavery and later on the tenant system, with all the attendant evils of absentee landlordism and bad agricultural practices, the upper or northern portion of the

---

[1] Atlanta, the largest urban center in the Southeast, is quite different industrially from the rest of this subregion. Likewise the agriculture of nearby counties, because of the metropolitan influence, is quite different from that of the rest of the Piedmont Region. Hence, the findings of this report do not apply to the Atlanta Area.

Piedmont developed an agriculture characterized by small family-sized farms with white owner operators. This system has been conducive to diversified farming and maintenance of soil resources in a much more productive state.[2] Attention will be directed to the agriculture of this portion of the Piedmont, since it is in the northern Piedmont that most of the textile industry is located.

Table 81.—Distribution of Persons, 10 Years Old and Over, Gainfully Occupied in the Textile Subregion, 1930

Industry	Total		Atlanta		Cities of 25,000 to 100,000 population [1]		Rural areas and cities of less than 25,000 population	
	Number	Per-cent	Num-ber	Per-cent	Num-ber	Per-cent	Number	Per-cent
Total population	2,530,911		270,366		279,010		1,981,535	
Total gainfully employed	1,039,150	100.0	130,154	100.0	128,212	100.0	780,784	100.0
Agriculture	380,108	36.6	684	0.5	1,811	1.4	377,613	48.4
Service industries	377,107	36.3	92,753	71.3	87,625	68.4	196,729	25.2
Manufacturing and allied industries	281,935	27.1	36,717	28.2	38,776	30.2	206,442	26.4
Total manufacturing and allied industries	281,935	100.0	36,717	100.0	38,776	100.0	206,442	100.0
Forestry and fishing	986	0.3	15	*	78	0.2	893	0.4
Extraction of minerals	3,484	1.2	57	0.2	264	0.7	3,163	1.5
Building	32,626	11.4	8,040	21.9	7,253	18.7	17,333	8.4
Chemical and allied	8,319	3.0	2,146	5.8	2,112	5.5	4,061	2.0
Clay, glass, and stone	4,589	1.6	567	1.5	872	2.2	3,150	1.5
Clothing	6,960	2.5	1,940	5.3	1,091	2.8	3,929	1.9
Food and allied	9,593	3.4	3,028	8.3	2,973	7.7	3,592	1.7
Automobile factories and repair shops	7,513	2.7	2,281	6.2	1,268	3.3	3,964	1.9
Blast furnaces and steel rolling mills	106	*	—		10	*	96	0.1
Other iron and steel	10,691	3.8	3,505	9.6	2,409	6.2	4,777	2.3
Saw and planing mills	10,875	3.9	321	0.9	891	2.3	9,663	4.7
Other wood and furniture	5,081	1.8	1,379	3.8	741	1.9	2,961	1.4
Paper, printing, and allied	6,254	2.2	2,903	7.9	1,161	3.0	2,190	1.1
Cotton mills	133,290	47.3	2,360	6.4	11,357	29.3	119,573	58.0
Knitting mills	5,849	2.1	122	0.3	490	1.3	5,237	2.5
Other textile	8,625	3.1	482	1.3	746	1.9	7,397	3.6
Independent hand trades	6,905	2.5	1,475	4.0	1,322	3.4	4,108	2.0
Other manufacturing	20,189	7.2	6,096	16.6	3,738	9.6	10,355	5.0

* Less than 0.05 percent.

[1] Spartanburg, Greenville, and Columbia, South Carolina; Augusta and Columbus, Georgia; Montgomery, Alabama.

Source: *Fifteenth Census of the United States: 1930*, Population Vol. III.

The northern Piedmont is about 300 miles long and 70 miles wide (figure 3, page XXVI). The surface of this area is rolling to hilly with sandy loam soils on the smoother lands and clay loam soils on the slopes where erosion has taken place. Both types of soils are fairly productive where the slope is not too steep.[3]

In 1930, 71 percent of the total land area in the northern Piedmont Region was in farms, and of the land in farms 48 percent was cropland.

[2] Hartman, W. A. and Wooten, H. H., *Georgia Land Use Problems*, Bulletin 191, Georgia Experiment Station, 1935, pp. 48–49.

[3] *Yearbook of Agriculture: 1932*, U. S. Department of Agriculture, pp. 916–919.

Seven-eighths of all farms were classified as cotton farms, and two-thirds of the farm income was derived from the cotton crop.[4] Small farms predominated and part-time farms were common. There were 2,752 part-time farms in the area in 1929, according to the census classification [5] (figure 1, page XXI).

The population of the Cotton Textile Subregion is predominantly white. Negroes constituted 32.4 percent of the total population in 1930. The urban population averaged 32 percent Negro, the rural-nonfarm population about 20.5 percent Negro, and the rural-farm population about 40 percent Negro. The relatively small number of Negroes in the rural-nonfarm population reflected the limited employment of Negroes in cotton mills, which are located mostly in rural areas. In 1930, 27 percent of the farms in the northern Piedmont were operated by Negroes. Prior to 1930, there was a considerable migration from rural areas to the larger cities and textile centers, these showing substantial increases in population between 1920 and 1930 while most of the rural counties either lost population or remained stationary.

Counties Covered in Field Survey

Wide variations among textile mills affect conditions of part-time farming so greatly that no one area properly represents the situation. Therefore, field surveys were conducted in two areas selected to illustrate marked contrasts: Greenville County, South Carolina, and Carroll County, Georgia.

In Greenville County a large number of mills are clustered around a city, the combination making for dense population, opportunity for employment in occupations outside the predominating industry, and readily available urban conveniences and social advantages. Several of the mills make fine fabrics and pay wages higher than the average in the industry.

In Carroll County, on the other hand, there are fewer mills and these are scattered in small villages or rural areas. They make chiefly coarse goods and pay wages lower than the average for the industry.

In other respects, the counties are quite similar. Both had considerable part-time farming in 1930; both are in predominantly cotton-growing areas, 29 percent of all farm land in Carroll County and 26 percent of the farm land in Greenville County being in cotton. Cotton acreage in both counties has increased in recent years. Size of farms,

---

[4] These data for the northern Piedmont Area were calculated from 1930 Census of Agriculture reports. Five counties surrounding Atlanta were omitted.

[5] Part-time farms included all farms whose operators worked 150 days or more at jobs not connected with the farm and whose products did not exceed $750. See Methodological Note (Appendix C) for definition of part-time farm used as basis of sample in this survey.

cotton yields, and value of products per farm were about the same, though value of farm lands and buildings per farm averaged 68 percent higher in Greenville County—probably a reflection in land values of denser population.

The population of Greenville County was 117,000 in 1930, while that of the city of Greenville and its metropolitan area was 64,000. The population of Carroll County was only 34,000 and that of the largest town, Carrollton, was only 6,000. In both counties in 1933, over 90 percent of the wage earners in manufacturing and of the wages collected came from the textile group: in Greenville, mostly from cotton mills; in Carroll, about half from cotton mills and a little less than half from knitting mills.

THE COTTON TEXTILE INDUSTRY

Growth and Distribution in the South

In any consideration of the possibilities of part-time farming in the Eastern Cotton Belt, the manner in which such activities can be and are combined with employment in the textile industry is of primary importance. The oldest and most conspicuous industry in the South, the cotton textile industry, or "cotton goods" industry, employs the greatest number of workers of any single industry, and in South Carolina it employs more workers than all other industries combined. Although there is considerable concentration of textile mills in the southern Piedmont Region of North Carolina and in northwestern South Carolina, the industry is one of the most widely scattered of any of the great factory industries. Figure 4 shows the distribution of cotton spindles in the three States of the area under consideration. Not only is the industry scattered among more than 120 counties, but often it is found in several communities of the individual counties. The 345 cotton manufacturing establishments in these 3 States in 1933 [6] were located in some 240 cities, towns, and villages.[7] Only 10 percent of the cotton millworkers in the Textile Subregion designated in figure 2 lived in cities having a population in excess of 25,000. Thus a great majority of the workers are within reach of farm lands.

The growth of the industry was founded on an immense supply of cheap labor, cheap power, and relatively low taxation. The last-named factor has ceased to be important, but the first remains an advantage of no mean proportions. By the end of the World War, the industry in the Southeast had almost caught up with that in the other great textile area, New England, in volume of output and in

---

[6] *Biennial Census of Manufactures: 1933*, p. 152.

[7] *Davidson's Textile Blue Book, 1934.* (This represents data collected in early 1934 and so is comparable with the *Biennial Census of Manufactures* covering 1933.)

importance. The growth of the cotton goods manufacturing industry during the 1920's in the South and its decline in New England were accompanied by a shift or migration southward, and by 1933 the South had nearly twice as many spindles in place and more than twice as many active spindles as New England. The South, predominating in the coarse goods industry, used three and one-half times as much cotton as New England in that year.

FIG. 4 – NUMBER OF COTTON SPINDLES IN PLACE

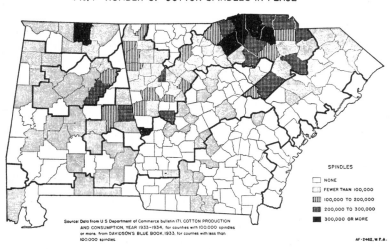

Source: Data from U.S. Department of Commerce bulletin 171, COTTON PRODUCTION AND CONSUMPTION, YEAR 1933–1934, for counties with 100,000 spindles or more, from DAVIDSON'S BLUE BOOK, 1933, for counties with less than 100,000 spindles.

SPINDLES

☐ NONE
▨ FEWER THAN 100,000
▥ 100,000 TO 200,000
▦ 200,000 TO 300,000
■ 300,000 OR MORE

AF-2462, W.P.A.

National Problems of the Industry

Throughout most of the 1920's the industry, or some branch of it, suffered from difficulties arising from excess capacity. Since it is a highly decentralized industry, made up of many small independent units and linked to a complicated selling system, competition and price cutting became major ills. So severe did they become that in 1926 [8] the industry in self-defense established the Cotton Textile Institute, which has endeavored to work out methods of voluntary control of production.

Indifferent success of this and several other such cooperative efforts made the leaders of the textile industry welcome the N. R. A. The cotton textile industry was the first to present a code. Its code, which was adopted and made effective July 17, 1933, provided for a maximum 40-hour week and limited machine hours to two 40-hour shifts. The minimum wage was set at $12 per week for the South and $13 per week for the North, with specified exemptions for learners, and

[8] Address of the Hon. Henry F. Lippitt, *Textile World*, October 23, 1926, p. 27.

later for outside employees, and with provisions for wage differentials based on skill. The N. R. A. set a differential in the minimum wage rate in the North and South, principally to offset the low rents charged in southern company villages.[9] Employment of any minor less than 16 years of age was prohibited.

The effect of the code was to increase the wage bill of the industry by approximately 65 percent,[10] the greatest increases in rates being in the lower paid brackets, and to spread payment to a greater number of employees. In Alabama, Georgia, and South Carolina, the number of wage earners in the industry in 1933 was above the number in 1929, and substantially above that in 1931 (table 82).

Table 82.—Wage Earners in the Cotton Goods Industry, 1921–1933

State	1921	1923	1925	1927	1929	1931	1933
United States total	412,058	471,503	445,184	467,596	424,916	329,962	379,445
5 New England States	185,941	194,891	164,074	154,634	127,041	90,127	90,596
Massachusetts	106,337	113,707	96,182	90,875	70,788	46,990	45,418
Rhode Island	29,328	33,993	29,276	26,203	21,833	13,089	13,077
New Hampshire	22,733	18,516	14,745	14,722	13,769	10,663	10,988
Connecticut	14,279	14,865	12,020	12,639	10,789	10,165	9,667
Maine	13,264	13,810	11,851	10,195	[1] 9,862	9,220	11,446
5 southern States	178,732	219,207	228,771	260,713	254,839	208,664	256,838
North Carolina	66,316	81,041	84,139	95,786	91,844	73,508	87,709
South Carolina	51,509	62,479	66,378	75,069	71,731	59,777	74,593
Georgia	35,237	47,479	48,612	56,607	55,368	44,102	57,238
Alabama	18,275	20,325	21,607	24,825	27,724	24,097	28,762
Virginia	7,395	7,883	8,035	8,426	7,672	7,180	8,536
All other States	47,385	57,405	52,339	52,249	43,036	31,171	32,011

[1] Includes 3 establishments in Vermont, 15 in Maine.

Source: *United States Census of Manufactures: 1921–1933.*

Since the N. R. A. was declared unconstitutional, May 27, 1935, evidence indicates that a majority of the cotton goods manufacturers have continued to adhere to the code hour and wage provisions.[11] Some of the smaller mills have not done this, but these make up only a relatively small part of the industry. Many of the mill executives interviewed during the summer of 1935 thought it would be possible to maintain N. R. A. standards indefinitely, but others feared that the pressure of competition would gradually force a decrease in wage rates and an increase in hours. Even as late as the summer of 1936,

[9] *N. R. A. Code for the Cotton Textile Industry*, Letter of Transmittal.

[10] *Wage Rates and Weekly Earnings in the Cotton Goods Industry from July 1933 to August 1934*, Mimeographed Report, 2d edition with minor corrections, Bureau of Labor Statistics, p. 12.

[11] From statements of trade association and mill executives (July 1935). See also *Cotton Textile Industry*, 74th Congress, Senate Document 126, p. 127; and Bowden, Witt, "Hours and Earnings Before and After the N. R. A.," *Monthly Labor Review*, Vol. 44, No. 1, January 1937. pp. 13–36.

the Cotton Textile Institute was confident of holding the majority of the mills in line for the principal gains of the N. R. A.

Competing Materials

Wool, linen, silk, and jute have always competed with cotton. The recent increase in the use of paper for containers, towels, napkins, and handkerchiefs has cut into important markets for cotton products. The increased use of rayon for clothing and household furnishings in the last decade also has decreased the market for fairly high-grade cotton fabrics. The use of cotton cloth as a tensile element in asphalt-surfaced, sand, or gravel roads has raised hopes for the opening of a large new outlet, provided, of course, that its use proves economical.

Exports and Imports

For generations, the export trade has been a minor but highly valued outlet for cotton goods. During the 1920's, exports of cotton cloth amounted to more than half a billion square yards a year, going chiefly to the Philippines, Cuba, Central America, and Canada. This trade has fallen off rapidly, and in 1934 it amounted to only 223 million square yards, or one-half of the previous amount. Exports to the Philippines dropped sharply. Imports, of which there were over 218 million square yards in 1923, dropped to 109 million in 1925 and to 40 million in 1934.[12]

The prime factor in these changes in international trade in textiles is the recent growth of the industry in the Orient. From 1926 to 1934, the index number for spindles dropped 18 percent in the United States and 19 percent in Great Britain, while in Japan the index number increased 63 percent, in China 38 percent, and in India 13 percent.[13] The Orient now supplies a large part of its own needs, and Japan has become an exporter of such proportions as to displace the United States, first in China, and more recently in the Philippines. Most recently Japan has begun to figure prominently in exports to the United States itself.

Prior to 1931, the United Kingdom supplied the bulk of cotton cloths imported into this country, and Switzerland was the leading source in the period 1931–1934. Late in 1934, the imports from Japan became important, and that country was the principal source of imports in 1935 and in early 1936. The cotton cloth imported from Japan is competing with domestic nainsooks and muslins manufactured in southern mills. The activity of the Japanese textile industry stands as a threat to this country's export rather than to its domestic trade, however, since the competition of imports from Japan is confined to

---

[12] *Cotton Textile Industry, op. cit.,* p. 99.

[13] *Idem,* p. 43.

only part of the textile field—that of print cloth—and since imports of countable cotton cloth from Japan were equivalent to only one-half of 1 percent of the total yardage of domestic production in 1935.

Starting June 20, 1936, further tariff protection was provided the domestic industry by new rates of duty on about 90 percent of the cotton cloth imported from Japan.[14] The proclaimed duties represent an increase over the existing duties of about 42 percent for both bleached cloth and printed, dyed, or colored cloth.

Outlook for Employment

In view of the situation as discussed above, it seems probable that the general trend of employment in the industry will be downward for some time to come. The perfecting of textile machinery has been so slow a process that technical improvements have not recently made striking changes in the amount of labor required. However, new labor-saving machines now in the experimental stage, such as the long-draft roving frame, eventually will displace several machines now being used. In addition, the probable retirement of obsolete plants, accompanied by increased efficiency in others, will mean less labor per unit of output even though an increase in demand may arise.

During the last decade, the application of scientific management principles to labor in the interest of economy and efficiency has resulted in considerable reduction of the labor force and rather radical reduction in the more skilled of the machine operations, such as weaving. It is probable, however, that the principal impact of this movement reached its crest during the hard times in textiles in the late 1920's or during the depression itself.

With prospects of a continued low or further declining foreign trade and increasing competition with cotton substitutes, employment in the cotton textile industry faces a still further set-back in the possible wholesale breakdown of the hour-reduction agreements achieved under the N. R. A. and continued by voluntary action. With longer hours, fewer workers can produce the necessary amount of goods.

On the other hand, textiles other than cotton goods are increasing in the South. The average number of workers in the knit goods industry in Alabama, Georgia, and South Carolina totaled 11,571 in 1933 in comparison with 2,607 in 1929.[15]

Also, a recent development in the South of mills for the finishing and dyeing of textiles probably will lead to some increase in employment. The average number of wage earners in the dyeing and finishing plants in South Carolina, where the southern development is

---

[14] United States Tariff Commission, Public Information Release, May 21, 1936.

[15] *Biennial Census of Manufactures: 1933*, p. 168; and *United States Census of Manufactures: 1929*, Vol. II, p. 300.

chiefly centered, was 4,561 for 1933, an increase of 135 percent over 1929.[16]

Labor

The labor force of the southern mills has been drawn from the native-born white stock of the farms of the South, so that large numbers of the workers have a farm background. Although there are now many second-generation millworkers, many of these also have had some farm experience. Negroes are employed only as sweepers and outside helpers and make up less than 7 percent of the total mill force on the average. The percentage of females among the employees varies from mill to mill but averages about 35 percent in the South.

Most tasks in textile mills require manual dexterity rather than physical strength. About 75 percent of the employees are classified as semiskilled, 15 percent as unskilled, with only a small group of mechanics and repairmen classified as skilled.[17] The period of training varies from a few weeks to 6 months or more. New workers are recruited from the nearby farms or mountain districts.

Child labor, long a matter for debate and criticism, has been gradually disappearing under improved State laws. The N. R. A. established 16 years as the minimum age for employment, but for several years prior to adoption of the code, it had been illegal to employ any child under 14 years of age in the cotton mills.[18]

Hours and Wages

Prior to the adoption of the N. R. A. code, the standard working week varied from 55 to 60 hours.[19] Many of the mills operated two shifts at these hours before the N. R. A. limited them to two shifts of 40 hours. Curtailment is effected sometimes by reducing numbers but more commonly by reducing the hours per week, both shifts being retained.

Pay is on a piece-work basis, except for a few workers, such as loom fixers and cleaners, whose output cannot be directly measured. Full-time wages in 1928 in Alabama, Georgia, and South Carolina averaged about $10 a week for spoolers, $12 for spinners, $14 to $16 for doffers and speeder tenders, and about $16 to $17 for weavers (table 83). Rates of pay declined from these figures between 1928 and 1933. Then, with the adoption of the N. R. A. code, hourly

[16] *Biennial Census of Manufactures: 1933*, p. 140; and *United States Census of Manufactures: 1929*, Vol. II, p. 271.

[17] See appendix table 30 for occupational distribution of sample.

[18] Alabama—Code of 1923, section 3494; Georgia—Code of 1926, Civil, section 3149 (1); South Carolina—Code of Laws 1922, Vol. 2, Criminal, chapter 7, section 413. See also, *Child Labor Facts and Figures*, Publication No. 197, U. S. Department of Labor, Children's Bureau, pp. 56–57.

[19] *Wages and Hours of Labor in Cotton-Goods Manufacturing, 1910 to 1928*, Bulletin 492, United States Bureau of Labor Statistics.

earnings rose sharply, almost doubling in many occupations (table 84). On the basis of a 40-hour week, the weekly earnings of the above series of occupations in 1934 were approximately $13.40 for spoolers, $12.80

Table 83.—Earnings in Selected Occupations in Cotton Mills, in Alabama, Georgia, and South Carolina, by Sex, 1928

Occupation and sex	Alabama			Georgia			South Carolina		
	Per hour	Per week full time	Per week actual time	Per hour	Per week full time	Per week actual time	Per hour	Per week full time	Per week actual time
Loom fixers, male	$0.395	$21.73	$19.82	$0.379	$21.30	$18.94	$0.377	$20.74	$16.44
Card grinders, male	0.365	20.08	17.60	0.349	19.72	18.32	0.359	19.75	16.87
Warp-tying machine tenders, male	0.348	19.14	17.88	0.336	18.85	18.49	0.354	19.47	15.86
Drawing-in machine tenders, male	0.318	17.49	15.45	0.341	19.40	19.08	0.351	19.31	16.50
Weavers, male	0.311	17.11	13.50	0.309	17.33	13.41	0.313	17.22	11.79
Weavers, female	0.299	16.45	12.39	0.292	16.35	11.97	0.277	15.24	10.09
Slubber tenders, male	0.286	15.73	11.74	0.317	17.82	13.99	0.311	17.11	11.07
Speeder tenders, male	0.276	15.18	10.94	0.307	17.16	12.79	0.296	16.28	10.48
Speeder tenders, female	0.258	14.19	10.31	0.294	16.55	12.87	0.274	15.07	10.30
Slasher tenders, male	0.286	15.73	12.50	0.304	17.12	15.87	0.286	15.73	12.02
Doffers, male	0.264	14.52	10.30	0.282	15.88	12.35	0.270	14.85	9.63
Warper tenders, female	0.269	14.80	11.35	0.251	14.01	11.59	0.287	15.79	11.40
Drawers-in-hand, female	0.216	11.88	9.30	0.284	15.68	14.01	0.266	14.63	8.98
Card tenders and strippers, male	0.234	12.87	9.31	0.248	14.01	10.25	0.262	14.41	9.34
Drawing-frame tenders, male	0.235	12.93	8.53	0.245	13.82	9.91	0.256	14.08	9.40
Drawing-frame tenders, female	0.195	10.73	7.80	0.208	11.63	8.26	—	—	—
Spinners (frame), female	0.215	11.83	8.60	0.222	12.45	9.09	0.215	11.83	7.09
Picker tenders, male	0.213	11.72	8.52	0.218	12.36	10.00	0.210	11.55	7.79
Creelers, female	0.205	11.28	8.26	0.201	11.30	8.94	0.212	11.66	7.51
Spooler tenders, female	0.183	10.07	7.53	0.210	11.68	9.29	0.186	10.23	6.74
Trimmers and inspectors, female	0.180	9.90	7.88	0.202	11.31	9.61	0.188	10.34	7.78

Source: Wages and Hours of Labor in Cotton-Goods Manufacturing, 1910 to 1928, Bulletin 492, United States Bureau of Labor Statistics.

Table 84.—Average Hourly Earnings in Selected Occupations in Southern Cotton-Textile Mills, by Sex, 1933–34

Occupation and sex	Average hourly earnings		
	July 1933	August 1933	August 1934
Loom fixers, male	$0.324	$0.499	$0.507
Card grinders, male	0.273	0.440	0.443
Warp-tying machine tenders, male	0.255	0.424	0.436
Weavers, male	0.235	0.395	0.401
Weavers, female	0.215	0.384	0.382
Slubber tenders, male	0.213	0.372	0.374
Speeder tenders, male	0.215	0.365	0.368
Speeder tenders, female	0.196	0.346	0.353
Doffers, male	0.195	0.344	0.349
Warper tenders, female	0.194	0.340	0.333
Drawers-in-hand, female	0.232	0.383	0.388
Card tenders and strippers, male	0.194	0.324	0.325
Drawing-frame tenders, male	0.191	0.328	0.338
Drawing-frame tenders, female	0.180	0.315	0.309
Spinners (frame), female	0.161	0.322	0.321
Picker tenders, male	0.173	0.309	0.313
Creelers, female	0.160	0.315	0.310
Spooler tenders, female	0.162	0.328	0.334
Trimmers and inspectors, female	0.160	0.309	0.310

Source: Hinrichs, A. F., "Wage Rates and Weekly Earnings in the Cotton-Textile Industry, 1933–34," Monthly Labor Review, March 1935, p. 615.

for spinners, $14 to $15 for doffers and speeder tenders, and $16 for weavers.

Seasonal Variation in Employment

While some mills experience a dull season in summer, thus allowing more time for gardening, most of the variations in employment are irregular in response to market conditions. There is very little demand for regular seasonal part-time employment in cotton mills. Trained workers among the families in the villages or vicinity, or floating labor, have been sufficient in recent years to take care of periods of increased activity.

The Mill Village

No discussion of incomes of cotton millworkers would be complete without some consideration of the services and facilities furnished them in the company-owned mill villages. These vary widely from mill to mill and what is furnished depends on the financial resources of the individual mill as well as on the sense of social responsibility and the ability of its management. The villages vary from a collection of shacks, badly in need of repair and with only the most primitive sanitary facilities, to well maintained homes with electric lights, water, sewerage, and gardens in a community with good schools, medical care, and recreational facilities.[20] Many company houses have additional land for farming activities, pasturage for cows, and pens for hogs.

The rental charged is most frequently 25 cents per room per week, the house ranging from three to six rooms. A recent study of 50 southern mill villages[21] showed the average rental to be 33 cents per room per week, including lights and water. The number of workers living in mill villages was 69.5 percent of the total number employed.

The low rents constitute an addition to the real income not shared by the 30 percent who do not live in company houses. Comparable housing by home ownership costs more than these rentals, and rents from private landlords are substantially higher. In addition, it is quite customary for the company to charge no rent when a mill is temporarily shut down.[22]

The mill villages were at first essential because mills were erected in isolated communities or on the outskirts of towns. Now the workers

---

[20] *Welfare Work in Mill Villages* by Harriet L. Herring, Chapel Hill: University of North Carolina Press, 1929, is a comprehensive study of North Carolina mill villages. The general features of the picture presented would apply in Alabama, Georgia, and South Carolina as well.

[21] From an address by President William D. Anderson before the American Cotton Manufacturers Association, April 25, 1935, Pamphlet, issued by Ralph E. Loper and Company.

[22] This practice is enforced by law in South Carolina. *South Carolina Acts of 1933*, Act No. 269.

have come to expect the company to provide them with houses at the customary low rentals. Employers, on the other hand, have in general accepted the extra housing cost as a part of their labor costs and as a price to pay for their ability to control the community. In recent years this control, exercised in strikes by way of evictions, has been the subject of considerable criticism.

A provision was inserted in the N. R. A. code for the industry setting up an agency "to consider the question of plans for eventual employee-ownership of homes in mill villages." After preliminary investigation, this provision was abandoned in view of the force of tradition, the habits of both employers and employees, and the undeniable social and economic difficulties of such a change.

FARMING ACTIVITIES OF PART-TIME FARMERS

Types of Part-Time Farmers

The part-time farmers included in the field survey in both counties (190 farmers in Greenville and 103 in Carroll) were chiefly operators of small acreages on which products were grown primarily for home use. There were a few cases with sufficient land and a large enough volume of sales to be considered commercial or semicommercial farmers. These were essentially different from the large group with only an acre or two of land, a small garden, a cow, a few chickens, and a pig. They usually were located in the open country, where they had considerable land, machinery, and work stock, and grew corn, cotton, or other field crops. They carried on at least one distinctly commercial farm enterprise, and in many cases they had been until recently full-time farmers.

The noncommercial group, however, was numerically of much greater importance in these counties than was the commercial group, and most of the discussion will be devoted to it, with occasional references to the other group for purposes of comparison. Since the population of the Cotton Textile Subregion is predominantly white, and opportunities for the employment of Negroes in industry limited, the field study for this subregion included only whites.

Location of Part-Time Farms

The location of the part-time farms included in the field enumeration is shown in figures 5 and 6. Grouped around the towns and cities, the majority of these farmers lived near enough to their places of employment so that transportation was not an important item. This was particularly true of the noncommercial group. In Greenville County 67 percent and in Carroll County 93 percent of this group lived less than 1½ miles from their work. Those few who were not within walking distance of their places of employment usually drove their own cars. Frequently two or more persons rode together to reduce transportation costs. It should be noted in this connection

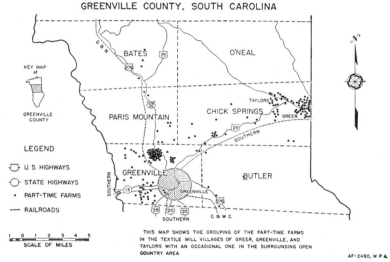

FIG. 5-LOCATION OF PART-TIME FARMS INCLUDED IN FIELD SURVEY
GREENVILLE COUNTY, SOUTH CAROLINA

that about one-third of the families surveyed in Greenville County and
two-thirds of those in Carroll County lived in textile mill villages.[23]

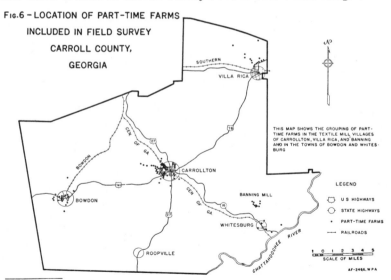

FIG.6 – LOCATION OF PART-TIME FARMS
INCLUDED IN FIELD SURVEY
CARROLL COUNTY,
GEORGIA

[23] Associated with these differences in location were certain social and economic
differences. Where these were significant, the data were analyzed on a county
rather than on a subregion basis.

In the Carrollton mill village, there were large areas of tillable land directly back of the mill houses and conveniently located pasturage for cows. Hence, a large majority of this mill's employees were part-time farmers. In Banning, the land was difficult to work because of the steep slopes and poor soil, and in Fullerville there was a lack of land suitable for gardens near the workers' homes. Therefore, there were only a few part-time farmers working in these two mills.

Farm Production

Almost four-fifths of the noncommercial part-time farmers surveyed had less than 2½ acres of cropland (appendix table 6), and the average amount was 1½ acres. Of the types of food produced—vegetables, dairy products, poultry products, and pork—nearly one-third of the noncommercial and over two-thirds of the commercial farmers reported all four (appendix table 12). Figure 7 shows graphically the proportion of noncommercial farmers in each county with varying sizes of the several farm production enterprises.

Gardens

All of the farms surveyed had vegetable gardens, except for 7 in nonmill villages and 13 in mill villages in Greenville County, where the only farming operation was keeping a cow (appendix table 11). Both Greenville and Carroll Counties have an average frost-free growing season of about 7 months, which means that there are about 5 months in which the less hardy vegetables may be consumed fresh from the garden. The hardy root crops and leafy vegetables may be available during the colder months. In this subregion, there was an average of 7½ months when some fresh vegetable or fruit was consumed on part-time farms (appendix table 14).

In Carroll County two-thirds of the gardens supplied three or more fresh vegetables over a period of 4 or 5 months, and about one-fourth of them for 6 or 7 months. Only one garden supplied three or more vegetables for more than 7 months. In Greenville County more variation was reported in the length of the garden season. It varied from 2 to 8 months for 82 percent of the cases, with five gardens supplying three or more vegetables for 9 months, and one for 12 months (appendix table 13). These facts suggest the possibilities for improvement of many of the gardens so that they can be made to produce over a longer period.

In view of these variations, it is noteworthy that so many of the gardens made sufficient contributions to the family living to reduce the grocery bill during the 6 summer months, the estimated individual reductions ranging from $1 to $14 monthly.[24] In Greenville County

---

[24] See Case Studies of Part-Time Farmers (Appendix A) for specific evaluation of the contribution of gardens.

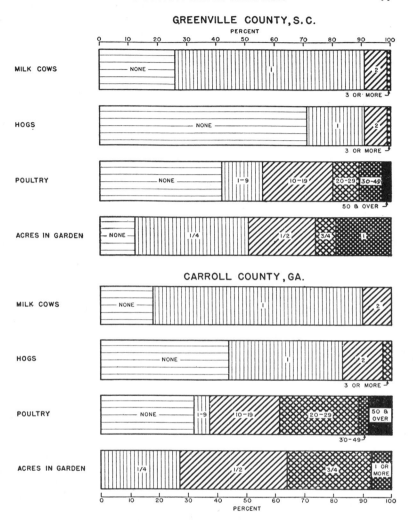

FIG.7— SIZE OF PRINCIPAL ENTERPRISES ON WHITE
NONCOMMERCIAL PART-TIME FARMS,
GREENVILLE COUNTY, S.C., AND
CARROLL COUNTY, GA., 1934

AF-2488, W. P. A.

82 percent of the families that had gardens reported reductions, the reductions averaging $7.60 per month.   In Carroll County 88 percent reported reductions, these averaging $3.75.   This difference was probably not entirely the result of better gardens in Greenville County, although the Greenville gardens were somewhat larger and produced over a longer period.   As will be shown later, incomes were considerably lower in Carroll County, and it is probable that expenditures for food were normally lower than in Greenville County.

The above figures do not measure the entire contribution of the garden.   During the garden season, the family may not only buy less groceries, but it may fare better in quality and variety of food consumed, while the canning and storing of vegetables serve to reduce the grocery bill for the winter months.

In the Textile Subregion, as a whole, less than one-fifth of the part-time farm families did no canning (appendix table 16).   In Carroll County all but 5 percent of the families did some canning, and the average quantity canned was 98 quarts.   This included fruits as well as vegetables, since some of the families had a few apple and peach trees (appendix table 15).   In Greenville County there was somewhat less canning, 26 percent of the families doing none.   The average for those who did canning was 86 quarts.   The more extensive canning of fresh fruit and vegetables in Carroll County may partially explain why summer grocery bills in that county were reduced less than in Greenville County.

Almost all of the commercial farm families in the subregion and over one-half of the noncommercial families stored vegetables (table 29, page 20).   Both sweet potatoes and Irish potatoes were frequently stored, the average amounts stored by the noncommercial part-time farmers being 12 bushels of sweet potatoes and 6 bushels of Irish potatoes (appendix table 17).   Other products occasionally stored were onions, peanuts, sorghum syrup, peas, beans, apples, and peppers.

Corn

Field corn was grown by 88 percent of the commercial part-time farmers, average production being approximately 100 bushels.   Less than 10 percent of the noncommercial part-time farmers produced corn, the average production being 21 bushels (appendix table 24).   All those producing corn used on an average about 10 bushels for meal and the remainder as feed for livestock.

Dairy Products

The ownership of a cow was very common in this area.   Practically all of the commercial and over three-fourths of the noncommercial group owned at least one cow (appendix table 11).   The average production of milk per cow was over 2,400 quarts a year (appendix table

20). About 2 quarts were used fresh, the remainder being used to make butter (appendix table 21). A few part-time farmers sold milk, and about half of the noncommercial farmers who kept cows sold butter. For those selling dairy products, the average value of sales was $66 in Greenville County and $98 in Carroll County. Dairy products accounted for about three-fourths of all sales of farm products.

It was customary for textile mills in this region to have a common pasture where each employee might graze his cow. These pastures were frequently overstocked and did not supply all of the roughage needed. Frequently cows were staked out along the roadsides or on vacant lots, but farmers who lived in mill villages or on part-time farms of 1 or 2 acres had to purchase most of the feed for their cows. For those who purchased all of the feed other than pasturage, the cost was usually from $60 to $75. The amount of roughage produced by many noncommercial part-time farmers was very small, averaging only about 1½ tons (appendix table 23).

Poultry Products

About two-thirds of the families in each county had poultry, flocks varying in size from 10 to 50 birds (appendix table 11). The consumption of home-produced eggs varied widely, the average being about 75 dozen a year, or 1½ dozen eggs per week for noncommercial farmers who had poultry (appendix table 18). For the households that had chickens, consumption of poultry amounted to about one 3-pound chicken every 2 weeks for noncommercial, and every week for commercial, part-time farm families (appendix table 19).

Pork

More than three-fourths of the commercial, and over one-half of the noncommercial, part-time farmers produced pork in 1934 (appendix table 22), although some of the mill villages had restrictions against keeping pigs. Most families had only one pig. Considering this, the poundage produced, averaging 385 pounds, was comparatively high.

Fuel

Only 9 percent of the part-time farmers in Greenville County and 3 percent in Carroll County cut wood for fuel on their farms. This is explained by the fact that many of them lived in villages, and only 12 percent in Greenville County and 8 percent in Carroll County had woodland.

Changes in Size of Farming Operations, 1929–1934

The group of families under consideration had about the same size of farming operations in 1934 as in 1929. A few more families had cows, but the average number of cows had not increased. There were no significant changes in the ownership of hogs or chickens. Gardens were the same average size in both years (appendix table 5). The data do not accurately measure the change in amount of part-time farming in the region, however, since they do not include families that may have given it up during this time.

Cash Receipts and Cash Expenses

In Greenville County 66 percent and in Carroll County 47 percent of the noncommercial part-time farmers sold some farm products. The average cash receipts for all products sold, however, was under $50 (appendix table 25). Cash expenses for the noncommercial group, exclusive of rent and taxes, averaged $107 in Greenville County and $66 in Carroll County, and on the average, those who sold more than $200 worth of farm products in Greenville County and more than $50 worth in Carroll County covered cash expenses.

The more favorable cash balance in Carroll County is explained by a combination of slightly higher receipts and considerably lower expenses. This probably is associated, at least in part, with the lower income status of the Carroll County group which made it urgent for them to take advantage of every possible source of income and to reduce expenses to the minimum. This was accomplished by selling as much of their farm products as possible and by hiring no labor to do work that could possibly be done by members of the family. The net effect was that the food products from the farm were obtained at a lower net cash cost.

Value and Tenure of Part-Time Farms

In Greenville County 45 percent and in Carroll County 16 percent of the part-time farmers owned their homes. Many part-time farmers lived in mill villages where there was little or no opportunity for home ownership. Outside the mill villages, the usual differences in economic status between owners and tenants appeared.

The procedure used for arriving at real estate values, namely, capitalizing the rental value at 5 percent, was not satisfactory for those living in mill villages because company rents were lower than normal. In Carroll County, there were too few cases outside the mill village for an analysis of differences between owners and tenants to be made. Therefore, calculations of real estate values were made only for those outside the mill village in Greenville County. Here real estate of owners was of considerably greater value than that leased by tenants, that of noncommercial owners being 65 percent higher than that of noncommercial tenants, and that of commercial owners being 71 percent higher than that of commercial tenants (table 17, page 12, and appendix table 7). Since the tenants operated considerably more land than did the owners, it is evident that the difference in values must have been chiefly in buildings, of which the dwelling was, of course, by far the most important. This fact indicates that better housing conditions prevailed among the owners. Commercial part-time farmers, on the whole, had more farm buildings than did noncommercial farmers (appendix table 9).

Owners had more machinery than did tenants (appendix table 10), although this was a minor item, since in Greenville County 87 percent and in Carroll County 93 percent of the noncommercial groups (composed mostly of tenants) had no machinery other than small hand tools. The average cost for the noncommercial farmers having machinery was only $65 (appendix table 10). Livestock was not a very important investment item, since the typical combination of a cow, a pig, and 15 hens was usually not worth much over $100.

The high value of the owners' real estate did not represent assets alone, however, since their mortgage indebtedness was greater than that of tenants. The average mortgage indebtedness for the noncommercial owners who were in debt was $1,443 (appendix table 8).

The owners in Greenville County who were not in mill villages earned substantially higher wages at their off-the-farm employment than did the nonmill-village tenants in all industries except building and construction, the 83 owners averaging $924 at off-the-farm employment, and the 48 tenants averaging $660. The higher wages were due both to the higher occupational level of the owners and to the fact that a larger proportion of owners were in industries paying higher wages. Larger earnings in this group had doubtless made possible the purchase of part-time farm homes.

Labor Requirements of Part-Time Farms and Their Relation to Working Hours in Industry

The 40-hour week established by the N. R. A. code was divided by most mills into a 5-day week. The two shifts which most mills operate change at about 2 or 3 o'clock in the afternoon. Thus workers have plenty of daylight hours for work on their part-time farms. In the service industries, the N. R. A. codes were either nonexistent or ineffective. The hours, except in those industries that are highly unionized, such as railroads, were generally more than 8 hours per day and averaged nearly 10. Workers in those industries, however, did approximately as much farming as did textile workers.

Among the noncommercial part-time farm households, work on the farm absorbed about 3½ hours a day from April through August, and considerably less time during the rest of the year (table 48, page 32). In terms of hours, the heads of households did less than half of the farm work. Commercial farms required over 10 hours of farm work a day from April through October, heads working over 4 hours a day on the average during the summer months.

The wife did some farm work on 75 percent of the farms in Greenville County and on 82 percent in Carroll County. Unemployed youth, workers too old for outside employment, and, to a small extent, children also helped. There were only 12 percent of the farms in Greenville County and 3 percent in Carroll County in which no member of the household other than the head worked. Labor was hired for the heavier work on field crops if the occupation of the head did not leave him sufficient time for it (appendix table 26).

EMPLOYMENT AND EARNINGS IN INDUSTRY

Employment in the textile industry was affected in 1934 by the N. R. A. order limiting hours to 30 per week for 12 weeks from June 4 to August 25, and by the textile strike in September. The former affected cotton mills in both counties studied, the latter chiefly in Carroll County. In addition, the knitting mills of Carroll County and the finishing plants of Greenville County suffered a seasonal slack period in the summer.

The Industrial Group

For comparative purposes, the enumerators were instructed to take schedules of industrial workers as follows: approximately 100 schedules of white textile workers, 30 of white workers in other manufacturing and mechanical industries, and 70 of white workers in the service group of industries in Greenville County, and 100 schedules of white textile workers in Carroll County.[25]

Industry and Occupation

The part-time farmers included in this study were selected without regard to the industry in which they worked (appendix table 29). In Carroll County, because of the lack of other manufacturing and service industries, 80 percent worked in cotton or knitting mills. In Greenville County, 58 percent of the part-time farmers were employed in textiles, the others being widely distributed among other manufacturing and service industries.

There was very little difference between the part-time farm and nonfarm groups in the proportions in various occupational classes (appendix table 30). There was considerable difference in skill between the occupational groups of Greenville and Carroll Counties, however. Roughly one-half of both part-time farmers and nonfarming industrial workers were classified as semiskilled in Greenville County, while 70 percent of the part-time farmers and 79 percent of the

---

[25] The term "industrial workers" covers a large group of individuals of such widely varying income, type of employment, and social status that it was decided to limit those to be included in this survey to the predominant industrial groups of the respective areas. Because of this arbitrary selection of industrial workers, there was some disparity between the occupational distribution of the nonfarming industrial workers and the part-time farmers. It was believed, however, that the industrial groups would be homogeneous enough in themselves to form a basis for comparison. See Introduction and Part I, chapter II, pp. 37–39.

nonfarming workers were in this classification in Carroll County (table 85). Proportionately fewer part-time farm and nonfarm workers were in the skilled group in Carroll County, however, partly because of the preponderance of cotton mill workers in Carroll County. All mill operators except loom fixers, mechanics, and foremen were classified as semiskilled.

Table 85.—Occupation of Heads of White Part-Time Farm and Nonfarming Industrial Households in the Textile Subregion, by Industry, 1934

Industry	Part-time farmers						Nonfarming industrial workers					
	Total	Proprietary	Clerical	Skilled	Semi-skilled	Unskilled	Total	Proprietary	Clerical	Skilled	Semi-skilled	Unskilled
CARROLL COUNTY												
All industries_____	103	1	6	17	72	7	98	—	5	11	77	5
Cotton mills_____	76	—	4	8	60	4	78	—	4	10	59	5
Knitting mills_____	7	—	—	—	7	—	20	—	1	1	18	—
GREENVILLE COUNTY												
All industries_____	190	9	30	54	88	9	216	2	37	63	108	6
Cotton mills_____	37	—	1	12	21	3	87	—	1	23	58	5
Other textile_____	73	—	2	18	53	—	24	—	—	2	21	1
Steam and street railroads_	—	—	—	—	—	—	12	—	—	8	4	—
Auto agencies and filling stations_____	10	4	6	—	—	—	11	—	11	—	—	—
Wholesale and retail trade_	22	5	16	—	—	1	22	2	17	—	3	—
Personal service [1]_____	—	—	—	—	—	—	15	—	4	1	10	—

[1] Barbers and laundry employees.

Earnings of Heads of Households

The part-time farmers included in this survey were, with very few exceptions, full-time workers in industry. A comparison of hourly rates of pay, hours worked per day, days worked per year, and average yearly earnings of part-time farmers and nonfarming industrial workers [26] shows differences that are explainable by better industrial conditions in Greenville County rather than by participation in part-time farming operations (table 86). In Carroll County, part-time farmers earned an average of $554 per year, the nonfarmers $447, the difference being due partly to the fact that many of the nonfarming industrial group worked in the Banning and Fullerville mills, one of which was closed for 2 months and the other for 3 months during 1934. In Greenville County, the part-time farmers averaged $816, the non-farming industrial workers $1,037. Here a few cases of very short time in the cotton mill group served to pull down the first average, while a few highly paid salesmen raised the average unduly in the nonfarm group. On the average, commercial part-time farmers in this subregion earned $733 a year in industry, noncommercial part-

[26] See appendix tables 32 and 34.

time farmers earned $722, and nonfarming industrial workers earned $853 (appendix table 34).

Table 86.—Rate of Pay, Working Time, and Annual Earnings [1] of Heads of White Part-Time Farm and Nonfarming Industrial Households in the Textile Subregion, 1934

Industry	Part-time farmers				Nonfarming industrial workers			
	Average hourly rate of pay	Average hours worked per day	Average full days worked	Average earnings	Average hourly rate of pay	Average hours worked per day	Average full days worked	Average earnings
CARROLL COUNTY								
All industries	$0.34	8.3	198	$554	$0.31	8.0	180	$447
Cotton mills	0.34	8.0	203	566	0.31	8.0	180	461
Knitting mills	†	†	†	†	0.30	7.9	181	428
GREENVILLE COUNTY								
All industries	0.43	8.6	228	816	0.48	8.5	257	1,037
Cotton mills	0.41	8.0	217	722	0.44	8.0	234	845
Other textile	0.47	8.0	213	841	0.43	8.0	230	800
Steam and street railroads	†	†	†	†	0.74	8.3	282	1,716
Auto agencies and filling stations	†	†	†	†	0.44	10.5	308	1,361
Wholesale and retail trade	0.37	9.1	238	784	0.44	9.3	280	1,117
Personal service [2]	†	†	†	†	0.39	9.5	294	1,050

† Average not computed for less than 10 cases.
[1] At principal off-the-farm employment (job with the largest earnings).
[2] Barbers and laundry employees.

Total Family Cash Income

There was no significant difference between the part-time farm and nonfarming industrial groups in average total family cash income from nonfarm sources, except for the differences in earnings of the heads, explained in the preceding section (table 59, page 44). In average number of employed members per household, in percentage of households with only the head employed, and in average earnings of members other than the head, the part-time farm and the nonfarm groups in Greenville County did not differ greatly (table 87). In Carroll County, the earnings of the other members of part-time farm and nonfarming industrial families differed in the same fashion that earnings of heads differed and for the same reason. In this county there was a greater total number employed per household than in Greenville County. There was no difference between the farm and nonfarm groups in this respect, however.

In both counties, there was a higher proportion of large families in the part-time farm group, the average being over one person more per household, than in the nonfarming industrial group (table 87). A farming operation is a greater help to a large family than to a small one. The reduction in cash outlay for food is greater, there is less waste of farm produce, and the dependent family members can help considerably with the farm work. These reasons may have prompted many of the heads of large households to go into farming or gardening.

Table 87.—Earnings and Employment of Members of Part-Time Farm and Nonfarming Industrial Households in the Textile Subregion, 1934

Item	Carroll County		Greenville County			
	All industries		All industries		Textile industry	
	Part-time farmers	Non-farming indus-trial workers	Part-time farmers	Non-farming indus-trial workers	Part-time farmers	Non-farming indus-trial workers
Average annual earnings of head at principal off-the-farm employment	$554	$447	$816	$1,037	$801	$835
Average annual earnings of members other than head per household	$487	$330	$280	$267	—	—
Average annual off-the-farm income per household [1]	$1,060	$801	$1,116	$1,308	$1,055	$1,131
Percent of households with only the head employed	28	21	56	57	55	49
Average number of employed members per household	2.1	2.0	1.7	1.6	1.7	1.7
Average size of household	5.2	4.0	5.4	4.2	5.3	4.3
Average number of dependents per employed worker	1.5	1.0	2.2	1.6	2.1	1.5
Average annual off-the-farm income per person	$203	$198	$209	$315	$200	$267

[1] Includes all off-the-farm sources.

The data presented here show that the part-time farm families in this area were able to get about as much industrial employment and earn about as much money as the comparable nonfarming industrial workers' families in the same locality. This indicates that cash income from industrial employment was not affected by whether or not the family did part-time farming. The characteristics of the individual, the amount and type of employment available, and wage scales are the important factors.

It should be emphasized that the earnings discussed here are for 1934, a year in which the N. R. A. was effective in the textile industry. Whether the industry will be able to maintain the N. R. A. wage rates in the face of keen competition and a large supply of available low-income labor on the farms of the South is problematical. These industrial incomes were substantially higher than farm incomes in the same counties in 1934, as will be discussed later. Some differential existed in 1929 also, but it has undoubtedly widened during the depression. Such differentials ordinarily exert a pressure toward reduction of earnings, but there are always resistances to be overcome. Two important elements of resistance in this case were the efforts of the textile manufacturers' organizations to maintain the N. R. A. scale, and the constant battle of the labor union, although weak in numbers, against any wage reduction.

LIVING CONDITIONS AND ORGANIZED SOCIAL LIFE

Living conditions and opportunities for participation in organized social life in this subregion depended to a great extent on whether the part-time farmer lived in the open country, in a mill village, or other village. The textile industry is so located in relation to good farm land that part-time farmers live either in the same communities as do nonfarming industrial workers or within easy commuting distance from town (table 62, page 51, and appendix table 28). Hence the problem of rural isolation is not a serious one.

In Greenville County, 30 percent of the part-time farmers lived in mill villages, 40 percent in the open country, and the rest in country or suburban villages. Of the nonfarming industrial group, about one-half lived in mill villages and the others in the city of Greenville or in other villages. In Carroll County, 55 percent of the part-time farmers and 85 percent of the nonfarm group lived in mill villages; very few were in the open country.

Living conditions of the mill village inhabitants depended in part upon the policies of the mill management in the maintenance of the village and furnishing of facilities. The type and general state of repair of the houses and the household facilities provided were fairly uniform in any one mill village, but these items and the general community facilities varied widely from village to village, as was pointed out above. It was observed by those making the study that, in general, housing and facilities in mill villages in which a considerable number of the workers were part-time farmers were somewhat better than the average, and living conditions of part-time farm families in such villages were better than those of nonfarming industrial workers. Electric power, which sometimes was not available in the open country without a private generating plant, was almost always supplied in the mill villages. The fact that a large proportion of the part-time farmers in Greenville County lived in the open country tended to place them at a disadvantage in this respect.

Housing

In general, the houses in Greenville County, both in mill villages and outside, were in better repair and had more conveniences than those in Carroll County. This was to be expected in view of the higher wages and investments in the former county. Slightly more part-time farm than nonfarm houses in both counties needed no repairs, but on the other hand somewhat more part-time farm houses needed such fundamental attention as general structural repairs (appendix table 40).

A typical mill-village dwelling in Carroll County, occupied by a part-time farm family of five persons, consisted of three rooms in a one-story, single-family house with electric lights but without running water. The building was in need of paint and minor repairs. The annual rental was $91, which included ¼ acre for a garden and pasturage for a cow. Mill-village dwellings of the nonfarming industrial families were often double houses, crowded together, and with no available land for gardens.

A typical dwelling of a part-time farm family of seven persons in Greenville County was a six-room, single-family house in good repair with electric lights, running water, and bathroom. The annual rental, which included 2½ acres of ground, was $78.

Part-time farmers had larger homes than industrial workers. The difference in size was greater in Carroll County where the dwellings of nonfarming industrial households were smaller than those of the part-time farmers for all but the largest size of household. Part-time farm families in Greenville County had larger dwellings than did those in Carroll County, due, for the most part, to the greater size of houses located outside the mill villages (appendix table 38).

In Carroll County approximately three-fourths of each group had electric lights, but only a few had running water or bath facilities. Nearly all families in Greenville County, except those living in the open country, had electric lights and running water. Electric lights were available to only about two-thirds of those living in the open country and running water to approximately one-fourth. Over one-third of the nonfarming industrial households but only one-fourth of the part-time farm households had bathrooms (appendix table 41).

Automobiles, Radios, and Telephones

Almost two-thirds of the part-time farmers had automobiles, as compared with two-fifths of the nonfarming industrial workers (appendix table 42). In Greenville County 41 percent of the part-time farmers were 1½ miles or more from their places of employment, and an automobile was required for transportation to and from work in many cases. Only 17 percent of the industrial workers were 1½ miles or more from their places of employment. Since 90 percent of the part-time farmers and all of the nonfarming industrial workers in Carroll County were less than 1½ miles from their places of employment, distance from work cannot explain the larger number of part-time farmers having automobiles.

Three-fourths of the part-time farmers and somewhat fewer of the nonfarming industrial workers in Greenville County had radios, while one-half of the part-time farmers and one-third of the nonfarming industrial workers in Carroll County had them. Telephones were so infrequent in all groups as to be insignificant. One-sixth of the part-time farmers and almost one-third of the nonfarming industrial group lacked all three of these facilities.

Home Ownership

The proportion of home owners was much greater among part-time farmers than among nonfarming industrial workers. In Greenville County, almost one-half of the part-time farmers, as compared with slightly over one-tenth of the nonfarming industrial workers, owned their homes; and in Carroll County, there was an even greater difference. This was associated with a somewhat greater proportion of the industrial households living in mill villages where there was little or no chance for ownership (table 88). However, when the comparison is limited to part-time farmers and nonfarming industrial workers living outside of mill villages, the part-time farm group still had a higher percentage of home owners. As has already been noted,[27] the low rents of those living in company villages gave them a considerable advantage over either owners or other tenants in cost of housing.

Table 88.—Tenure Status of Part-Time Farmers and Nonfarming Industrial Workers in the Textile Subregion, 1934

Tenure status	Greenville County				Carroll County	
	All industries		Textile industry		All industries	
	Part-time farmers	Non-farming industrial workers	Part-time farmers	Non-farming industrial workers	Part-time farmers	Non-farming industrial workers
Total_____	190	216	110	111	103	98
Owners_____	86	28	35	2	16	1
Tenants:						
Mill village_____	56	105	57	105	58	83
Nonmill village_____	48	83	18	4	29	14

Education

Children 7–16 years of age of both part-time farming and non-farming industrial groups who had attended school during 1933–34 had made approximately normal progress [28] (table 76, page 64). However, 4 percent of the part-time farm children in Greenville County between these ages had not attended school, as against 9 percent of those in nonfarming industrial households. In Carroll County, however, 18 percent of the children of both groups were not in school during the 1933–34 term. Most of these children were 7 years of age and had not yet started to school, or had left school between the ages of 14 and 16. Only four children in Greenville County and three in Carroll County were employed (table 75, page 63).

One-half of the heads of part-time farm households in the Textile Subregion had completed grade school and most of those had attended high school (appendix table 46). Of those not completing grade school, two-fifths had completed four grades or less. There was no significant difference between the education of part-time farmers and nonfarming industrial workers (appendix table 46).

Greenville County had a free public library service with over 100 distributing points outside the city of Greenville receiving some form of library service.[29] The main library in Greenville supplied books to

---

[27] See p. 93.

[28] See Part I, pp. 62 and 64.

[29] Frayser, Mary E., *The Libraries of South Carolina*, Bulletin 292, South Carolina Agricultural Experiment Station, 1933.

branch libraries, reading rooms, rural schools, crossroad stores, filling stations, post offices, churches, clubs, and homes. More than three-fifths of the part-time farm and approximately one-half of the non-farming industrial families made use of this service (table 78, page 66).

Library services were available to very few households in Carroll County, and less than one-fourth of either the part-time farm or non-farming industrial households which had library facilities made use of them.

Social Participation

Participation in organized social activities was usually confined to the local community, although occasional families in villages near Greenville were able to attend meetings in the city. In Greenville County, the villages were well organized. The church was the center of social life, and members of both part-time farm and nonfarming industrial households had an opportunity to participate in church, Sunday School, adult church organizations, Parent-Teacher Associations, labor unions, and young people's organizations (appendix table 48). In some of the mill villages, community houses formed a center for many social activities, such as athletic contests, club meetings, plays, Boy Scouts, Girl Scouts, and other groups. A baseball league, including teams from a number of mills, played about four games a week during the season.

In Greenville County, there was an equal amount of participation in church and adult church organizations by members of part-time farm and nonfarming industrial families, but participation in Sunday School, and particularly in young people's organizations, was much greater among part-time farm families. Labor unions were available to only about two-fifths of the families in both groups, and participation was slight.

Greenville County textile workers in the part-time farm group averaged 91 attendances at meetings per person, as against 78 for the nonfarming industrial households in 1934 (table 80, page 68). Extremely small households participated less in community social organizations than did larger households because children, especially children of school age, tended to increase the interest of the family in community activities. This was responsible, to some extent, for the favorable showing of part-time farm families in Greenville County.

Carroll County villages showed less variation in the number of available social organizations, and participation in them by both part-time farm and nonfarm families was considerably less than by those in Greenville County. In church, Sunday School, and church organizations, however, there was more participation by members of part-time farm households than by those of nonfarming industrial households. The average number of attendances per person was 56 and 29, respectively, for part-time farm and nonfarming industrial households (table 80, page 68). This difference was related to the scarcity of social organizations in some of the mill villages where industrial workers lived.

The part-time farm groups in both Greenville County and Carroll County furnished a larger proportion of the leadership of local organizations than did the industrial households (appendix table 49). An average of nearly one out of every two part-time farm households in Greenville County furnished an officer for a local organization, as compared to one out of six for the nonfarming group. In part-time farm households, 21 husbands, 31 wives, 34 children, and 5 other members were officers of 1 or more organizations, whereas only 10 husbands, 12 wives, and 6 children in the nonfarming industrial households held office. In Carroll County, only four persons from the part-time farm and one from the nonfarming industrial group held office.

ECONOMIC STATUS OF PART-TIME AND FULL-TIME FARMERS

The survey indicated that the part-time farmer suffered no handicap in employment or earnings, and in some phases of living conditions and social life, he had a slight advantage over the nonfarming industrial worker. Since the part-time farmers were farmers as well as industrial workers, it is pertinent briefly to compare them with full-time farmers.

The 1930 Census showed that the average value of products sold or traded by farmers in Greenville County, plus receipts from boarders and lodgers, was $777 in 1929. Deductions for the three major expenses—feed, fertilizer, and labor—which averaged $171, left $606 as the farm income. This amount may be compared with the off-the-farm cash income, $1,116, for part-time farm households in Greenville County in 1934 (table 87).

In Carroll County, the gross receipts on full-time farms were $758. Chief expenses totaled $193, leaving a net cash income of $565, which may be compared with the $1,060 off-the-farm income of part-time farmers in 1934.

The use of 1929 data for farm incomes for comparison with 1934 part-time farm incomes requires a word of explanation. Farm incomes were somewhat higher in these counties in 1929 than they were in 1934. The value of crops harvested in 1929 reported by the census was $695 per farm in Greenville County as compared with $393 in 1934,[30] and $604 in Carroll County for 1929 as compared with $510 for 1934. In the absence of actual net income data for full-time farmers in 1934, these figures may be used as rough indices of net incomes for the 2 years, since farm receipts vary much more from

---

[30] Value of crops harvested was calculated by using quantities reported by the census for the counties and prices reported for the States.

year to year than do farm expenses in this subregion. The value of farm real estate, a further index of agricultural conditions, was substantially lower in both counties in 1934 than in 1929. These facts indicate that if 1934 net income data for full-time farmers were available, the comparison would be even less favorable to this group than that indicated above.

RELIEF

Very little relief was received in 1934 by either part-time farmers or nonfarming industrial workers included in the study. Employment in the textile mills, the major industry of the subregion, was as high or higher in 1934 than in 1929. Most of the textile workers on the relief rolls in Greenville County were, according to a local relief official, either too old to work in the mills or were members of the floater class. Since only those having at least 50 days of industrial employment during 1934 were included in the survey, many on relief undoubtedly were excluded.

There were only three part-time farm cases enumerated in the sample, all in Carroll County, in which the amount of relief received during 1934 exceeded $10. One industrial household received $19 from private relief sources, due to 5 months' unemployment of the head, during which time his leg was amputated. A part-time farmer, having had only 94 days of industrial employment during the year, received $75 of public relief to care for doctors' bills and to replace mattresses following a contagious disease in the household. The third case was an 11-person part-time farm household which was handicapped by dependents and unemployment. This household received $60 during 1934.

Only 2.1 and 1.4 percent, respectively, of the part-time farm and nonfarming industrial households in the sample in Greenville County received any relief in 1934, as against 13.6 and 9.2 percent in Carroll County. In Greenville County, the relief reported was from public sources. More than one-half of the Carroll County relief cases, however, received this help from the Red Cross or other private agencies. In the subregion as a whole, the average time part-time farm families receiving relief had had assistance was almost 1½ years, and that for nonfarm families was slightly less (appendix table 36).

Chapter II

THE COAL AND IRON SUBREGION
OF ALABAMA

GENERAL FEATURES OF THE SUBREGION

THE COAL and Iron Subregion of Alabama is located at the southern end of the Appalachian Range. The presence of deposits of coking coal, iron ore, and limestone has led to the development of an industrial area based on iron and steel manufacturing and coal mining (figure 8).

Included in this industrial area are 10 counties, with the city of Birmingham at the geographical center. Jefferson County, in which Birmingham is located, is the most populous and the most highly industrialized of the group. Most of the iron mining, a substantial part of the coal mining, and the bulk of the iron and steel manufacturing of the area are concentrated in this county. Walker County is an important coal producer, and coal is also mined in Tuscaloosa, Bibb, Shelby, St. Clair, and Blount Counties.

Outside of Jefferson County, there are two minor industrial centers where most of the remaining iron and steel manufacturing of the subregion is located. These are the adjacent towns of Gadsden and Alabama City (combined population about 32,600) in Etowah County, and Anniston (population 22,300) in Calhoun County. Cotton goods manufacturing is the most important industry of Talladega County, and is also found in the other counties of the subregion, except Bibb and Blount. The relative importance of the various industries in this subregion and in Jefferson County is indicated by the number of persons occupied in each industry (table 89).

The pre-eminence of Jefferson County and of Birmingham dates from 1897 when real development in the manufacture of steel started, although a small beginning in steel manufacture was made in 1888. Rapid expansion of the local steel business took place after the United

113

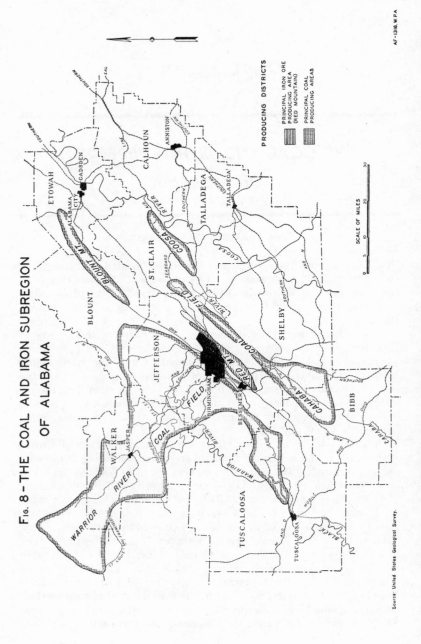

Fɪɢ. 8–THE COAL AND IRON SUBREGION OF ALABAMA

PRODUCING DISTRICTS

PRINCIPAL IRON ORE PRODUCING AREA (RED MOUNTAIN)

PRINCIPAL COAL PRODUCING AREAS

SCALE OF MILES

Source: United States Geological Survey.

AF-1316, W.P.A.

Table 89.—Distribution of Persons, 10 Years Old and Over, Gainfully Occupied in the Coal and Iron Subregion and in Jefferson County, Alabama, 1930

Industry	Coal and Iron Subregion		Jefferson County, Alabama	
	Number	Percent	Number	Percent
Total population	820,228		431,493	
Total gainfully employed	312,252	100.0	173,001	100.0
Agriculture	60,215	19.3	6,409	3.7
Service industries	131,135	42.0	93,456	54.0
Manufacturing and allied industries	120,902	38.7	73,136	42.3
Total manufacturing and allied industries	120,902	100.0	73,136	100.0
Forestry and fishing	705	0.6	111	0.2
Coal mines	26,438	21.8	13,543	18.5
Other extraction of minerals	6,762	5.6	5,505	7.5
Building	11,560	9.6	8,351	11.4
Chemical and allied	3,206	2.6	2,572	3.5
Clay, glass, and stone	3,167	2.6	2,187	3.0
Clothing	1,108	0.9	846	1.2
Food and allied	3,098	2.6	2,483	3.4
Automobile factories and repair shops	2,280	1.9	1,636	2.2
Blast furnaces and steel rolling mills	16,070	13.3	12,950	17.7
Other iron and steel	18,311	15.2	13,189	18.1
Saw and planing mills	4,163	3.4	505	0.7
Other wood and furniture	1,455	1.2	692	0.9
Paper, printing, and allied	2,273	1.9	1,493	2.0
Cotton mills	8,796	7.3	566	0.8
Knitting mills	572	0.5	13	*
Other textile	1,360	1.1	121	0.2
Independent hand trades	1,837	1.5	1,258	1.7
Other manufacturing	7,740	6.4	5,115	7.0

*Less than 0.05 percent.

Source: *Fifteenth Census of the United States: 1930*, Population Vol. III.

States Steel Corporation bought the Tennessee Coal, Iron and Railroad Company in 1907. By 1914, the Steel Corporation had spent over 20 million dollars for improvements and additions to the Tennessee Company's properties.[1]

Under the impetus of this development, population in the subregion increased 58 percent between 1910 and 1930. Jefferson County secured a major portion (68 percent) of this increase. From a population of about 12,000 in 1870, the county had increased to 431,500 in 1930. Birmingham, a cotton field in 1870, had grown to a city of a quarter of a million in 1930, receiving 60 percent of the population increase. Eleven percent of the increase went into other urban areas of the county.

A large migration into this subregion from other areas has resulted in two factors of importance for consideration in this study. First, the migration has resulted in a concentration of population in the biologically and economically active age groups, which means fewer dependents per person capable of working. In 1930, 50 percent of the population of the subregion were in the 20- to 44-year age group, as compared with 35 percent for Alabama as a whole in this group, and

[1] Cotter, Arundel, *The Authentic History of the United States Steel Corporation*, New York: Moody Magazine and Book Company, 1916, p. 204.

38 percent for the United States.[2] Second, many of the migrants have come from surrounding rural areas, bringing with them a background of farm experience.

In 1930, the Coal and Iron Subregion had a larger proportion of whites (69 percent) than had Jefferson County (61 percent), with its concentration of industries employing unskilled labor. The ratio of Negro to white population in this county has remained almost constant during the entire period of industrial development.

Jefferson County suffered severely in the depression, as did other steel centers. From 1929 to 1933, the average number of wage earners in the manufacturing industries of the county declined 42 percent, total wages declined 64 percent, and value of products 64 percent.[3] In the same period, the coal production of the county decreased 50 percent in amount and 62 percent in total dollar value.[4] Since the business of the local service industries is largely dependent on manufacturing and mining pay rolls, these figures give an indication of the loss of income suffered by all workers in this area during the depression.

Cotton farming is the predominant type of agriculture in northern and central Alabama. However, the metropolitan development in the vicinity of Birmingham has had a modifying influence upon the agriculture of the immediately surrounding area. The production of dairy and truck crops for the local market has been stimulated. As a result Jefferson, Shelby, Walker, and Winston Counties may be considered a separate type of farming area.

Farm production in this area is limited by the rough topography and by the unproductiveness of some of the soils. In 1934, only 40 percent of the total land area was in farms, and of the land in farms, 37 percent was cropland.[5] In Jefferson County, only 28 percent of the total land area was in farms, and of the land in farms, only 42 percent was cropland.[6]

The 1930 Census of Agriculture reported a considerably larger number of part-time farms in Jefferson and Walker Counties than in any other county in the State.[7] In Jefferson County, there were 496 part-

---

[2] *Fifteenth Census of the United States: 1930*, Population Vol. III, Part I, p. 37.

[3] *United States Census of Manufactures: 1933; Fifteenth Census of the United States: 1930*, Manufactures Vol. III.

[4] *Coal, 1929 and 1933*, United States Bureau of Mines.

[5] *United States Census of Agriculture: 1935.*

[6] *Idem.*

[7] *Fifteenth Census of the United States: 1930*, Agriculture Vol. III, Part 2, county table 1. Those farms were classified as part-time whose operator spent 150 days or more at work in 1929 for pay at jobs not connected with his farm, or reported an occupation other than farmer, provided the value of the products of the farm did not exceed $750. This presupposes the census definition of a farm as comprising at least 3 acres unless it produced $250 worth of farm products or more.

time farms, or 15 percent of all farms, and in Walker County 427 part-time farms, or 12 percent of all farms.

THE INDUSTRIES OF THE SUBREGION

Iron and Steel Manufacturing

The low mountainous ridges and narrow valleys around Birmingham contain the principal raw materials for iron and steel manufacturing: iron ore, coking coal, and limestone and dolomite for fluxing. They exist in quantities estimated to last over 300 years at the 1925 peak production rates [8] and are located so close to the furnaces that the cost of transportation is lower for the Birmingham district than for any other district in the country.

Several important disadvantages partially counterbalance the advantage of low transportation costs. The iron ore is low grade, averaging about 36 to 37 percent metallic iron, compared with an average of over 50 percent for the United States.[9] Most of it has to be mined by underground drilling and blasting instead of by the open pit methods used on the Lake Superior ranges. The principal disadvantage of the Birmingham district is its distance from the great steel consuming areas since freight rates are an important item in price competition. Hence, the market for Birmingham's iron and steel products is primarily in the South, with some export via the Black Warrior River and the Gulf to Central and South America and the West Indies. About 86 percent of the pig iron of this district is consumed in local plants making steel, cast-iron pipe, and machinery.[10] A large part of the steel also is used in local plants.

Another important industry of this district is the manufacture of cast-iron pipe, of which Alabama produces more than 40 percent of the country's supply.[11] A little over one-half of the employees of the cast-iron pipe industry in Alabama are in Jefferson County.

Before 1929 the principal products of the Alabama steel industry were railroad and structural steel. Since 1929 there has been a slump in requirements of the railroads and the construction industry, which has been offset to some extent, however, by the increased activity of the sheet mills.

The dominant position in the steel industry is held by the Tennessee Coal, Iron and Railroad Company (commonly referred to as the T. C. I. Company). The total rated productive capacity of this company's units is about 50 percent of the pig iron and 80 percent of the steel

---

[8] Burchard, E. F., "Alabama Ores Equal Lake Supply," *The Iron Age*, March 24, 1927.

[9] *Minerals Yearbook: 1934*, United States Bureau of Mines.

[10] White, Langdon, "The Iron and Steel Industry of the Birmingham, Alabama, District," *Economic Geography*, Vol. XV, p. 359.

[11] *Biennial Census of Manufactures: 1933*.

making capacity of the State.[12]   It owns and operates mines, quarries, furnaces, and mills for all stages in steel manufacturing from the extraction of the raw materials to the finished products, a railroad for the transport of its materials, and a fleet of barges on the Black Warrior River.   The Gulf States Steel Company's Alabama City Works at Gadsden is the only other large producer of steel.   Three other companies, the Sloss-Sheffield Steel and Iron Company, the Republic Steel Corporation, and the Woodward Iron Company, also owning mines and quarries, produce pig iron.

Trend of Production and Employment

The peak of production for iron ore was reached in 1925, and for pig iron, steel, and cast-iron pipe in 1926.   The low point for the production of iron ore was reached in 1932, and for cast-iron pipe a year later. The severity of the depression in these industries is indicated by the ratios of minimum annual production to maximum, which were as low as 19.6 percent for iron ore, 22.6 percent for pig iron, 22.9 percent for cast-iron pipe, and 28.6 percent for rolled steel products.[13]   There has been some recovery since these low points, pig iron production in 1934 amounting to 40 percent of maximum, and rolled steel production to 49 percent of maximum.   However, operations during the last half of the year were decidedly less than during the first half.

Generally speaking, the steel industry in Alabama has followed the trend of the industry as a whole.   It did not share in the high peak of the country's output in 1929, however, because it did not supply the automobile business, which was largely responsible for that demand. The prosperous years for the cast-iron pipe industry coincided with the period of great building activity and of suburban housing development, which passed its peak about 1927.

Employment in iron and steel manufacturing has decreased because of technological improvements as well as loss of demand for products. The output of iron ore per man increased 79 percent from 1923 to 1931.   Employment in the mines dropped from an average of 7,710 men working 294 days in 1923 to approximately 2,800 men working only 106 days in 1932.[14]

Replacement of old blast furnaces by more efficient ones resulted in a decrease of 55 percent in the number employed in this industry in Alabama between 1923 and 1929 (table 90).[15]   In 1933, only 964

---

[12] *Directory of the Iron and Steel Works of the United States and Canada*, 22d Edition, American Iron and Steel Institute, 1935, pp. 370, 372, and 373.

[13] *Annual Statistical Reports of the American Iron and Steel Institute*.

[14] *Minerals Yearbook: 1934*, United States Bureau of Mines, p. 339.

[15] For a discussion of technological improvements in blast furnaces and their effects on productivity, see *Productivity of Labor in Merchant Blast Furnaces*, Bulletin 474, United States Bureau of Labor Statistics.

men were employed in this industry.   Coke and cast-iron pipe plants have drastically reduced workers also, the former employing in 1933 less than one-half and the latter barely one-third of the number employed during the peak years of the middle twenties.

Table 90.—Average Number of Wage Earners Employed in Iron and Steel and Allied Industries in Alabama, 1923–1933

Year	Total excluding steel	Total including steel	Iron mining	Coke plants	Blast furnaces	Steel works and rolling mills	Cast-iron pipe
1923	25,236	32,163	7,710	2,071	5,343	6,927	10,112
1925	25,569	33,238	7,155	1,932	4,861	7,669	11,621
1927	22,928	—	6,172	1,759	4,157	(¹)	10,840
1929	18,837	28,090	5,498	1,606	2,398	9,253	9,335
1931	13,419	—	3,672	1,147	1,468	(¹)	7,132
1933	8,516	—	2,940	804	964	(¹)	3,808

¹ Data not given.

Source: *Minerals Yearbook: 1933 and 1934,* United States Bureau of Mines, and *United States Census of Manufactures.*

❧ *Hours and Wages*

In most of the Alabama ore mines, the 10-hour day was standard in the years prior to 1933.   In 1931, the average pay of all employees in iron and steel and allied industries was 38½ cents per hour, and actual weekly earnings averaged $12.08.[16]   In 1933, the 8-hour day was adopted by most of the important mines and some pay raises were made.   The 123 white ore mine employees included in the present study received an average of 59 cents per hour in 1934 and the 83 Negroes an average of 48 cents per hour.

The 8-hour day was adopted by most blast furnaces and steel mills in 1923, though continuous night and day operation for the 7-day week remained until 1931.[17]   The N. R. A. code for the iron and steel industry, approved August 19, 1933, limited hours to 8 per day, and to an average of 40 per week for any 6-month period, with a maximum of 48 in any 1 week.   The "spread work" system in effect during the depression, however, has reduced hours of labor for the great majority of workers to considerably below nominal full-time hours.   The code also set a minimum wage rate of 27 cents per hour for the Birmingham district with provision for differentials above the minimum rate for those already earning a higher wage rate.   Average earnings per hour for the industry as a whole increased 37 percent from June 1933 to April 1934.[18]

[16] *Wages and Hours of Labor in Metalliferous Mines, 1924 and 1931,* Bulletin 573, United States Bureau of Labor Statistics.

[17] *Wages and Hours of Labor in the Iron and Steel Industry, 1931,* Bulletin 567, United States Bureau of Labor Statistics.

[18] *N. R. A. Code for the Iron and Steel Industry* (Amendment No. 1), Letter of Transmittal, p. 6.

Bituminous Coal Mining

The principal coal producing areas of Alabama are the Black Warrior River, Cahaba, Coosa, and Blount Mountain fields (figure 8). Part of the Black Warrior River area, which is the largest field, lies in Jefferson County.

The coal mined in Alabama is used principally for production of by-product coke and for railroad fuel. In 1929, coke production accounted for 38.5 percent of Alabama's coal output, railroad fuel 28.5 percent, electric utilities 1.7 percent, and all other uses 31.3 percent.[19] A large number of the mines are owned by steel and iron makers who consume their own product in making coke for the blast furnaces. Production by "captive" mines (i. e., those owned by and producing for steel and iron companies) was about 48 percent of the total output of the district in 1924.

The principal market for Alabama coal is within the State itself, in southwestern and western Georgia, and in Florida. The markets in Mississippi and Louisiana have dwindled to small proportions because of the introduction of natural gas. Natural gas is now used extensively in Birmingham itself. The burning of fuel oil by ships has cut sharply the demand for bunker coal at Mobile and New Orleans.

The production of coal in Alabama declined steadily from a peak of 21 million tons in 1926 to a low of less than 8 million in 1932.[20] The reduction in output has been relatively somewhat greater in Alabama than in the country generally.

Employment and Mechanization

The peak in numbers employed in Alabama coal mines was reached in 1923, when approximately 30,000 men were engaged. By 1929 the number had decreased to 25,200,[21] and by 1933 to 18,200.[22] Beginning in 1929, there was also a drastic curtailment in number of days worked, which reached a low of 107 days (average) in 1932.

The proportion of the coal mined in Alabama by machine cutting, the oldest mechanized process, has been steadily increasing since 1922. Loading of coal into the mine cars by mechanical devices is a newer development[23] and has greater effect in reducing employment because loading has always been one of the most labor-consuming operations

---

[19] Trapnell, W. C. and Ilsley, Ralph, *The Bituminous Coal Industry With Survey of Competing Fuels*, Division of Research, Statistics, and Finance, Federal Emergency Relief Administration, May 1935, p. A–40.

[20] *Mineral Resources of the United States, 1930*, United States Bureau of Mines, Part II; and *Minerals Yearbook: 1933*, United States Bureau of Mines.

[21] *Mineral Resources of the United States, 1930, op. cit.*, p. 651.

[22] *Minerals Yearbook: 1934, op. cit.*

[23] See "Employment in Relation to Mechanization in the Bituminous Coal Industry." *Monthly Labor Review*, February 1933.

in the mines.   The percentage of Alabama coal mechanically loaded reached a maximum of approximately 19 percent in 1929.

The effect of mechanization on employment is difficult to measure statistically because of the peculiarities of timekeeping in the coal-mining industry, the "spread work" system, and changes in the length of the working day.   In general, however, the output per man-day increased between 1929 and 1931, and then decreased.   Part of the decrease in output per man-day in 1933 and 1934 was due to the shorter working day introduced by the N. R. A. code.

Hours and Wages

There was a steady decline of wage rates in the coal-mining industry from 1922 to 1931, and a precipitous drop from 1931 to 1933.[24]   Average hourly earnings of miners and loaders, based on time "at face," [25] fell 42 percent, from 45 cents in 1929 to 26 cents in 1933; and bimonthly earnings fell 63 percent, from $33.58 to $12.45 between 1929 and 1933.   The N. R. A. code for the bituminous coal district including Alabama set an 8-hour day, which later was amended to a 7-hour day and a 5-day week.   Basic minimum rates for outside unskilled labor, set first at 30 cents, were later amended to 40 cents an hour, and those for inside skilled labor were set at 42½ and later at 54 cents an hour. [26]

A large proportion of the coal miners in Alabama are members of the United Mine Workers, and wage rates in most of the mines are set by agreement between that organization and the mine operators.   After the N. R. A. was declared unconstitutional by the Supreme Court on May 28, 1935, the wage rates in effect under N. R. A. were continued by such an agreement until September 1935, when a new agreement was negotiated.   This new contract raised wage rates slightly while retaining the 7-hour day and 5-day week.   It is effective until April 1, 1937.

Seasonal Variation in Employment

There is some regular seasonal swing in production of the Alabama coal mines, with October, December, and January usually the busiest months, and April, May, June, and July the slackest.   The mines usually work with a full labor force and shut down entirely (except for maintenance crews) when orders are filled.

Outlook for Employment

Birmingham's iron, steel, and coal mining industries and the railroads are to a certain extent interdependent.   The demand for coal depends principally on the iron and steel and railroad fuel require-

[24] *Wages and Hours of Labor in Bituminous Coal Mining, 1933,* Bulletin 601, United States Bureau of Labor Statistics.

[25] Time "at face" means time at the working place in the mine.

[26] *N. R. A. Code for the Bituminous Coal Industry.*

ments. At the same time, hauling coal is an important source of railroad revenue, and the railroads are large consumers of steel.

The principal factors affecting the future activity of the iron and steel industries in Alabama may be summarized as follows:

The demand for pig iron is affected directly by requirements for steel, cast-iron pipe, machinery, etc. Increased use of scrap in steel making reduces this demand.

The market for steel products depends largely on railroad buying, construction activity, and industrial expansion in the South. A large potential demand for steel has accumulated during the depression, due to the deferring of maintenance expenditures by railroads and industrial plants.

The market for cast-iron pipe depends on resumption of building activity and expansion of gas and water utility systems, which are not likely to reach the proportions of the boom years of the 1920's in the near future. The market for Alabama cast-iron pipe is not limited to the South.

The favorable situation of the iron and steel plants of this district with respect to raw material makes for stability of the industry.

It is evident that a revival of general business activity to predepression levels would increase total employment in the iron and steel and allied industries of Alabama. Because of technological advances, however, return to anything like the amount of employment during the peak period of 1925 to 1926 would be possible only with an output considerably beyond former high levels. In recent years there have been large numbers of underemployed men on the pay rolls, and these will probably be restored to full-time work before many new men are hired. The number employed will depend, of course, on the number of hours per week that will be considered to be full time when industrial production approaches normal. This is an uncertain quantity, but the number is quite likely to exceed the maximum set by the N. R. A. code.

Because of its dominant position in the steel business of the Birmingham district, the policies of the United States Steel Corporation are an important factor in the employment situation here.

The consumption of coal by manufacturing plants, electric utilities, and domestic users will probably be adversely affected by increased use of water power and natural gas and other fuels. Therefore, with the return of general business to normal activity, the consumption of Alabama coal will most likely be somewhat below its normal level of the past. Future coal mine employment will depend on two opposing factors: recovery of market demand and mechanization. The use of mechanical loaders in Alabama mines has been relatively small, but with recovery in demand for coal, there is likely to be an increase in the use of these devices.

Retention of the 7-hour day in effect since April 1934 will increase the number of miners required for a given output, as compared with the number employed under the former working day which averaged nearly 9 hours.

FARMING ACTIVITIES OF PART-TIME FARMERS
Location of Part-Time Farms

The pattern of part-time farming in the Birmingham area has been largely set by the interaction of two factors peculiar to the area: the limitation of land, and the fact that much of the land available for farming is owned by large employers of industrial labor who have for a long time [27] encouraged gardening by their employees.

The iron and steel industry is centered in two long, narrow valleys, Jones and Opossum, enclosed by rough mountainous ridges. These valleys, varying from 1 to 2 miles in width and separated only by a low ridge, are largely taken up by the metropolitan development of the Birmingham district. Hence, the amount of land available for farming is quite limited in relation to the number of industrial workers who might be interested in part-time farming.

Most of the land available is not very productive. The soil, which is largely Clarksville stony loam,[28] erodes badly. Because of its structure and the topography, it does not hold water well, suffering periodically from drought. And yet, because of its availability, this soil is used extensively for gardening by the industrial workers.

Coal and iron workers live, for the most part, in company houses in villages and mining camps, or in cities and towns near their places of employment. House lots are usually about 50 x 100 feet in size and offer so little opportunity for gardening that the companies often make available plots of land on unoccupied company property. The practice of the T. C. I. Company is a case in point. It allots 1 acre or less to a family, offers to plow the plots for 50 cents each, and employs a man to help improve garden practices. At times when mules used at the mines are not needed, they are made available for use in cultivating the gardens; garden seeds are furnished; ammonium sulphate (a coke oven by-product used for fertilizer) is made available; and prizes are offered for the best gardens.

These advantages are largely counterbalanced by the fact that the plots are often located at some distance from the homes, thus discouraging the keeping of livestock and adding to the effort necessary in cultivation.

In spite of these handicaps, part-time farming was popular in this district before the depression, 52 percent of the white families and 28 percent of the Negro families having farmed for at least 6 years (appendix table 4). Part-time farming increased markedly during the depression, following the reduction in working hours and wages

---

[27] As early as 1908, the Tennessee Coal, Iron and Railroad Company, in order to encourage gardening by miners, built wire fences around their yards and hired an agricultural expert. See Mims, Edwin, *The Advancing South*, New York: Doubleday, Page and Co., 1926, p. 102.

[28] Smith, H. C. and Pace, E. S., *Soil Survey of Jefferson County, Alabama*, U. S. Department of Agriculture, 1910.

FIG. 9—LOCATION OF PART-TIME FARMS INCLUDED IN FIELD SURVEY
CHARLESTON COUNTY, SOUTH CAROLINA

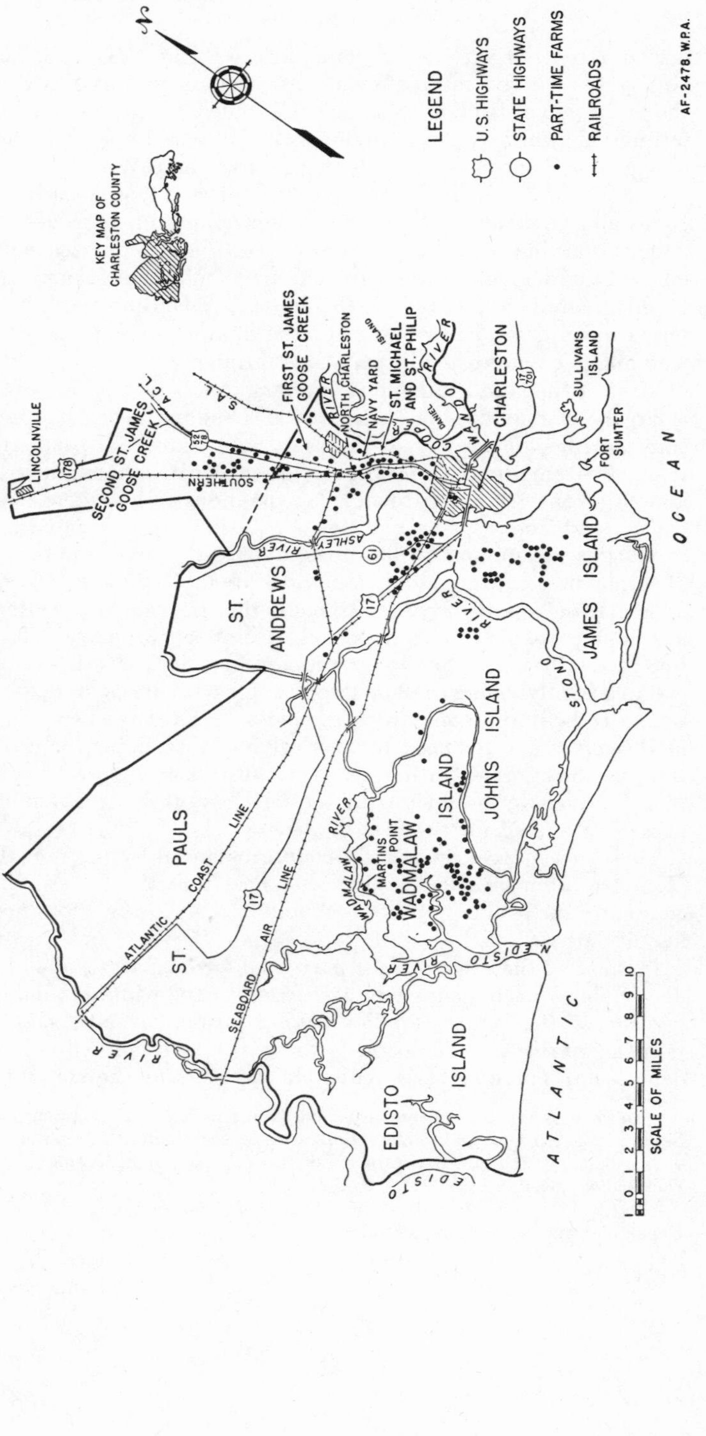

(appendix table 5). Aid given by the T. C. I. Company to its employees, for example, was made contingent upon cultivation of a garden, and after the introduction of Federal relief, the company continued to encourage gardening.

Many families not coming under company programs have purchased or rented land for farming purposes. So common had small-scale part-time farming become in this area that the 328 cases (204 whites and 124 Negroes) covered by the survey (figure 9) constituted only a small proportion of the number actually engaged in part-time farming at the time. It is also important to note that the greater part of the industrial workers in the group classed as nonfarmers actually did some gardening, although they did not produce $50 worth of food and hence were classified as part-time farmers.

Farm Production

The relative scarcity of land available for farming is indicated by the fact that 60 percent of the white farmers surveyed and 80 percent of the Negroes had only 1½ acres or less of cropland (appendix table 6). Only 15 (7 percent) white part-time farmers and only 1 Negro had 10 acres or more. Most of the Negroes had only ¼ or ½ acres in gardens (appendix table 11 and figure 10).

Barely 18 percent of the whites and 4 percent of the Negroes reported all of the four chief types of production (vegetable, poultry products, dairy products, and pork). One-third of the whites and nearly two-thirds of the Negroes had only vegetables or vegetables and poultry (appendix table 12).

Gardens

All of the Negroes and all except seven of the white part-time farmers had gardens. At Birmingham, the average frost-free growing season is almost 8 months.[29] This means that there are about 6 months in which the less hardy vegetables can be used fresh from the garden. In addition, a number of hardy vegetables, both root and leafy, may be available during the colder months. Ninety-one percent of the whites and seventy-three percent of the Negroes had three or more fresh vegetables for at least 5 months. Nearly two-thirds of the white families had three or more fresh vegetables for at least 7 months (appendix table 13). Only 3 percent of the whites had three or more fresh vegetables for 10 months or longer, but more than one-third had at least one fresh vegetable for that period (appendix table 14). No Negro family had three or more fresh vegetables for as long as 10 months but 16 percent had at least one vegetable for that period.

During the 6 summer months, the products of the garden reduced the purchase of groceries from the amount normally bought to a

---

[29] *Yearbook of Agriculture: 1934*, U. S. Department of Agriculture, p. 731.

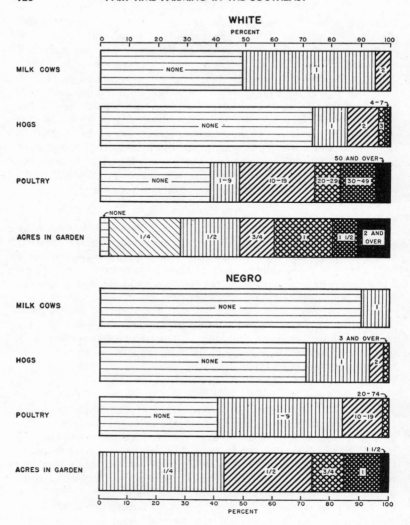

Fɪɢ.10− SIZE OF PRINCIPAL ENTERPRISES ON PART-TIME
FARMS, BY COLOR OF OPERATOR,
JEFFERSON COUNTY, ALA., 1934

AF-2470, W.P.A.

considerable extent. Seventy-six percent of the white part-time farmers with gardens and fifty-seven percent of the Negroes estimated that their grocery bills were reduced, the reduction averaging $10 per month for the white families and $5.50 per month for the Negroes. The fact that 24 percent of the whites and 43 percent of the Negroes surveyed reported no reductions was perhaps not surprising, considering the small size of gardens in this area. Rather, it is surprising that 11 percent of the whites reported reductions estimated at over $20, and over 12 percent of the Negroes reported reductions estimated at more than $10.

These reductions do not measure the entire contribution of the garden since the diet is improved in quality and variety during the garden season. Furthermore, canning and storage of garden products tend to reduce the grocery bill during the winter months.

Canning of fruits and vegetables was done by 87 percent of the white families and 55 percent of the Negro families, the average quantity canned being 110 and 47 quarts, respectively. Of the 204 white families, 23 canned 200 quarts or more (appendix table 16). Vegetables were stored by 86 percent of the whites and by all of the Negroes (table 29, page 20). Sweet potatoes were the most common vegetable stored, 65 percent of the white families storing an average of 22 bushels, and 83 percent of the Negro families storing an average of 15 bushels. More than one-half of the whites, but only about one-eighth of the Negroes stored Irish potatoes, the average amount being 7 and 3 bushels, respectively (appendix table 17). A popular item in this area was peanuts, 29 percent of the whites storing an average of 10 bushels, and 60 percent of the Negroes storing an average of 3 bushels. Onions, peppers, beans, and peas were stored by relatively smaller numbers, while okra, cabbage, figs, peaches, walnuts, grapes, and apples were stored occasionally.

Corn

Over one-third of the white part-time farmers grew corn, the average production being 68 bushels. In view of the small areas cultivated by the Negroes, it was surprising that as many as three-fifths grew corn, producing an average of 21 bushels (appendix table 24). Both white and Negro households had from 5 to 15 bushels of the corn ground into meal, and the remainder was fed to livestock.

Dairy Products

Considering the smallness of the farms and the great reduction in incomes during the depression in this area, it is noteworthy that one-half of the white part-time farmers had cows (appendix table 11). Milk production during 1934 averaged over 3,000 quarts per cow (appendix table 20). Butter was made by all but one of the families whose cow produced milk, butter consumption averaging 234 pounds a year (appendix table 21). Of the 103 white families with cows, 47 sold dairy products. The average receipts from such sales were $75.

In the matter of dairy products, the production by Negroes was far behind that of the whites, instead of being roughly half that of the white part-time farmers, as in the case of other farm activities. Only 13 Negro families (10 percent) had cows, and milk production averaged 2,700 quarts in 1934, a little less than the average for the whites. Butter production averaged only 176 pounds per year for those producing butter.

In general, of course, the products were consumed by the family. Two or three quarts of milk were used fresh, the remainder being used for making butter. The buttermilk was used as food and the surplus was fed to pigs and chickens.

Most of the feed for cows was purchased, since only a few of the whites and none of the Negroes had pastures, and only 14 white families and 2 Negro families grew any roughage (appendix table 23.) Frequently cows were staked out along the roadsides or on vacant lots. Purchased feed usually cost from $50 to $75.

Poultry Products

Almost two-thirds of the white part-time farmers and almost as many of the Negro farmers had poultry (appendix table 11). The flocks of white farmers usually contained from 10 to 20 birds, while those of the Negroes contained fewer than 10 birds. The white part-time farmers with chickens reported an average of 113 dozen eggs consumed a year or over 2 dozen a week, while Negroes reported only 8 or 9 eggs a week (appendix table 18). An average of 70 pounds of dressed chicken a year, or less than 1½ pounds a week, was consumed by white part-time farmers, while Negro families consumed about half that amount (appendix table 19).

Pork

One or more pigs were kept on 27 percent of the white part-time farms and on 29 percent of the Negro farms (appendix table 11). Most of the families had only one or two pigs, but a few had more. The quantity of home-produced dressed pork consumed or stored was considerably higher for the whites (376 pounds) than for the Negroes (217 pounds) (appendix table 22).

Fuel

In view of the metropolitan nature of the area, it is not surprising that few families were able to cut fuel on their land. Only nine white and eight Negro part-time farmers had any woodland, and of these only four white farmers and five Negroes cut wood for fuel. Arrangements are frequently made whereby employees of the coal mining companies may secure coal for fuel at wholesale prices.

Cash Receipts and Cash Expenses

Less than one-half of the white and only one-tenth of the Negro part-time farmers sold any farm products, sales from all products averaging $33 for the whites and $4 for the Negroes (appendix table 25). Among the whites, dairy products were most frequently sold, and they accounted for 54 percent of the total sales.

Cash expenses of both groups were for plowing, seeds, fertilizer, and livestock feed. For the whites, expenses exclusive of rent and taxes averaged $73, for Negroes only $15 (appendix table 25). The 24 white part-time farmers who sold as much as $100 worth of products more than covered their cash outlay. For the remainder, expenses were somewhat in excess of receipts, this excess representing the net cost in cash of the products used by the family.

Value and Tenure of Part-Time Farms

Only 34 percent of the white and 19 percent of the Negro part-time farmers owned their homes (appendix table 43), and some of these had to rent land for farming purposes. However, the average investment for the farming enterprise was rather small. Farming lands were frequently owned by the employers and the rent paid, if any, was nominal.

Very few families had work animals or any equipment other than a few simple hand tools. The average cost for those having machinery was only $30 for whites and only half that amount for Negroes (appendix table 10). For the relatively few farmers with the combination of a cow, a pig, and a flock of chickens, the investment did not amount to over $100.

Labor Requirements of Part-Time Farms and Their Relation to Working Hours in Industry

During 1934, underemployment in this area was so widespread that the work necessary for cultivation of gardens and small farms took up only part of the workmen's spare time. Slightly more than 4 hours a day were spent on farm work by white part-time farm families during the growing season. The heads of the households put in more than half of the total time required for the farm work (table 48, page 32). About one-fourth of the white households contained young men between the ages of 16 and 24, inclusive, who helped with the farm work, and on 57 percent of the farms the wife did part of the work (appendix table 27). It is quite possible that the essential farm work could have been done in somewhat less time than that actually spent, since in many instances the farm work filled in spare time.

Negro part-time farm families worked an average of over 6 hours a day from April through August, although their enterprises were only about half as large or productive as were those of the white part-time farmers. Slightly less than half of this worktime represented labor of the heads of the households, the balance that of other members. One-half of these households contained one or more persons from 16 to 24 years of age, who worked about 1½ hours a day for about 7 months of the year.

EMPLOYMENT AND EARNINGS IN INDUSTRY

The outstanding fact concerning employment and earnings in this area is the drastic reduction in hours and wages that has occurred since 1929. The principal industries of the region, depending largely upon the market for iron and steel, were severely hit by the depression, which led to decreases in the number employed as well as in the earnings of those still retaining some employment. On the average, total family income from nonfarm sources for whites, including both farm and nonfarm households,[30] was 46 percent lower in 1934 than in 1929 (table 60, page 46).

Negro workers in this area, even more than the whites, have borne the full brunt of the depression, the average total family income from industrial employment being 58 percent lower in 1934 than in 1929. A large proportion of the Negroes were unskilled workers and were the first to be laid off when a mill or factory was shut down. Not only were heads of families underemployed, but members other than the heads had great difficulty in finding work.

Industry and Occupation

Part-time farmers included in the field survey were selected without regard to the industry in which they worked. However, most of them, both whites and Negroes, were engaged in one of the three major industries of the region: coal mining, iron mining, or iron and steel manufacturing. Sixteen percent of the whites and eleven percent of the Negroes were in other manufacturing industries, transportation, trade, and miscellaneous industries (appendix table 29).

For purposes of comparison with the part-time farmers, a group of 222 white and 346 Negro nonfarming industrial workers[31] were included in the enumeration. These were selected to represent the three chief industries of the area.

There was one marked difference in occupational grouping between part-time farmers and nonfarming industrial workers. Among the whites, only 16 percent of the part-time farmers were in the unskilled group, as compared with 30 percent in the nonfarming industrial group. Among the Negroes, 59 percent of the part-time farmers as compared with 70 percent of the nonfarming industrial workers were in the unskilled group (appendix table 30). This may be without

---

[30] See following section on Industry and Occupation.
[31] For explanation of the selection of industrial workers, see pp. XXX–XXXI.

significance, the result of the relatively small sample or of the limits set on the selection of the nonfarm sample, or it may indicate a slight occupational advantage among the part-time farmers.

While there was thus some difference in general occupationa grouping between part-time farm and nonfarming industrial workers, there was a greater difference between whites and Negroes. More than one-half of the whites, as compared with only one-seventh of the Negroes, were in skilled occupations. In the blast furnaces and steel rolling mills the number of skilled workers among the Negroes was somewhat higher, amounting to 20 percent (table 91). Less than one-fourth of the whites as compared with two-thirds of the Negroes were in unskilled occupations. The predominance of unskilled workers among the Negroes, a common characteristic of southern labor, was particularly striking in the heavy industries represented in this area. In general, whites filled the ranks of electricians, machinists, mechanics, and especially of foremen.

Table 91.—Occupation of Heads of Part-Time Farm and Nonfarming Industrial Households in the Coal and Iron Subregion, by Industry and by Color, 1934

Occupation	Part-time farmers					Nonfarming industrial workers				
	Total	Coal mining	Iron mining	Blast furnaces and steel rolling mills	All others	Total	Coal mining	Iron mining	Blast furnaces and steel rolling mills	All others
WHITE										
Total	204	14	54	93	43	222	61	69	76	16
Proprietary	2	—	—	—	2	—	—	—	—	—
Clerical	17	—	3	8	6	11	4	4	3	—
Skilled	105	7	35	45	18	120	29	48	34	9
Semiskilled	47	1	2	28	16	23	2	1	13	7
Unskilled	33	6	14	12	1	68	26	16	26	—
NEGRO										
Total	124	10	22	77	15	346	132	61	142	11
Proprietary	—	—	—	—	—	—	—	—	—	—
Clerical	—	—	—	—	—	6	—	—	6	—
Skilled	19	1	4	14	—	46	11	5	30	—
Semiskilled	32	—	2	25	5	53	1	3	42	7
Unskilled	73	9	16	38	10	241	120	53	64	4

Earnings of Heads of Households

Since no significant differences in earnings in 1934 were found between white part-time farmers and nonfarming industrial workers, the two groups are not presented separately. More than one-third of the white workers earned less than $500, over three-fifths earned less than $750, and only one-fifth earned more than $1,000 (table 92). The low annual earnings were due principally to part-time work. The high hourly rates, averaging 59 cents, reflect the large proportion of skilled workers (table 93).

Slightly over one-half of the Negro part-time farmers, but only about one-fifth of the Negro nonfarmers, worked in a steel plant

Table 92.—Earnings From Industrial Employment [1] of Heads of Households in the Coal and Iron Subregion, by Color, 1934

Earnings from industrial employment	Total		Coal mining		Iron mining		Blast furnaces and steel rolling mills		All others	
	White	Negro	White	Negro	White	Negro	White	Negro	White	Negro
Total	426	470	75	142	123	83	169	219	59	26
$1 to $99	1	1	—	—	—	—	—	—	1	1
$100 to $249	26	124	5	41	4	32	12	47	5	4
$250 to $499	124	276	21	90	51	43	44	128	8	15
$500 to $749	111	59	13	11	36	7	46	37	16	4
$750 to $999	81	10	24	—	13	1	34	7	10	2
$1,000 to $1,249	40	—	7	—	8	—	14	—	11	—
$1,250 to $1,499	14	—	2	—	3	—	5	—	4	—
$1,500 to $1,999	20	—	2	—	4	—	10	—	4	—
$2,000 to $2,499	6	—	1	—	2	—	3	—	—	—
$2,500 or more	3	—	—	—	2	—	1	—	—	—
Average earnings	$733	$363	$723	$336	$682	$324	$751	$390	$805	$408

[1] At principal off-the-farm employment (job with the largest earnings).

which was shut down entirely for 5 months in 1934. As a result, the average earnings of part-time farmers in that year ($337) were somewhat smaller than the average earnings of the nonfarming industrial workers ($372) (appendix table 34). Since the differences in earnings between Negro part-time farmers and nonfarming industrial workers were not due to the farming activities carried on by the part-time farmers, the earnings of the two groups are discussed together hereafter.

Twenty-seven percent of the Negroes earned less than $250, fifty-eight percent earned $250–$499, and only fifteen percent earned $500 or more. The average earnings for iron and steel workers were slightly higher than for miners (table 92).

Table 93.—Rate of Pay [1] of Heads of Households in the Coal and Iron Subregion, by Color, 1934

Hourly rate of pay	Total		Coal mining		Iron mining		Blast furnaces and steel rolling mills		All others	
	White	Negro	White	Negro	White	Negro	White	Negro	White	Negro
Total	426	470	75	142	123	83	169	219	59	26
10 to 19 cents	2	—	—	—	—	—	—	—	2	—
20 to 29 cents	8	18	1	3	1	1	3	13	3	1
30 to 39 cents	41	214	4	54	9	12	23	127	5	21
40 to 49 cents	72	144	17	60	19	34	26	49	10	1
50 to 59 cents	119	84	24	23	36	33	47	26	12	2
60 to 69 cents	91	9	11	1	40	3	32	4	8	1
70 to 79 cents	46	—	11	—	10	—	13	—	12	—
80 to 89 cents	20	1	4	1	1	—	11	—	4	—
90 to 99 cents	11	—	1	—	3	—	6	—	1	—
$1.00 or more	16	—	2	—	4	—	8	—	2	—
Average hourly rate of pay	$0.59	$0.41	$0.59	$0.42	$0.59	$0.48	$0.59	$0.39	$0.58	$0.37

[1] At principal off-the-farm employment (job with the largest earnings).

The low earnings of heads of both white and Negro households of all groups in 1934 were due not so much to low hourly rates as to the lack of full-time employment. Some mills shut down entirely for part of the year, retaining only a small maintenance force. Several of the larger mines and mills operated for 6 months or less during 1934. Others gave partial employment throughout the year, either on a curtailed working schedule or on a "spread work" system.

More than one-half of the white part-time farmers and nonfarming industrial workers were employed less than 150 days in 1934 (appendix table 32). The average for the whole group of whites was only 153 days, and for white iron miners only 138 days (table 94). The situation of the Negroes was even worse because of the predominance of unskilled workers who were more commonly laid off during shutdowns. Eighty-five percent of the Negroes had less than 150 days of work, and the average for the group was only 114 days. The average for those in iron mining was only 92 days. Only a little more than 6 percent of the Negro heads of households were employed for as much as 200 days during 1934.

Table 94.—Number of Days Heads of Households in the Coal and Iron Subregion Were Employed off the Farm,[1] by Color, 1934

Number of days employed off the farm	Total		Coal mining		Iron mining		Blast furnaces and steel rolling mills		All others	
	White	Negro	White	Negro	White	Negro	White	Negro	White	Negro
Total_____	426	470	75	142	123	83	169	219	59	26
50 to 99 days_____	103	209	18	71	40	61	36	69	9	8
100 to 149 days_____	132	191	18	59	47	19	55	102	12	11
150 to 199 days_____	92	40	21	9	16	1	40	28	15	2
200 to 249 days_____	61	25	13	3	10	1	28	19	10	2
250 to 299 days_____	18	2	2	—	4	—	6	1	6	1
300 days or more___	20	3	3	—	6	1	4	—	7	2
Average days employed__	153	114	156	105	138	92	153	125	186	142

[1] At principal off-the-farm employment (job with the largest earnings).

Total Family Cash Income

Total family incomes of white part-time farm households from nonfarm sources were greater ($899) than the incomes of nonfarm households ($810), while the per capita income was approximately the same, $176 and $179, respectively. Among the Negroes the reverse was true, the incomes of part-time farm families averaging $370 and those of nonfarming industrial families averaging $432, with per capita averages of $74 and $103, respectively (table 95). This difference in income between the two Negro groups may be due primarily to the fact, already cited, that over one-half of the Negro part-time farmers but only one-fifth of the nonfarming industrial workers surveyed were employed in a steel plant that remained closed for 5 months in 1934.

The scarcity of employment opportunity was such that very few members of the households other than the heads had any work. Few of the young people who had recently become of working age had found employment. Only 20 percent of the young people 16 to 24 years of age in white part-time farming households and 9 percent of the young people in Negro part-time farming households had any employment in 1934 (table 58, page 43, and appendix table 47).

Table 95.—Cash Income From Nonfarm Sources of Part-Time Farm and Nonfarming Industrial Households in the Coal and Iron Subregion, by Color, 1934

Size of household	Part-time farm households				Nonfarming industrial households			
	Number of cases		Income per capita		Number of cases		Income per capita	
	White	Negro	White	Negro	White	Negro	White	Negro
Total	204	124	$176	$74	¹ 221	346	$179	$103
1 person	1	1	†	†	—	2	—	†
2 persons	8	13	†	165	21	68	397	206
3 persons	28	22	324	126	50	84	241	122
4 persons	50	20	216	74	52	79	197	115
5 persons	45	26	180	76	36	42	162	98
6 persons	28	14	142	56	32	27	134	64
7 persons	21	14	169	57	19	19	128	67
8 persons or more	23	14	87	51	11	25	139	67
Average income per household	$899	$370			$810	$432		

† Average not computed for less than 10 cases.
¹ Total family income unknown for 1 case.

The occupations of the young white people were widely varied. Their earnings ranged from $20 to $1,500 annually with an average of $369. The fact that 21 youth earned less than $200 indicates that many were employed only part-time. Among the Negroes, there was less variety in the occupations. Their earnings ranged from $15 to $624 and averaged $205.

Only about one-fourth of the white part-time farm and one-sixth of the nonfarming industrial families had one or more members other than the head employed in 1934 (appendix table 35). The earnings of these other members averaged $467 per employed person for the part-time farm group and $432 for the nonfarming industrial group. This contribution increased the average family income of white part-time farm households by $160 and of nonfarming industrial households by $77 (table 59, page 44). Sixteen percent of the Negro part-time farm and nineteen percent of the nonfarming industrial households had one or more members other than the head employed during at least part of 1934. Their earnings averaged $174 and $245, respectively, per employed person. This amounted to an average of $25 for all part-time farm households and $59 for nonfarming industrial households.

Changes in Family Income, 1929–1934

The incomes of workers enumerated in this area were greatly reduced between 1929 and 1934. Among the whites, 85 percent of the households had lower incomes in 1934 than in 1929, 11 percent remained in the same income class, and only 4 percent had risen to a higher income class. Table 96 shows the extent of the decrease by income groups. As might be expected, the most drastic reductions occurred in the higher income groups. On the average, the incomes of all white households had decreased 46 percent.

A typical case was that of a condenser operator in a steel mill whose earnings were reduced from $900 to $477. He was the only wage earner for a family of six persons. A more drastic reduction—from $1,500 to $230—was made in the case of a drill runner in an iron mine. The family consisted of the head, his wife, and eight children. Such a marked reduction was not typical, but occurred frequently. In both of the cases cited above, the earnings of the head constituted the entire family income from off-the-farm sources. Both cases received relief in 1934, $95 for the steel mill employee and $25 for the iron miner.

Table 96.—Changes in Family Income From Nonfarm Sources in the Coal and Iron Subregion, by Color, 1929–1934

Total family income, 1934	Total family income, 1929										
	Total	$1–$99	$100–$249	$250–$499	$500–$749	$750–$999	$1,000–$1,249	$1,250–$1,499	$1,500–$1,999	$2,000–$2,499	$2,500 or more
WHITE											
Total	1 411	—	—	6	26	41	77	50	126	49	36
$1 to $99	1	—	—	1	—	—	—	—	—	—	—
$100 to $249	12	—	—	1	1	1	3	—	6	—	—
$250 to $499	107	—	—	2	14	20	27	11	18	10	5
$500 to $749	101	—	—	2	7	8	30	17	27	6	4
$750 to $999	80	—	—	—	3	10	10	11	29	8	9
$1,000 to $1,249	46	—	—	—	—	1	5	8	18	11	3
$1,250 to $1,499	17	—	—	—	1	—	—	2	11	1	2
$1,500 to $1,999	30	—	—	—	—	1	1	1	13	10	4
$2,000 to $2,499	12	—	—	—	—	—	1	—	3	2	6
$2,500 or more	5	—	—	—	—	—	—	—	1	1	3
Average family income, 1934	$848	—	—	†	$528	$591	$620	$757	$936	$1,158	$1,349
NEGRO											
Total	2 447	1	5	41	110	99	109	35	31	12	4
$1 to $99	1	—	—	—	—	—	1	—	—	—	—
$100 to $249	99	—	2	12	33	23	20	1	5	2	1
$250 to $499	248	—	2	26	62	62	62	20	13	6	2
$500 to $749	70	—	1	3	11	14	20	10	9	2	—
$750 to $999	21	1	—	—	4	4	2	4	4	2	—
$1,000 to $1,249	6	—	—	—	—	2	4	—	—	—	—
$1,250 to $1,499	—	—	—	—	—	—	—	—	—	—	—
$1,500 to $1,999	1	—	—	—	—	1	—	—	—	—	—
$2,000 to $2,999	1	—	—	—	—	—	—	—	—	—	1
Average family income, 1934	$411	†	†	$334	$358	$413	$417	$497	$479	$466	†

† Average not computed for less than 10 cases.
1 Exclusive of 15 white cases for which 1929 income was unknown.
2 Exclusive of 23 Negro cases for which 1929 income was unknown.

The average family income of all Negro households in 1934 from all sources other than the farm was only 42 percent of the average income of the same families in 1929, $411 as compared with $975. Eighty-six percent of the Negro households received less income in 1934 than in 1929; 11 percent remained in the income group; and only 3 percent were in a higher income group. As with the whites, the reductions were relatively greater in the higher income groups (table 96).

The meaning of the reductions may be gained by citing two examples. The income for one Negro part-time farm family was reduced from $920 in 1929 to $192 in 1934. During 1934, the head of the household, an iron miner, received only 12 days of employment a month for 5 months. Although there was a son 27 years of age, and a daughter 26 years of age, the head was the only wage earner. Such reductions, though greater than the average, occurred frequently. The added contribution of the garden was not sufficient for self-support and the family received $140 of public relief. Similarly, the wages of a Negro brickmason helper in a steel mill dropped from $1,000 to $475. Since a family of 10 depended upon his earnings, such a reduction was a serious loss. The children were all under 16 years of age and therefore too young to seek employment. This latter family was able to maintain self-support by the aid of the garden and by mortgaging the home for $600.

LIVING CONDITIONS AND ORGANIZED SOCIAL LIFE

Since the part-time farmers surveyed in this subregion lived in the same urban and suburban environment as did the nonfarming industrial workers, the living conditions and proximity to urban facilities of the two groups were similar (table 62, page 51).

Housing of White Households

The only significant difference between dwellings of white part-time farmers and of white nonfarming industrial workers was that the former had slightly larger houses, averaging 5.2 rooms per dwelling, while the houses of the latter averaged 4.5 rooms (appendix table 38). This advantage of slightly more than half a room per dwelling does not mean that housing conditions of part-time farmers were superior to those of nonfarming industrial households, since the part-time farm households were somewhat larger in size. Approximately two-thirds of each group had the relatively high standard of one room per member of the household (appendix table 39).

The state of repair and the available conveniences were about the same for the two groups. About 40 percent of all the houses needed no repairs. More than one-half were in need of paint, new floors, siding, window panes, porch repairs, papering, or other minor repairs. Approximately one-fifth needed roof repairs and one-tenth needed general structural repairs (appendix table 40). Almost all of the houses had electric lights and running water while about half of them had bathrooms (appendix table 41).

Housing of Negro Households

In general the living conditions of Negroes in the Coal and Iron Subregion were somewhat above the average for southern Negroes. The houses of the families surveyed averaged 3.5 rooms, with 37 percent of the part-time farm and 51 percent of the nonfarm families averaging one person or less per room (appendix tables 38 and 39). The size of the houses did not increase with the size of the household as consistently as among the whites.

The typical Negro dwelling consisted of two, three, or four rooms, and was either part of a double house or a single family residence. The dwellings varied from rough shacks to well-kept modern homes. Approximately one out of four dwellings needed no repairs (appendix table 40). More than one-half were in need of paint, screens, siding, porch repairs, window panes, new floors, plastering, papering, or other minor repairs. One out of three dwellings needed roof repairs, while one out of six required such major repairs as new foundations, frames, and sills. Approximately one-half had electric lights, six out of seven had running water, and one out of seven had a bathroom (appendix table 41).

Automobiles, Radios, and Telephones

Radios were found in the homes of almost three-fourths of both groups of white workers, and in the homes of more than one-fifth of the Negro workers (appendix table 42). Telephones were rare in all groups. Only 8 percent of the white part-time farm and 4 percent of the white nonfarming industrial households had telephones; and only two Negro families had them. Automobiles were owned by 46 percent of the white part-time farmers as compared with 38 percent of the nonfarmers. This difference is related to the fact that 66 percent of the part-time farmers lived 1½ miles or more from their places of employment, as compared with only 27 percent of the nonfarming industrial group who lived at that distance (appendix table 28). Less than 5 percent of the Negro part-time farmers owned cars, although 38 percent of them lived 2½ miles or more from their places of employment. However, cars were not necessary in all cases, since street cars or buses were available to many, and since the most common means of getting to work for both whites and Negroes was for several neighbors to drive together in one car.

Home Ownership

Approximately one-third of the white part-time farmers owned their homes, as compared with only 18 percent of the nonfarming industrial workers (appendix table 43). Among the Negroes, there was no difference between the part-time farm and the nonfarming industrial groups, about one-fifth of each owning their homes. Most of the white and Negro coal and iron miners lived in company villages, so it is perhaps noteworthy that so many workers owned their homes.

Education

Elementary and secondary schools were available for all children, Negroes as well as whites. Less than 5 percent of all children from 7 to 16 years of age, inclusive, were not in school (table 75, page 63). Most of these were 7-year-old children who had not yet started to school. There was comparatively little retardation in school of eit er white or Negro children (table 76, page 64).

Heads of white households had completed about seven grades on an average. Less than one-half of either white group had completed grade school, and only about 1 out of 9 of the part-time farmers and 1 out of 11 of the nonfarming industrial workers had completed high school. Negro heads of households had completed approximately four grades (appendix table 46). Only about 13 percent had completed grade school, and only 2 percent had been graduated from high school.

More than 80 percent of both white groups reported library facilities available, but only 49 percent of the part-time farm and 58 percent of the nonfarming industrial households with such facilities had made any use of them (table 78, page 66). Although three-fourths of the Negro part-time farm and 43 percent of the Negro nonfarming industrial households reported library facilities, only one in six and one in eight of these households, respectively, made any use of the facilities.

Social Participation of White Households

Organized social life in this area offered a considerable variety of activities. The church was an important center of social life with both adult and young people's organizations. Church services and Sunday Schools were available to nearly all white households. School clubs, athletic teams, and fraternal orders were more frequently available to, and more often attended by, members of nonfarming than of farming households (appendix table 48). Boy Scouts, Girl Scouts, women's organizations, and special interest groups were also more often available to the nonfarming industrial households, but were seldom attended by either group. About one-third of both groups of white households reported membership in labor unions, while others said that they would be members if they could pay the dues.

Although the nonfarming industrial households participated in more organizations than did part-time farm households, their total numerical attendance per person in 1934 was slightly less, being 70 as against 78 for the part-time farm group (table 80, page 68). Similarly, while members of part-time farm households furnished somewhat more leadership to local organizations than did nonfarming industrial households, the leadership was confined to a smaller number of organizations. About 37 percent of the part-time farm households in comparison with 24 percent of the nonfarming industrial households had a member who was an officer in some organization (appendix table 49).

Social Participation of Negro Households

The church was by far the most important factor in the social life of Negroes in this area. Nearly all families attended church and Sunday School regularly, while adult church organizations and young people's organizations were available to nearly all and were well attended. Approximately 40 percent of the heads of Negro households attended labor union meetings. Whites and Negroes were members of the same unions. Parent-Teacher Associations, athletic teams, fraternal orders, school clubs, and women's organizations were generally available and attended by occasional households. Practically no participation in Boy Scouts and Girl Scouts was reported. The average number of attendances per person in 1934 was about 90 (table 80, page 68).

Leadership was confined largely to the church and related organizations. On an average, 1 out of 16 persons in these households held an office in some organization (appendix table 49).

RELIEF

It is evident that small farming operations, such as those being carried on in this area, are quite inadequate for the support of a family. Also, the data show that such operations have not compensated for the decline in industrial earnings and have not served to keep either white or Negro families off relief. Thirty-two percent of the white part-time farm group and twenty-eight percent of the white nonfarming industrial group received public relief at some time during 1934 (table 61, page 47). The average amounts received were $50 and $58, respectively. However, only 22 percent of those who had been part-time farmers for 5 years or more received relief in 1934. During the period, 1929–1935, those who received some relief had received it for an average period of 1½ years (appendix table 36).

Seventy-eight percent of the Negro part-time farm group and fifty-eight percent of the Negro nonfarming industrial group received public relief at some time during 1934. The average amounts received were almost identical: $56 and $55, respectively. The higher proportion of Negro part-time farmers than of nonfarming industrial workers on relief was associated with less steady employment. Those workers with the least employment were the most likely to receive relief. Also, due to the fact that they had more time available and lower incomes, they were most likely to undertake farming activities.

Chapter III

THE ATLANTIC COAST SUBREGION

GENERAL FEATURES OF THE SUBREGION AND OF CHARLESTON COUNTY

THE COUNTIES which comprise the Atlantic Coast Subregion (figure 2, page XXIV) are part of the larger region designated on the type of farming map (figure 3, page XXVI) as the Atlantic Coast Flatwoods. Most of this region is covered by forest. Only 33 percent of the total land area in the portion located in Georgia and South Carolina was in farms in 1934, and of the land in farms only 15 percent was in crops harvested that year.[1]

From an agricultural standpoint, the truck-farming area centering in Beaufort and Charleston Counties, South Carolina, is the most important area of any considerable size in the whole region. These two counties together include 50 percent of the total value of farm land and buildings for the entire Flatwoods Region of Georgia and South Carolina.[2]

In the Atlantic Coast Subregion nearly all of the industry, except some lumbering and naval stores operations, is clustered in and around the three seaports of Brunswick, Charleston, and Savannah. In 1930, 44 percent of the 107,100 persons gainfully employed in nonagricultural pursuits in this subregion lived in Chatham County, Georgia, which includes Savannah; 33 percent lived in Charleston County, South Carolina; and 8 percent lived in Glynn County, Georgia, where Brunswick is located.

Charleston County

The considerations leading to the selection of Charleston County for study in this region were as follows: (1) It includes one of the three leading seaports; (2) it includes part of the principal truck-farming area; (3) it includes a considerable number of part-time farms; and (4) the relief load has been relatively high. The 1930 Census of

---

[1] *United States Census of Agriculture: 1935.*
[2] *Idem.*

Agriculture reported 347 part-time farms in Charleston County, accounting for 18 percent of the total number of farms. In October 1934, the number of families receiving relief in Charleston County amounted to 28 percent of the number of families recorded in the 1930 Census of Population.

Population

The population of Charleston County was 62 percent urban in 1930. That year, for the first time in its history, a majority (55 percent) of the population of the city of Charleston was white. While the white urban population had increased from 1920 to 1930, the Negro urban population had declined as a result of considerable emigration. The total urban population, which had increased gradually since the Civil War, showed a decline of 8 percent during this decade.

In 1930, the rural nonfarm population was 61 percent Negro and the rural farm population was 83 percent Negro. The total rural population declined between 1920 and 1930, but the decline was relatively less than that for the urban population.

Agricultural Features

The great majority of the rural population, both farm and nonfarm, is directly dependent upon agriculture. In 1930, 77 percent of the gross farm income of the county was derived from the sale of potatoes and other vegetables. Hence, the truck-crop industry is of major importance.

For some distance inland, the area to the south of the city of Charleston is comprised of islands separated from the mainland by a series of narrow tideways commonly referred to as rivers. Much of it is marshy and covered with woods, but there are also considerable areas of sandy soil well adapted to the production of truck crops. The normal annual rainfall is about 45 inches, with the heaviest precipitation in the summer months.[3] The normal frost-free growing season is 9 months, from February 28 to December 1.[4] Thus, soil and rainfall are adapted to vegetable growing and the season is long enough for two or even three crops of certain types.

More significant perhaps than the length of the growing season is the fact that it normally begins early enough to permit farmers to harvest their first crop of vegetables at a time when the markets are not well supplied from competing areas. Their potato crop reaches northern and eastern markets before the North Carolina crop but after the Florida and Texas crops. The time when the crop is marketed is all-important from the standpoint of prices received. The significance of seasonal price movements is further evidenced by the fact that

---

[3] *Yearbook of Agriculture: 1935*, U. S. Department of Agriculture, p. 707.
[4] *Idem*, p. 709.

the local trucking area does not supply the markets of Charleston during off-seasons, but devotes all of its resources to producing for the seasons when high prices prevail.

Some of the produce leaves by motor truck but shipment by rail predominates. In 1934, a total of 3,150 carloads of vegetables were shipped from Charleston. Of these 2,028 were carloads of potatoes, 838 of cabbages, and the remaining 284 of miscellaneous vegetables. Potatoes are shipped chiefly in May, cabbages from November through January and again in May. Shipments of other vegetables reach their height in May and June, but there is some movement throughout the year.[5]

Of the 3,733 farms [6] in Charleston County reported by the 1935 Census of Agriculture, only 20 percent were operated by whites. However, these 20 percent included 83 percent of all land in farms. All farms operated by whites averaged 209 acres in size and those operated by Negroes averaged 11 acres. The commercial agriculture of the county is carried on for the most part on a relatively small number of large-scale truck farms operated by whites. Many Negro operators of small farms depend for part of their living upon labor on the large commercial farms. Only 30 percent of all the farmers in the county reported hiring labor in 1929.[7] For those hiring labor, the average expenditure was about $1,230. Ninety-six percent of those reported as farm laborers in the 1930 Census were Negroes.[8]

The demand for vegetables varies decidedly with general business conditions. The effects of the last two general depressions resulted in small shipments in 1920 and 1932. Aside from this type of fluctuation and occasional fluctuations in yields resulting from weather conditions, production has remained fairly uniform. There is reason to believe that with further increases in business activity production of vegetables will also increase. However, any expansion beyond the volume produced during the twenties seems unlikely in view of the limitations imposed by the available area of good vegetable land and by markets for the crop. There is an adequate supply of labor in the area to produce such a volume of vegetables. Increases in production would merely mean more employment to be shared by the large underemployed labor force.

---

[5] "Car-Lot Shipments of Fruits and Vegetables in South Carolina During 1934," *Market News Service*, United States Bureau of Agricultural Economics.

[6] The number of farms reported by this census was almost double the number reported by the 1930 Census, but approximately the same as the numbers reported by the 1925 Census and the 1920 Census. This difference in number of farms is probably accounted for chiefly by the difference in the number of small Negro holdings enumerated as farms. With a 91 percent increase in number of farms between the 1930 and 1935 Censuses, there was only an 8 percent increase in acres of cropland harvested and a 30 percent decrease in the acreage of potatoes, the principal crop.

[7] *Fifteenth Census of the United States: 1930*, Agriculture Vol. III, Part 2.

[8] *Idem.*

Area Covered and Cases Enumerated

Field enumeration was limited to the Charleston peninsula and to the four nearest townships across the Ashley River. This area included most of those who work in the urban industries since a high bridge toll renders commuting from across the Cooper River to the north of the city impractical. It also includes a portion of the truck farming section.

Records were secured from 213 white and Negro families that met the above requirements. Their location is shown in figure 11. This represents a nearly complete census of white part-time farmers (according to the definition used) in the eight minor civil divisions included in the enumeration. The enumeration of Negro part-time farmers was equally complete in and near Charleston, but less nearly complete in the rural portion of the county where farm laborers were found in large numbers.

INDUSTRIES OF CHARLESTON COUNTY

Charleston is primarily a seaport and trading center. A majority of the workers are employed in the service industries. Some of these workers derive their incomes from serving the local population, while others are dependent directly on the commerce of the city with other areas. Manufacturing, while not employing directly as many people as the group of service industries, is a very important element in the economic life of the city. Therefore, discussions of both port commerce and manufacturing are included in this section. These activities not only employ large numbers of people directly, but they are also the principal factors determining the city's general prosperity, and hence its industrial employment opportunities.

Charleston's situation between the Ashley and Cooper Rivers, with ample waterfront and anchorage space only 7½ miles from the open sea, is ideal for a port.

Before the Civil War, Charleston was the business center and principal port of the Southeast. When railroad building began, railroads were projected from Charleston to the interior and were partly built before construction was stopped by the Civil War. Before the South could recover from the effects of the war, the expansion of railroads from northern ports to the West and Northwest had established the overseas traffic of these regions through the northern ports. Some of the Middle West's foreign trade has been diverted through New Orleans, but the South Atlantic ports have not shared in it.

The port of Charleston is dependent on the Southeast for its traffic. In the development of this traffic other ports more favored by the railroads, notably Savannah, have surpassed Charleston. Probably the development of Savannah is due in large part to the fact that it is the terminus of the Central of Georgia Railway, and also is served by

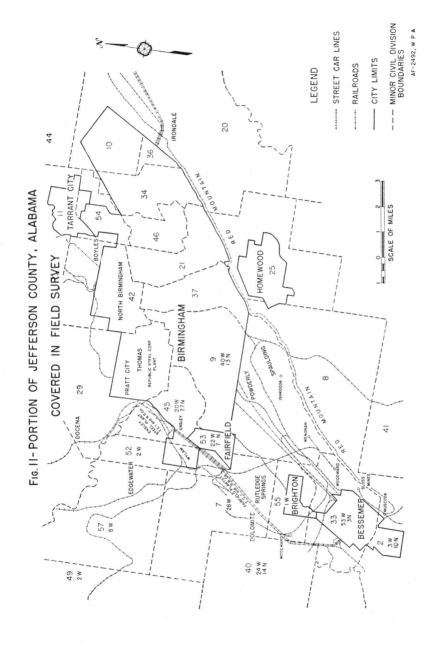

Fig. 11 – PORTION OF JEFFERSON COUNTY, ALABAMA COVERED IN FIELD SURVEY

LEGEND

······ STREET CAR LINES

+—+—+ RAILROADS

——— CITY LIMITS

— — — MINOR CIVIL DIVISION BOUNDARIES

AF-2492, W P A

SCALE OF MILES

four other railroads.   Charleston is served by three railway systems: the Southern, the Atlantic Coast Line, and the Seaboard Air Line.

Charleston has 44 piers, wharves, and docks, which are owned by the Port Utilities Commission, and by railroads, steamship companies, and other private interests.   The United States Navy has a yard for the construction and repair of naval vessels located on the Cooper River about 4 miles north of the city limits.

The water-borne commerce of the port of Charleston (exports, imports, and coastwise traffic) showed a downward trend from 1925 to 1932 but recovered somewhat in 1933 and 1934.   Petroleum products, the principal item of tonnage handled in the years 1924 to 1934, inclusive, declined from a peak of 1,680,000 tons in 1925 to less than one-half of that amount in 1933.   Coal exports reached a high level in 1926, due to the strike of British miners in that year, and then fell to negligible amounts in 1929 and succeeding years.   The total of all other items also decreased, due mainly to the drop in imports of fertilizer materials, the principal item in this group.   The total traffic in all commodities, except petroleum, coal, and fertilizer materials, varied between a high of 751,000 tons in 1926 and a low of 482,000 tons in 1931.[9]   Lumber and cotton are important items in this miscellaneous group.

Savannah is Charleston's principal competitor for port business. Savannah's water-borne commerce also showed a downward trend from 1925 to 1932 and an upturn in 1933 and 1934 in the total of all items except petroleum products.[10]   Savannah's traffic in petroleum products increased greatly in this period.   Evidently, some of Charleston's petroleum business was lost to Savannah.   The principal items of Savannah's water-borne trade are petroleum, fertilizers, cotton, sugar and molasses, lumber, and naval stores.

Service Industries

Of the 43,200 gainfully occupied persons living in Charleston County in 1930, 55 percent were service workers (table 97).   Of the largest group, "Other domestic and personal service," 88 percent were Negro women.   Wholesale and retail trade, the next most important group, was made up of about 55 percent white men, 18 percent white women, 25 percent Negro men, and 2 percent Negro women.   More than 60 percent of the railroad workers were white men.   "Other transportation and communication" included the workers in the shipping industry.   Many of this group were Negro longshoremen and dock laborers.   The public service group included the Navy Yard workers, largely skilled shipbuilding mechanics.

[9] *The Ports of Charleston, S. C., and Wilmington, N. C.*, Port Series No. 9, Revised 1934, Corps of Engineers, United States Army.

[10] *Idem*, Port Series No. 10, 1925 and 1935 (Revised 1935).

Table 97.—Distribution of Persons, 10 Years Old and Over, Gainfully Occupied in Service Industries in Charleston County, South Carolina, 1930

Industry	Total		White		Negro	
	Num-ber	Per-cent	Male	Female	Male	Female
Total_____	23,704	100.0	8,498	2,960	4,887	7,359
Construction and maintenance of streets_____	226	0.9	91	1	132	2
Garages, greasing stations, etc_____	160	0.7	110	2	48	—
Postal service_____	174	0.7	115	17	42	—
Steam and street railroads_____	1,516	6.4	924	38	548	6
Telegraph and telephone_____	311	1.3	143	157	10	1
Other transportation and communication_____	2,040	8.6	750	27	1,256	7
Banking and brokerage_____	368	1.6	267	72	25	4
Insurance and real estate_____	566	2.4	415	123	17	11
Automobile agencies and filling stations_____	389	1.6	288	26	74	1
Wholesale and retail trade_____	4,523	19.1	2,512	799	1,109	103
Other trade_____	83	0.3	47	18	18	—
Public service (not elsewhere classified)_____	2,065	8.7	1,701	87	273	4
Recreation and amusement_____	252	1.1	69	76	86	21
Other professional and semiprofessional service_____	2,299	9.7	664	953	310	372
Hotels, restaurants, and boarding houses_____	1,222	5.2	179	309	355	379
Laundries, cleaning and pressing_____	324	1.4	88	22	83	131
Other domestic and personal service_____	7,186	30.3	135	233	501	6,317

Source: *Fifteenth Census of the United States: 1930*, Population Vol. III.

The shipping business of Charleston varies with the seasons, because of the seasonal nature of fertilizer shipments. The first 3 months of the year are the busiest time, and summer is the dullest. The demand for stevedore labor varies with the tonnage and kind of goods handled. Petroleum products, which form a large part of Charleston's port traffic, and coal require little or no dock labor for handling.

Manufacturing

"Manufacturing and allied industries" accounted for 23 percent of the gainfully employed in Charleston County in 1930 (table 98). Building is the only important nonmanufacturing industry in this group. Although Charleston County is on the seacoast, fishing is a means of livelihood for comparatively few persons.

The principal manufacturing industries of Charleston County are fertilizer and lumber, each represented by several establishments. There are also a cigar factory, a factory making jute bagging for cotton bales, an asbestos products plant, a wood-preserving concern, and a petroleum refinery. A cotton mill was in operation in 1929, but has since gone out of business. Average employment remained fairly steady between 1929 and 1933, the losses in the fertilizer and forest products groups being offset by an increase in other industries. Total wages for 1933 were about two-thirds of the 1929 figure. Even before the depression, however, manufacturing activity in Charleston County was declining. On the average, 7,000 wage earners were employed in 1919, 6,200 in 1927, and 5,300 in 1929.[11]

---

[11] *Biennial Census of Manufactures.*

Table 98.—Distribution of Persons, 10 Years Old and Over, Gainfully Occupied in Manufacturing and Allied Industries in Charleston County, South Carolina, 1930

| Industry | Total | | White | | Negro | |
	Number	Percent	Male	Female	Male	Female
Total_____	10,021	100.0	4,198	618	4,211	994
Forestry and fishing_____	267	2.7	87	2	177	1
Extraction of minerals_____	25	0.2	10	3	12	—
Building_____	1,829	18.3	860	15	945	9
Chemical and allied_____	1,923	19.2	638	55	1,210	20
Clay, glass, and stone_____	46	0.4	19	2	25	—
Clothing_____	117	1.2	39	14	44	20
Food and allied_____	659	6.6	215	28	252	164
Automobile factories and repair shops_____	228	2.3	183	2	42	1
Iron and steel_____	1,220	12.2	841	21	357	1
Saw and planing mills_____	634	6.3	155	4	430	45
Other woodworking_____	253	2.5	74	4	158	17
Paper, printing, and allied_____	203	2.0	150	37	16	—
Cotton mills_____	173	1.7	83	45	29	16
Other textile_____	321	3.2	49	12	86	174
Independent hand trades_____	403	4.0	57	87	58	201
Other manufacturing_____	1,720	17.2	738	287	370	325

Source: *Fifteenth Census of the United States: 1930*, Population Vol. III.

With the exception of a very few small plants, all of the manufacturing industry of Charleston is located within the corporate limits of Charleston or on the peninsula north of the city. The bagging factory and the cigar factory are in the city. Most of the fertilizer plants, the large sawmills, the wood-preserving plant, and the petroleum refinery are on the narrow neck just north of the city. The asbestos plant is in North Charleston.

Since fertilizer manufacturing is a highly seasonal business, a great part of the year's operations is crowded into the months of February, March, and April. The low point is in the summer, and employment then gradually increases through the rest of the year as stock is accumulated for the next spring's business.

Most of the wage earners in fertilizer manufacturing are unskilled Negroes. In 1923, the average wage in this industry in the South was 13.7 cents per hour.[12] The minimum rate of pay under the N. R. A. code, effective November 10, 1933, was 25 cents per hour in the South, and this rate was maintained in the Charleston factories during the summer of 1935 after the N. R. A. had ceased to function.

The fertilizer industry has been on the downgrade since the World War. Because its customers are farmers, it has felt the full impact of the agricultural depression. There are many small concerns in the business, and it is highly competitive. The N. R. A., with its open price provisions, rescued the industry from a state approaching demoralization, but its future is rather uncertain. Any considerable

---

[12] "Code of Fair Competition for the Fertilizer Industry," letter from the N. R. A. Administrator to the President.

shift in the South from cotton raising to diversified farming will be likely to result in decreased use of commercial fertilizers.

The lumber industry mostly employs unskilled Negroes and wages are low. This industry had an N. R. A. code which set the minimum pay at 23 cents per hour in the South and limited working hours to 40 per week, but wages have been reduced and hours lengthened since code enforcement stopped.

The largest single manufacturing establishment in Charleston is a cigar factory, which normally employs several hundred persons. A large majority of the workers are white women who operate the cigar-making machines. Some Negro women are employed as strippers. N. R. A. code wage rates and hours were being maintained in 1935. The minimum rates were 22½ cents per hour for certain strippers classed as show workers, 25 cents for other strippers and unskilled laborers, and higher rates for cigar makers. Maximum hours were set at 40 per week for most employees, except during the two peak seasons of the year.

In the industries of Charleston, the unskilled work is generally done by Negro men. White men are usually skilled or semiskilled workers or foremen.

Outlook for Employment

While no detailed analysis of the industries of Charleston has been attempted, the foregoing description may serve as a basis for a few generalizations as to the probable future trend of industrial employment.

The shipping and fertilizer businesses, and to a certain extent the trade industries of Charleston, depend on commerce with the city's agricultural hinterland; hence, these industries will probably tend to rise or fall with the fortunes of southern agriculture. Any substantial increase in employment in these industries must await a solution of the agricultural problem.

There is no indication that any marked change in the numbers employed in manufacturing in Charleston County is likely to take place within the next few years. Manufacturing activity and population both declined in the decade from 1920 to 1930. However, manufacturing employment has remained fairly steady throughout the depression, the 1933 average being about equal to 1929, and the 1931 average only 8 percent less. Charleston has no raw materials other than the products of southern farms and forests. In fact, none of the important local industries, except the forest products group, draws its raw material from local sources. The principal advantage that Charleston has to offer to manufacturers is low freight rates by water to eastern seaboard cities and foreign ports, particularly those in Cuba and the Caribbean Islands.

FARMING ACTIVITIES OF PART-TIME FARMERS
Types of Part-Time Farmers

Most of the part-time farmers enumerated in this study, both white and Negro, produced farm products chiefly for their own use. About one-third of the white group, however, in addition to production for family use, conducted operations on a scale beyond that normally expected to supply the needs of a single family. Among the 24 farms involved, there were 14 truck farms, 3 dairy farms, 2 combined truck and dairy farms, 2 cotton farms, 2 poultry farms, and 1 general farm. No study of the success of the commercial part of these farming ventures has been attempted, but comparisons have been made between their self-sufficing aspects and those of the noncommercial farms.

The average acreage in cropland was 26 acres for white commercial part-time farmers, 3 acres for white noncommercial part-time farmers, and around 4 acres for Negroes (appendix table 6). Over one-third of the white farmers had less than 1½ acres, but only one-fifth of the Negroes had as small a plot as this. Another third of the whites had from 1½ to 9 acres, while nearly three-fourths of the Negroes had crop acreages of this size.

Farm Production

One-fourth of the whites and less than 6 percent of the Negroes produced all four types of food products: vegetables, dairy products, poultry products, and pork. On the other hand, 90 percent of the whites and nearly 70 percent of the Negroes had more than one type of enterprise (appendix table 12).

Gardens

Gardens were practically universal among the part-time farmers, all except two whites and two Negroes having them (appendix table 11 and figure 12). Since the area is adapted to vegetable growing and marketing channels are well developed, many produced vegetables for sale or at least sold their surplus. Most of the commercial group had what amounted to commercial truck farms. Only five in the noncommercial group sold as much as $100 worth of products, and less than one-fifth of the Negroes sold $50 worth or more (appendix table 25).

Since Charleston has an average frost-free growing season of 9 months, there are about 7 months in which the less hardy vegetables may be consumed fresh from the gardens (appendix table 14). The more hardy vegetables may be available during the colder months. However, nearly three-fourths of the gardens of the white farmers supplied three or more fresh vegetables for only 4 months or less. One-eighth of the Negroes' gardens supplied at least three vegetables for 4 months or more (appendix table 13). Usually gardens were planted only in the spring.

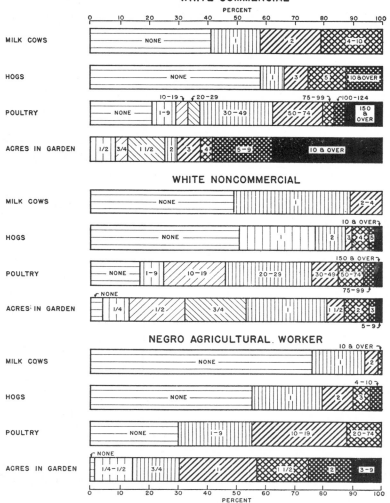

FIG. 12 – SIZE OF PRINCIPAL ENTERPRISES ON PART-TIME
FARMS, BY TYPE OF FARM AND BY
COLOR OF OPERATOR,
CHARLESTON COUNTY, S.C., 1934

AF-2468, W.P.A.

Despite this fact, the gardens, especially of the white families, contributed fairly well to their living. Two-thirds of the whites with gardens and well over one-third of the Negro families with gardens reported that their grocery bills were less in the 6 summer than in the 6 winter months, the average reduction being $6.60 and $3.50 per month, respectively. In one white family the reduction was over $20 per month, and in two Negro families it was over $10.

Canning and storage of vegetables did not extend the contribution of the garden very much in this area. Less than one-fifth of the white part-time farm families and only two of the Negro part-time farm families did any canning (appendix table 16). Storage of vegetables was somewhat more common (table 29, page 20). One-half of the whites stored sweet potatoes and about one-fourth stored Irish potatoes, the amounts usually ranging from 10 to 20 bushels (appendix table 17). These vegetables were stored by the Negroes in somewhat smaller quantities. Storage of other vegetables by either whites or Negroes was too limited to be significant.

Corn

Field corn was grown by four-fifths of the white commercial and by about one-half of the white noncommercial part-time farmers, their average production being 310 bushels and 48 bushels, respectively (appendix table 24). Practically all of this was used as feed for livestock, only four families reporting use of corn for food. Over three-fourths of the Negroes grew corn, their production averaging 21 bushels. Thirty-five percent of the Negro families consumed an average of 7 bushels for food.

Dairy Products

About half of the white farmers had one or more cows (appendix table 11). One-fifth of the Negroes had cows, but only a few of them had more than one. Milk production during 1934 averaged 2,440 quarts per cow for the white commercial part-time farmers and 1,770 quarts for the white noncommercial part-time farmers (appendix table 20). However, only two-thirds of the whites and ·one-fourth of the Negroes who had cows made any butter (appendix table 21), the amounts averaging 3 pounds a week for the whites and less than 2 pounds for the Negroes. Only nine of the white noncommercial part-time farmers sold dairy products.

Most of the white commercial group produced roughage, averaging 11 tons (appendix table 23). Few of the white noncommercial or the Negro part-time farmers produced roughage and when they did it was in such small quantities that they had to purchase additional feed for their cows. The pasture season is quite long in this area, but the soil does not produce good pasturage.

Poultry Products

Over four-fifths of the white noncommercial part-time farmers and 70 percent of the Negro part-time farmers had poultry, the most common size of flocks being from 10 to 30 birds (appendix table 11). The flocks of the white commercial group were somewhat larger than those of the white noncommercial group and egg and meat production was more than twice as high; consumption by the former averaged 152 dozen eggs and 117 pounds of dressed poultry in 1934, and that by the latter averaged 84 dozen eggs and 67 pounds of dressed poultry (appendix tables 18 and 19). Nearly all of the flocks of the Negroes contained less than 20 birds, which produced an average of only 47 dozen eggs. Consumption of home-produced poultry by the Negroes averaged less than one chicken a month.

Pork

Two-fifths of the white and one-sixth of the Negro part-time farm families raised pork for their own use. Home-grown pork was a fairly important contribution to the living of these families, the consumption or storage being 531 pounds in 1934 for white commercial part-time farmers, 306 pounds for the white noncommercial part-time farmers, and 230 pounds for the Negro part-time farmers (appendix table 22).

Fuel

Only 21 of the white and 16 of the Negro part-time farmers had some woodland and cut fuel for their own use. Six other whites and thirty-seven other Negroes were able to cut wood in nearby woodlots. The quantity used ranged from 5 to 15 cords.

Fish

The Negro part-time farmers who lived on the islands in the south-western part of the county had favorable opportunities for fishing close at hand. Seventeen Negro families on Wadmalaw Island reported catching fish for home use throughout the year, the quantities ranging from 20 to 500 pounds per family. In addition, each of these families reported gathering oysters for home use in the winter months, the quantities ranging from 4 to 50 bushels. Sea food was thus an important item in the living of these families.

Cash Receipts and Cash Expenses

Only 21 of the white noncommercial part-time farmers sold farm products, the average being $30 (appendix table 25). Dairy products accounted for 71 percent of the sales. Cash expenses were in most cases in excess of cash receipts. On the average, however, those who sold over $50 worth of farm products more than covered cash expenses exclusive of rent and taxes. Comparatively, the Negroes did somewhat better; 56 percent sold some products, and though the average cash receipts were only $38, all who sold anything more than covered expenses. For the 62 who sold no products, cash expenses, exclusive of rent and taxes, averaged only $7. Expenses of the whites averaged $62 and of the Negroes $26.

Value and Tenure of Part-Time Farms

One-half of the white and two-fifths of the Negro part-time farmers owned their homes (appendix table 7). The real estate of owners was of considerably greater value than that leased by tenants, averaging approximately twice as high for the noncommercial whites and Negroes, and 68 percent higher for the commercial whites. The acreage operated by white owners and tenants was approximately the same, the difference in real estate value being accounted for largely by more buildings and better homes for the owners. Negro owners had larger farms than did the tenants, the averages being 9 and 4 acres, respectively.

There was a great difference in real estate values between the whites and Negroes. Average values of white part-time farms ranged from $2,293 for noncommercial tenants and $4,400 for noncommercial owners to $4,584 for commercial tenants and $7,705 for commercial owners, while those for Negroes averaged $599 for tenants and $1,242 for owners (table 17, page 12).

Investment in implements and machinery was not an important item for any except white commercial part-time farmers. Three-fourths of the white noncommercial group and one-half of the Negroes had only small hand tools. The average cost for those having implements and machinery was only $33 for the white noncommercial farmers and $35 for the Negroes (appendix table 10).

Two-thirds of the white owners held their farms free of debt (appendix table 8). The owners of commercial part-time farms with debts had a much larger average mortgage indebtedness than did the owners of noncommercial part-time farms. For the noncommercial group, the total mortgage indebtedness of owners who were in debt averaged $466. Only five of the white tenants reported any mortgage indebtedness. The indebtedness for these few averaged $235.

Only 44 percent of the Negro owners reported any mortgage indebtedness, and the amount reported by those who were in debt averaged $99. Among the tenants, 14 percent reported mortgage indebtedness averaging $42.

White owners earned more at employment off the farm than did tenants, but the reverse was true for Negroes employed in agriculture. For Negroes employed in some industry other than agriculture, earnings away from the home farm averaged the same for owners and tenants (table 99).

Table 99.—Earnings at Off-the-Farm Employment of Heads of Households in the Atlantic Coast Subregion, by Type of Farm, by Tenure, and by Color, 1934

Type of farm, tenure, and color	Number of cases	Average earnings
WHITE		
Commercial part-time farm owners	13	$1, 223
Commercial part-time farm tenants	11	856
Noncommercial part-time farm owners	22	1, 040
Noncommercial part-time farm tenants	25	656
NEGRO		
Owners employed in agriculture	[1] 33	90
Tenants employed in agriculture	[1] 57	141
Owners employed in nonagriculture	20	331
Tenants employed in nonagriculture	28	326

[1] The actual earnings of 2 owners and 2 tenants were unknown.

Labor Requirements of Part-Time Farms and Their Relation to Working Hours in Industry

On commercial part-time farms, members of the household averaged about 6 hours of work per day during the busy season, of which roughly three-fourths was by the head (table 48, page 32). About half of this group had full-time jobs, and all but three commercial farmers hired outside labor (appendix table 26). On the noncommercial part-time farms, the average number of hours worked by all members was 4 hours a day in spring and early summer, divided fairly equally between the head and other members of the household (table 48, page 32, and appendix table 27).

Almost half of the household heads in the noncommercial group worked at industries in which the 8-hour day prevailed, thus having plenty of time for farm work. The remainder, employed for the most part in agriculture or service industries, worked longer hours but apparently found sufficient time for work on the farm.

Among the Negro part-time farmers, the average number of hours spent by all members of the household was larger than that spent by the white commercial part-time group from April through June. The large amount of time relative to the size of the enterprises was due to the fact that a few had sufficient acreage in truck or cotton crops to employ considerable labor. The members of the family other than the head did well over half of the work. In the rural areas, all members of the family worked as laborers on commercial farms. Hence, an abundance of family labor accustomed to farm work was available on most part-time farms. Negroes employed in industry worked only 8 hours per day, those on truck farms 10 hours; but all considered that they had ample time for their own farming operations.

EMPLOYMENT AND EARNINGS IN INDUSTRY

White workers in the industries of Charleston were largely skilled or semiskilled workers and foremen. Steady employment was the rule for those workers who had jobs, with the exception of those engaged in the building industry. Even in such a seasonal industry as fertilizer manufacture, white workers were regularly employed throughout 1934. The high proportion of skilled workers resulted in higher average earnings than those which prevailed in the Textile Subregion.

Only nine white agricultural laborers were found, but low wages and irregular employment placed them on an economic level definitely below that of the other part-time farmers. The commercial part-time farmers, on the other hand, were on an income level definitely above that of the other part-time farmers. About half of them had part-time jobs which frequently paid high hourly rates. Only the white noncommercial part-time farmers with off-the-farm employment in agriculture are included in this section.[13]

Negro workers in Charleston County were largely laborers on truck farms and unskilled workers in Charleston industries. Both groups had extremely low annual earnings due to irregular employment and low wage rates. The farm laborers, who received even lower wages than did the urban workers, have not been included in the text tables for this section.

The Industrial Group

A group of 103 white nonfarming industrial workers was included in the study for comparative purposes. The term "industrial workers" covers a large group of individuals of widely varying incomes and social status. For the purposes of this study, it would have been desirable to select a few homogeneous groups of workers employed in the same industries as were the part-time farmers. However, in Charleston white part-time farmers were distributed throughout many small industries rather than concentrated in a few large ones. The enumerators were instructed to take approximately 100 schedules from workers in industries other than forestry, sawmills, and woodworking.

For comparison with the Negro part-time farmers, 105 Negro industrial workers who did no farming were included in the study. However, there were certain differences between the farming and nonfarming groups with respect to the industries in which they were employed that must be kept in mind in making any comparison of incomes. In the first place, most of the Negro part-time farmers in Charleston County were truck-farm laborers who, in addition to this work which was of a more or less irregular nature, operated small farms of their own. Farm laborers who did no farming on their own account were not included. It was found that some types of urban workers, such as longshoremen and those engaged in domestic and personal service, rarely undertake part-time farming, because their work is such that they must live in the city where there is little or no land

---

[13] For distribution of all workers, see appendix table 29 ff.

available for gardening. The few Negroes employed in rural industries were on a definitely lower income level than those in the urban industries.

Industry and Occupation of Heads of White Households

The white part-time farmers were selected without any regard to the industry in which they worked. Table 100 gives the distribution by industries of the white noncommercial part-time farmers and of the nonfarming industrial workers. The part-time farm group was subdivided into those who were employed in industries of a distinctly rural nature, such as operating country stores and driving school buses, and those who were employed in urban industries. This was done because the former group was distinctly different from the industrial workers with respect to employment and income, while the latter group was roughly similar, except for the large group of 42 workers in the asbestos factory. No part-time farmers were found who were employed in that plant.

Table 100.—Industry of Heads of White Noncommercial Part-Time Farm and Nonfarming Industrial Households in the Atlantic Coast Subregion, 1934

Industry of head	Part-time farmers [1]		Nonfarming industrial workers
	Rural industries	Urban industries	
Total	10	29	103
Manufacturing and mechanical industries:			
Building	1	1	2
Cigar and tobacco factories	—	1	3
Food and allied	1	—	—
Iron and steel	—	3	7
Saw and planing mills	1	1	—
Printing, publishing, and engraving	—	—	2
Textile	—	1	2
Electric light and power	—	2	4
Fertilizer factories	—	1	1
Other chemical factories	—	4	3
Asbestos products	—	—	42
Other manufacturing and mechanical	—	—	1
Transportation and communication:			
Construction and maintenance of streets	2	—	—
Steam and street railroads	—	5	5
Other transportation and communication	1	3	5
Trade:			
Automobile agencies and filling stations	—	—	2
Wholesale and retail trade	4	5	9
Other trade	—	—	1
Public service	—	2	12
Domestic and personal service	—	—	2

[1] Exclusive of 8 white noncommercial farmers with off-the-farm employment in agriculture.

The principal difference in occupational levels between the part-time farm and nonfarm groups in urban industries was in the higher proportion of clerical and semiskilled workers in the nonfarm group (table 101 and appendix table 30). Most of the latter were employed in the asbestos factory. On the other hand, a larger proportion of the part-time farmers were skilled workers.

Table 101.—Occupation of Heads of White Noncommercial Part-Time Farm and Nonfarming Industrial Households in the Atlantic Coast Subregion, 1934

Occupation of head	Part-time farmers		Nonfarming industrial workers
	Rural industries	Urban industries	
Total	10	29	103
Proprietary	3	2	1
Clerical	1	—	13
Skilled	2	15	33
Semiskilled	4	9	49
Unskilled	—	3	7

Industry and Occupation of Heads of Negro Households

Most of the Negro part-time farmers with employment in urban industries worked in the fertilizer factories or in transportation (table 102). These two industries, together with trade and domestic and personal service, accounted for the majority of the nonfarming industrial workers.

Table 102.—Industry of Heads of Negro Part-Time Farm and Nonfarming Industrial Households in the Atlantic Coast Subregion, 1934

Industry of head	Part-time farmers[1]		Nonfarming industrial workers
	Rural industries	Urban industries	
Total	13	35	105
Fishing	1	—	—
Manufacturing and mechanical industries:			
Building	5	—	9
Cigar and tobacco factories	—	—	2
Food and allied	—	—	3
Iron and steel	—	—	1
Lumber	—	2	—
Printing, publishing, and engraving	—	1	—
Textile	—	—	3
Electric light and power	—	—	2
Independent hand trades	—	—	1
Fertilizer factories	—	14	17
Other chemical factories	—	—	4
Other manufacturing and mechanical	—	3	2
Transportation and communication:			
Construction and maintenance of streets	4	—	1
Steam and street railroads	—	10	2
Other transportation and communication	—	2	29
Trade:			
Wholesale and retail trade	1	—	11
Other trade	1	—	—
Public service	—	3	2
Professional service	—	—	2
Domestic and personal service	1	—	12
Industry not specified	—	—	2

[1] Exclusive of 94 Negro part-time farmers engaged in agriculture, mostly as farm laborers.

The Negro nonfarming industrial group had a somewhat higher proportion of skilled and semiskilled workers than did part-time farmers in nonagricultural occupations (table 103). The more highly skilled nonfarming industrial workers included carpenters, blacksmiths, bakers, and brickmasons. All except three of the part-time farmers engaged in agriculture were farm laborers.

Table 103.—Occupation of Heads of Negro Part-Time Farm and Nonfarming Industrial Households in the Atlantic Coast Subregion, 1934

Occupation of head	Part-time farmers			Nonfarming industrial workers
	Agriculture	Rural industries	Urban industries	
Total_____	94	13	35	105
Proprietary_____	—	1	—	3
Clerical_____	—	1	—	1
Skilled_____	3	2	1	12
Semiskilled_____	—	1	5	23
Unskilled:				
Farm laborer_____	91	—	—	—
Servant_____	—	—	2	13
Other unskilled_____	—	8	27	53

Earnings of Heads of White Households

The total annual earnings of white noncommercial part-time farmers employed in urban industries averaged about the same as those of the nonfarm group. These part-time farmers in general received slightly higher hourly rates, because there were proportionately more skilled workers among them. However, this was offset by the fact that they worked fewer days. The greater average time worked by the white nonfarming industrial group is partly explained by the inclusion of several city fire department employees who worked 7 days a week throughout the year. The white noncommercial part-time farmers working in rural industries received lower pay, worked fewer days, and earned considerably less money than did the other two groups (tables 104, 105, and 106, and appendix tables 32 and 34).

Table 104.—Rate of Pay [1] of Heads of White Noncommercial Part-Time Farm and Nonfarming Industrial Households in the Atlantic Coast Subregion, 1934

Hourly rate of pay	Part-time farmers		Nonfarming industrial workers
	Rural industries	Urban industries	
Total_____	10	29	103
10 to 19 cents_____	1	1	1
20 to 29 cents_____	5	3	8
30 to 39 cents_____	2	1	36
40 to 49 cents_____	1	5	16
50 to 59 cents_____	—	7	18
60 to 69 cents_____	—	6	8
70 to 79 cents_____	—	2	7
80 to 89 cents_____	—	2	5
90 to 99 cents_____	—	2	3
$1.00 or more_____	1	—	1
Average hourly rate of pay_____	$0. 36	$0. 54	$0. 48

[1] At principal off-the-farm employment (job with the largest earnings).

Table 105.—Number of Days Heads of White Noncommercial Part-Time Farm and Nonfarming Industrial Households in the Atlantic Coast Subregion Were Employed off the Farm,[1] 1934

Number of days employed off the farm	Part-time farmers		Nonfarming industrial workers
	Rural industries	Urban industries	
	10	29	103
Total_____	3	4	3
50 to 99 days_____	—	1	3
100 to 149 days_____	2	2	13
150 to 199 days_____	—	9	11
200 to 249 days_____	2	7	38
250 to 299 days_____	3	6	35
300 days or more_____			
Average days employed_____	215	230	261

[1] At principal off-the-farm employment (job with the largest earnings).

Table 106.—Earnings [1] From Industrial Employment of Heads of White Noncommercial Part-Time Farm and Nonfarming Industrial Households in the Atlantic Coast Subregion, 1934

Earnings from industrial employment	Part-time farmers		Nonfarming industrial workers
	Rural industries	Urban industries	
	10	29	103
Total_____	2	2	1
$100 to $249_____	2	3	10
$250 to $499_____	2	4	14
$500 to $749_____	3	6	30
$750 to $999_____	1	2	21
$1,000 to $1,249_____		5	13
$1,250 to $1,499_____	—	6	11
$1,500 to $1,999_____	—	1	3
$2,000 or more_____			
Average earnings_____	$588	$1,058	$1,020

[1] At principal off-the-farm employment (job with the largest earnings).

Earnings of Heads of Negro Households

There was a slight difference in wage earnings between the Negro nonfarming industrial workers and the Negro part-time farmers in urban industries. Both of these groups were at a distinctly higher earning level than the rural Negroes (table 107 and appendix table 34). The difference in average cash earnings of part-time farmers employed as farm laborers and those employed at other rural jobs is partially but not entirely offset by the fact that the former frequently had the use of a house and a small piece of land rent-free.

The low annual earnings of the rural Negroes were due partly to the small number of days they were employed, but even more to the low rates of pay—an average of 8 cents an hour for those in agriculture and 14 cents an hour for those in rural industries (table 108 and appendix table 32). The Negro part-time farmers worked an average of 144 days in 1934 and the nonfarming industrial workers were employed off the farm an average of 173 days (table 109). Employment for all groups was irregular and subject to seasonal fluctuations.

Table 107.—Earnings [1] From Industrial Employment of Heads of Negro Part-Time Farm and Nonfarming Industrial Households in the Atlantic Coast Subregion, 1934

Earnings from industrial employment	Part-time farmers			Nonfarming industrial workers
	Agriculture	Rural industries	Urban industries	
Total	[2] 90	13	35	105
$1 to $99	47	4	5	5
$100 to $249	37	5	11	25
$250 to $499	6	4	12	50
$500 to $749	—	—	4	19
$750 to $999	—	—	—	3
$1,000 to $1,249	—	—	3	1
$1,250 to $1,499	—	—	—	1
$1,500 to $1,999	—	—	—	—
Average earnings	$116	$171	$352	$388

[1] At principal off-the-farm employment (job with the largest earnings).
[2] Excludes 4 cases in which Negro farm laborers worked with a mule or horse. Only the total earnings of this combination were reported.

Table 108.—Rate of Pay [1] of Heads of Negro Part-Time Farm and Nonfarming Industrial Households in the Atlantic Coast Subregion, 1934

Hourly rate of pay	Part-time farmers			Nonfarming industrial workers
	Agriculture	Rural industries	Urban industries	
Total	[2] 90	13	35	105
Less than 10 cents	68	4	1	—
10 to 19 cents	22	7	9	27
20 to 29 cents	—	1	20	51
30 to 39 cents	—	—	3	17
40 to 49 cents	—	1	—	5
50 to 59 cents	—	—	1	2
60 to 69 cents	—	—	1	2
70 to 79 cents	—	—	—	1
Average hourly rate of pay	[3] $0.08	$0.14	$0.25	$0.25

[1] At principal off-the-farm employment (job with the largest earnings).
[2] Excludes 4 Negro farm laborers who worked with a mule or horse. Only the total earnings of this combination were reported.
[3] This does not include rent of house and land which were frequently furnished by employers.

Table 109.—Number of Days Heads of Negro Part-Time Farm and Nonfarming Industrial Households in the Atlantic Coast Subregion Were Employed off the Farm,[1] 1934

Number of days employed off the farm	Part-time farmers			Nonfarming industrial workers
	Agriculture	Rural industries	Urban industries	
Total	94	13	35	105
50 to 99 days	28	2	11	24
100 to 149 days	32	4	8	19
150 to 199 days	16	2	1	15
200 to 249 days	11	2	6	14
250 to 299 days	2	2	6	11
300 days or more	5	1	3	22
Average days employed	144	173	170	189

[1] At principal off-the-farm employment (job with the largest earnings)

Total Cash Income of White Households

In white households, cash income other than earnings of the head was in nearly all cases derived from earnings of other members of the family. In over three-quarters of the cases, however, there was no member of the family employed except the head (table 8, page 4, and appendix table 35). There were very few cases of income from investments or other sources.

The average total family incomes of the noncommercial part-time farm group in urban industries and the nonfarm group were about the same (table 110). Per capita incomes of the part-time farm families averaged somewhat less than those of the industrial workers because of the higher proportion of large families in the former group.

Table 110.—Cash Income From Nonfarm Sources of White Noncommercial Part-Time Farm and Nonfarming Industrial Households in the Atlantic Coast Subregion, by Size of Household, 1934

Size of household	Part-time farm households in urban industries		Nonfarming industrial households	
	Number of cases	Income per capita	Number of cases	Income per capita
Total	29	$222	103	$265
1 to 3 persons	8	451	30	422
4 to 5 persons	7	312	40	269
6 to 7 persons	7	176	22	192
8 persons or more	7	150	11	218
Average income per household	$1,264		$1,244	

Total Cash Income of Negro Households

The average family cash income and income per capita for all sizes of Negro families were lower for the part-time farmers in urban industries than for the nonfarming industrial workers (table 111). In both

Table 111.—Cash Income From Nonfarm Sources of Negro Part-Time Farm and Nonfarming Industrial Households in the Atlantic Coast Subregion, by Size of Household, 1934

Size of household	Part-time farm households						Nonfarming industrial households	
	Agriculture		Rural industries		Urban industries			
	Number of cases	Income per capita	Number of cases	Income per capita	Number of cases	Income per capita	Number of cases	Income per capita
Total	94	$39	13	$44	35	$79	105	$127
1 to 3 persons	30	72	4	84	12	149	54	173
4 to 5 persons	23	47	4	59	9	86	32	108
6 persons or more	41	29	5	26	14	55	19	98
Average income per household	[1] $206		$223		$411		$503	

[1] This does not include rent of house and land which were frequently furnished by employers.

of these groups half of the families had some member other than the head working (appendix table 35) and the average number employed per household was the same, but these other members in the nonfarm group earned more. The part-time farm families more frequently lived in rural areas where their members could secure employment only as farm laborers or at other jobs paying low wages. The differences in earnings per capita were further increased by the fact that the part-time farm group included a higher proportion of large families than did the nonfarming industrial group.

Among the three part-time farm groups, average incomes per household show approximately the same relationships as average earnings for heads. The group of farm laborers' households is raised slightly relative to the other two groups by the fact that more members were employed.

LIVING CONDITIONS AND ORGANIZED SOCIAL LIFE

The geography of Charleston County is such that little land for farming is available except at some distance from the city of Charleston. Two-thirds of the white part-time farmers studied lived in the open country, most of them on the peninsula north of the city but a few on the islands south of the Ashley River (table 62, page 51). This means that many of the white part-time farmers have had to forego certain living facilities that are available to the city dweller. The nonfarm group, on the other hand, lived in the city or in the village of the asbestos company at North Charleston. Rural-urban differences between the living conditions of the two white groups are evident in the data which follow.[14]

Living conditions of both part-time farm and nonfarming industrial Negro workers reflected their small incomes. Ninety percent of the part-time farmers lived in the open country. In spite of the lower incomes of the farm laborers, their living conditions were about the same as those of the other part-time farmers; hence, in the following discussion, all part-time farmers are treated as a single group. The differences between this group and the nonfarming industrial workers are typical of the differences between rural Negroes and city Negroes in the South. The industrial workers lived in the city except for a small group of fertilizer workers who lived in villages just north of the city limits.

Housing of White Households

Although a considerable number of the dwellings of white households were reported as needing paint and minor repairs, most of them were in fairly good condition. Only 1 out of 5 houses in both groups

---

[14] Because of differences in living conditions as a result of differences in economic status, pointed out in the preceding section, white commercial farmers and white noncommercial farmers with off-the-farm employment in agriculture are omitted from most of the analysis.

needed roof repairs and 1 out of 7 part-time farm houses, as compared with 1 out of 20 nonfarm houses, was in need of general structural repairs (appendix table 40). The dwellings of noncommercial part-time farmers were somewhat larger on the average than those of nonfarmers (appendix table 38).

Dwellings of white part-time farmers showed considerable variation. Two extreme cases may be cited to show the range of conditions. A six-room frame house for a family of six, constructed in 1932, in excellent repair and with electric lights, running water, and bath, was somewhat above the average. A three-room frame house, also occupied by a family of six, constructed in 1885, with rotting porch, no paint, and no modern conveniences, was below the average. Some houses had been constructed recently, but a number of them had never been completed. Many lacked paint, partitions, porch flooring, etc. Approximately half of the white noncommercial part-time farm families had electric lights, running water, and bath facilities (appendix table 41).

There was less variation in the condition of dwellings of white industrial workers. Typical families lived in four-room apartments of two-family houses or in four-room bungalows. Practically all dwellings of white nonfarming industrial workers had such conveniences as electric lights, running water, and bathrooms.

Housing of Negro Households

The typical Negro part-time farm dwelling was a two-, three-, or four-room shack, unpainted, unplastered, with leaky roof, no windows, and otherwise in poor condition. Only 1 out of 18 part-time farm families lived in homes which needed no repairs, as against 1 in 5 of the nonfarming industrial families (appendix table 40). However, industrial workers lived mainly in congested tenements, in some cases with as many as 10 persons in 2 or 3 rooms. Negro homes in Charleston are not segregated from those of the whites, but are fairly well distributed throughout the poorer sections of the city. Some of the houses occupied by several Negro families were once residences of wealthy white families. Many of these houses were in need of porch repairs and paint, and few had any screens. The roofs, however, were usually in good condition, and the houses had been plastered, although the plaster was usually dirty and cracked. In certain sections of Charleston, the older houses were interspersed with rows of Negro shacks constructed of slab lumber and unplastered. With respect to size of dwelling, there was little difference between the part-time farm and nonfarming industrial groups (appendix table 38).

Nearly all of the Negro nonfarming industrial workers had running water, but in many cases it came from a faucet situated in the yard or court, which frequently supplied several families. Only 1 out of 4 industrial workers' homes had electric lights, and only 1 out of 10 had a bathroom. In some cases, the houses were wired for electricity, but it was not utilized either because of the occupant's inability or his unwillingness to pay the electric bills. Bathrooms with running water were extremely rare in Negro homes. In most cases, toilet facilities were provided by a small house in the yard, resembling a privy but connected with the city sewerage, and utilized by several families. Only one Negro part-time farmer had electric lights, and only four had running water (appendix table 41).

Automobiles, Radios, and Telephones

Among the whites, automobiles were more frequently owned by noncommercial part-time farmers than by nonfarming industrial workers, largely because of their need of some means of transportation to work (appendix table 42). Twenty-six of the entire group of noncommercial part-time farmers [15] lived 2½ miles or more from their places of employment; the average was more than 4 miles (appendix table 28). Practically all of those engaged in urban industries drove to work in their own automobiles. Slightly more than one-half of both the noncommercial farm and the nonfarm groups had radios, while few members of either group had telephones.

Few Negro workers had automobiles, radios, or telephones. Ten of the Negro nonfarming industrial workers had radios, two had automobiles, and three had telephones. None of the Negro part-time farmers had telephones, and only one part-time farmer had a radio. Eighteen part-time farmers, including six farm laborers, owned automobiles. The cars, however, were usually 7 to 10 years old, three were not in running order, and in only two cases were they used in driving to work.

Home Ownership

Home ownership was much more common among white noncommercial part-time farm than among nonfarming industrial households. The numbers owning their homes were 22 and 16, respectively (appendix table 43), all of the part-time farm owners being engaged in nonagriculture. Part-time farm tenants effected a substantial saving in rent by living outside of the city. Their average annual rent amounted to $114, as against $225 paid by nonfarming industrial households living in the city.

Home ownership was fairly common among Negro part-time farmers, but was infrequent among nonfarming industrial workers. About 40 percent of the part-time farmers owned their own homes as against 6 percent of the nonfarming industrial workers. The average amount of rent paid was $42 per year for part-time farmers engaged in industry, as against $95 for nonfarming industrial workers living

---

[15] All of whom were engaged in nonagriculture.

in the city. As previously stated, the Negro farm laborers were frequently furnished with a house and plot of land rent-free by their employers.

Education

The opportunities for securing an education were approximately the same for children of white noncommercial part-time farmers and of white nonfarming industrial workers. There were only two one-teacher elementary schools for whites left in the county.[16] The term was 9 months for all schools. School buses were commonly used to transport rural children to both elementary and high schools. Children 7–16 years of age in the part-time farm group had made approximately normal progress in school, while those in the non-farming industrial group were retarded 1 year on the average (table 76, page 64). All children of these ages in the part-time farm group were in school, as were all but three of the children of nonfarming industrial workers (table 75, page 63).

About one-third of the heads of both white noncommercial part-time farm and white nonfarming industrial households had attended high school (appendix table 46). On the average, both groups had nearly completed grade school.

All of the industrial workers and most of the noncommercial part-time farmers had library service available (table 78, page 66). Charleston was one of the three counties in South Carolina having a county-wide library service.[17] Books were provided for nearly all of the white population of the county, including all children in school.

Negroes living in the country were at a decided disadvantage with respect to securing an education. Most rural elementary schools were one- and two-teacher schools having terms of 6 months or less.[18] All city schools had 9-month terms. There were only two Negro high schools in the county: one in Charleston and the other in Lincoln-ville. The Lincolnville High School, which had only 89 students, was located in a remote corner of the county, more accessible to parts of Dorchester and Berkeley Counties than to Charleston County.

Children of Negro part-time farm households showed an average retardation in school of 3 years (−3.3 for farm laborers and −2.9 for other part-time farmers) as compared to an average retardation of almost 2½ years for the nonfarming industrial group (table 76, page 64). This reflects the meager educational facilities provided for Negro children in rural areas. A total of 41 out of 215 children of Negro part-time farmers between the ages of 7 and 16 did not attend school

---

[16] *Annual Report of the State Superintendent of Education of South Carolina, 1934.*

[17] Frayser, Mary E., *The Libraries of South Carolina*, Bulletin 292, South Carolina Agricultural Experiment Station, 1933.

[18] *Annual Report of the State Superintendent of Education of South Carolina, 1934.*

during 1933-34, as compared to only 7 out of a total of 87 children in the nonfarming industrial group. Two children of each group were employed, but most of the remainder were too young to secure employment (table 75, page 63).

Heads of Negro households also were handicapped by a lack of schooling. Thirty-five percent of the Negro part-time farmers and twenty-five percent of the nonfarming industrial workers reported no school attendance (appendix table 46). On the average, Negro part-time farmers had completed two grades as compared to four grades for the nonfarming industrial workers.

Libraries were not reported as being available to Negro part-time farm families (table 78, page 66). Although libraries were accessible to 82 of the nonfarming industrial Negroes, most of whom lived in the city, only 17 reported making any use of them. A limited number of books from the county circulating library were available to the Negro elementary schools but not to the high schools.[19]

Social Participation

Church and Sunday School were accessible to all families, white and Negro, and members of nearly all households attended one or both of these organizations (appendix table 48). Adult church organizations and young people's organizations were available to nearly all white and Negro nonfarming industrial households and to somewhat fewer of the white noncommercial part-time farm households. But attendance by part-time farm families was as great as that by nonfarm families among the whites and, in the case of Negroes, it was greater. Of the organizations not centered around the church, Parent-Teacher Associations and fraternal orders were most important for white families. Such organizations as Boy Scouts and Girl Scouts were rarely found in the country although they were frequently available for white children in the city. However, the children of only five white nonfarming industrial and two white part-time farm families were members of these organizations. Except for railroad workers, labor unions were not an important factor in Charleston. A Farm Bureau, agricultural cooperatives, and 4–H Clubs were not reported, indicating that the white noncommercial and the Negro part-time farm families had no contact with the Agricultural Extension Service.

Although white noncommercial part-time farm households had fewer social organizations available, they took advantage of them to a greater extent than did white nonfarming industrial households. The average number of times of attendance per person at all organizations in 1934 was 61 and 56, respectively, for the 2 groups. Negro attendances per person in 1934 averaged 63 times for the nonfarming industrial households, and 55 times for the part-time farm households (table 80, page 68).

---

[19] Frayser, Mary E., *op. cit.*

RELIEF

The number of Charleston County cases receiving relief among the groups studied was so small (appendix table 36) and the circumstances surrounding the cases so diverse that relief data afforded no direct evidence as to the value of part-time farming in keeping families off relief.   There was no significant difference between part-time farmers and nonfarming industrial workers in amount of relief allowances. However, consideration of the value of the contribution of many of the part-time farms indicated that by producing some of their own food a number of families may have kept themselves off the relief rolls or may have reduced the amount of relief needed.

A rehabilitation program for the relief population involving part-time farming must depend on recovery or expansion of the urban industries to provide the necessary jobs, since the existing rural industries employ very few workers and the establishment of others is not probable.   Such recovery or expansion is likely to be slow (see page 149).

Even if industry were stimulated in Charleston, there would be enough labor to fill a considerably increased demand without going outside of the city proper.   In March 1935, there were 7,900 persons eligible for employment on the Charleston County relief rolls.[20]

The possibilities for rehabilitation of relief clients in this subregion by the part-time farming method appear limited.   Part-time farmers can produce a considerable portion of their household food, but a cash income is needed to secure the other necessities which must be purchased.   Hence, it is essential that these people have some industrial employment.   It cannot be assumed that any group that may be selected and provided with small farms will be able to obtain jobs for themselves in private industry.   Skilled workers in one of the urban industries would have the best chance of getting a job.   Unskilled workers, located at any considerable distance from places of employment, would be greatly handicapped in the keen competition for such work as may be available.

Another consideration is whether or not relief families would be successful in carrying on small-scale farming operations.   Those with a farm background and reasonable amounts of energy and initiative would have a good chance of being successful, although it is likely that, as a rule, they would require some supervision.

---

[20] *Workers on Relief in the United States in March 1935, A Census of Usual Occupations* (in preparation), Division of Social Research, Works Progress Administration, 1937, table VII.

Chapter IV

THE LUMBER SUBREGION OF ALABAMA, GEORGIA, AND SOUTH CAROLINA

GENERAL FEATURES OF THE SUBREGION AND OF SUMTER COUNTY

THE AREA designated as the Lumber Subregion is a large and rather heterogeneous region covering about one-third of Alabama, Georgia, and South Carolina (figure 2, page XXIV). It is a region of farms and forests, but is primarily agricultural, approximately two-thirds of the gainfully occupied persons being engaged in farming (table 112). The lumber industry is a much less important source of employment than is agriculture, but it is the only important manufacturing industry. Since the principal virgin forests have been removed, lumbering has been carried on in only a limited way in much of this area as well as other parts of the Southeast. Scattered throughout this area are villages, towns, and small cities which serve principally as centers of trading and transportation and of the wood products industries.

Sumter County

Sumter County, located in central South Carolina, was selected for the field study because it is in general similar to the rest of the subregion with respect to industry, and because the 1930 Census indicated that it has a large number of part-time farms as compared with other counties of the subregion.

The county is representative with respect to agriculture of the type of farming area designated in figure 3 (page XXVI) as the "Eastern coastal plain and sand hills." This area is located chiefly in the eastern portion of the Lumber Subregion but also extends into the Naval Stores Subregion.

Table 112.—Distribution of Persons, 10 Years Old and Over, Gainfully Occupied in the Lumber Subregion and in Sumter County, South Carolina, 1930

Industry	Lumber Subregion (excluding Macon, Georgia)		Sumter County, South Carolina	
	Number	Percent	Number	Percent
Total population	2,104,888		45,902	
Total gainfully employed	828,723	100.0	18,286	100.0
Agriculture	564,493	68.1	10,182	55.6
Service industries	174,874	21.1	5,336	29.2
Manufacturing and allied industries	89,356	10.8	2,768	15.2
Total manufacturing and allied industries	89,356	100.0	2,768	100.0
Forestry and fishing	6,324	7.1	133	4.8
Coal mines	610	0.7	—	—
Other extraction of minerals	1,706	1.9	9	0.3
Building	9,987	11.1	398	14.4
Chemical and allied	1,863	2.1	55	2.0
Clay, glass, and stone	1,279	1.4	50	1.8
Clothing	521	0.6	25	0.9
Food and allied	3,289	3.7	180	6.5
Automobile factories and repair shops	2,732	3.1	137	4.9
Iron and steel	2,514	2.8	146	5.3
Saw and planing mills	34,388	38.4	809	29.2
Other wood and furniture	3,765	4.2	489	17.7
Paper, printing, and allied	1,315	1.5	21	0.8
Cotton mills	7,051	7.9	6	0.2
Knitting mills	766	0.9	39	1.4
Other textile	740	0.8	8	0.3
Independent hand trades	3,225	3.6	86	3.1
Other manufacturing	7,281	8.2	177	6.4

Source: *Fifteenth Census of the United States: 1930,* Population Vol. III.

Population

The population of Sumter County, 46,000 in 1930, was entirely rural with the exception of 12,000 in the city of Sumter. Slightly more than one-half (56 percent) of the population of the city was white in 1930, but the rural population was predominantly Negro (76 percent).[1] The city, which serves as a trading center for the county and also carries on some manufacturing, based chiefly upon the products of the forests of nearby areas, has grown steadily since 1880 when its population was about 2,000. From 1910 to 1930, the population of the township of Sumter, which includes the city, increased 42 percent, while that of the remainder of the county (making allowance for changes in boundaries) decreased slightly.

Agricultural Features

Sumter County is located partly in the sand hills and partly in the coastal plain. The western portion of the county is representative of the sand hills while the remainder is fairly level country with sand and sandy loam soils interspersed with swampy areas along the rivers and streams. The county was originally covered with forests, but

[1] *Fifteenth Census of the United States: 1930,* Population Vol. III, Part 2, pp. 794 and 795.

clearing the land for farming began at an early date.[2] In 1935, 69 percent of the land area of the county was in farms.[3] Most of the remainder was forest land, and in addition 41 percent of the land in farms was woodland.

Cotton became the chief crop shortly after the Civil War and has been the chief source of income since that time. Of the land in farms, 45 percent was in crops harvested in 1934, and 31 percent of the cropland harvested was in cotton. In 1929, the last year for which income data are available, 59 percent of the farm income was from the sale of cotton and cottonseed.[4] In that year, 73 percent of the farms were classified as cotton farms. The next most important cash crop, tobacco, accounted for 9 percent of the farm income.

Cotton farming in Sumter County received a severe setback in the early twenties as a result of the ravages of the boll weevil.[5] The number of farms decreased 20 percent from 1920 to 1930 but increased 3 percent between 1930 and 1935. The acreage of land in farms increased 27 percent during this 5-year period. Cotton acreage declined, but there was an increase in the number of livestock and in the acreage of feed crops.

There is a great diversity in the form of land tenure of the rural population of the county.[6] According to the 1935 Census, 602 white owners and managers operated 34 percent of the total cropland harvested, 612 white croppers and other tenants operated 19 percent, 474 Negro owners and managers operated 9 percent, and 2,382 Negro croppers and other tenants operated 38 percent. Thus, there is a tendency for the farm lands to be concentrated in the hands of the white owners.

Industry

In general, Sumter County is similar to the rest of the subregion with respect to type of industry, but there are some differences. The proportion of workers engaged in nonagricultural pursuits is somewhat higher in the county than in the subregion as a whole (table 112). While the principal manufacturing industries of both Sumter County and the subregion belong to the forest products group, the county has relatively more woodworking plants, as distinguished from sawmills, than has the subregion generally. The

---

[2] Bennett, Frank and Others, *Soil Survey of Sumter County, South Carolina*, U. S. Department of Agriculture, Bureau of Soils, 1908, p. 8.

[3] *United States Census of Agriculture: 1935.*

[4] *Fifteenth Census of the United States: 1930*, Agriculture Vol. II, Part 2, pp. 69 and 73; Vol. III, Part 2, p. 313; and *Yearbook of Agriculture: 1932*, p. 661.

[5] The *United States Census of Agriculture: 1925* showed the 1924 crop to be 62 percent below that of 1919.

[6] Jensen, W. C. and Others, *An Economic Study of Sumter County Agriculture*, Bulletin 288, Clemson Agricultural College, 1933, pp. 9 and 34.

distribution of numbers employed in manufacturing and allied industries in 1930 for the subregion and for Sumter County has changed
somewhat since that year, owing to the severe depression in the
lumber industry.

The original stands of yellow pine timber in the county were cut
some years ago. At present the lumber cut is mostly hardwoods
from the swamps that border the Wateree River and other streams.
These hardwoods are the raw material for Sumter's woodworking
industries.

Except for a few sawmills, nearly all of the manufacturing plants
of the county are located in the city of Sumter or on its outskirts.
The principal factories are two large sawmills (cutting mostly hardwoods), a planing mill, two veneer plants, a cooperage stock plant,
two furniture factories, and a casket factory. The largest employers
of labor are the furniture factories, one of the veneer plants, and
the cooperage stock plant. The latter concern is a subsidiary of a large
sugar refining company and produces staves and heading stock for
sugar barrels exclusively. The sawmills and woodworking plants
employ about 80 percent of all the factory employees of the county.

The lumber and woodworking industries of Sumter County have
fared relatively better during the depression than have those elsewhere in the subregion, probably because the local industry is not
dependent on the construction business for a market, much of the
lumber cut being consumed in the local factories. In "lumber and
timber," which includes the sawmills and veneer and cooperage stock
plants, the decline from 1929 to 1933 in average number employed
was about 15 percent and in wages 40 percent, as compared with
declines of 60 percent and 75 percent, respectively, for the total of
the same industry for the three States of Alabama, Georgia, and South
Carolina.[7]

Area Covered and Cases Enumerated

Field enumeration centered around Sumter. All of Sumter and
the two adjacent townships of Concord and Privateer were covered,
as well as adjacent portions of four other townships. In these areas
a complete census was not made,[8] occasional cases being passed by

---

[7] *United States Census of Manufactures: 1929 and 1933.*

[8] According to recently published data from the 1935 Census of Agriculture,
1,210 farm operators in Sumter County worked 50 days or more at off-the-farm
employment during 1934. These data afford no basis for determining the com-
pleteness of enumeration in this field study because most of these farm operators
are not classified by the census as to the industry in which they were employed;
no breakdown between Negroes and whites is available; and the criteria for a
farm were different from those of the present study. Moreover, the present
study was limited to those who had done some farming and were employed off
the farm at least 50 days during both 1933 and 1934.

when some difficulty or delay would have been involved in securing the essential information. However, most of the part-time farmers who worked in the city of Sumter and lived in the outskirts or in the nearby open country areas were included. In addition, smaller samples of part-time farmers who lived and worked in the more rural portions of the county were included.

Records were taken from 208 families; 76 were white and 132 were Negro. Figure 13 shows their tendency to cluster about Sumter, with a thinner distribution over the more isolated portions of the county.

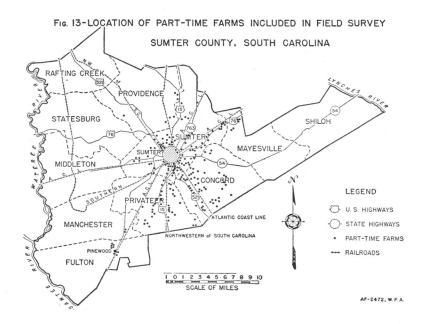

Fɪɢ. 13-LOCATION OF PART-TIME FARMS INCLUDED IN FIELD SURVEY

SUMTER COUNTY, SOUTH CAROLINA

LUMBER AND WOODWORKING INDUSTRIES

The major part of the cash income of part-time farm families in the Lumber Subregion is earned by work off the farm in the lumber and woodworking industries.

The best timber stands of Alabama, Georgia, and South Carolina are found in the coastal plain, the principal species being longleaf, slash, and loblolly pines, cypress, and hardwoods. In this area, most of the cutting of old growth timber was done long ago, so that now there are large areas of second growth of merchantable size.

Lumber Consumption in the United States [9]

Consumption of lumber, both total and per capita, has been declining in the United States since 1906. Peak consumption was nearly 45 billion board feet. In 1932, when the lowest level of the depression was reached in this industry, consumption was less than 12 billion board feet.

The principal reasons for the downward trend of lumber consumption are the cessation of agricultural expansion and the postwar agricultural depression, and the displacement of wood by other materials, such as brick, fiberboard, steel, concrete, etc., in such former large wood-users as the construction industry, automobile manufacture, box-making, and freight car construction.

The country's normal annual lumber requirements are estimated in the *Copeland Report* at 31 to 34 billion board feet, approximately the same as, or a little less than, consumption in 1929.

Among the important factors which will affect future lumber consumption are population growth, changes in construction practices, use of new materials, development of new uses for wood, and the rate of replacement of dwellings.

Employment in the Lumber Industry in Alabama, Georgia, and South Carolina

The term "lumber industry" as used here covers logging camps, sawmills, planing mills, veneer mills, and cooperage stock plants. The number employed in the lumber industry in Alabama, Georgia, and South Carolina reached a peak of about 66,800 in 1923, and dropped to about 25,000 in 1933.[10]

Employment in the wood-using industries in these three States is relatively very small. The most important of these industries are furniture and box and crate manufacture, which employed roughly 4,000 workers in the 3 States in 1933. However, these constitute only about 3 percent of the total workers in these industries in the United States.[11]

Hours and Wages

The lumber industry in the South has always been characterized by low wages and long hours, largely because its labor force is drawn from the farm population, which is notoriously a low income group. A study of wages and hours in the lumber industry made by the Bureau of Labor Statistics in 1932 showed an average hourly rate of pay of about 13½ cents and average weekly earnings of $5.67 to $6.49 in sawmills in Alabama, Georgia, and South Carolina.

[9] The discussion in this section is based on "Our National Timber Requirements," by Frank J. Hallauer in *A National Plan for American Forestry*, 73d Congress, 1st Session, Senate Document No. 12, hereinafter referred to as the *Copeland Report*.

[10] *United States Census of Manufactures.*

[11] *Idem.*

Wages were greatly below previous levels in 1932, the year of severe depression in the lumber industry.[12] Some laborers were paid less than 8 cents per hour. Average wages in this year were roughly 60 percent of the 1930 figure.

An indication of the variation in wage rates from year to year can be obtained from the average wage per wage earner in the Census of Manufactures data. This "census average wage" does not truly represent an average annual income per worker, but it may be used as an index of full-time earnings.[13] Full-time earnings were fairly constant from 1923 to 1929, but they fell sharply during the depression (table 113).

Table 113.—Index of Wage Rates in Lumber, Timber, and Planing Mill Industries in Alabama, Georgia, and South Carolina, 1923–1933

Year	Total wages	Average number of wage earners	Average wage per wage earner	Index of full-time earnings, 1929=100
1923	$40,370,507	66,769	$605	98
1925	42,329,738	65,938	642	104
1927	40,902,554	64,137	638	103
1929	39,246,526	63,376	619	100
1931	12,709,075	26,145	486	79
1933	9,609,719	25,120	383	62

Source: *United States Census of Manufactures.*

Prior to adoption of the N. R. A. code, full-time hours in the sawmills in these States were usually 60 per week. In the Bureau of Labor Statistics study referred to above, it was found that of the 45 sawmills studied in 1932 in the 3 States, 28 were operated 60 hours per week, 10 less than 60 hours, and 7 longer than 60 hours. The minimum was 48 and the maximum 72 hours per week.

The N. R. A. code, approved August 19, 1933, provided for a maximum of 40 hours per week, with certain exceptions. The minimum wage allowed in the South varied from 23 to 26 cents per hour in the several divisions of the industry. Enforcement of the code was abandoned early in 1935, before the Supreme Court decision declaring all of the codes unconstitutional was handed down.

Seasonal Variation

There is very little seasonal variation in the lumber industry in the South. Hardwood logging operations are frequently shut down when high water makes the swamps impassable; and much independent logging is done by farmers at times when they do not need to work

---

[12] *Wages and Hours of Labor in the Lumber Industry in the United States, 1932,* Bulletin 586, United States Bureau of Labor Statistics.

[13] For a discussion of the census average wage, see *Earnings of Factory Workers, 1899 to 1927,* by Paul F. Brissenden, United States Census Monograph X.

on the farms.   These factors result in only minor fluctuations in
employment, however.

Type of Labor

A large majority of the workers in the lumber industry are unskilled.
According to the 1930 Census, the unskilled group, which includes
laborers, teamsters, lumbermen, raftsmen, and woodcutters, made up
about 70 percent of the total labor force of the industry. The remainder
was about equally divided between the skilled and semiskilled groups.

Because of the heavy nature of the work, women are not employed
in this industry except in clerical and kindred positions.

Like other industries in the South which require large numbers of
unskilled workers for heavy tasks, a majority of the labor force of the
industry in this area are Negroes.   The proportion of Negroes is somewhat lower in planing mills than in sawmills and logging camps.

Lumbering is a rural industry.   In the three States, about 18 percent
of the labor force is drawn from the urban population; 55 percent is
drawn from the rural-nonfarm population; and 27 percent from the
rural-farm population.[14]

Outlook for Employment

The future of forest products industries will depend on the solution
of many pressing problems, such as the ownership and management
of forest lands, the balancing of timber drain and growth, taxation of
forest lands, and development of new uses for forest products.   These
problems have been studied intensively by the Forest Service and
other agencies for many years.[15]   To work them out will take a long
time, and the results cannot be forecast now.   However, probabilities
for the near future and possibilities for long-time development will be
indicated here.

Lumber Industry

Employment in the lumber industry in this area would appear to
be somewhat limited by the saw-timber drain that the forests will be
able to stand.   With normal demand, the South would easily be able
to regain lumber sales at least equal to its 1929 amount, provided it
had a sufficient stand of merchantable timber.   In the *Copeland
Report*, it was estimated that the 1925–1929 annual rate of saw-timber
drain in the South was nearly four times the annual growth, and it was
stated that, because of the resultant severe depletion of growing stock,
a continuation of the 1925–1929 drain seems impossible.[16]   The later

---

[14] *Fifteenth Census of the United States: 1930*, Population Vol. III, Part 1, pp.
91 and 463; Part 2, p. 783.

[15] The major forest problems are very fully discussed in the *Copeland Report*,
op. cit.

[16] *Copeland Report*, *op. cit.*, pp. 222 and 224.

and more accurate figures of the Southern Forest Survey may change the estimates of drain and growth somewhat,[17] but it seems clear that the lumber cut in the South must remain substantially below the 1925–1929 rate for many years. A reduction in the lumber cut will mean an approximately proportionate decrease in employment in the industry.

Pulp and Paper Industry

The greatest possibilities for increased employment in forest industries in the South lie in the expansion of such wood-using industries as the pulp and paper industry. However, the desirability of this development from the standpoint of maintenance of the forests and stability of employment will depend largely on the forest policies that will be adopted. If sound practices are followed, the pulp and paper industry can be expanded and at the same time the growing stock can be built up. At the present time, however, a large proportion of the pulpwood operations in the South are based on destructive methods.[18]

The employment possibilities in an expansion of the paper industry in Sumter County are indicated by the fact that in 1929 imports of foreign pulps, pulpwoods, and paper (mostly newsprint) were equivalent to full-time employment for more than 70,000 wage earners.[19] Although domestic supplies of spruce for pulpwood have been diminished, processes for making newsprint paper from young second-growth southern pines have recently been developed and have been successful on an experimental scale.[20]

Woodworking Industries

Some increase in employment may be gained by the expansion of wood-using industries, but as has been pointed out above, the numbers engaged in these industries are relatively small. From the standpoint of numbers employed, furniture manufacture is the most important of these industries.

---

[17] The Southern Forest Survey found that "the drain for the year 1934 in the deep South was only about one-third of the 1925–1929 production, and in those units where such computation has been made, the findings of the survey tend to show growth and drain figures much closer together than those used in the *Copeland Report*. The 1934 drain was exceeded by from 20 to 30 percent in 1935." Letter from I. F. Eldredge, Director, Southern Forest Survey.

[18] Eldredge, I. F., Spillers, A. R., and Kahler, M. S., *The Expansion of the Pulp and Paper Industry in the South,* Forest Survey Report. This report presents data for several areas in the South within which the development of the pulp and paper industry is possible.

[19] *Copeland Report, op. cit.,* p. 270.

[20] Curran, C. E. and Behre, C. E., *National Pulp and Paper Requirements in Relation to Forest Conservation,* 74th Congress, 1st Session, Senate Document No. 115, p. 18.

The furniture factories draw largely on the South for their supplies of hardwoods, but nearness to consuming areas is more important to them than nearness to raw materials. These factories are located mostly in the northeastern States with the southern branch of the industry concentrated in and around High Point, North Carolina.

FARMING ACTIVITIES OF PART-TIME FARMERS

Types of Part-Time Farmers

The 76 white part-time farmers included in the field survey were of 2 types. One group had small farms, usually including about an acre of cropland. They produced chiefly food for home use and sold nothing more than an occasional seasonal surplus. They hired little or no labor. The 37 part-time farmers of this type will be referred to as noncommercial.

The remaining white part-time farmers had larger enterprises, producing principally for market. These farms ranged for the most part from 20 to 50 acres, and averaged 40 acres (appendix table 6). They all had 2 or more acres of cotton or tobacco and 15 or more acres of corn. The work on these farms was usually done, at least in part, with hired labor since only a few of the heads of families had sufficient time from their outside employment or sufficient family labor to carry on a one-mule farm, the minimum-sized commercial farming unit.

Of the Negro part-time farmers included in the field study, 63 were farm laborers and 69 were industrial workers. Most of the farm laborers were contract hands. They usually worked as contract laborers for 7 months, and received about $8 per month in cash, plus their rent, fuel, and certain supplies, usually 3 pounds of meat and a peck of meal per week. During the remainder of the year, they worked when needed, usually for about 50 cents per day. It was customary for the landlord to furnish them a plot of land large enough for a garden, and sometimes 2 or 3 acres for corn and cotton, as well as a mule and implements for cultivating the land. Thus, these Negroes divided their time between production of food and occasionally a little cotton at home, and work for large commercial farmers. They are included in the present study to describe a situation which accounts for an important amount of the part-time farming in the county.[21]

About three-fourths of the nonagricultural Negro part-time farmers lived in the open country, and their farms averaged twice as large as those of the farm laborers, 9.7 acres compared with 4.8 acres. However, the farming operations of the two groups were so similar that they will not be considered separately in this section.

---

[21] Special tabulations of 1930 Census data indicated that many of the farms classified as part-time were of this type.

Farm Production

Four principal types of food were produced for home use: vegetables, dairy products, poultry products, and pork. Three-fourths of the white commercial part-time farmers, almost two-fifths of the white noncommercial farmers, and about one-fourth of the Negro farmers produced all four types. Much larger proportions of each group produced at least three of the four types (appendix table 12).

Gardens

All but two of the white and three of the Negro part-time farmers had gardens (appendix table 11). Those of the white commercial part-time farmers averaged somewhat larger than those of the white noncommercial farmers, but in both groups most of the gardens contained only 1 acre or less. Among the Negroes, two-thirds of the gardens contained less than ½ acre (figure 14).

Sumter County has an average frost-free growing season of about 8 months. Thus, there are about 6 months in which the less hardy vegetables may be consumed fresh from the garden. The more hardy vegetables, such as parsnips, collards, and kale, may be used directly from the garden during the colder months. There was considerable variation among the farms studied in the length of the garden season. Measured by the number of months in which three or more fresh vegetables were used, this ranged from 1 to 9 months among the whites, averaging over 4 months, and from a few weeks to 7 months among the Negroes, averaging almost 3½ months (appendix table 13). The Negroes had at least one fruit or vegetable available for an average of 8 months during the year, and the whites for almost 9 months (appendix table 14).

Almost three-fourths of all families reported that the gardens reduced their grocery bills during the summer months. The average was $5.90 for the white and $3.60 for the Negro families reporting reductions.

Canning and storage of vegetables extended the period of garden contributions. Almost three-fourths of the white part-time farmers and over one-third of the Negro part-time farmers did some canning. The amounts canned were small, however, averaging only 83 quarts for the whites and 37 quarts for the Negroes (appendix table 16). Storage was more important. Over three-fifths of all the families stored sweet potatoes, the white noncommercial part-time farmers averaging 27 bushels, and the Negroes averaging 29 bushels. White commercial part-time farmers stored over twice as many bushels as the other groups. Thirty-eight percent of the whites and thirty percent of the Negroes stored Irish potatoes, the white noncommercial part-time farmers storing an average of 9 bushels and the Negroes an average of 10 bushels a year (appendix table 17). Peas, onions, lima beans, pecans, peanuts, and apples were also stored occasionally.

WHITE COMMERCIAL

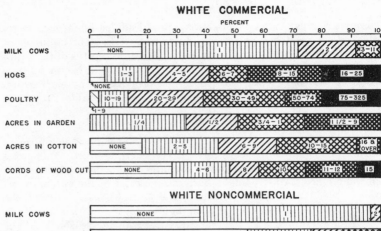

WHITE NONCOMMERCIAL

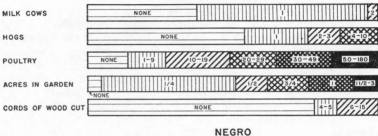

NEGRO

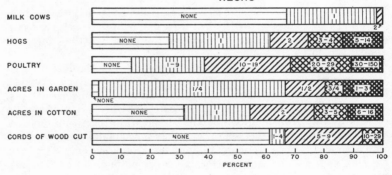

Fɪɢ.14—SIZE OF PRINCIPAL ENTERPRISES ON PART-TIME
FARMS, BY TYPE OF FARM AND BY
COLOR OF OPERATOR,
SUMTER COUNTY, S.C., 1934

Corn

Corn was grown by all except one of the white commercial part-time farmers, by almost two-fifths of the white noncommercial part-time farmers, and by over four-fifths of the Negro part-time farmers, the average production being 281, 41, and 49 bushels, respectively (appendix table 24). White families used an average of 10 bushels and Negroes an average of 20 bushels for food, the remainder being fed to livestock. Eight Negroes sold some corn.

Dairy Products

Four-fifths of the white commercial, three-fifths of the white noncommercial, and one-third of the Negro part-time farmers kept at least one cow and a few kept two or more (appendix table 11). During 1934, milk production averaged 1,375 quarts per cow for the white commercial, 1,941 quarts for the white noncommercial, and 1,265 quarts for the Negro part-time farmers (appendix table 20). Butter was made on most of the farms that had cows, the white families consuming an average of over 2 pounds and the Negroes almost 1½ pounds a week (appendix table 21). Very little milk or butter was sold by part-time farmers in this area.

Poultry Products

Poultry flocks were almost as common as gardens in this area. All of the white commercial, all except 5 of the white noncommercial, and all except 17 of the Negro part-time farmers had flocks (appendix table 11). The size of the flocks varied greatly. The flocks of white farmers contained, as a rule, less than 75 birds. All but 4 flocks on Negro farms contained less than 50 birds. Consumption of home-produced eggs averaged 3 dozen and 2 dozen a week for white commercial and noncommercial farmers, respectively, and 1⅓ dozen eggs per week for the Negro families (appendix table 18). Consumption of home-produced poultry averaged 3 pounds per week for the whites and nearly 1½ pounds per week for the Negroes (appendix table 19).

Pork

All except one of the white commercial part-time farm families produced pork, consuming or storing an average of 583 pounds a year. About two-thirds of both the white noncommercial and the Negro part-time farm families produced pork, consuming or storing an average of 249 and 263 pounds, respectively (appendix table 22).

Feed Crops

The white commercial part-time farmers grew most of the feed for their cows and other livestock. Six white noncommercial part-time farmers grew part of their feed in spite of their limited amount of land (appendix table 23). Occasionally as much as $50 worth of feed was purchased for the cow. Few of the white noncommercial group and of the Negroes had any pasturage and that of the commercial group was quite limited.

Fuel

All but six of the white commercial part-time farms included some woodland, and in all but five cases the families with woodland cut their own fuel, the amounts varying from 4 to 15 cords. On one farm, $200 was secured from the sale of wood. Only 5 of the white noncommercial and only 20 of the Negro part-time farms included woodland. However, eight of the white farmers and most of the Negroes cut fuel on land owned by their employers.

Cash Receipts and Cash Expenses

Only 15 of the 37 noncommercial part-time farmers sold any farm products, and none of these sold as much as $100 worth. Sales for the 15 averaged $15. For the entire noncommercial group, cash expenses, exclusive of rent and taxes, averaged $55 (appendix table 25).

In the commercial group of 39 part-time farmers, there were 29 small-scale cotton farmers growing from 2 to 18 acres of cotton, and 1 small-scale tobacco farmer growing 4 acres of tobacco. For this group, the net farm cash income[22] averaged $165 and ranged from minus $285 to $645. There were six others who kept livestock and grew feed crops but had very little to sell. For five of these, expenses were greater than receipts. Of the three remaining cases, one was a dairy farmer and two were cotton farmers who also had important truck crop enterprises. For these three, the net cash incomes from farm enterprises ranged from $800 to $1,400.[23]

Over two-thirds of the Negro part-time farmers grew an acre or more of cotton. In most cases, however, less than 5 acres were grown and 16 acres were the most grown on any one farm. Cotton was practically the only product grown for sale, and total sales amounted to less than $100 on over two-thirds of the part-time farms. In most cases, the cotton sold for enough to more than cover all direct cash farm expenses. Hence, the part-time farmers received in return for their own labor and that of their families the products described above plus a small net cash income (appendix table 25).

---

[22] The difference between cash farm receipts and cash farm expenses, including rent and taxes, but excluding purchases of livestock in excess of normal replacements.

[23] Schedule data are on file in the Division of Social Research, Works Progress Administration.

Value and Tenure of Part-Time Farms

The value[24] of the white commercial part-time farms was considerably greater than that of the white noncommercial part-time farms, and in both groups the real estate of the owners was of considerably greater value than that leased by the tenants (table 17, page 12). The proportion of owners was higher among the commercial than among the noncommercial part-time farmers (appendix table 7).

Only 26 of the Negro part-time farmers owned their homes. The owners had houses and farms of considerably greater average value than those of the renters.

Implements and machinery represented an average investment of $136 on the white commercial part-time farms having machinery, while only three white noncommercial part-time farmers had any farm equipment other than small hand tools (appendix table 10).

Only 35 of the Negro part-time farmers owned farm implements and machinery other than small hand tools. Most of the Negro farm laborers used mules and machinery owned by their employers. In only four cases was the investment more than $100.

Mortgage indebtedness was reported occasionally, but when found, it was usually small except in the case of the owners of white commercial part-time farms. Of the 25 farmers in this group, 16 were in debt and their indebtedness averaged $1,300. Only four of the Negroes who owned their homes, and none of those who rented them, were in debt for as much as $250 (appendix table 8).

Labor Requirements of Part-Time Farms and Their Relation to Working Hours in Industry

A working week of five 8-hour days predominated during 1934 as a result of the N. R. A. maximum for the lumber and woodworking industries. Those in service industries worked longer hours. A small number of whites and one-half of the Negroes were farm laborers, whose standard work week was made up of five and one-half 10-hour days. Employment for this group, however, was irregular, and all Negroes averaged only 191 days in 1934 (appendix table 32).

The heads of the households were able to spend some time in the mornings and evenings and on Saturdays on their part-time farms. Heads in the white commercial group averaged about 3½ hours, in the white noncommercial group about 2 hours, and in the Negro group about 3 hours per day during the summer season (table 48, page 32). In this area the other members of the families worked more than the head. In 83 percent of the white families and in 87 percent of the Negro families, the wife worked on the farm (appendix table 27). Members of white commercial part-time farm families spent an average of 7 hours a day in farm work, in addition to con-

---

[24] Real estate values were arrived at by capitalizing the actual rent or theoretical rental value of property at 5 percent.

siderable hired labor (appendix table 26), and those in white non-commercial part-time farm families averaged over 3 hours a day during the garden season. Negro families spent a total of 8 to 9 hours a day in farm work during the spring and summer months, but this labor was not all employed in producing food for home use. Little labor was hired, most of it being done by members of the family.

EMPLOYMENT AND EARNINGS IN INDUSTRY

Minimum wage rates and hours of work in the lumber and wood-working industries were set by an N. R. A. code during 1934. As compared to 1929, there was a shorter working day.

Eight of the white part-time farmers in the sample were engaged in agriculture. They have been omitted from the discussion of earnings [25] because of the small number of cases involved and because they constitute a distinct group. Seven were farm laborers on a contract basis with about the same income as Negro contract laborers, and one was a farm overseer with a considerably higher income than the other part-time farmers.

The Industrial Group

For comparison with white part-time farmers, a sample of 92 non-farming industrial workers in the lumber and woodworking industries was included in the study.[26] A group of 103 nonfarming Negroes who were employed in woodworking industries was enumerated for comparison with Negro part-time farmers.

Industry and Occupation

The part-time farmers were selected without regard to the industry in which they were employed. In the area covered, only 68 white part-time farmers engaged in nonagricultural industries were found, of whom 25 were in lumber and woodworking industries. Of the 69 Negro workers employed in industries other than agriculture, 28 were in lumber and woodworking industries (appendix table 29).

Building and construction, the industry next in importance to lumber and woodworking, included seven white carpenters, a brickmason, and a painter. Four school bus drivers, three truck drivers, and an auto mechanic were included under "Other transportation and communication." There were two salesmen in filling stations, one manager and one owner of filling stations, and four salesmen in retail stores. The two cases in personal service were truck drivers for a laundry.

Most of the white workers in these industries were either skilled or semiskilled laborers, the bulk of the unskilled work being performed by Negroes (appendix table 30). Although a larger proportion of the white part-time farmers in lumber and woodworking industries were

---

[25] They are included, however, in appendix table 29 ff.

[26] For criteria used in their selection, see Introduction, pp. XXX–XXXI.

classified as skilled workers, their earnings were not significantly different from those of the white nonfarming industrial workers.[27] For this reason, the two groups are not presented separately in the discussion of earnings of heads of white households which follows.

All except 1 of the 63 part-time farming Negroes engaged in agriculture were farm laborers. The proportion of unskilled nonagricultural workers was greatest in the service industries and least in the building and construction industry. About half of those engaged in lumber and woodworking industries were unskilled workers. The occupational distributions of part-time farmers and nonfarming industrial workers engaged in the lumber and woodworking industries were roughly similar, about half of each group being unskilled laborers.

Earnings of Heads of White Households

Annual earnings of heads of white households employed in lumber and woodworking industries averaged somewhat less than those of heads in service industries, but more than those of heads in "Other manufacturing and mechanical" industries (table 114). The low

Table 114.—Earnings[1] From Industrial Employment of Heads of White Households in the Lumber Subregion, 1934

Earnings from industrial employment	Lumber and wood-working	Other manu-facturing and mechanical industries	Service industries
Total	117	17	26
$100 to $249	3	3	4
$250 to $499	26	6	4
$500 to $749	61	5	6
$750 to $999	15	2	4
$1,000 to $1,249	6	1	4
$1,250 to $1,499	4	—	—
$1,500 to $1,999	2	—	4
Average earnings	$655	$500	$809

[1] At principal off-the-farm employment (job with the largest earnings).

annual earnings of this latter group were due to the small number of days worked. About half of this group were in the building industry in which work has been very irregular during the last few years. Most of the lumber and woodworking employees had steady employment, about four-fifths of them working 200 days or more during 1934 (table 115). Workers in service industries were employed slightly fewer days but at a higher average hourly rate of pay, 45 cents, as against 35 cents for the lumber and woodworking group (table 116). Hours and rates of pay in lumber and woodworking industries were regulated by an N. R. A. code during 1934. Eight hours was the

[27] Average annual earnings in 1934 were $662 and $654, respectively, for the white part-time farmers and the white nonfarming workers in the lumber and woodworking industries.

usual length of the working day in that year.   As compared to annual earnings in 1929, wages were substantially less in 1934.   The average reduction for the 87 workers who were employed in lumber and wood-working industries in both 1929 and 1934 was 29 percent.   With the subsequent collapse of the N. R. A., hours of work were increased and wage rates further reduced.   A local employer expressed the opinion that this adjustment had resulted in little change in weekly earnings.

Table 115.—Number of Days Heads of White Households in the Lumber Subregion Were Employed off the Farm,[1] 1934

Number of days employed off the farm	Lumber and wood-working	Other manu-facturing and mechanical industries	Service industries
Total	117	17	26
50 to 99 days	2	4	4
100 to 149 days	5	3	2
150 to 199 days	17	5	3
200 to 249 days	35	3	4
250 to 299 days	46	1	7
300 to 349 days	9	1	5
350 days or more	3	—	1
Average days employed	237	167	226

[1] At principal off-the-farm employment (job with the largest earnings).

Table 116.—Rate of Pay[1] of Heads of White Households in the Lumber Subregion, 1934

Hourly rate of pay	Lumber and wood-working	Other manu-facturing and mechanical industries	Service industries
Total	117	17	26
10 to 19 cents	1	2	1
20 to 29 cents	35	2	5
30 to 39 cents	51	4	7
40 to 49 cents	17	5	2
50 to 59 cents	5	2	3
60 to 69 cents	4	—	4
70 to 79 cents	3	—	2
80 to 89 cents	1	2	2
Average hourly rate of pay	$0. 35	$0. 40	$0. 45

[1] At principal off-the-farm employment (job with the largest earnings).

Earnings of Heads of Negro Households

Differences in earnings between Negro part-time farmers engaged in the lumber and woodworking industries and nonfarming workers in the same industries were not significantly related to the farming activities carried on by the part-time farmers; hence, the two groups are not presented separately in this discussion.

Among nonagricultural workers, those employed in building and construction had the lowest annual incomes, due to irregular employ-ment, in spite of slightly higher average hourly rates (tables 117, 118, and 119).   The higher average earnings of lumber and woodworking employees were due to steadier employment, 94 out of the total of 131

Table 117.—Earnings [1] From Industrial Employment of Heads of Negro Households in the Lumber Subregion, 1934

Earnings from industrial employment	Agriculture	Nonagriculture		
		Lumber and wood-working	Building and con-struction	Other industries
Total	63	131	15	26
$1 to $99	5	2	2	4
$100 to $249	56	16	6	7
$250 to $499	1	70	3	11
$500 to $749	—	43	4	2
$750 to $999	1	—	—	—
$1,000 to $1,249	—	—	—	1
$1,250 to $1,499	—	—	—	—
$1,500 to $1,999	—	—	—	1
Average earnings	$150	$416	$301	$377

[1] At principal off-the-farm employment (job with the largest earnings).

Table 118.—Number of Days Heads of Negro Households in the Lumber Subregion Were Employed off the Farm,[1] 1934

Number of days employed off the farm	Agriculture	Nonagriculture		
		Lumber and wood-working	Building and con-struction	Other industries
Total	63	131	15	26
1 to 49 days	—	1	1	—
50 to 99 days	5	4	7	6
100 to 149 days	3	16	2	3
150 to 199 days	23	17	2	4
200 to 249 days	24	48	3	3
250 to 299 days	4	40	—	4
300 to 349 days	2	3	—	3
350 days or more	2	3	—	3
Average days employed	195	218	121	206

[1] At principal off-the-farm employment (job with the largest earnings).

Table 119.—Rate of Pay[1] of Heads of Negro Households in the Lumber Subregion, 1934

Hourly rate of pay	Agriculture	Nonagriculture		
		Lumber and wood-working	Building and con-struction	Other industries
Total	63	131	15	26
Less than 10 cents	57	—	—	5
10 to 19 cents	5	6	3	7
20 to 29 cents	1	105	5	7
30 to 39 cents	—	20	4	3
40 to 49 cents	—	—	2	1
50 to 59 cents	—	—	1	1
60 to 69 cents	—	—	—	—
70 to 79 cents	—	—	—	1
80 to 89 cents	—	—	—	1
Average hourly rate of pay	$0.087	$0.24	$0.28	$0.24

[1] At principal off-the-farm employment (job with the largest earnings).

working 200 days or more during 1934. A number of these workers reported hourly rates less than the code minimum of 23 cents, and six reported rates of less than 20 cents an hour. As compared with 1929, the average annual earnings of lumber and woodworking employees were somewhat reduced in 1934. The average earnings of 93 heads who were employed in these industries in both 1929 and 1934 were 11 percent less in the latter year.

Agricultural laborers had incomes considerably lower than those of workers employed in other industries. It was customary for contract farm laborers to work for their employer as needed during the growing season or throughout the year, and in return to receive a definite amount in cash, a stipulated amount of meat and meal, a house, wood as needed for fuel, 2 or 3 acres of land, and use of farm implements. The payments were sometimes based on a daily rate and sometimes on a lump sum for a year or part of a year.

The average cash earnings of this group in 1934 were about $100, and the estimated average value of the payments in kind, including rent, was $50. The number of days worked varied considerably, but averaged a little less than 200. The usual length of the working day was 10 hours. The computed hourly rate of pay, based on total earnings including payments in kind, was less than 10 cents per hour for all but six of these laborers.

Total Cash Income of White Households

Total cash incomes of white part-time farm households from nonfarm sources were slightly greater than were those of nonfarming industrial households, while per capita incomes were somewhat less (table 120). When households of similar size were compared, part-time farm households of two to four persons had larger per capita incomes than nonfarming industrial households, while those containing five to seven persons had smaller per capita incomes. Practically

Table 120.—Cash Income From Nonfarm Sources of White Part-Time Farm and Non-farming Industrial Households in the Lumber Subregion, by Size of Household, 1934

Size of household	Part-time farm households		Nonfarming industrial households	
	Number of cases	Income per capita	Number of cases	Income per capita
Total	68	$152	92	$188
2 to 3 persons	13	274	34	247
4 persons	12	216	18	210
5 persons	14	163	14	191
6 to 7 persons	15	139	20	144
8 persons or more	14	105	6	†
Average income per household	$863		$834	

† Average not computed for less than 10 cases.

the entire family income from nonfarm sources for both groups was from wage earnings.

White commercial part-time farmers worked approximately the same number of days and had the same annual earnings as white noncommercial part-time farmers. In addition to this off-the-farm income, commercial farmers had a very considerable cash income from sale of farm products, which exceeded farm expenses by $300 on the average.

In approximately one out of three families of both groups, one or more members other than the head were employed (appendix table 35). Employed female members in part-time farm households earned an average of $143, and employed male members other than the head earned an average of $392, as compared to $175 and $436 in the nonfarming industrial group. One-third of the young people 16–24 years of age in part-time farm families and almost one-half of those in nonfarm families were employed (table 58, page 43).

Fifteen women in each group were engaged in bedspread manufacturing. The manufacturer delivered the bedspreads and returned to collect them at the end of the week. The women tufted and embroidered the spreads at home. The earnings seldom amounted to more than $1 or $2 a week. The average amount earned by the women in this employment in 1934 was $53. Other women were employed in personal and domestic service, retail stores, nursing, sewing, and teaching. Most of the employed male members of the household other than the head were in woodworking industries or in retail stores.

Total Cash Income of Negro Households

Negro part-time farm families whose heads were engaged in nonagricultural work had an average of $98 a year less income from industrial employment than did nonfarming industrial households. Part of this difference was due to the irregular employment of part-time farmers engaged in the building trades. In addition, members other than the head contributed less to part-time farm households. The earnings of both heads and other members of agricultural part-time farm households were considerably less than those of the other groups. Besides having smaller family incomes, part-time farm families were larger than nonfarming industrial households (appendix table 2), and their per capita incomes were therefore relatively smaller (table 121).

The employment and earnings of members of Negro households other than heads are shown in table 122. Although a larger number of members other than heads were employed in families of Negro farm laborers, they usually worked on the farms during the busy season only and their earnings were small. Most of the male members of households in which the head was engaged in industrial work were employed in woodworking or service industries. Female mem-

Table 121.—Cash Income From Nonfarm Sources of Negro Part-Time Farm and Non-farming Industrial Households in the Lumber Subregion, by Size of Household, 1934

| Size of household | Part-time farm households | | | | Nonfarming industrial households | |
| | Agriculture | | Nonagriculture | | | |
	Number of cases	Income per capita	Number of cases	Income per capita	Number of cases	Income per capita
Total	63	$42	69	$83	103	$143
2 to 3 persons	20	70	14	136	54	206
4 to 5 persons	17	52	27	102	32	132
6 to 7 persons	15	39	13	82	14	86
8 persons or more	11	24	15	54	3	†
Average income per household	$219		$448		$546	

† Average not computed for less than 10 cases.

bers were usually employed in domestic and personal service, with the exception of 15 in the nonfarming industrial group who were engaged in embroidering bedspreads. As in the case of white women, the earnings of one person seldom amounted to more than $1 or $2 a week. Over half of the young people 16–24 years of age in part-time farm families and two-fifths of those in nonfarming industrial families were employed (table 58, page 43).

Table 122.—Employment and Earnings of Members Other Than the Heads of Negro Part-Time Farm and Nonfarming Industrial Households in the Lumber Subregion, 1934

| Item | Part-time farm households | | Nonfarming industrial households |
	Agriculture	Nonagriculture	
Total	63	69	103
Number of households with employed members	60	36	59
Number of members employed:			
Male	28	18	14
Female	81	32	60
Average earnings:			
Male	$47	$185	$281
Female	26	50	84

LIVING CONDITIONS AND ORGANIZED SOCIAL LIFE

Part-time farmers generally lived in the open country or villages and were frequently without conveniences common to urban dwellers [28] (table 62, page 51). Nonfarming industrial households lived in the city of Sumter or on the outskirts, with the exception of the workers in a logging camp 25 miles from Sumter. Those in the logging camp had no modern conveniences, and they had no social organizations

---

[28] The eight white part-time farmers engaged in agriculture had about the same living conditions as Negro contract laborers.

nearer than the ones in the village of Pinewood, 6 miles distant. Workers living on the outskirts of Sumter generally had electric lights but not city water.

Housing of White Households

Dwellings of white part-time farmers were somewhat larger for each size of household and in better condition than were those of nonfarming industrial workers (appendix tables 38 and 40). On the average, they contained 4.5 rooms as against 3.7 rooms for the homes of the nonfarmers. Approximately two-fifths of the part-time farm houses and one-fourth of the nonfarming industrial houses needed no repairs (appendix table 40). Paint, screens, weatherboarding, porch repairs, flooring, and papering were needed by nearly one-half of the part-time farm and by three-fourths of the nonfarm dwellings. One-third of the part-time farm houses and over one-fourth of the non-farming industrial houses needed roof repairs, while a few needed more extensive repairs.

The availability of electricity and running water depended largely on the location of the home. Electric power lines were available to people living in the city of Sumter or in the immediate vicinity, while city water was generally available only to families within the city limits.

Since most of the white part-time farmers lived in the open country, only 3 had running water, 2 had bathrooms, and 12 had electric lights (appendix table 41). There are a few power lines leading out of Sumter, but cost of installation and service is practically prohibitive for the vast majority of rural residents. A few part-time farmers whose houses were wired for lights were found close to town, but because of the high rates, they had been forced to abandon the use of electricity. In the city of Sumter were 57 nonfarming industrial families and of these, 53 had running water, 47 had bathrooms, and 43 had electric lights. Of the 26 nonfarming industrial households on the outskirts of Sumter, 16 had electric lights only, and 3 had electric lights and running water. None of the nine nonfarming industrial white families who lived in a logging camp 25 miles from Sumter had any of these conveniences.

Better than average conditions were represented by a part-time farm family of five persons living on the outskirts of Sumter in a four-room dwelling with electric lights and radio, although without running water. The house was in good condition, having been constructed in 1929. The annual rent for the place, which included 3 acres of land, was $101.

Conditions somewhat below the average were represented by a carpenter with a family of 10 living in an old 5-room house which had never been painted, was in need of porch and window repairs, and had a leaky roof.   No conveniences were available.   Annual rent of $130 was paid for the farm, which included 25 acres of land.

Housing of Negro Households

The typical dwelling of a Negro contract farm laborer was a shack of two, three, or four rooms owned by his employer.   It was usually constructed of rough boards and was without paint, plaster, or screens. Frequently the roof leaked, window panes were broken, and porch and floor repairs were needed.

Negro part-time farmers engaged in the industries in Sumter were also without modern conveniences, but their houses were in a better state of repair than were those of farm laborers.   Better than average conditions were represented by a family of four living in a single-family frame house of five rooms constructed in 1925 and kept in good condition.   A number of dwellings were fairly comfortable but lacked screens, paint, or other minor repairs.   Approximately one-fourth needed roof repairs, and many of these dwellings were old and dilapidated (appendix table 40).

The dwellings of nonfarming industrial workers were smaller than those of part-time farmers (appendix table 38), but they had more modern conveniences.   Twenty-four dwellings of nonfarmers, but only two of part-time farmers, had running water; 20 nonfarmers, but only 2 part-time farmers, had bathrooms; and 11 nonfarmers, but only 2 part-time farmers had electric lights (appendix table 41).   The five nonfarming industrial families living in the logging camp had fairly new dwellings which were crudely constructed and without conveniences.

Automobiles, Radios, and Telephones

Very few of the white or Negro families had telephones and few of the Negro families had radios.   As compared with the part-time farmers, a relatively high proportion of the white nonfarming industrial workers had radios, partly because a greater number of this group had electricity in their homes (appendix table 42).

More than two-thirds of the white part-time farmers owned automobiles, while only one-third of the nonfarming industrial workers had them.   An automobile was the chief means of getting to work for those who lived at a distance, and those who had cars usually drove them.   A few rode with relatives or friends.   Three-fifths of the white part-time farmers and less than one-fifth of the nonfarmers lived 1½ miles or more from their places of usual employment (appendix table 28).

Twenty-three Negro part-time farmers, including five employed in agriculture, and seventeen of the nonfarming industrial workers had automobiles.   Only one farm laborer and one nonfarming industrial worker lived more than 2½ miles from their places of employment.

Twenty-four of the part-time farmers engaged in nonagricultural industries were located 3 miles or more from their places of employment. Most of these rode in their own or friends' cars, or rode bicycles. Several who lived 3 or 4 miles from their places of employment walked to and from work daily.

Home Ownership

Home ownership, by both whites and Negroes, was greater among part-time farmers than among nonfarming industrial workers. Thirty-seven, or one-half, of the white part-time farmers, but only two of the nonfarming industrial workers, owned their homes (table 69, page 59). Tenants on white noncommercial part-time farms paid $75 rent per year on the average, which provided a small plot of land in addition to the house. This was less than the average of $110 paid by the nonfarming industrial tenants, most of whom lived in Sumter. As already pointed out, however, the rent for nonfarm dwellings more frequently included such facilities as running water, bathroom, and electric lights.

Twenty-three, or one-third, of the Negro part-time farmers working in industry owned their dwellings, as compared to only eleven owners among the nonfarming industrial workers. Only three of the Negro workers in agriculture owned their houses. One of these was an overseer for a pigeon farm, who had an income of $750, and another had a son employed in a furniture factory in Sumter. Both of these workers had houses which were in excellent condition and both owned automobiles. The third family owned a farm of 23 acres, but the dwelling seemed to be little better than those of the farm laborers.

Education

Children of school age of white part-time farm and nonfarming industrial households had made slightly less than normal progress in school, both groups being retarded about three-fourths of a year on the average (table 76, page 64). Only 10 children between the ages of 7 and 16 in the families studied were not in school. Four of these were 7 years of age and had not yet started to school; two were 15 and three were 16 years of age and had dropped out. Only one, a boy of 16, was employed (table 75, page 63).

Heads of white households had completed six grades in school on the average (appendix table 46). There was no significant difference in this respect between part-time farmers and nonfarming industrial workers. Slightly less than one-half of either group had completed grade school, and only three members of each group had completed high school.

The term for white children varied from 7 to 9 months, and transportation to and from school was frequently furnished.[29] Library

---

[29] *Annual Report of the State Superintendent of Education of South Carolina, 1934*

service was available more frequently to nonfarming industrial families, but was used more often by part-time farm families. While 31 part-time farmers with off-the-farm employment in nonagriculture reported having a library available, only 16 used it during the year. Although the library was available to 90 of the nonfarming industrial families, only 10 made any use of it (table 78, page 66).

There were three Negro schools in Sumter in addition to a Negro college, which also had a grammar school and a high school in connection with it. Most of the schools in rural districts were one- and two-teacher schools which had terms of less than 7 months.

Negro children were somewhat retarded in school. Children of farm laborers were retarded more than 2½ years on the average, while children of the other part-time farmers and of the nonfarming industrial workers were retarded about 1½ years. Of the children 7 to 16 years of age in the families studied, 26 were not in school, and of these 7 had some employment during 1934. Negro heads of households had had very little education (appendix table 46). This low level of educational achievement for heads reflects the limited opportunities available to Negroes in past years.

Social Participation

Organized social life, particularly for Negroes, was centered largely around the church and related organizations (appendix table 48). Although a considerable variety of social organizations were available in Sumter, many of them were not attended by the white factory employees. In fact, their participation in social life was limited largely to church, Sunday School, and the labor union. Adult church organizations, young people's organizations, 4-H Clubs, fraternal orders, athletic teams, and women's organizations were the types most frequently attended by members of white part-time farm households. Of those reporting labor unions available, about the same proportions of both groups attended. Not only did the nonfarming industrial group participate in fewer organizations, but the average number of attendances per person in 1934 was less. This number was 48 for the nonfarming industrial group as against 69 for the part-time farm group (table 80, page 68).

Only six members of white part-time farm households and one member of a white nonfarming industrial household held offices in social organizations during 1934 (appendix table 49).

Among the Negroes, the members of part-time farm households in which the head had nonagricultural employment showed the greatest participation in organized social life. The average number of attendances per person during 1934 was 84 for this group, 68 for the group in which the head was a farm laborer, and 67 for the nonfarming industrial group.

Negro leadership was largely confined to the church and related organizations. Among members of Negro households, 38 held offices in social organizations: 18 in church; 9 in Sunday School; 4 in adult church organizations; 2 each in young people's organizations, in women's organizations, and in fraternal orders; and 1 in a Parent-Teacher Association. Of these officers, 21 were from nonagricultural part-time farm households, and 6 from agricultural part-time farm households, while 11 were from nonfarming industrial households.

RELIEF

Only five white part-time farm households and seven white non-farming industrial households included in the survey received any relief during 1934. The amounts they received varied from $27 to $169, averaging $74. Fourteen Negro part-time farm households and seven nonfarming industrial households received relief in 1934, the amounts ranging from $5 to $200. In general, those receiving relief had unsteady employment. During the period 1929–1935, only 11 percent of the whites and very few more Negroes received any relief (table 61, page 47, and appendix table 36).

The number of cases receiving relief was too small for any conclusions to be drawn regarding the value of part-time farming in keeping families off relief. However, from a consideration of the net value of the farm contribution to the family living, it would appear beyond doubt that the farm, even when it is too small to provide cash crops, is an aid in tiding industrial workers over short periods of unemployment. For complete self-support, a minimum of industrial employment, or some cash crop, is necessary.

Chapter V

THE NAVAL STORES SUBREGION OF ALABAMA AND GEORGIA

GENERAL FEATURES OF THE SUBREGION AND OF COFFEE COUNTY

THE NAVAL stores[1] producing area, located mainly in the southern tier of counties in Alabama, northern Florida, and southeastern Georgia, is distinctly rural and sparsely populated, with its population primarily dependent on the farms and forests. The towns and small cities of the region serve mainly as trading and transportation centers. A portion of this area, lying in the States of Alabama and Georgia, has been designated for purposes of this study as the Naval Stores Subregion (figure 2, page XXIV). Coffee County, centrally located in the Georgia portion of this subregion, was chosen as generally representative of the area, and the field study was conducted in that county.

Coffee County

The topography of Coffee County is level to gently rolling. The soils are sandy and sandy loams with clay subsoils.[2] Rainfall is adequate for most crops, but considerable areas are swampy and poorly drained. Twenty-four percent of the land area of Coffee County was cropland in 1934 and most of the remainder was forest and woodland.[3] Over one-half of this forest and woodland was in

---

[1] The chemical products of the pine tree, specifically turpentine and rosin, are known as "naval stores," probably because in the past they included tar and pitch which were used in wooden ships.

[2] No soil survey has been made of Coffee County, but the Bureau of Soils of the U. S. Department of Agriculture has made surveys in three adjacent counties, Jeff Davis, Ben Hill, and Ware, where soil conditions are quite similar.

[3] *United States Census of Agriculture: 1935.*

farms, that is, was owned or rented by farmers. The original pine forests of the county were cut over some years ago and have become restocked with second growth longleaf and slash pines, which are now being worked for turpentine and rosin.

The population of Coffee County, 19,700 in 1930,[4] was entirely rural with the exception of the 4,200 persons living in the city of Douglas. This city is centrally located, and there were 3 small outlying villages with populations of 830, 651, and 66 in 1930.[5] Making allowances for two changes in county boundaries[6] the population of the county has approximately trebled since 1890.

Agriculturally, Coffee County represents the flue-cured tobacco growing area of Florida and Georgia (figure 3, page XXVI), which is more limited in extent than is the Naval Stores Subregion. The county is located near the center of this agricultural area, and in 1929 was the leading tobacco producing county in it. That year, 45 percent of the farm income of the county was from the sale of tobacco and 23 percent from the sale of cotton.[7]

Coffee County is primarily agricultural with a relatively small amount of industrial employment. Only 22 farms, or 1 percent of all farms in the county, were classified as part-time by the 1930 Census of Agriculture.[8] There were, however, 168 farms which reported 75 days or more of off-the-farm employment for the operator.[9] This latter group included in addition to those classified as part-time many more on which the operator either worked away from the farm less than 150 days or produced more than $750 worth of farm products.

Although 27 percent of the population of the county were Negroes, only 15 percent of the farm operators were Negroes. Of the 2,090 farms in the county reported by the 1935 Census of Agriculture, 772 were operated by white owners and managers, 1,014 by white croppers and other tenants, 41 by Negro owners, and 263 by Negro croppers and other tenants. Sixty-five percent of all land in farms was operated by white owners and managers, their farms averaging 239 acres in size as compared with 82 acres for the white croppers and other tenants.

The number of farms in the county has remained fairly constant for 15 years, being approximately the same in 1935 as it was in 1920. However, the acreage of land in farms decreased 10 percent from 1920 to 1930, but increased again by 6 percent prior to 1935.[10] During this

---

[4] *Fifteenth Census of the United States: 1930*, Population.

[5] *Idem.*

[6] In 1905 and 1919 parts of Coffee County were set off to form new counties.

[7] *United States Census of Agriculture: 1935.*

[8] For census definition of part-time farms, see p. XVI, footnote 2.

[9] Special tabulation of census data.

[10] *Fifteenth Census of the United States: 1930*, Agriculture, and *United States Census of Agriculture: 1935.*

last 5-year period there was a decrease in the acreage of cash crops and an increase in the acreage of feed crops. The change in total acreage in farms, however, was brought about chiefly by a 25 percent increase in the acreage of woodland.

Coffee County is fairly representative of the Naval Stores Subregion with respect to industry as indicated by the distribution of workers by industries in 1930 (table 123). The principal industries of the area are naval stores and lumber.

The principal manufacturing establishments in Coffee County are the turpentine stills which are scattered throughout the area, and the repair shops of the Florida and Georgia Railroad at Douglas. In the "Other manufacturing" group the railroad shops are the most important. They normally employ about 125 men.

In Coffee County, 71 records were taken from white part-time farm families.[11] While this was not a complete census of all cases meeting the above requirements, it probably included about three-fourths of them. The entire county was covered, but those cases were omitted where some delay or difficulty would have been involved in securing the necessary information.

Because the population of the Naval Stores Subregion is predominantly white, this report deals only with whites.

Table 123.—Distribution of Persons, 10 Years Old and Over, Gainfully Occupied in the Naval Stores Subregion and in Coffee County, Georgia, 1930

Industry	Naval Stores Subregion		Coffee County, Georgia	
	Number	Percent	Number	Percent
Total population	887, 018		19, 739	
Total gainfully employed	321, 044	100. 0	7, 126	100. 0
Agriculture	191, 267	59. 6	4, 287	60. 2
Service industries	76, 273	23. 7	1, 619	22. 7
Manufacturing and allied industries	53, 504	16. 7	1, 220	17. 1
Total manufacturing and allied industries	53, 504	100. 0	1, 220	100. 0
Forestry and fishing	3, 237	6. 1	53	4. 3
Extraction of minerals	406	0. 7	2	0. 2
Building	4, 803	9. 0	88	7. 2
Chemical and allied	1, 143	2. 1	9	0. 7
Clay, glass, and stone	195	0. 4	1	0. 1
Clothing	805	1. 5	4	0. 3
Food and allied	2, 523	4. 7	25	2. 1
Automobile factories and repair shops	1, 442	2. 7	31	2. 5
Iron and steel	2, 431	4. 5	102	8. 4
Saw and planing mills	9, 537	17. 8	182	14. 9
Other wood and furniture	1, 164	2. 2	100	8. 2
Paper, printing, and allied	443	0. 8	5	0. 4
Cotton mills	2, 230	4. 2	1	0. 1
Other textile	164	0. 3	—	—
Independent hand trades	1, 470	2. 8	28	2. 3
Other manufacturing [1]	21, 511	40. 2	589	48. 3

[1] "Other manufacturing" includes workers on turpentine farms and in distilleries.

Source: *Fifteenth Census of the United States: 1930,* Population Vol. III.

[11] An additional 26 cases were enumerated, but they were so heterogeneous as to size of farming enterprises, type and amount of industrial employment, and sources of cash income, that they were eliminated from the study.

THE GUM NAVAL STORES INDUSTRY
The Industry

There are two principal types of turpentine and rosin: "gum turpentine" and "gum rosin," and "wood turpentine" and "wood rosin." Gum naval stores are obtained by distilling the oleoresin (gum) exuded from the pine tree when it is wounded. Wood naval stores are obtained by destructive distillation or steam and solvent extraction from the resinous stumps and other wood left in the forest after cutting the virgin pine stands. Small amounts of by-products, known as sulphate turpentine and liquid rosin, are obtained from the sulphate process of papermaking. In recent years the gum distillation process has produced approximately 85 percent of the country's turpentine and nearly 80 percent of the rosin output.[12] Unless otherwise stated the following discussion will be devoted exclusively to gum naval stores.

Location of the Industry

Naval stores are produced in quantity in this country by only two species of pines—longleaf and slash. Slash pine, which is more favored because it gives relatively higher yields and its gum is more liquid, grows in the Coastal Plain from the southern corner of South Carolina to the Mississippi River.

Present distribution of the industry is indicated in figure 15, which shows the number of processors (gum distillers) by counties as determined by the Southern Forest Survey in 1934. The total number of processors in the active belt was 1,110. The area of greatest concentration was in the survey's Georgia Unit #1[13] which produced about 45 percent of the country's output of gum naval stores in the 1933–34 season.

Method of Production

The production of gum naval stores is a relatively simple and crude process. In advance of the operating season, which begins in March, the first streak is cut in the trees to be turpentined, and the cups and gutters for collecting the gum are hung. To maintain the flow of gum, fresh streaks must be cut periodically, usually once each week. This successive "chipping" gradually lengthens the scar, or "face," on the tree as the season proceeds. When the cups are filled with the gum, they are emptied into barrels[14] (this process is called "dipping"), which

---

[12] *Annual Naval Stores Report, 1934–35*, U. S. Department of Agriculture.

[13] This concentration was due mainly to the presence here of second-growth timber, which was of a size and age to attract the industry when the last of the large stands of old-growth pine were worked out in Louisiana, Mississippi, and Texas.

[14] On the average, for every 50 gallons of turpentine 3⅓ round barrels of rosin (500 pounds gross weight) are produced. One 50-gallon cask of turpentine and 3⅓ round barrels of rosin are therefore known as a unit. Production figures are frequently quoted in units.

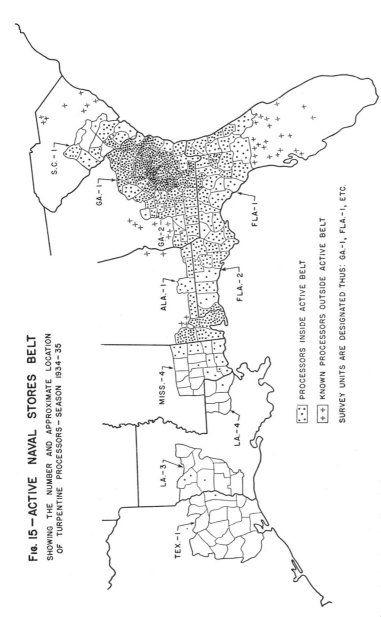

Fig. 15 – ACTIVE NAVAL STORES BELT

SHOWING THE NUMBER AND APPROXIMATE LOCATION
OF TURPENTINE PROCESSORS – SEASON 1934–35

PROCESSORS INSIDE ACTIVE BELT

KNOWN PROCESSORS OUTSIDE ACTIVE BELT

SURVEY UNITS ARE DESIGNATED THUS: GA.–1, FLA.–1, ETC.

Source: Southern Forest Experiment Station,
Forest Survey Release No. 17.

AF–2482, W P A

are then hauled to the still.   There the turpentine and rosin are separated by distillation.

The work of chipping, dipping, and stilling the gum continues from March until November.   At the end of the season the gum which has hardened on the face of the tree (called "scrape") is removed and stilled.   Some operators continue to chip the trees at longer intervals throughout the winter, but the yield of gum is small.   During the winter, the labor force is usually engaged in repairing tools, in thinning and fire-protection operations in the woods, and in raising the cups and gutters on some of the trees and installing new ones.   Thus, employment is held fairly steady throughout the year.

When a tree has all the faces it can stand (two or three, depending on diameter) and the faces have been lengthened by successive chipping to such a height that further working is unprofitable, the tree is considered worked out, and can be cut for pulpwood, ties, or lumber, thus bringing an additional income to the forest owner.   The number of years a tree can be worked depends on its size and the width of the streaks cut.   Under careful operation, each face may be worked for as much as 7 years.

Types of Producers and the Labor Force

Naval stores operators usually work their own or leased timber· They may also buy crude gum from producers who own no stills or they may still gum for these producers for a cash charge per barrel. Sales are usually made through naval stores factors, who in many cases finance the entire operation.

The labor force of a typical operation consists of a stiller, a still hand, one or more woods riders who supervise the woods work, the woods laborers, and the necessary teamsters or truck drivers.   The proprietor (operator) usually manages the business and keeps the accounts.   A great majority of the operators have only a single still. The operator, stiller, and woods riders are usually white.   A great majority of the laborers are Negroes.   Payment for chipping and dipping may be made on a time, piecework, or share basis.

Camps

The still is usually located in the woods or in the open country near the operator's timber.   Nearly all of the operators have camps for their woods laborers.   A typical layout of this type in Coffee County, Georgia, consists of a still, a commissary, and about 25 two-room or three-room cabins for workers and their families.

Trend of Production

The country's output of gum naval stores showed a declining trend from 1912 to 1918, then an increase to a peak in 1927, and a decrease during the depression.   Production of wood naval stores increased sharply in the early 1920's.

The declining production of gum turpentine and rosin from 1912 to 1918 coincided with a drop in exports, which was due to the World War, and also with the period in which the old-growth timber was being worked out. The postwar rise in output was roughly paralleled by rising exports. In fact, from 1910 to 1930, the amount of gum and wood naval stores available for domestic consumption (production less exports) has shown in general a level trend.[15]

Competing Materials

Gum and wood naval stores have the same general uses. The principal use for turpentine is in the manufacture of paint and varnish. Some is also consumed in making shoe polish and other products, but a very large proportion of the turpentine is sold over the counter by retailers to ultimate consumers.

Competing with turpentine are petroleum distillates, known as mineral thinners, which are used as thinners for paint and as solvents for varnish because they are much cheaper than turpentine. At present, about 10 gallons of these mineral thinners are used by the paint and varnish industry to every gallon of turpentine.

Rosin is used principally in the manufacture of varnish, lacquers and laundry soap, and for paper sizing. The principal competitors of rosin are synthetic resins used in varnish and lacquer making. At present there is no evidence of a trend toward the further displacement of turpentine and rosin. On the other hand, new uses for turpentine and rosin may also be developed.[16]

Problems of the Industry

The future of the industry is largely dependent upon the adoption of better forest practices, improved methods of handling and marketing, and the expansion of markets through development of new uses for turpentine and rosin.

Reform in forest practices is needed. The Forest Service, as a result of years of research, has worked out the principles to be followed to obtain the maximum return from the pine forests while maintaining their productivity. However, for various reasons approved methods are not generally followed. Financial pressure has frequently caused owners of timberlands to attempt to derive an income from the trees at the earliest possible moment rather than wait several years for a larger ultimate return. This has in many cases led to the turpentining of trees considerably smaller than the 9-inch diameter minimum recommended by the Forest Service, resulting in a low yield of gum, and little or no return from the cutting of worked-out trees for timber.

[15] *The Naval Stores Review* (Savannah), April 1934, and *The Journal of Trade* (Savannah), April 1934.

[16] Research in this field has been undertaken by the U. S. Department of Agriculture, but it is too early to indicate results.

Management of the pine forests for sustained yields has not been generally adopted in this country, where the practice of leasing a tract, obtaining what it would yield, and then moving on has prevailed.[17]

The processing methods followed in the industry are very crude, resulting in a lower-grade product than could otherwise be obtained. Some stills have recording thermometers for controlling the stilling, but in most cases the stiller regulates his fires according to the sound issuing from the discharge pipe. Rosin grades are determined by color, the lighter colors bringing the higher price, but frequently little attempt is made to keep out dirt which discolors it. Improvement might be obtained by shipping the gum to large centrally located stills where better control of the process could be exercised, and a more uniform, higher-grade product made. This centralization would only slightly reduce employment opportunities in the rural areas, because the labor involved in the stilling operation is only a small part of the total.

Wood naval stores, on the other hand, are produced by a relatively few chemical companies at large central plants. These concerns can keep in contact with industrial consumers, and adjust the quality and quantity of their output to the changing needs of these consumers. The gum naval stores industry consists of about 1,200 individual producers, who have no contact with consumers and little knowledge of market requirements.

Since 1929, prices received for turpentine and rosin have been so low as to bring about a condition of distress in the industry, and consequently, wages have been depressed to extremely low levels and profits have about vanished. Prices fluctuate widely from year to year depending on the amount produced, stocks on hand, and business activity.[18]

This distressed condition has led to efforts to obtain better prices through marketing associations or agreements, but they have not met with much success. In 1931, Congress passed a bill which declared gum turpentine and gum rosin to be agricultural commodities, and as such entitled to the benefits of any farm relief legislation. A cooperative marketing association was then formed, and an attempt made to maintain prices by withholding part of the supply from the market. This effort collapsed after 3 months, prices dropped to new lows, and the association had large stocks left on its hands.[19]

Outlook for Employment

It does not appear that any marked change is likely to take place in the next few years in the general level of activity of the industry

---

[17] *A Naval Stores Handbook*, Miscellaneous Publication 209, U. S. Department of Agriculture, p. 36.

[18] Braun, E. W. and Gold, N. L., *Some Facts Respecting Prices and Income in the Naval Stores Industry*, U. S. Department of Agriculture.

[19] *Gamble's International Naval Stores Yearbook for 1932–33*, pp. 2–3.

other than the recovery that can be expected if and when world trade revives. Of course, technical progress may bring about changes in demand for turpentine and rosin which may be either harmful or beneficial to the industry, or improved practices within the industry itself may enable it to extend its markets, but such changes usually develop slowly.

The amount of timber available for gum production is sufficient for present requirements, and the amount of second growth coming to maturity appears to be sufficient to allow an expansion of the naval stores industry to two or three times its present size within the next 20 years.[20] The industry may decline temporarily in certain areas where the maturing stock of trees is insufficient to replace the ones that are worked out, but this will probably be offset by increases in other areas, thus causing a shift in the geographical distribution of the industry. Such shifts can be avoided by sustained yield management where the condition of the forests is favorable.

FARMING ACTIVITIES OF PART-TIME FARMERS

Industry and farming activities are closely related in the Naval Stores Subregion, chiefly because of the proximity of the turpentine forests to the farm land, and because the work of gathering gum from which turpentine is distilled is similar to agricultural labor. In recent years, many farmers have turned to gum production as a means of supplementing their reduced farm incomes. They worked part-time in the turpentine industry either as wage hands of turpentine producers, or as independent operators of small areas, usually their own land. The latter usually sold their gum to a stiller, or had it processed and sold the turpentine and rosin.

In 1934, the Southern Forest Survey found 8,460 of these small turpentine producers in Georgia Survey Unit #1 (figure 15).[21] There were 1,150 of them in Alabama Survey Unit #1, but very few in Florida. In the belt surveyed, there were 11,250 turpentine producers of this class, whose production in the 1933–34 season was about 19 percent of the total production of all classes of producers in this area.

Types of Part-Time Farmers

Thirty-seven farmers who worked part-time in the turpentine industry, and who operated cotton and tobacco farms quite similar to those operated by full-time farmers throughout the county, were included in the sample studied for this survey. They will be spoken of as commercial part-time farmers.

---

[20] Letter from I. F. Eldredge, Director, Southern Forest Survey.

[21] *Statistics on Gum Naval Stores Production*, Forest Survey Release No. 17, Southern Forest Experiment Station.

An entirely different type of part-time farmer in this subregion was the full-time worker in miscellaneous (nonturpentine) jobs (appendix table 29) who had taken up small-scale farming activities as a means of supplementing industrial earnings. Thirty-four of these industrial workers were studied. These workers lived in Douglas or in the villages of Ambrose, Broxton, and Nichols, and their farming activities were limited chiefly to vegetable growing. They will be spoken of as noncommercial part-time farmers.

Size of Farms

The part-time farms of the town workers were usually not much more than family garden plots and the largest included only 6 acres of cropland. Those of the commercial farming group, who had part-time employment in the turpentine industry, ranged in size from 16 to 74 acres of cropland (appendix table 6).

Farm Production

Production for home use was important on all of these part-time farms. Four chief types of food were produced: vegetables, dairy products, poultry products, and pork. Nearly two-thirds of the commercial group produced all four types, while on the other hand about the same proportion of the noncommercial group produced only vegetables (appendix table 12).

While gardens were common to both commercial and noncommercial groups, and were about the same size for each, cows, hogs, and poultry were generally found only on the commercial farms (appendix table 11 and figure 16). As an additional enterprise, nearly all of the noncommercial group and about two-thirds of the commercial group cut their own firewood.

Gardens

All but one of the entire group of part-time farmers had gardens varying in size from ¼ acre to 2 acres.[22] There is considerable variation in the contribution that a garden of a given size may make to the family living. This depends upon the number of different vegetables grown, the yields, and the manner in which the various crops are planned seasonally. In southern Georgia, the winters are mild, but cold periods of a few days' duration are of common occurrence. Freezing weather is rare. Vegetables, particularly the more hardy types, may be grown almost continuously if temporary protection is given them during periods of cold weather. The average frost-free growing season is about 9 months.[23]

---

[22] Three gardens were completely washed out by heavy rains in 1934 and hence produced nothing.

[23] Wood, Percy O. and Others, *Soil Survey of Jeff Davis County, Georgia*, U. S. Department of Agriculture, Bureau of Soils, 1914, pp. 7–9.

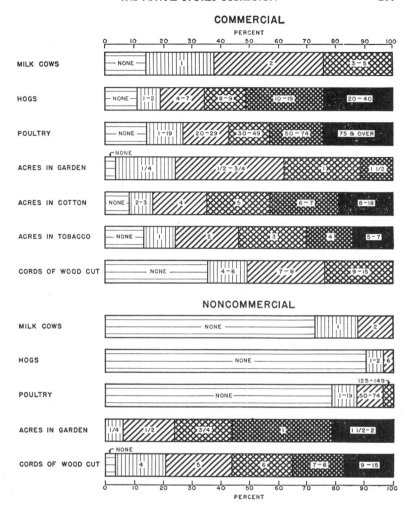

FIG.16– SIZE OF PRINCIPAL ENTERPRISES ON WHITE
PART-TIME FARMS, BY TYPE OF FARM,
COFFEE COUNTY, GA., 1934

AF-2476, W.P.A.

The length of the garden season on the farms studied, as measured by the time during which three or more fresh vegetables were available, ranged from 1 to 12 months and averaged about 4½ months (appendix table 13). For an average of 8½ months, at least one fruit or vegetable was available (appendix table 14). Several of the best gardens supplied cabbages, turnips, and collards from October through March. From one garden, in addition to these winter vegetables, carrots, onions, and radishes were supplied during the early spring months and pumpkins in the late fall, with a much greater variety available during the summer. These facts suggest that most of the gardens could be made to contribute more by the planting of early and late crops.

During the 6 summer months in particular, the products from the garden reduced to a considerable extent the purchase of food. Fifty-seven percent of all part-time farmers with gardens reported that their grocery bills were less in summer than in winter, the amount of the reduction averaging $3.70 per month. About four-fifths of those with only a garden reported a reduction in their grocery bills, this reduction averaging $4.70. Those with livestock and field crops used fewer purchased foods because they depended in large measure upon such home-grown staples as corn meal, sorghum syrup, sweet potatoes, and pork throughout the year. As a result, the substitution of home-grown vegetables during the summer made less of a reduction in their grocery bills than was true for those with less extensive farming operations.

As pointed out in the other subregion reports, such figures do not measure the entire contribution of the garden. In the first place, during the garden season the family may not only buy less groceries, but it may also fare better in quality and variety of food consumed. In the second place, to the extent that vegetables are canned or stored (table 29, page 20), they serve to reduce the grocery bill during the winter months. Two-thirds of the noncommercial group and nearly half of the commercial group did some canning, the average for both groups being 111 quarts (appendix table 16).

In a few cases, sweet potatoes (appendix table 17) and pecans were stored for winter use. Another field crop commonly grown for food by the commercial farmers was sugar cane. Usually from ¼ to 1 acre was devoted to this crop and from 20 to 50 gallons of syrup were stored for use throughout the year.

Dairy Products

More than three-fourths of the commercial part-time farmers, but only one-fourth of the noncommercial farmers, had one or more cows (appendix table 11 and figure 16). These animals, known locally as "piney woods cows," are of mixed breed and are given very little care, being left to pick up most of their forage by roaming through the "piney woods." As might be expected, they are inferior milk producers, but can be kept with little expense. Those on the commercial farms studied produced on the average slightly over 1,000 quarts of milk for the year, while those on noncommercial farms produced almost 1,300 quarts (appendix table 20). Families with more than one cow usually had fresh milk throughout the year and those with one cow had it for all but 2 or 3 months.

Most of the families who kept cows made butter, the average for the commercial farmers being 191 pounds, and for the noncommercial farmers only 86 pounds a year (appendix table 21). Only six part-time farmers sold dairy products.

Poultry Products

All but five of the commercial group, but only seven of the noncommercial group, kept poultry (appendix table 11). Flocks were quite variable in size. The poultry was given very little attention and egg production was low. Thirteen families sold eggs. The quantity of home-produced eggs consumed averaged about 2½ dozen a week for the commercial group (appendix table 18).

In addition to eggs, most of the families with poultry flocks consumed chicken as well and in three cases small quantities were sold. The amount consumed was small, however, being about one chicken a month on the average (appendix table 19).

Pork

Thirty-three of the commercial farmers, but only three of the noncommercial group, kept hogs (appendix table 11 and figure 16). Four-fifths of the commercial farmers had three hogs or more. Pork production for all commercial farmers who had hogs averaged 1,263 pounds, and for noncommercial farmers only 220 pounds a year (appendix table 22). In only two cases was pork sold directly for cash. Most of it was salted and stored on the farm. It is customary in this region to take salt pork to the local storekeeper from time to time to exchange for other supplies. Because of the difficulties involved, no attempt was made in the present study to determine just how much was used at home and how much was traded. Most of the families, however, had several hundred pounds of salt pork to eat during the year, pork being one of the principal articles in their diets. While the pork traded for supplies has not been figured in the cash income, it amounts, in effect, to a small increase in the family purchasing power. In a few cases, sharecroppers gave one-half of their pork to the landlord as rent, but usually a share of the pork was not included in the rental agreement.

Feed Crops

Practically all of the feed used was home grown. Since the noncommercial part-time farms were small and had very little livestock the growing of feed crops was almost entirely limited to the commercial group (appendix table 23). All of this group grew corn, the average per farm being 24 acres, and the average production 228 bushels (appendix table 24). This was nearly all fed to the livestock, since only a small proportion was needed for food. Only six commercial part-time farmers sold corn. Peanuts, cowpeas, velvet beans, and soybeans were the crops usually grown for roughage. Frequently, these were planted with corn and sometimes with, or following, tobacco. Sometimes they were cured and stored as hay for winter use and sometimes the livestock was turned into the lot to feed off the crop.

Fuel

Most of the commercial but only two of the noncommercial part-time farms included woodland. However, since this is largely a wooded region, all could readily cut their own firewood. Twenty-four commercial families cut an average of 9 cords, and thirty-three noncommercial families an average of 6 cords.

Cash Receipts and Cash Expenses

Only four of the farmers in the noncommercial group sold any farm products, and the maximum value of products sold was $51. For this group cash farm expenses, exclusive of rent and taxes, varied from $6 to $59 and averaged $25 (appendix table 25).

All the commercial part-time farmers grew cotton or tobacco, and nearly four-fifths of them grew both. Cotton acreages varied from 2 to 18 acres, and tobacco acreages from 1 to 6½ acres. Most of the remaining land was given over to the production of feed crops. The average value of the tobacco crop on these farms was slightly more than double the average value of the cotton crops.

On the owned and cash rented commercial farms, cash receipts ranged from $116 to $1,668 and averaged $583. Cash farm expenses, including rent and taxes, ranged from $87 to $460 and averaged $240. In only three cases were expenses greater than receipts.

Value and Tenure of Part-Time Farms

In view of the usual difficulties in arriving at significant real-estate values, the very simple procedure was adopted, as in the other sub-region studies, of recording the rental charge if the property was rented; or, if owned by the operator, of recording his estimate of what he could rent it for. The resulting rental values were capitalized at 5 percent to give a figure to serve as a rough index of value.

The value of farms in the open country was greater than that of homes in town since the farms included not only dwellings but also other buildings (appendix table 9) and farm land. In both cases, the real estate of owners was of considerably greater value than that of tenants (appendix table 7).

Only three of the noncommercial group had any implements and machinery other than small hand tools. Each of these three had a plow representing an original investment of $6.50. None of this group had work stock. Only a few had livestock and their gardening required an almost negligible investment in addition to the usual investment in a home. Since most of them rented their homes, their indebtedness consisted of chattel mortgages, not exceeding $400 in any case.

The commercial owners and tenants [24] had an investment in implements and machinery of from $25 to $200, averaging $115 (appendix table 10). Typically, this included three to five one-horse plows, a two-horse steel-beam plow, a fertilizer distributor, a harrow, and a wagon. Occasionally, tobacco transplanters and stalk cutters were also included.

Eight of the commercial farm owners had mortgages on their farms. These ranged from $500 to $1,900. About three-fourths of the commercial part-time farmers had chattel mortgages of varying amounts, the maximum being $450. This usually represented claims on furniture, mules, and automobiles. The indebtedness had increased substantially since 1929. Indebtedness of the commercial farm owners averaged $718, and that of the commercial farm tenants $108 (appendix table 8).

Fourteen of the commercial owners and tenants (exclusive of sharecroppers) kept one mule, and seven kept two. The other three borrowed or hired work stock.

Labor Requirements of Part-Time Farms and Their Relation to Working Hours in Industry

While the busy season on farms coincides in a general way with that in the turpentine industry, a fairly satisfactory basis for combining the two has been worked out. The commercial part-time farmers who worked as chippers and dippers in the turpentine forests usually were allotted slightly over one-third as many trees as were included in a unit for a full-time worker. The work on these trees required about eight 12-hour days a month from April through October, and somewhat less through the winter. There was some flexibility in the time for performing the 8 days of work each month; hence, each farmer could work out an adjustment between farming and turpentine work which suited his particular situation.

The commercial part-time farmers averaged nearly 9 hours of work a day on their farms through the spring and summer (table 48, page 32). In addition to the usual amount of family labor (appendix table 27), most of them had some of their work done by hired labor, the amount varying with the scale of their operations (appendix table 26).

---

[24] Exclusive of 13 sharecroppers.

Among the group of noncommercial farmers, those working in the railroad shops in Douglas had their working day curtailed to 6 hours in 1934. Most of the other town workers had an 8-hour day. Since their farm usually consisted of an acre or less of garden, they all had time to do this farm work. It required about 2 hours per day during the summer and could be done at the end of the regular working day. Little work was done by other family members.

EMPLOYMENT AND EARNINGS IN INDUSTRY

Incomes of industrial workers in this subregion are generally low. In the naval stores industry the laborers are very poorly paid, wages tending to be roughly on the same level as those for agricultural laborers. This is probably because the work is similar to agricultural labor. Earnings of workers in the railroad shops and in other enterprises in Douglas are higher than those of the turpentine laborers, but lower than those of similar white workers in the other subregions studied.

For comparative purposes, a sample of 49 white nonfarming industrial workers engaged in gum naval stores production was included in the study.

Industry and Occupation

The noncommercial part-time farmers were employed in a variety of industries (appendix table 29). The largest single group consisted of skilled and semiskilled workers in the car and railroad shops (appendix table 30). The others were scattered among the trades, communication, and mechanical industries.

Most of the work in the turpentine industry is unskilled labor in the woods. All of the commercial part-time farmers in this industry were woods laborers, except two who were woods riders (supervisors). About two-thirds of the nonfarming industrial group were laborers, and the remaining third included two woods riders and a semiskilled group of stillers, still hands, and truck drivers.

Earnings of Heads of Households

The off-the-farm employment of the commercial part-time farmers was distinctly secondary to their farm work, the source of the major part of their cash incomes. They worked only part time at turpentining, averaging 83 days employment in 1934, for which they received an average of $95 (appendix tables 32 and 34). The full-time turpentine workers had, on the average, 221 days of work and received $260 in annual earnings. Hourly earnings were from 8 to 12 cents for the laborers and somewhat more for the others (table 124). This industry never had an N. R. A. code.

Employees in the naval stores industry are frequently furnished with houses, rent-free. Forty-three of the forty-nine nonfarming

Table 124.—Rate of Pay [1] of Heads of White Part-Time Farm and Nonfarming Industrial Households in the Naval Stores Subregion, 1934

Hourly rate of pay	Part-time farmers			Non-farming industrial workers
	Commer-cial	Noncommercial		
		Car and railroad shops	Other industries	
Total	37	11	23	49
Less than 10 cents	14	—	1	24
10 to 19 cents	19	—	6	19
20 to 29 cents	2	2	6	4
30 to 39 cents	1	4	6	1
40 to 49 cents	—	2	3	—
50 to 59 cents	—	3	1	—
60 to 69 cents	—	—	—	—
70 to 79 cents	1	—	—	1
Average hourly rate of pay	$0.13	$0.38	$0.27	$0.12

[1] At principal off-the-farm employment (job with the largest earnings).

industrial workers paid no rent. Although this represents an addition to real income, it is usually not taken into account in setting wage or piecework rates, all employees being on the same basis whether living in a rent-free house or not.

The noncommercial part-time farmers carried on small-scale farming operations in their spare time. Their average annual earnings from industrial employment were over $500, or considerably higher than average annual earnings of workers in naval stores employment. Workers in railroad shops had a 6-hour day during 1934, but their annual earnings were about the same as those of workers in other nonnaval stores industries, the shorter day being offset by higher hourly rates of pay.

Total Family Cash Income

A major part of the cash income of the commercial part-time farmers came from the sale of farm products. The net cash farm income (receipts less cash expenses, including rent and taxes) in 1934 averaged $333 for owners and $360 for tenants, exclusive of croppers.[25] A small amount of cash was earned by members of the family other than the head (appendix table 35), 14 members earning an average of $55. There were also a few cases of income from other sources, such as Agricultural Adjustment Act payments and turpentine leases.

Total family cash incomes from all sources averaged $545 for owners and $453 for tenants other than the 13 sharecroppers, omitting earnings from bootlegging in 3 cases. The value of farm products consumed by the family or traded for other goods is not included in these income figures.

[25] The net cash farm income of the 13 sharecroppers averaged $159 and the total family cash income averaged $267.

Cash incomes of the noncommercial part-time farm families averaged $621 in 1934, the principal item being the earnings of the head (table 59, page 44). Outside labor of 10 other members contributed an average of $147 per worker, and there was a small amount of income from other sources. The farm contributed food to the family, but no cash income except in four cases.

This family income is not comparable with the figures given for the commercial part-time farmers because rent and taxes have been figured as farm expenses for the commercial group.

Total cash incomes of the nonfarming turpentine workers' families averaged $290. There were 23 working members other than the heads and they earned an average of $63 during the year.

Variation in Earnings in the Naval Stores Industry

Earnings of workers in the naval stores industry, while very low in 1934, are likely to improve as the industry and agriculture in the region recover. An idea of the increase in wages in this industry that might be expected with such recovery can be obtained from a consideration of past levels of earnings. No wage studies are available, but the ratio of wages to the average number of wage earners as reported by the Census of Manufactures can be used as an index. This ratio, the "census average wage," does not truly represent average actual earnings, but where there has been no substantial change from year to year in the relative amount of part-time work by the wage earners included in the census figures, the average wage is a fair index of changes in full-time earnings [26] (table 125).

Table 125.—Index of Wage Rates in the Gum Turpentine and Rosin Industry, 1919–1933

Year	Total wages	Average number of wage earners	Average wage per wage earner	Index of full-time earnings 1929=100
1919	$16,972,881	28,067	$605	162
1921	9,512,177	27,422	347	93
1923	15,448,590	34,328	450	120
1925	15,090,076	29,413	513	137
1927	16,953,054	37,913	447	120
1929	15,036,175	40,157	374	100
1931	7,280,389	28,257	258	69
1933	5,501,000	26,285	209	56

Source: *United States Census of Manufactures.*

LIVING CONDITIONS AND ORGANIZED SOCIAL LIFE

Turpentine orchards and stills are scattered throughout the rural areas. Hence, commercial part-time farmers who worked in the turpentine industry and nonfarming workers in the industry lived in the open country and experienced the same lack of conveniences

---

[26] For a discussion of the census average wage, see *Earnings of Factory Workers, 1899 to 1927,* by Paul F. Brissenden, United States Census Monograph X.

and of organized social life as full-time farmers. Noncommercial part-time farmers, most of whom lived in Douglas, had a more varied social life and their dwellings were in much better condition than those of the commercial part-time farmers or of the nonfarming turpentine workers. They frequently had such conveniences as running water and electric lights, but only a few had bathrooms.

Housing

Dwellings of commercial part-time farmers were typical of farm dwellings in general in this area. The walls of the houses were usually constructed of rough boards with narrow vertical strips nailed over the cracks between them. They were unpainted, unplastered, and most were in a poor state of repair (appendix table 40). They usually contained four, five, or six rooms and were without such modern conveniences as running water and electric lights. Many had no glass windows and where these were found, panes were frequently missing.

The dwellings of the noncommercial part-time farmers were typical of those in small towns and villages. Their houses had substantial foundations, weatherboarding on the walls, and were plastered inside and painted outside. The average size of all part-time farmhouses was 4.9 rooms (appendix table 38). Of the 27 families living in Douglas, 17 had running water, 5 had bathrooms, and 11 had electric lights. Seven families lived in villages, and of these none had running water and only one had electric lights. Over 70 percent of the part-time farm families had no such conveniences (appendix table 41).

As previously mentioned, the houses of the nonfarming turpentine workers were usually furnished rent-free by their employer. They were smaller than the farmhouses, averaging 3.6 rooms. None had electric lights and only one in the sample studied had running water. A number of these houses were fairly new.

Automobiles, Radios, and Telephones

Only a few families reported having automobiles, radios, or telephones. The only family reported as having a telephone was in the noncommercial part-time farm group. Five noncommercial and three commercial part-time farm families and one nonfarming household had radios. Automobiles were owned by 10 nonfarming turpentine workers, and by 5 commercial and 6 noncommercial part-time farmers (appendix table 42). This lack of communication facilities tended to intensify the isolation of the turpentine workers in scattered communities or on farms.

Home Ownership

Sixteen of the commercial part-time farmers owned their homes, as compared with only four of the noncommercial part-time farmers (table 69, page 59, and appendix table 7). None of the nonfarming workers in the turpentine industry owned their homes. Home ownership was rather a disadvantage for turpentine workers because it prevented them moving about and because employers usually furnished houses rent-free.

Education

Children of nonfarming workers in the turpentine industry were retarded about 2 years in school on the average (table 76, page 64). This is indicative of inadequate school facilities in some of the rural areas and the low cultural and economic level of this group. Children 7–16 years of age in the commercial part-time farm households, who had the advantage of better schools, were retarded less than 1 year, while those in the noncommercial part-time farm group had made approximately normal progress.

Part-time farmers had completed an average of six grades in school, as compared with less than five for the nonfarming industrial workers (appendix table 46).

Social Participation

Very few social organizations were found in the rural areas of Coffee County because the people required to support them were widely scattered and had low incomes. Monthly church services, and sometimes Sunday Schools, were the only organized activities in which commercial part-time farm families participated.

In Douglas, where most of the noncommercial part-time farmers lived, there were Parent-Teacher Associations, athletic teams, labor unions, and fraternal orders in addition to the usual church organizations.

Participation in social organizations of the families enumerated in Coffee County was much lower than that of families in the other areas studied (appendix table 48). The average number of meetings of all social organizations attended per person in 1934 was 19 for the noncommercial part-time farm group, 14 for nonfarming industrial households, and only 4 for commercial part-time farm families (table 80, page 68). A considerable number of the households did not participate at all in organized social life. This included 15 commercial and 7 noncommercial part-time farm households, and 14 nonfarming industrial households. There were only three part-time farm households and five nonfarming industrial households in which one or more persons held office in social organizations in 1934 (appendix table 49).

RELIEF

Only two commercial and four noncommercial part-time farmers and five nonfarming turpentine workers reported receiving public relief during 1934. The amounts of relief received ranged from $3 to $75, and averaged $23.   The small number of cases reporting relief is partly due to the fact that nearly all workers who qualified as part-time farmers in the Coffee County sample had steady employment throughout the year.   Since those families whose heads had worked less than 50 days off the farm during 1934 were automatically excluded from the category of part-time farmer, this excluded most of the cases receiving relief.

Only 10 percent of the part-time farmers had received any relief during the period 1929–1935.   Slightly less than 30 percent of the nonfarming industrial workers had received relief (table 61, page 47, and appendix table 36).

Appendixes

Appendix A

CASE STUDIES OF PART-TIME FARMERS

From WHAT has gone before, it may be seen that part-time farmers are not a homogeneous group of people, but may be considered in many respects as a fairly representative cross section of the population of a given area. The only thing which part-time farmers have in common is the specified twofold source of income. A description chiefly in statistical terms of such a group of people may not accurately describe any one family in the group, or convey a concrete picture of the activities of the people under consideration. For this reason, descriptions of actual representative cases of part-time farming are introduced.

COTTON TEXTILE SUBREGION
Textile Millworker, Greenville County, South Carolina

This man was 34 years old, a millworker, and a typical noncommercial part-time farmer. His household consisted of his wife and four children ranging from 7 to 15 years. They lived in the open country 7 miles from Greenville to which both parents commuted daily in their 1931 Ford to work in a textile mill. The head was a weaver and in 1934 worked 8 hours a day for 5 days a week, except for 3 months during the summer when employment was curtailed to a 30-hour week. His total earnings were $864. The wife worked in the same mill, also as a weaver, for 4 months and added $300 to the family income.

This family rented a five-room house and 4½ acres of land for $100 a year. The house, while fairly substantial, was 25 years old, needed painting, and was unattractive in general appearance. It did not have a telephone, electric lights, or running water.

Two and one-half acres were planted in crops in 1934. These crops included 1½ acres of field corn, ¼ acre each of sweet corn and peanuts, and ½ acre of other vegetables, including Irish and sweet potatoes, tomatoes, okra, peas, snap beans, lettuce, peppers, squash, cucumbers, onions, turnips, and melons. This garden furnished a good supply of

221

vegetables from June through October, with turnips somewhat earlier and later. The grocery bill was only $20 per month during the summer, as compared with $25 during the winter. In addition, 59 quarts of vegetables were canned for winter use, and potatoes, peas, beans, and peanuts were stored. Sales from the garden amounted to $9. The corn crop of 15 bushels was fed to the pig and chickens. Six pear trees and a fig tree together yielded 1½ bushels of fruit.

The livestock consisted of a cow, a pig, and eight chickens. The cow produced 2,500 quarts of milk during the year, but was dry for 2 months. Two quarts of milk were consumed per day. In addition to the sweet milk, the family had almost 3 quarts of buttermilk per day and about 5 pounds of butter a week for 10 months.

The pig was killed in November, and its dressed weight was 200 pounds. Most of the meat was cured for use throughout the year. The eight hens laid 25 dozen eggs over a period of 8 months.

The family did practically all of the work on the farm, paying only $5 for hired machine work. The head worked on the farm all day Saturday and 1 or 2 hours after work during most of the year. His wife fed the chickens and sometimes did the milking. Cash expenses exclusive of rent were $70 for the year. The feed cost was considerably reduced by the fact that the landlord allowed the use of a pasture for the cow.

The exact cash value of the farm's contribution is difficult to determine. In the first place, the quantities of garden products consumed are not definitely known, since the family used them as needed from day to day. When a particular vegetable or other product was available in abundance, the family used much more of it than it would have done had it been necessary to purchase it.

It should also be noted that the quantity of products grown on this farm would be worth more to a larger family than to a smaller one. This is so because larger quantities of one product could be used in a given period by the larger family, thus reducing the waste from surplus. The variety of products is therefore very important since with a greater variety more can be utilized to advantage.

Recognizing these difficulties it still seems worth while to estimate a value for this production.

600 qts. milk	@ 10¢	$60. 00
200 lbs. butter	@ 25¢	50. 00
800 qts. buttermilk	@ 3¢	24. 00
200 lbs. pork	@ 10¢	20. 00
25 doz. eggs	@ 20¢	5. 00
64 qts. canned vegetables and fruits	@ 25¢	16. 00
15 bu. sweet potatoes stored	@ $1	15. 00
2½ bu. peas, beans, and peanuts	@ $1	2. 50
Fresh vegetables and fruits		75. 00
Total value		267. 50

The chief guide in arriving at the prices used in the above calculations was the prices paid to millworkers in this area in 1934 when they sold farm products to one another.

Although this family had moved from Greenville to the farm only 2 years before, the head, who had had 5 years of previous farming experience, was managing this small place very well and wanted a larger farm. The children were all in school and all members of the family were going to church and Sunday School regularly. There were no organized social activities in this community. The parents had attended school through the elementary grades.

Textile Millworker, Carroll County, South Carolina

This household, a noncommercial part-time farm family, consisted of a man and wife, aged 29 and 39, respectively, and their two daughters, aged 4 and 2. They lived in the Mandeville Mill Village, only ¼ mile from the mill where both husband and wife worked. Each worked an 8-hour day for 5 days a week during 1934 except for the month of September during the textile strike. They worked on different shifts, however. The head ran a waste machine on the afternoon shift and earned $516, and his wife was a spinner on the morning shift, earning $480.

This family rented a three-room, company-owned house with ½ acre of land for $90 a year. Rents in this village were higher than those usually charged in mill villages. The house was in fair condition except for the need of paint. It had electric lights, but no telephone or running water. The family had a radio, but no automobile.

Virtually all of the land except that on which the house was located was used as a garden in 1934. The vegetables grown were tomatoes, okra, peas, snap beans, lima beans, cabbages, lettuce, peppers, squash, cucumbers, beets, onions, turnips, collards, and sweet corn. A good supply of vegetables was available from June through September, with turnips and collards in October and November. The wife canned 44 quarts of vegetables. The grocery bill was reduced an average of $8 per month during the 6 summer months.

The livestock consisted of a cow, a pig, and 11 chickens. The cow produced 2,600 quarts of milk during the year, being dry only 1 month. Two hundred pounds of butter were made. The family sold $27 worth of milk, butter, and buttermilk, and had on the average 2 quarts of milk a day and 4 pounds of butter a week for 11 months. The pig was slaughtered in December, and its dressed weight was 250 pounds. The chickens laid throughout the year, producing about 30 dozen eggs. Ten chickens were raised. The roosters were eaten and the pullets replaced the hens that were culled from the laying flock. In this way, the family had 10 chickens to eat at various times during the year.

The mill supplied a shed for the livestock and pasturage for the cow. All other feed was purchased at a cost of $80, most of which was for the cow. Cash farm expenses, exclusive of rent, totaled $106. Deducting the $27 received from sales of dairy products leaves $79 as the cash cost of the farm products used by the family. The value of these products, at the prices used in the calculations for the farm in Greenville County, would be as follows:

650 qts. milk	@ 10¢	$65
200 lbs. butter	@ 25¢	50
600 qts. buttermilk	@ 3¢	18
30 doz. eggs	@ 20¢	6
20 lbs. chicken	@ 25¢	5
250 lbs. pork	@ 10¢	25
44 qts. canned vegetables	@ 25¢	11
Fresh vegetables		50
Total value		230

The garden was considerably smaller than the one on the Greenville County farm, and there were no fruit trees on the place. Consequently, in spite of the greater variety of products grown, smaller quantities were available for preserving for winter use. The smaller size of the family also meant that fewer vegetables could be used. As a result of these considerations, the value of the products of the garden was estimated at $50, as compared with $75 for the Greenville County farm.

The head and his wife did all of the work on this farm in 1934. The wife milked the cow and fed all of the livestock in the evening while her husband was working, and he did these chores in the morning. She also helped him with the gardening.

The head was a full-time farmer until 4 years ago, when he moved into town and began working in the mill. Since then, he has been a part-time farmer at two places in this mill village. He thinks part-time farming very much worth while.

This family takes no part in the many organized social activities in the village except for attending church and Sunday School. The head completed three grades in school and his wife five.

Unusually Successful Part-Time Farmer, Greenville County, South Carolina

Mr. Pickens [1] was one of the most successful part-time farmers in the Greenville Area. He was 38 years of age, his wife 28, and four children ranged from 4 to 12 years. Mr. Pickens was a weaver in one of the larger cotton mills in Greenville. He had been with the mill for 7 years, and had rarely been without employment, a record considerably above the average for cotton mill weavers. This mill makes fine goods, thus requiring a skilled labor force, and wages are correspondingly higher than in most mills. Mr. Pickens earned a little over $1,000 in 1934. In addition to his work in the mill, he owned and operated a 15-acre farm about 5 miles from his place of employment.

[1] The name used is fictitious.

When he was 11 years old his father was permanently disabled. His mother ran the farm for a few years, but it eventually became necessary for them to sell at a sacrifice. When he was about 12 years of age, he started to work in a textile mill. When he was 18, he entered school at Berea College but left during his first year to join the Navy Medical Corps in 1917. After the war, he was honorably discharged and returned to work in a mill near Greenville where the other members of his family were then employed. He saved money while he was working in the mill and bought 4 acres outside the city limits. At the end of 3 or 4 years he had improved this land to such an extent that he was able to sell for more than twice the amount he had paid. With the money received for his first venture, he purchased a 100-acre farm in the lower part of Greenville County and went into commercial farming.

His farming venture promised to be very successful, but his wife (he married shortly before moving to the farm) was not satisfied with rural life and was in poor health besides. So the family moved back to the city of Greenville where they lived for a time in the mill village. Five years ago, however, they decided to move to a small farm near enough to town for Mr. Pickens to keep his employment and for the family to enjoy advantages offered by proximity to the city.

During his 5 years of operation of his present farm, Mr. Pickens had built a six-room, two-story brick house, doing most of the work himself, and at the time of the survey was completing the inside finishing. He had wired the house for electricity and had installed plumbing. He had improved his farm to the point where it produced all of the vegetables, dairy products, and meat which the family needed. He was building up a small fruit orchard and a vineyard, and already had small bush fruits and berries well established. Each year he has mapped out some plan of permanent improvement on the place.

In 1934, Mr. Pickens had 1½ acres of garden, 3 acres of corn, 1 acre of wheat, and 2 acres of pea-vine hay. He had vegetables from the garden during all but 2 months of the year, and in addition Mrs. Pickens canned 80 quarts of vegetables and 52 quarts of fruit. Since he grew 50 bushels of grain and 3 tons of hay, and had 5 acres of pasture, Mr. Pickens spent only $10 for feed for his cow, 2 heifers, 2 hogs, and 150 chickens. In addition, he had corn and wheat ground for home use; he had a good supply of milk and eggs throughout the year; and also had 225 pounds of dressed poultry, 700 pounds of pork, and 140 pounds of veal.

Mr. Pickens did practically all of the work himself with what little help his children were capable of giving. He spent only $8 for hired labor. He sold practically nothing, although he had considerable surplus which he gave away.

The family was active in the social life of the local neighborhood, and both Mr. and Mrs. Pickens were regarded as "pillars of the church." Mrs. Pickens was an officer in the circulating library. Mr. Pickens was contributing part of his land fronting on the road for the building of a women's club house.

The family favored part-time farming as a mode of living. Mr. Pickens said: "A man likes to feel that he is building himself a home that is his. You can't do that in the mill village. Another thing—you feel independent when you have a place of your own that you can depend on in an emergency. You don't feel cramped. Your kids have plenty of room to play in and they learn to work and not get into mischief.

"I am almost 40 years old, and I know that I have earned as good money as I will ever earn. Pretty soon I will have to take less, and before many years I will have to quit the mill, although I will not be too old to work for a living. Now if I have a place where I can raise all I need to eat and something extra to sell, I will be set for my old age. If I can save up money while I am working and not spend it for food and rent, I can give my kids a better education than I have."

COAL AND IRON SUBREGION
A White Iron Mine Worker

This man, the head of a household of eight, was 48 years old, and a blacksmith at an iron mine. In 1929, he earned $2,100 at this job, but after July 1934, the mine was closed. As a result, even though his wages were 70 cents per hour, he earned only $616 during the year.

Three sons, aged 19, 21, and 22, had completed high school, but were still at home. The oldest had a job in 1934 as a clerk in a grocery store and earned $650. The other two had no industrial employment. The remaining children were two daughters aged 8 and 5, and a small granddaughter.

The home was located in Bessemer, a mile from the mine, and was rented from the company for $11 per month. It was a five-room house equipped with electric lights and running water, but had no telephone or bathroom. It was in fairly good repair except for lack of paint. The family had a radio and a 1928 model car.

In 1934, the company allowed this man free use of 1½ acres of land located about ½ mile from his home. He planted ¼ acre of peanuts, ¼ acre of sweet corn, and 1 acre of various other garden crops. There were eight fig trees on the place which yielded 8 bushels of figs, of which 90 quarts were canned and the remainder used fresh. The vegetables grown included Irish potatoes, sweet potatoes, tomatoes, okra, peas, snap beans, lima beans, cabbages, lettuce, peppers, squash, cucumbers, beets, onions, radishes, turnips, and collards. The garden season lasted from May through October, with radishes and turnips in March and April as well. A total of 90 quarts of tomatoes, okra, and corn were canned. Twelve bushels of Irish potatoes, twenty bushels of sweet potatoes, and ten bushels of peanuts were stored for winter use. As a result, the grocery bill was only $2 per month more during the winter than during the summer. In addition, $50 worth of corn and tomatoes were sold.

The only livestock was a cow which produced 3,200 quarts of milk in 1934. The family used 3 or 4 quarts of sweet milk and over 1 quart of buttermilk per day, and made 100 pounds of butter during the year, or about 2 pounds per week. All of the cow's feed, except that supplied by a few cornstalks and peanut vines, had to be purchased, the total cost being $72. The only other expenses were $20 for labor, $4 for fertilizer, and $2 for supplies.

The approximate value of the production of this farm, using prices which prevailed in this area when products were sold at the farm, was as follows:

1, 200 qts. milk	@ 10¢	$120
100 lbs. butter	@ 25¢	25
400 qts. buttermilk	@ 3¢	12
180 qts. canned vegetables and fruits	@ 25¢	45
32 bu. potatoes	@ $1	32
10 bu. peanuts	@ 70¢	7
Fresh vegetables and fruits		75
Total value		316

The head of this family and one son worked about 4 hours per day each on the garden from April through October. The wife milked and fed the cow, spending about 1 hour per day at this work throughout the year.

This miner had carried on part-time farming on this place for 4 years. He had had no previous farming experience, but was much interested in farming and was continually trying out new crops, new varieties, and new methods. He had completed the fifth grade in school.

A number of community social organizations, including church and related groups, athletic teams, school clubs, a labor union, library and women's organizations, were available. However, participation by members of this family was limited. The head of the family rarely took part in any religious activities, but attended his labor union meetings regularly. The wife attended church about twice a month. The children went to Sunday School, and one of them attended a young people's society.

A White Steel Millworker

The head of the household was a rigger in a steel mill in Ensley. In 1934, he worked 20 days per month until August, but only 14 days during the remaining 5 months of the year. His pay was 50 cents per hour and his total earnings $616. This was the entire cash income of the family. In 1929, he earned $1,000 at the same job. He was 42 years of age and was not incapacitated for work in any way. Besides his wife, the family included four children from 1 to 10 years of age. The three oldest were in school in 1934.

The home was a six-room house in good repair, owned by the family. It had a bathroom, running water, electric lights, and a radio, but no telephone. It was located in the open country 3 miles from the mill where the head of the family was employed. He drove to work in his 1929 Chevrolet.

There was about ¼ acre of land in the house lot, and an additional acre was rented. All of the land except that occupied by the house and yard was used for a garden. Vegetables and fruits were grown, including Irish and sweet potatoes, tomatoes, okra, peas, snap beans, lima beans, cabbages, lettuce, peppers, beets, carrots, onions, radishes, turnips, watermelons, sweet corn, peanuts, popcorn, blackberries, and strawberries. From 3 to 13 vegetables were available from March through October. Forty quarts of vegetables and forty quarts of berries were canned; 8 bushels of Irish potatoes and 15 bushels of sweet potatoes were stored.

A cow was kept, and from the 2,200 quarts of milk produced the family had over 1 quart of fresh milk and nearly 2 quarts of buttermilk per day, as well as about 2 pounds of butter per week during the whole year. A small pig was raised and slaughtered in December, providing the family with 150 pounds of pork. Forty pounds were eaten fresh and the rest was cured for use throughout the year. The pig was fed surplus skim milk and buttermilk as well as other waste food, and the cow was fed cornstalks and peanut vines and was staked out along the roadside. As a result, the cost of purchased feed was only $40.

The value of the products of this farm may be estimated as follows:

400 qts. milk	@ 10¢	$40
100 lbs. butter	@ 25¢	25
600 qts. buttermilk	@ 3¢	18
80 qts. canned vegetables and fruits	@ 25¢	20
23 bu. potatoes	@ $1	23
150 lbs. pork	@ 10¢	15
Fresh vegetables and fruits		75
Total value		216

Farm products were valued at less than those of the preceding farm chiefly because of the smaller production of the cow.

All of the farm work except plowing was done by the head of the family. He worked about 4 hours a day on the average during the summer and about 2 hours a day during the remainder of the year. The company charged $2 for plowing the garden. Total expenses other than rent and taxes were $45. No farm products were sold.

This family moved out of town and undertook part-time farming late in 1932, but the head had had 5 years of earlier farming experience. The organized group life in the community was rather limited. There were a church and related religious group activities, athletic teams, a Parent-Teacher Association, and a woman's organization. The participation of this family was confined to occasional church and regular Sunday School attendance, and regular attendance at the Parent-Teacher Association by the wife. There was a library in the community, but it was not used by any member of the family.

A Negro Steel Millworker

The head of the family was 50 years of age, and worked in 1934 as a ladle liner in a steel mill in Ensley. He was employed regularly 20 days per month until July, when the mill was closed. His rate of pay was 37 cents per hour and his total earnings $385. In 1929, when he was fully employed at the same job, he received $1,050. In 1934, the family received $90 from the relief agency.

Five children ranged from 2 to 15 years of age. The two older ones were in school in 1934. The family lived in a five-room house, 16 years old but in good condition, which was rented from the company for $11 per month. It had running water but no bathroom and no electricity. It was ½ mile from the mill. The family owned a 1925 automobile.

The acre of cropland nearby which the company furnished was planted half in corn and half in garden vegetables. These included sweet potatoes, tomatoes, okra, peas, snap beans, lima beans, cabbages, lettuce, peppers, squash, beets, carrots, onions, turnips, collards, and peanuts. Three or more fresh vegetables were available from May through October. In addition, 14 quarts of tomatoes and snap beans were canned, and 12 bushels of sweet potatoes were stored. There were five peach trees which yielded 10 bushels of fruit, of which 100 quarts were canned. Twelve bushels of corn and four bushels of peanuts were stored for winter use. Some of the corn was ground for use as food and the remainder fed to the three chickens, which were eaten during November and December.

The value of the contribution of this farm to the family living may be estimated as follows:

16 lbs. chicken	@ 25¢	$4. 00
114 qts. canned vegetables and fruits	@ 25¢	28. 50
12 bu. potatoes	@ $1. 00	12. 00
4 bu. peanuts	@ 70¢	2. 80
4 bu. peaches	@ $1. 50	6. 00
Fresh vegetables		70. 00
Total value		123. 30

All the farm work was done by the family. The head, his wife, and their 15-year-old son each worked about 2 hours per day on the crops from April through September. There were no direct cash expenses in connection with the operation of the farm other than about $3 for seed and fertilizer. The family had been doing part-time farming for 3 years, but had no previous farming experience.

The community in which this family lived had a number of organizations, but the family limited its participation to regular attendance at church and Sunday School.

A Negro Iron Ore Miner

This man was 34 years old, and his family consisted of a wife and six children. He worked 64 days in 1934 as a mucker in an iron ore mine, receiving 45 cents per hour. His total earnings were $230. In 1929, when fully employed at this same job, he received $720. In 1934, the family received $120 from the relief agency.

This family lived in Bessemer in a two-room house, rented from the company for $5 per month. The house needed extensive repairs, and had not been repainted since it was built 22 years ago. It had running water, but no bathroom and no electric lights.

An acre of company-owned land located ¼ of a mile from the home was used rent-free for a garden. One-half acre was devoted to corn and the remainder to 14 kinds of vegetables. Three or more vegetables were used from the garden from May through October, while turnips were also used during March, April, November, and December as well, and collards during the latter 2 months. In addition to fresh vegetables, 2 bushels of Irish potatoes, 30 bushels of sweet potatoes, 25 bushels of corn, and 4 bushels of peanuts were stored for winter use. The six peach trees on the place yielded 2 bushels of fruit, from which 6 quarts were canned.

Twelve hens were kept and twelve chicks were raised during the year. About a dozen eggs per week were produced throughout the year, and 80 pounds of chicken were used during the second half of the year. The value of the farm products consumed by the family may be estimated as follows:

50 doz. eggs	@ 20¢	$10. 00
80 lbs. chicken	@ 25¢	20. 00
6 qts. canned fruits	@ 25¢	1. 50
32 bu. potatoes	@ $1. 00	32. 00
10 bu. corn	@ $1. 00	10. 00
4 bu. peanuts	@ 70¢	2. 80
1½ bu. peaches	@ $1. 50	2. 25
Fresh vegetables		65. 00
Total value		143. 55

The head of the family worked on the farm an average of 6 hours per day during the summer, and 1 hour per day during the remainder of the year. He paid $10 for hired machine work. Feed for the chickens, in addition to the corn and other surplus garden products grown, cost $5. The only other cash expenditure was $2 for garden seeds.

This family had been doing part-time farming for 3 years, and the head previously had had 5 years of farm experience. The members of the family attended church and Sunday School regularly. The head of the family attended labor union meetings, and the wife went regularly to meetings of a woman's club.

ATLANTIC COAST SUBREGION

A White Service Industry Employee

Mr. Andrews,[2] 40 years old, was a railroad section foreman. His family consisted of his wife and five children, who ranged from 8 to 18 years of age. He was representative of part-time farmers who were skilled workmen or foremen. He worked regularly throughout 1934 for six 8-hour days per week, with 1 week's vacation, and earned approximately $1,500.

This family lived rent-free in a house owned by the railroad. Three-fourths of an acre of cropland went with the house. In addition, discarded railroad ties were used for fuel, and the cow was pastured along the railroad right-of-way. All of these advantages were equivalent in effect to an annual addition of about $175 to the family income.

The land was planted in 1934 in a variety of vegetables, including tomatoes, okra, peas, snap beans, lima beans, peppers, squash, cucumbers, radishes, collards, and sweet corn. Collards were used from December through March, radishes in April, and the other vegetables through May, June, and July. The grocery bill was reduced $6 per month, or 12 percent, during the summer by the garden contribution.

The livestock consisted of a cow and a small flock of chickens. The cow was dry for 2 months of the year, but produced 2,000 quarts of milk during the remaining 10 months. Two or three quarts of fresh milk per day were consumed and the remainder was made into butter. Thus the family had 3 pounds of butter per week for home consumption, and about 3 quarts of buttermilk per day.

Twelve hens were kept and ten chicks raised during the year. Thirty dozen eggs were produced over a 9-month period.

Although it is difficult to determine the farm's contribution with precision, its value can be roughly estimated as $187.50. Prices used are those which prevailed in the area when farm families sold products to one another.

800 qts. milk	@ 10¢	$80. 00
125 lbs. butter	@ 25¢	31. 25
800 qts. buttermilk	@ 3¢	24. 00
30 doz. eggs	@ 20¢	6. 00
25 lbs. chicken	@ 25¢	6. 25
Fresh vegetables		40. 00
Total value		187. 50

The entire farm work, with the exception of the plowing, was done by the family. During the summer, Mr. Andrews spent about 1 hour a day in the garden. The older boys cared for the livestock before and

---

[2] The name used is fictitious.

after school. Farm expenses totaled only $10 for feed, $3 for plowing, and $2 for supplies.

This family lived in the open country 6 miles from the city. They owned a 1933 Chevrolet sedan, used chiefly for pleasure. The house was in good repair but had no running water, no electricity, and no telephone.

An Unusually Successful White Part-Time Farmer

Mr. Williams[3] was 45 years old, with a wife, two children, and two grown stepdaughters. He earned $36 per week as a millwright in Charleston until the depression, when he was forced to become a part-time machinist at $350 per year. He undertook part-time farming at that time to establish greater security for himself and his family.

The family lived on a rented 4½-acre plot with a six-room cottage about ½ mile from his plant and, at the time of the survey, he had rented an additional 2½ acres of cropland. Mr. Williams said that without his farm, he could not have kept off relief during the period when his income was curtailed.

This man made intensive use of his cropland. In 1934, he grew 19 kinds of vegetables, and had at least 2 kinds of fresh vegetables during every month of the year. Following the early vegetables, first a corn crop and then a crop of pea-vine hay were planted, and enough feed was grown for the livestock on his farm: a Shetland pony, 5 pigs, and 50 chickens. Besides supplying home needs approximately $200 worth of crops was sold.

From the poultry, the family had about 4 dozen eggs a week throughout the year, and an average of one chicken a week. Four hundred pounds of pork also were used during the year. The approximate value of home-consumed products was as follows:

120 doz. eggs	@ 20¢	$24
200 lbs. chicken	@ 25¢	50
400 lbs. pork	@ 10¢	40
140 qts. canned vegetables	@ 25¢	35
Fresh vegetables		75
Total value		224

Mr. Williams worked about 4 hours a day on his farm throughout the 6 summer months, and from 1 to 2 hours a day during the remainder of the year. In 1934, he held a full-time job as watchman, yet did all the farm work except that of gathering vegetables. Cash expenses were $50 for fertilizer, $20 for supplies, and $20 for rent for the land exclusive of the house. Hence, at the above prices, Mr. Williams received a net return in cash and in products of $334.

Mr. Williams' investment in farm equipment was small. Besides hand tools, he had a plow, a harrow, and a cultivator, and his only work animal was the Shetland pony.

---

[3] The name used is fictitious.

The Williams' house had running water, inside bathroom, and electric lights. The family had a radio and a 1929 Ford.

A Negro Fertilizer Factory Employee

This man was 54 years of age. His family consisted of a wife, a son 30 years old, two daughters 19 and 20 years of age, and the son of one of the daughters. The head of the household had full employment of six 8-hour days per week during February, March, and part of April 1934. His wages were 25 cents per hour, and his total earnings were $130 per year. His wife did washing and ironing for several families and earned $150. In addition, the family received relief amounting to $130 during the time the head was unemployed. The family had been receiving relief since 1933. This situation was typical of fertilizer factory workers, many of whom are employed only in the spring, but it was not typical of the entire Negro group studied.

The family owned a four-room house and little more than an acre of land in a suburban village 2 miles from the head's place of employment. They had lived in this place for 23 years. The house was in a poor state of repair, with no electric lights and no running water. However, the family kept a 1926 Chevrolet touring car for pleasure purposes.

One-fourth of the cropland was used to grow sweet potatoes, and the rest was planted in tomatoes, okra, peas, snap beans, lima beans, peppers, turnips, and sweet corn. These vegetables were available during May, June, July, and August. No vegetables, other than 12 bushels of sweet potatoes, were stored. The family grocery bill was reduced $4 per month, or one-third, during the summer months by use of the home-grown vegetables.

Twenty-five hens, that produced slightly more than a dozen eggs per week, were kept, and twelve chickens were raised and eaten during 1934.

The value of the farm products used by this family was:

60 doz. eggs	@ 20¢	$12. 00
25 lbs. chicken	@ 25¢	6. 25
12 bu. sweet potatoes	@ $1	12. 00
Fresh vegetables		40. 00
Total value		70. 00

The head of this family was able to do all of the farm work, since most of it came after the fertilizer season was over. His operating expenses, exclusive of taxes, were only $10.

A Negro Farm Laborer

The head of this family worked 130 days in 1934 as a truck-farm laborer. His employment was distributed throughout the entire year, but there were two peak periods: one in April and May, and the other in October and November. At the rate of 8 cents an hour, his annual earnings were $83. His wife and four children, 10 to 20 years, worked for the same truck farmer during the busy seasons and earned a total of $84, making the total family cash income $167.

This family owned a 12- by 20-foot cabin with 1 acre of land on Wadmalaw Island, 20 miles from Charleston, and 16 miles from a hard-surfaced road. The family was allowed the use of 2½ acres of cropland by the truck farmer, rent-free. This was a common practice in this area. The house was unplastered and unpainted, and had no conveniences.

The head had never gone to school, and the wife had had only 2 years of schooling. The oldest child had 4 years of schooling; the 19-year-old boy had completed the fourth grade; and the 15-year-old girl, the third grade.

Two acres of the cropland were planted unsuccessfully in corn in 1934, the 5 bushels harvested being fed to the mule. Of the remaining land, ¼ acre was planted in sweet potatoes, and ¼ acre in tomatoes, okra, peas, lima beans, peppers, squash, and watermelons. With the exception of a few peppers in September, the farm products were available only in June and July, since all were planted at the same time. No vegetables were preserved or stored.

The chickens laid 20 dozen eggs during the spring months, and two fowls were eaten. The head caught 100 pounds of fish in the river during the year, and gathered 20 bushels of oysters during the winter months. Five cords of wood for fuel were cut on the land owned by the employer. Cash farm expenses totaled only $5. No farm products were sold.

The farm's production, plus wood, fish, and oysters, was:

20 doz. eggs	@ 20¢	$4
8 lbs. chicken	@ 25¢	2
100 lbs. fish	@ 10¢	10
20 bu. oysters	@ 50¢	10
Fresh vegetables		20
5 cords wood	@ $5	25
Total value		71

Both farm and general conditions were typical of those of truck-farm laborers in this area.

LUMBER SUBREGION
A White Commercial Part-Time Farmer

This man, with his wife and eight children, lived on a rented 25-acre farm 10 miles from Sumter, South Carolina, and 1 mile from a hard-surfaced road. He was a carpenter employed by a contractor in Sumter, and commuted with a relative who owned a car. His employment in 1934 was not steady. He worked 20 days a month from May through September, but only about 10 days a month during the remainder of the year. Working a 10-hour day and receiving 22½ cents an hour, his total earnings were $382 for the year. These earnings were somewhat below the average for all part-time farmers studied, but fairly representative of those in the building industry where employment was quite uncertain.

The entire farm was in crops in 1934, with the exception of about an acre of woodland. The crops were, approximately, 15 acres of corn, 7 acres of cotton, and 1 acre of sweet potatoes. About ¼ acre was used for a garden. Of the 175 bushels in the corn crop, 150 bushels were used for feed, 15 bushels for food, and 10 bushels were sold. The 4 bales of cotton produced were sold, together with the seed, for $320. The 50 bushels of sweet potatoes produced were used by the family. The garden supplied tomatoes, okra, peas, lima beans, and cabbages during July, August, and September. Turnips and onions were supplied 2 months earlier, and collards a month later. The only food canned was 8 quarts of peaches from the three trees on the place.

Enough feed was produced on the farm for the mule, the cow, the 7 pigs, and the 26 chickens. The cow was milked throughout the year, her total production being 1,460 quarts. About 1½ quarts of fresh milk were used daily, and the remainder was churned. About 100 pounds of butter were made during the year. Four hogs were butchered in the fall, and their total weight dressed was 800 pounds. Fifty pounds of pork were sold, and the remainder was used by the family. The hens laid throughout the year. Only 6 dozen eggs were sold, the family keeping 200 dozen for home consumption. Poultry was eaten from time to time throughout the year, since chickens were raised to replace those culled from the flock. About 200 pounds of poultry were used. In addition to these food products, the farm supplied 6 cords of firewood.

Using prices which approximated those which prevailed when products were sold at the farm, the value of the production of this farm may be estimated as follows:

500 qts. milk	@ 10¢	$50
104 lbs. butter	@ 25¢	26
400 qts. buttermilk	@ 3¢	12
200 lbs. chicken	@ 25¢	50
200 doz. eggs	@ 20¢	40
750 lbs. pork	@ 10¢	75
8 qts. canned fruits	@ 25¢	2
50 bu. potatoes	@ $1	50
Fresh vegetables and fruits		50
6 cords firewood	@ $5	30
Value of products used		385
Receipts from products sold		333
Total value		718

Cash expenses of running this farm were $60 for hired labor, $130 for rent, $32 for fertilizer, and $21 for several minor items, bringing the total to $243. With total sales of $333, the cash balance was $90. While the farm operator worked only about 2 hours a day on the farm, his wife and three oldest children (13 to 17 years) worked on the place 4 to 5 hours a day through the summer and even longer during the cotton-picking season. The two oldest children, both daughters, had left school after completing the seventh grade. The others were still in grade school, commuting 3 miles by school bus.

The family had been living on this farm for 10 years. The dwelling was a very old, poorly-kept house, which had never seen paint, and had never been finished inside. The roof leaked and the boards in the floor of the porch had rotted. Electricity and running water were not available. The family had no automobile or radio. While several organized social activities existed in the community, the members of this family took part in none, other than church and Sunday School.

A White Saw and Planing Mill Employee

This man, with a wife and two daughters, lived 3 miles out of Sumter on a rented 2½-acre farm. He was a skidder operator at a Sumter saw and planing mill, and during 1934 worked a total of 240 days: 5½ days a week for 8 months, and about half that time from July to October. His working day was 8 hours, his rate of pay 35 cents per hour, and his total earnings $672.

The older daughter, who was 19 years of age, had completed high school and was employed as a clerk in a 5- and 10-cent store in Sumter, earning $432. Thus the total family cash income was $1,104, somewhat above the average. The younger daughter attended high school in Sumter and expected to be graduated in another year.

Of the farm's 2½ acres, 2 acres were planted in corn and ¼ acre was in garden in 1934. The vegetables produced were sweet potatoes, tomatoes, okra, snap beans, lima beans, cabbages, cucumbers, onions, radishes, watermelons, cantaloupes, and mustard. Three or more vegetables were used fresh during the 5 months from May to September. Thirty-two quarts of tomatoes and thirty quarts of peas were canned for winter use; and 15 bushels of sweet potatoes were stored. Thirty bushels of corn were raised; 20 bushels were fed to livestock and 10 bushels were ground into corn meal for home use. There were two apple and two peach trees from which about 5 bushels of fruit were picked. Eight cords of firewood were cut on a nearby farm wood lot.

The livestock on the place included a cow, 5 pigs, and 12 hens. The cow was dry during 2 months of 1934, but supplied the family with a quantity of milk, of which about 1½ quarts were used every day. Two pounds of butter a week were made, and an abundance of buttermilk was used during the 10 months. Two pigs weighing about 150 pounds each were killed in the fall, and the pork was cured for use throughout the year. The hens produced 60 dozen eggs, and in addition 100 chicks were raised and 240 pounds of fowl were eaten by the family during the year. All the feed for the livestock was produced on the farm.

The value of the products of this farm may be estimated as follows:

420 qts. milk	@ 10¢	$42
80 lbs. butter	@ 25¢	20
300 qts. buttermilk	@ 3¢	9
240 lbs. chicken	@ 25¢	60
60 doz. eggs	@ 20¢	12
300 lbs. pork	@ 10¢	30
60 qts. canned vegetables	@ 25¢	15
15 bu. sweet potatoes	@ $1	15
10 bu. corn	@ $1	10
Fresh vegetables and fruits		60
Total value		273

Nearly all of the farm work was done by the head and his wife, who each spent at least 2 hours a day on the farm throughout the year and more during the spring months. The older daughter helped regularly with some of the chores. The only farm expenses were $10 for hired labor and $10 for fertilizer. No farm products were sold.

This family moved out of town and undertook part-time farming 3 years ago. The head had had no previous farm experience. The rent for their five-room house and the farm, which included a barn, garage, and poultry house, was $60. The dwelling was in good condition, but did not have running water, electric lights, telephone, or radio. The family had a 1928 automobile, which was used in getting to and from work and school. While within easy reach of the organized social activities of Sumter, the family took part only in church and Sunday School.

A Negro Woodworking Employee

This man, the head of a family of seven, worked as a clipping machine operator in a veneer manufacturing plant in Sumter, South Carolina. He was employed only 5 days a month during January, February, and March, but worked from 20 to 25 days a month during the remainder of the year, a total of 225 days. He worked 8 hours a day at 28 cents per hour, earning $504 during 1934. This was the sole cash income of the family.

This family lived 4 miles out of town in a fairly new three-room house on 2 acres of land. The house was without running water, electricity, or radio. The family did not have an automobile and the head went to work on a bicycle. There was a county school ½ mile away which the three oldest children attended. The dwelling, barn, poultry house, and land were rented for $42 a year.

An acre of corn and ¼ acre of garden were cultivated by the family. Twenty-five bushels of corn were produced; 20 bushels were fed to the pig and the chickens, and 5 bushels were ground into grits for home use. Garden vegetables included Irish potatoes, sweet potatoes, peas, cabbages, peppers, carrots, turnips, collards, and watermelons. Three or more fresh vegetables were used from May through September, with cabbages and collards during the winter months as well. In addition, 5 bushels of Irish potatoes and 15 bushels of sweet potatoes were stored. The pig was butchered in November when it weighed 125 pounds. The 20 hens laid 75 dozen eggs during the summer months, and in addition 120 pounds of fowl were eaten during the year.

The value of the contribution of this farm to the family living may be estimated as follows:

100 lbs. chicken	@ 25¢	$25
75 doz. eggs	@ 20¢	15
120 lbs. pork	@ 10¢	12
5 bu. potatoes	@ $1	5
15 bu. sweet potatoes	@ $1	15
5 bu. corn	@ $1	5
Fresh vegetables		40
Total value		117

All farming was done by the family, with the exception of a few days' work received in trade from a neighbor in return for plowing his ground. The operator spent about 1 hour per day on the farm, leaving most of the work to his wife and two oldest children. The family averaged from 4 to 9 hours of farm work per day, depending on the season. Cash expenses included $4 for feed, $2 for fertilizer, and $1 for supplies.

The family had lived at this place for 3 years, but had engaged in part-time farming continuously since 1928. The head had always lived on a farm. All members of the family attended church and Sunday School each week. The head belonged to a fraternal order and a labor union. The only other organization reported as available was a 4-H Club to which none of the children belonged.

A Negro Contract Farm Laborer

This man of 35, with a wife and five children, lived in a three-room house on 2½ acres of land which he received rent-free from his farm employer. In 1934 he contracted to work on this farm for 7 months at 60 cents per day, and besides his house and land, he received fuel, the use of a mule for working his land, and farm implements. During the remaining 5 months of the year he worked by the day, as needed, and this amounted to from 10 to 12 days per month. The usual length of the working day was 10 hours. He received wages estimated at $152, $122 of which was in cash, and the remainder in food supplies and rent. His wife earned $35 for work for the same farmer.

The available land was used to grow 1 acre of corn, 1 acre of cotton, and ¼ acre of vegetables. The vegetables included Irish potatoes, sweet potatoes, tomatoes, peas, lima beans, cabbages, cucumbers, beets, onions, collards, and watermelons. Three or more vegetables were available only during June, July, and August, with only collards during the winter months. Four bushels of Irish potatoes and six bushels of sweet potatoes were stored. Twenty bushels of corn were produced, of which half was ground for home use and half fed to livestock. The acre of cotton produced 1 bale of lint which, with the seed, sold for $81, the only cash farm receipts.

The only livestock was a young pig, which was not butchered during the year, and seven hens. The hens laid only 15 dozen eggs during the year, but 25 young chicks were raised and 40 pounds of fowl were eaten.

The value of the products of this farm may be estimated as follows:

40 lbs. chicken		@ 25¢	$10
15 doz. eggs		@ 20¢	3
4 bu. potatoes		@ $1	4
6 bu. sweet potatoes		@ $1	6
10 bu. corn		@ $1	10
Fresh vegetables			40
Value of products used			73
Receipts from products sold			81
Total value			154

No labor was hired. The head of the household worked an average of 1 hour a day on the place throughout the year. Most of the work was done by the wife with the help of the two oldest children, 10 and 12 years of age, when they were not attending school. The only farm expenses were $10 for fertilizer and $4 for ginning the cotton.

The dwelling was a crude three-room shack in a generally dilapidated condition. The family had lived in this place for 5 years. All members attended church and Sunday School regularly, and the wife attended a women's organization monthly. The children were retarded in school, the girl of 12 having completed only the second grade, and the two girls of 10 and 8 having completed only the first grade.

NAVAL STORES SUBREGION

A Turpentine Worker

This part-time farmer is typical of the group of commercial farmers who have employment in the turpentine industry, with respect to outside employment and food production for home use. Since the man is a farm owner, he is in certain respects not representative of the tenants and sharecroppers. In 1934, this farmer had a commercial farm business slightly larger than the average for the group. He was not in debt, and his economic status was a little above average for farm owners.

The farmer in question was 36 years old, with a wife and four children ranging from 4 to 14 years. He had been farming continuously since he was 16 years of age, but took up turpentining only 3 years ago.

His 150-acre farm was located in the open country 7 miles from town. It included 95 acres of woodland and 55 acres of cropland. The woodland was leased to a turpentine operator for 3 years for $200. The cash crops in 1934 were 6 acres of cotton and 3 acres of tobacco. The 3½ bales of cotton and 2,600 pounds of tobacco produced sold for $200 and $490, respectively. In addition 23 acres of corn, 6 acres of peanuts, and 2½ acres of pea-vine hay were grown for feed. Enough feed was produced, together with the pasturage which the woodland supplied, to carry all of the livestock. The livestock included 2 mules, 2 cows, 7 head of young cattle, 25 hogs, 25 chickens, and 30 goats.

Like most other farmers in the county, this man had recently been increasing his livestock because of low farm prices and the curtailment programs for cash crops. Consequently, most of the livestock was young and did not add to the income during 1934. The two cows were of the "piney woods" variety, and had to pick up most of their feed in the woods. However, they produced about 2,200 quarts of milk during the year. About 4 quarts per day were used fresh, and about 1½ pounds of butter a week were made from the remainder. Thus, the family had milk and butter throughout the year.

Twelve hogs were butchered in December and their total dressed weight was 2,900 pounds. About 100 pounds of meat were used fresh, and 2,300 pounds were salt-cured and stored. In addition, 500 pounds of lard were stored.

The family used about 700 pounds of pork and lard during the year, and exchanged the remainder for other supplies. This surplus pork production added the equivalent of approximately $125 to the family income.

The poultry flock was given no attention and produced only 5 dozen eggs during the whole year. Five 4-pound fowls were eaten. The flock of goats foraged in the woods. Twenty-one kids were sold for $16.

In addition to the livestock products, about 1 acre of garden crops was cultivated for home use. The garden had a fair variety of vegetables, including Irish potatoes, sweet potatoes, tomatoes, okra, peas, snap beans, lima beans, cabbages, peppers, squash, cucumbers, onions, collards, and cantaloupes. Since it was a summer garden, most of the vegetables were available only during May, June, and July. Collards and cabbages were used earlier and sweet potatoes later in the season. Approximately 60 quarts of tomatoes, 22 quarts of peas, 10 quarts of snap beans, and 16 quarts of cabbage—a total of 108 quarts—were canned. In addition, 26 gallons of syrup, produced from ¼ acre of sugar cane, were stored for use during the year.

The estimated value of the contribution of this farm to the family living was as follows:

1,460 qts. milk	@ 10¢	$146
80 lbs. butter	@ 25¢	20
300 qts. buttermilk	@ 3¢	9
20 lbs. poultry	@ 25¢	5
5 doz. eggs	@ 20¢	1
700 lbs. pork and lard	@ 10¢	70
26 gal. sugar syrup	@ 50¢	13
108 qts. canned vegetables	@ 25¢	27
Fresh vegetables		50
8 cords wood	@ $5	40
Value of products used		381
Receipts from products sold and traded		835
Total value		1,216

This farmer worked from daylight to dark on his place from March through September, with the exception of about 2 days a week when he worked off the farm in the turpentine woods. He cured tobacco, an operation which requires almost continuous tending of the fires for 4 or 5 days at a time. Hence for a part of the time, he worked longer hours than the 14-hour day that was customary. His wife and the two older boys, aged 14 and 10, worked 10 hours a day on the farm during June, July, and August, helping in the cotton chopping, and in the tobacco and cotton harvesting. The only labor hired was for harvesting hay and tobacco.

Wages paid hired labor totaled $35. The chief expense item was $115 for fertilizer, and total cash expenses were $192.

The off-the-farm job consisted of dipping gum about eight 10-hour days a month throughout 1934. There were no certain days that the operator had to work, but he was assigned a definite task to perform each month. He received 10 cents an hour, and his total earnings from this work were $92.

The three oldest children went to a country school 2 miles away. The family lived in a crudely constructed six-room house, unpainted and unplastered. They had a radio but no electric lights, running water, telephone, or automobile.

An Industrial Worker

The part-time farmer to be described was outstanding among the industrial workers in Douglas, Georgia, in his success in gardening and poultry keeping. He was a young man of 28 with two small children. He had done some gardening ever since his marriage 5 years earlier, and when his earnings were reduced, he had expanded his acreage of vegetables and added a flock of chickens.

This man was an apprentice machinist in the railroad shop. He received 42 cents an hour in 1934, but since he worked only part time, his total earnings were only $464—lower than they had been 5 years earlier when he was just getting started at this same job.

The home was located at the edge of town about a mile from the railroad shop. A comfortable seven-room house with running water and electric lights, together with 4 acres of land, was rented for $60 a year. Two acres of corn and two acres of a large variety of vegetables were planted. The various crops were planted in rotation so that several fresh vegetables were available throughout the year. In addition, 52 quarts of vegetables were canned; and 15 bushels of sweet potatoes, a supply of pumpkins, 10 bushels of corn, and 18 gallons of cane syrup were stored for home consumption. Vegetables worth $50 were sold.

A flock of 60 hens was kept. During the year birds were culled from the flock from time to time and dressed for home use. About 80 pounds of chicken and 25 dozen eggs were available for family use. The poultry was fed on home-grown corn and no feed was purchased. Six cords of firewood were cut on a nearby farm.

The value of the food and fuel production may be estimated as follows:

80 lbs. poultry	@ 25¢	$20
25 doz. eggs	@ 20¢	5
15 bu. sweet potatoes	@ $1	15
18 gal. cane syrup	@ 50¢	9
10 bu. corn	@ 80¢	8
52 qts. canned vegetables	@ 25¢	13
Fresh vegetables		60
6 cords wood	@ $5	30
Total value		160

The only cash expenses were $10 for hired labor and $16 for seed and fertilizer. The head of the family had ample time to take care of the garden and the chickens with only 24 hours of outside work a week.

It was evident that by means of his farming activities this man had raised the level of living of his family considerably above what it would have been had he been entirely dependent on his rather low industrial earnings. He had the reputation of being the hardest working man in town. He had taken several agricultural courses in the local branch of the State College, and at the time of the survey was taking a correspondence course in mechanical engineering. The head was active in community affairs, attending lodge and labor union meetings regularly. Members of the family attended Sunday School and church once or twice a month.

Appendix B

SUPPLEMENTARY TABLES

Appendix Table 1.—Age of Heads of Part-Time Farm and Nonfarming Industrial Households, by Color and by Subregion, 1934

Age of head	Textile	Coal and Iron		Atlantic Coast		Lumber		Naval Stores
	White	White	Negro	White	Negro	White	Negro	White
PART-TIME FARM HOUSEHOLDS								
Total	293	204	124	71	142	76	132	71
Under 20 years	3	—	—	—	2	—	—	—
20 to 24.9 years	24	—	2	3	8	3	17	10
25 to 29.9 years	33	11	9	3	20	8	28	14
30 to 34.9 years	49	24	13	8	10	8	16	15
35 to 39.9 years	49	37	23	13	22	12	20	10
40 to 44.9 years	44	36	27	14	15	13	18	5
45 to 49.9 years	32	33	20	13	22	19	14	6
50 to 54.9 years	30	33	15	4	16	6	6	5
55 to 59.9 years	16	20	5	7	10	6	5	3
60 to 64.9 years	13	10	10	6	17	1	8	3
Median age	39	42	43	43	43	43	36	34
NONFARMING INDUSTRIAL HOUSEHOLDS								
Total	314	222	346	103	105	92	103	49
Under 20 years	6	—	—	—	3	1	—	1
20 to 24.9 years	35	5	12	14	17	13	23	11
25 to 29.9 years	70	26	42	14	18	23	28	17
30 to 34.9 years	50	47	62	20	14	14	12	9
35 to 39.9 years	45	29	83	16	22	15	15	3
40 to 44.9 years	30	32	51	17	5	11	11	3
45 to 49.9 years	28	23	48	10	8	4	9	2
50 to 54.9 years	32	28	29	5	7	5	2	1
55 to 59.9 years	11	21	10	4	4	3	3	1
60 to 64.9 years	7	11	9	3	7	3	—	1
Median age	35	41	39	36	35	33	30	29

Appendix Table 2.—Size of Part-Time Farm and Nonfarming Industrial Households, by Color and by Subregion, 1934

Size of household	Textile	Coal and Iron		Atlantic Coast		Lumber		Naval Stores
	White	White	Negro	White	Negro	White	Negro	White
PART-TIME FARM HOUSEHOLDS								
Total	293	204	124	71	142	76	132	71
1 person	1	1	1	1	2	—	—	—
2 persons	16	8	13	12	18	9	22	3
3 persons	40	28	22	8	26	9	12	16
4 persons	65	50	20	9	12	14	22	11
5 persons	56	45	26	9	24	14	22	17
6 persons	46	28	14	13	22	8	17	9
7 persons	21	21	14	7	15	8	11	8
8 persons	20	13	3	4	6	5	11	4
9 persons	13	4	4	2	5	2	4	3
10 persons	8	3	3	4	6	5	3	—
11 persons or more	7	3	4	2	6	2	8	—
Average size of household	5.3	5.1	5.0	5.2	5.2	5.3	5.3	5.0
NONFARMING INDUSTRIAL HOUSEHOLDS								
Total	314	222	346	103	105	92	103	49
1 person	1	—	2	—	—	—	—	1
2 persons	64	21	68	10	22	13	27	10
3 persons	83	50	84	20	32	21	27	11
4 persons	53	53	79	21	16	18	20	13
5 persons	47	36	42	19	16	14	12	6
6 persons	30	32	27	16	11	10	8	3
7 persons	14	19	19	6	3	10	6	2
8 persons	9	4	11	7	2	6	—	2
9 persons	8	6	4	2	2	—	2	1
10 persons	4	1	4	2	—	—	—	—
11 persons or more	1	—	6	—	1	—	1	—
Average size of household	4.1	4.5	4.2	4.8	4.0	4.5	3.8	3.9

Appendix Table 3.—Farm[1] Experience of Heads of Part-Time Farm and Nonfarming Industrial Households, by Type of Farm, by Color, and by Subregion, 1934

Number of years head had lived on a farm since 16 years of age	Textile		Coal and Iron		Atlantic Coast			Lumber			Naval Stores	
	White				White			White			White	
	Commercial	Noncommercial	White	Negro	Commercial	Noncommercial	Negro	Commercial	Noncommercial	Negro	Commercial	Noncommercial
PART-TIME FARM HOUSEHOLDS												
Total	43	250	204	124	24	47	142	39	37	132	37	34
None	—	37	71	42	—	3	17	1	5	7	—	17
1 year	—	5	10	2	—	—	1	—	—	—	—	1
2 years	—	16	9	9	1	3	2	1	—	3	—	3
3 to 4 years	1	33	35	18	5	14	10	3	5	1	—	5
5 to 9 years	8	66	39	19	3	10	9	6	8	28	7	5
10 to 14 years	8	41	17	12	5	6	21	5	10	22	6	2
15 to 19 years	8	22	14	5	3	2	14	5	4	17	7	—
20 to 29 years	8	19	8	6	5	5	27	9	3	31	6	1
30 to 39 years	6	9	1	4	2	—	27	7	2	15	6	—
40 to 49 years	3	2	—	1	—	4	14	2	—	8	5	—
Unknown	1	—	—	6	—	—	—	—	—	—	—	—
Average years on a farm[2]	20	11	8	10	14	12	22	20	13	19	22	6
NONFARMING INDUSTRIAL HOUSEHOLDS												
Total	314		222	346	103		105	92		103	49	
None	144		136	151	80		82	36		45	9	
1 year	12		9	17	3		4	5		2	5	
2 years	19		13	30	6		2	7		5	6	
3 to 4 years	44		27	54	4		4	9		14	6	
5 to 9 years	49		27	52	5		5	20		18	14	
10 to 14 years	20		6	23	1		2	7		7	4	
15 to 19 years	11		1	11	—		2	4		4	3	
20 to 29 years	13		2	5	4		3	2		4	1	
30 to 39 years	2		1	1	—		1	2		4	1	
Unknown	—		—	2	—		—	—		—	—	
Average years on a farm[2]	8		6	6	8		10	8		10	7	

[1] Following the census definition, a farm was defined as a tract of land of at least 3 acres unless its agricultural products were valued at $250 or more. Hence, those who had had farm experience on small acreages only appear in this table as having had no experience.
[2] For those having lived on a farm.

Appendix Table 4.—Number of Years Head of Household Had Been a Part-Time Farmer Since December 31, 1928, by Color and by Subregion

Number of years head had been a part-time farmer	Textile	Coal and Iron		Atlantic Coast		Lumber		Naval Stores
	White	White	Negro	White	Negro	White	Negro	White
Total	293	204	124	71	142	76	132	71
1 year[1]	2	2	—	—	—	—	—	—
2 years	57	23	54	15	5	7	3	1
3 years	25	32	28	22	13	16	18	29
4 years	28	24	6	8	10	12	18	14
5 years	18	17	1	3	9	6	9	5
6 years	163	106	35	23	105	35	84	22

[1] Practically all of these cases were eliminated by definition. See pp. XXX–XXXI.

Appendix Table 5.—Number of Livestock and Size of Garden on 573 Part-Time Farms, 1929 and 1934, by Color of Operator and by Subregion

Number of livestock and acres in garden	Textile White 1929	Textile White 1934	Coal and Iron White 1929	Coal and Iron White 1934	Coal and Iron Negro 1929	Coal and Iron Negro 1934	Atlantic Coast White 1929	Atlantic Coast White 1934	Atlantic Coast Negro 1929	Atlantic Coast Negro 1934	Lumber White 1929	Lumber White 1934	Lumber Negro 1929	Lumber Negro 1934	Naval Stores White 1929	Naval Stores White 1934
Total	163	163	106	106	35	35	23	23	105	105	35	35	84	84	22	22
Cows:																
None	37	29	70	47	29	26	11	9	84	83	17	10	61	53	17	12
1	104	111	31	53	5	9	6	8	19	19	14	19	22	28	4	4
2 or more	22	23	5	6	1	—	6	6	2	3	4	6	1	3	1	6
Average for those owning cows	1.2	1.2	1.2	1.1	1.2	1.0	2.4	2.8	1.1	1.1	1.2	1.2	1.0	1.1	1.2	1.6
Hogs:																
None	76	88	89	79	25	19	16	13	71	57	13	9	28	17	18	16
1	56	42	10	13	5	12	2	2	15	26	3	5	18	35	—	1
2	26	25	5	8	3	3	1	2	7	11	2	1	17	10	1	1
3 or more	5	8	2	6	2	1	4	6	12	11	17	20	21	22	3	4
Average for those owning hogs	1.5	1.7	2.0	2.0	2.0	1.4	3.6	4.3	2.4	1.9	9.6	7.0	2.8	2.7	28.0	13.0
Poultry:																
None	52	53	40	38	18	12	7	4	35	28	4	—	15	10	16	14
1 to 9	12	15	6	9	6	15	2	3	15	24	1	3	17	20	—	1
10 to 19	37	46	22	23	8	6	2	3	45	39	4	7	24	26	—	2
20 to 29	26	23	18	13	1	—	4	4	6	10	13	9	16	19	2	—
30 to 49	18	12	12	16	—	1	3	4	3	4	8	9	9	7	—	—
50 or more	18	14	8	7	2	1	5	5	1	—	5	7	3	2	4	5
Average for those owning poultry	33	27	43	29	20	11	42	53	15	14	43	47	21	18	58	49
Acres in garden:																
None	12	10	12	4	6	—	2	—	23	—	—	—	11	2	1	—
¼	54	55	53	28	19	19	2	2	7	—	13	14	53	56	1	2
½	34	36	15	22	1	4	8	6	28	16	9	4	7	11	8	6
¾	16	25	4	7	3	7	3	3	10	15	1	2	1	5	2	2
1	26	11	11	19	1	4	3	3	16	28	10	9	11	7	7	8
1½	7	11	4	15	—	1	2	2	2	17	—	2	1	1	2	3
2	6	5	2	10	2	—	1	1	11	16	1	1	—	1	1	—
3 or more	8	10	5	1	3	—	3	6	8	13	1	3	—	1	—	1
Average for those having a garden	0.9	0.9	0.8	1.0	0.9	0.5	1.3	4.4	1.3	1.6	0.7	1.1	0.4	0.5	0.9	1.0

Appendix Table 6.—Acres of Cropland on Part-Time Farms, by Type of Farm, by Color of Operator, and by Subregion, 1934

Acres of cropland	Textile White Commercial	Textile White Noncommercial	Coal and Iron White	Coal and Iron Negro	Atlantic Coast White Commercial	Atlantic Coast White Noncommercial	Atlantic Coast Negro	Lumber White Commercial	Lumber White Noncommercial	Lumber Negro	Naval Stores White Commercial	Naval Stores White Noncommercial
Total	43	250	204	124	24	47	142	39	37	132	37	34
None	1	15	4	—	—	1	2	—	1	—	—	—
1 acre	—	196	123	100	2	23	27	1	14	17	—	25
2 acres	—	13	29	18	1	6	30	—	7	27	—	6
3 to 4 acres	3	13	19	4	1	8	47	2	9	44	—	2
5 to 9 acres	3	9	14	1	3	7	28	—	5	11	—	1
10 to 19 acres	17	2	12	—	8	2	7	4	1	17	1	—
20 to 29 acres	13	1	3	1	—	—	—	10	—	14	9	—
30 to 49 acres	4	—	—	—	2	—	1	13	—	2	17	—
50 to 74 acres	2	—	—	—	1	—	—	5	—	—	10	—
75 acres or more	—	—	—	—	3	—	—	4	—	—	—	—
Unknown	—	1	—	—	—	—	—	—	—	—	—	—
Average acres of cropland	20.4	1.5	2.9	1.5	26.4	3.0	4.1	40.4	2.9	7.4	41.3	1.5

Appendix Table 7.—Value of Part-Time Farms,[1] by Type of Farm, by Color and Tenure of Operator, and by Subregion, 1934

Value of farm	Textile White Commercial Own-er	Textile White Commercial Ten-ant	Textile White Noncommercial Own-er	Textile White Noncommercial Ten-ant	Atlantic Coast White Commercial Own-er	Atlantic Coast White Commercial Ten-ant	Atlantic Coast White Noncommercial Own-er	Atlantic Coast White Noncommercial Ten-ant	Atlantic Coast Negro Own-er	Atlantic Coast Negro Ten-ant	Lumber White Commercial Own-er	Lumber White Commercial Ten-ant	Lumber White Noncommercial Own-er	Lumber White Noncommercial Ten-ant	Lumber Negro Own-er	Lumber Negro Ten-ant	Naval Stores White Commercial Own-er	Naval Stores White Commercial Ten-ant	Naval Stores White Noncommercial Own-er	Naval Stores White Noncommercial Ten-ant
Total	16	16	67	32	13	11	22	25	55	87	25	14	12	25	26	106	16	8	4	30
Less than $500	—	—	1	—	—	—	—	6	5	40	—	—	—	2	1	6	—	—	—	5
$500 to $999	1	4	1	2	—	3	—	1	23	31	2	—	—	7	16	47	—	—	—	16
$1,000 to $1,999	5	6	28	14	—	1	5	5	18	15	5	4	4	7	6	39	1	5	1	4
$2,000 to $2,999	3	4	22	10	—	—	1	7	7	—	9	4	7	9	3	8	10	2	2	5
$3,000 to $3,999	2	1	8	4	—	2	7	2	1	1	6	4	1	—	—	2	2	1	1	—
$4,000 to $4,999	5	1	7	2	5	5	5	1	1	—	3	2	—	—	—	1	2	—	—	—
$5,000 or more	—	—	—	—	8	—	4	3	1	—	—	—	—	—	—	3	1	—	—	—
Average value	$4,331	$2,552	$3,528	$2,141	$7,705	$4,584	$4,400	$2,293	$1,242	$599	$3,780	$3,214	$2,332	$1,500	$1,876	$1,217	$3,000	†	†	$1,800

† Average not computed for less than 10 cases.

[1] Exclusive of 328 white and Negro cases in the Coal and Iron Subregion, 162 white cases in the Textile Subregion (59 mill-village cases in Greenville County and 103 cases in Carroll County), and 13 white sharecroppers in the Naval Stores Subregion.

Appendix Table 8.—Total Debt[1] of Part-Time Farm Households, by Type of Farm, by Color, by Tenure, and by Subregion, January 1, 1935

Total debt, January 1, 1935	Textile / White / Commercial / Owner	Textile / White / Commercial / Tenant	Textile / White / Noncommercial / Owner	Textile / White / Noncommercial / Tenant	Coal and Iron / White / Owner	Coal and Iron / White / Tenant	Coal and Iron / Negro / Owner	Coal and Iron / Negro / Tenant	Atlantic Coast / White / Commercial / Owner	Atlantic Coast / White / Commercial / Tenant	Atlantic Coast / White / Noncommercial / Owner	Atlantic Coast / White / Noncommercial / Tenant	Atlantic Coast / Negro / Owner	Atlantic Coast / Negro / Tenant	Lumber / White / Commercial / Owner	Lumber / White / Commercial / Tenant	Lumber / White / Noncommercial / Owner	Lumber / White / Noncommercial / Tenant	Lumber / Negro / Owner	Lumber / Negro / Tenant	Naval Stores / White / Commercial / Owner	Naval Stores / White / Commercial / Tenant	Naval Stores / White / Noncommercial / Owner	Naval Stores / White / Noncommercial / Tenant
Total	20	23	82	168	70	134	23	101	13	11	22	25	55	87	25	14	12	25	26	106	16	21	4	30
None	9	16	40	153	39	89	2	86	7	9	16	22	31	75	9	9	6	22	11	87	1	3	3	9
$1 to $49				5		12	1	3				1	15	10		1	1	1	4	13	2	7		9
$50 to $99		3			1	6	1						4		3				2	3	3	6	1	7
$100 to $249		3	3	4	3	6	1	3		2	1	1	2	1	1	2	2	1	5	3		4		4
$250 to $499	2	1	7	3	2	3	1	1	2					1	1	2	2		3		1			1
$500 to $749	1		6	1	2		4	2			2	1	2		1				1		5	1		
$750 to $999	2		4		3		4	3	2		3				5		1	1						
$1,000 to $1,999	4		11	1	15	11	6	2							2						3			
$2,000 to $2,999	1		8	1	2	4	1								1						1			
$3,000 to $3,999			1			2			1						1									
$4,000 or more	1		2		2	1			1						1									
Unknown					1		2	1					1											
Average total debt for those having debts	$1,602	$160	$1,443	$438	$1,377	$920	$955	$560	$2,291	$175	$466	$275	$99	$42	$1,298	$105	$437	$650	$191	$56	$718	$108	†	$87

† Average not computed for less than 10 cases.

[1] Mortgage indebtedness (real estate and chattel).

Appendix Table 9.—Buildings Other Than Dwellings on Part-Time Farms, by Type of Farm, by Color of Operator, and by Subregion, 1934

Buildings other than dwellings	Textile White Commercial	Textile White Noncommercial	Coal and Iron White	Coal and Iron Negro	Atlantic Coast White Commercial	Atlantic Coast White Noncommercial	Atlantic Coast Negro	Lumber White Commercial	Lumber White Noncommercial	Lumber Negro	Naval Stores White Commercial	Naval Stores White Noncommercial
Total	43	250	204	124	24	47	142	39	37	132	37	34
None	—	4	8	14	—	—	36	—	—	—	—	1
Barn only	1	2	4	—	—	—	4	—	—	2	—	—
Barn and garage	—	2	6	—	—	—	—	—	—	—	—	—
Garage only	—	7	15	2	1	2	—	—	—	—	—	—
Barn and other buildings	14	77	31	8	2	3	36	11	7	63	31	3
Garage and other buildings	3	44	54	3	4	13	3	1	9	6	—	1
Barn, garage, and other buildings	22	51	45	—	16	17	6	25	14	15	4	1
Other buildings only	3	63	41	97	1	12	57	2	7	46	2	28

Appendix Table 10.—Cost of Implements and Machinery on Part-Time Farms, by Type of Farm, by Color of Operator, and by Subregion, 1934

Cost of implements and machinery	Textile White Commercial	Textile White Noncommercial	Coal and Iron White	Coal and Iron Negro	Atlantic Coast White Commercial	Atlantic Coast White Noncommercial	Atlantic Coast Negro	Lumber White Commercial	Lumber White Noncommercial	Lumber Negro	Naval Stores White Commercial	Naval Stores White Noncommercial
Total	43	250	204	124	24	47	142	39	37	132	37	34
None	8	223	168	122	6	36	71	4	34	97	13	31
$1 to $4	2	4	5	—	—	—	1	—	—	—	—	—
$5 to $14	3	9	13	1	1	3	23	2	1	6	—	3
$15 to $24	4	6	8	1	2	4	20	1	—	6	—	—
$25 to $49	6	4	3	—	4	1	6	5	1	5	1	—
$50 to $99	7	—	5	—	1	3	20	10	1	14	9	—
$100 to $149	6	2	1	—	1	—	—	3	—	2	8	—
$150 to $199	1	—	1	—	1	—	1	5	—	—	6	—
$200 or more	6	2	—	—	8	—	—	7	—	1	—	—
Unknown	—	—	—	—	—	—	—	2	—	1	—	—
Average cost for those having machinery	$241	$65	$30	†	$339	$33	$35	$136	†	$60	$115	†

† Average not computed for less than 10 cases.

Appendix Table 11.—Number of Livestock and Size of Garden on Part-Time Farms, by Type of Farm, by Color of Operator, and by Subregion, January 1, 1934

Number of livestock and acres in garden	Textile White Commercial	Textile White Noncommercial	Coal and Iron White	Coal and Iron Negro	Atlantic Coast White Commercial	Atlantic Coast White Noncommercial	Atlantic Coast Negro	Lumber White Commercial	Lumber White Noncommercial	Lumber Negro	Naval Stores White Commercial	Naval Stores White Noncommercial
Total	43	250	204	124	24	47	142	39	37	132	37	34
Cows:												
None	3	58	101	111	10	23	113	7	14	88	5	25
1	27	169	94	13	4	19	24	21	22	41	9	5
2	9	22	9	—	5	3	5	8	1	3	14	4
3 or more	4	1	—	—	5	2	—	•3	—	—	9	—
Poultry:												
None	6	96	78	51	5	8	43	—	5	17	5	27
1 to 9	1	27	21	53	2	4	35	1	5	33	1	1
10 to 19	11	60	52	17	1	10	47	4	8	39	4	2
20 to 29	8	39	18	—	1	14	11	10	6	28	6	—
30 to 49	10	15	24	2	6	4	5	11	7	11	5	—
50 or more	7	13	11	1	9	7	1	13	6	4	16	4
Hogs:												
None	16	153	150	88	14	24	78	2	20	34	4	31
1	15	67	24	27	2	12	34	2	8	46	1	1
2	7	25	22	6	—	5	15	1	2	17	2	1
3 or more	5	5	8	3	8	6	15	34	7	35	30	1
Horses and mules:												
None	9	238	180	120	5	35	75	4	35	103	14	34
1	23	10	23	3	10	11	61	18	2	27	14	—
2 or more	11	2	1	1	9	1	6	17	—	2	9	—
Acres in garden:												
None	1	19	7	—	—	2	2	—	2	3	1	—
¼	—	87	51	53	—	4	1	13	17	84	8	2
½	4	70	40	37	2	9	17	7	4	18	11	6
¾	6	38	25	14	1	10	23	1	5	8	3	7
1	8	18	40	16	—	13	38	8	6	13	10	12
1½	11	7	19	4	3	3	25	2	1	2	4	6
2 or more	13	11	22	—	18	6	36	8	2	4	—	1

Appendix Table 12.—Types of Food Produced for Home Use on Part-Time Farms, by Type of Farm, by Color of Operator, and by Subregion, 1934

Food products	Textile White Commercial	Textile White Noncommercial	Coal and Iron White	Coal and Iron Negro	Atlantic Coast White Commercial	Atlantic Coast White Noncommercial	Atlantic Coast Negro	Lumber White Commercial	Lumber White Noncommercial	Lumber Negro	Naval Stores White Commercial	Naval Stores White Noncommercial
Total	43	250	204	124	24	47	142	39	37	132	37	34
Vegetables only	1	10	31	35	4	3	44	—	2	9	1	20
Dairy products only	1	11	3	—	—	1	2	—	—	—	—	—
Poultry products only	—	1	1	—	—	1	1	—	—	1	—	—
Vegetables and dairy products	—	30	17	2	1	2	2	—	1	3	—	—
Vegetables and poultry products	1	17	35	42	3	9	53	—	5	20	—	6
Vegetables and pork	—	4	13	11	—	1	2	—	1	7	1	4
Vegetables, dairy and poultry products	7	44	43	5	8	10	15	1	4	10	3	1
Vegetables, dairy products, and pork	1	34	10	2	—	1	—	1	2	—	3	2
Vegetables, poultry products, and pork	2	12	12	22	2	9	16	8	6	48	4	—
Vegetables, dairy and poultry products, and pork	30	79	36	5	6	10	8	29	14	32	22	1
Other combinations	—	8	3	—	—	—	—	—	2	2	3	—

Appendix Table 13.—Number of Months Three or More Fresh Vegetables Were Consumed on Part-Time Farms, by Color of Operator and by Subregion, 1934

Number of months 3 or more fresh vegetables were consumed	Textile	Coal and Iron		Atlantic Coast		Lumber		Naval Stores
	White	White	Negro	White	Negro	White	Negro	White
Total	293	204	124	71	142	76	132	71
None	23	7	1	12	29	3	16	3
1 month	5	—	1	1	23	2	6	3
2 months	15	2	—	9	50	6	14	—
3 months	35	4	4	15	22	14	26	22
4 months	67	6	27	15	10	20	30	18
5 months	59	22	37	8	4	13	26	8
6 months	37	37	33	6	4	8	11	7
7 months	32	75	16	2	—	4	3	1
8 months	14	36	4	2	—	3	—	4
9 months	5	9	1	—	—	3	—	1
10 months or more	1	6	—	1	—	—	—	4
Average number of months 3 or more fresh vegetables were consumed	4.5	6.8	5.3	3.4	1.9	4.3	3.4	4.4

Appendix Table 14.—Number of Months Any Fresh Vegetable or Fruit Was Consumed on Part-Time Farms, by Color of Operator and by Subregion, 1934

Number of months any fresh vegetable or fruit was consumed	Textile	Coal and Iron		Atlantic Coast		Lumber		Naval Stores
	White	White	Negro	White	Negro	White	Negro	White
Total	293	204	124	71	142	76	132	71
None	19	3	—	1	2	2	3	3
1 to 2 months	3	1	—	5	9	1	3	—
3 to 4 months	9	2	2	3	37	1	10	1
5 months	16	2	9	7	14	6	7	3
6 months	25	10	34	3	28	5	12	4
7 months	51	28	26	9	10	4	15	4
8 months	65	40	10	6	10	7	14	8
9 months	44	45	23	9	7	17	19	21
10 months	37	36	9	8	18	11	19	16
11 months	9	13	4	8	7	9	20	7
12 months	15	24	7	12	—	13	10	4
Average number of months any fresh vegetable or fruit was consumed	7.4	8.8	7.6	8.1	6.0	8.8	8.1	8.6

Appendix Table 15.—Part-Time Farms Producing Fruits, Berries, or Nuts, by Type of Farm, by Color of Operator, and by Subregion, 1934

Fruits, berries, or nuts produced	Textile		Coal and Iron		Atlantic Coast			Lumber			Naval Stores	
	White				White			White			White	
	Commercial	Noncommercial	White	Negro	Commercial	Noncommercial	Negro	Commercial	Noncommercial	Negro	Commercial	Noncommercial
Total	43	250	204	124	24	47	142	39	37	132	37	34
None	6	154	85	77	16	40	113	16	25	78	24	26
1 or more	37	96	119	47	8	7	29	23	12	54	13	8
Peaches	24	65	86	45	4	4	18	20	10	41	6	—
Apples	21	36	21	4	3	—	—	12	4	5	—	—
Figs	2	13	50	5	3	2	8	3	2	4	1	—
Grapes	5	13	22	4	3	3	—	4	3	3	2	—
Pears	3	7	17	7	3	3	3	2	3	4	4	1
Plums	1	1	10	5	—	1	5	4	—	3	3	—
Cherries	1	6	3	—	—	—	—	—	—	—	—	—
Other fruit	1	1	3	—	—	—	—	—	—	—	—	—
Strawberries	10	20	13	2	1	—	—	—	—	—	—	4
Blackberries	14	23	8	—	—	—	—	—	—	4	6	4
Huckleberries	—	—	—	—	—	—	—	1	—	3	1	—
Berries unknown	6	8	9	1	—	—	1	6	1	11	—	—
Walnuts	1	—	1	1	—	—	—	—	—	—	—	—
Pecans	1	—	1	1	1	1	1	5	3	1	5	3

Appendix Table 16.—Quantity of Fruits and Vegetables Canned on Part-Time Farms, by Color of Operator and by Subregion, 1934

Quarts of fruits and vegetables canned	Textile	Coal and Iron		Atlantic Coast		Lumber		Naval Stores
	White	White	Negro	White	Negro	White	Negro	White
Total	293	204	124	71	142	76	132	71
None	55	27	56	56	140	20	85	31
1 to 19 quarts	30	9	31	4	2	7	20	—
20 to 49 quarts	67	40	19	4	—	16	15	5
50 to 99 quarts	71	47	11	1	—	14	8	15
100 to 199 quarts	48	58	3	2	—	16	4	16
200 quarts or more	22	23	4	4	—	3	—	4
Average quarts canned by those doing canning	91	110	47	111	†	83	37	111

† Average not computed for less than 10 cases.

Appendix Table 17.—Quantity of Sweet Potatoes and Irish Potatoes Stored [1] on Part-Time Farms, by Type of Farm, by Color of Operator, and by Subregion, 1934

Quantity	Textile White Commercial	Textile White Noncommercial	Coal and Iron White	Coal and Iron Negro	Atlantic Coast White Commercial	Atlantic Coast White Noncommercial	Atlantic Coast Negro	Lumber White Commercial	Lumber White Noncommercial	Lumber Negro	Naval Stores White Commercial	Naval Stores White Noncommercial
SWEET POTATOES STORED												
Total	43	250	204	124	24	47	142	39	37	132	37	34
None	9	178	71	21	9	26	43	6	23	48	34	29
1 to 2 bushels	1	9	5	6	—	—	1	—	—	—	—	—
3 to 4 bushels	—	7	5	10	—	2	8	—	—	3	1	—
5 to 9 bushels	6	22	21	20	—	4	33	1	1	5	—	2
10 to 14 bushels	5	16	26	26	3	3	26	1	2	20	—	1
15 to 19 bushels	6	5	15	11	5	4	16	2	4	9	—	2
20 to 29 bushels	10	5	25	15	1	2	7	7	2	17	2	—
30 to 39 bushels	2	4	9	9	1	3	2	1	3	7	—	—
40 bushels or more	4	4	27	6	5	3	6	21	2	23	—	—
Average bushels stored by those storing sweet potatoes	24	12	22	15	53	19	13	60	27	29	†	†
IRISH POTATOES STORED												
Total	43	250	204	124	24	47	142	39	37	132	37	34
None	11	158	83	108	13	42	135	20	27	93	37	34
1 to 2 bushels	2	26	23	11	—	—	1	1	—	1	—	—
3 to 4 bushels	4	21	21	—	—	1	—	—	1	4	—	—
5 to 9 bushels	7	23	44	4	—	2	1	5	3	21	—	—
10 to 14 bushels	12	13	25	—	2	—	2	9	5	4	—	—
15 to 19 bushels	2	3	4	1	2	1	—	1	1	5	—	—
20 to 29 bushels	—	4	3	—	2	1	3	2	—	2	—	—
30 to 39 bushels	3	1	1	—	—	—	—	—	—	—	—	—
40 bushels or more	2	1	—	—	5	—	—	1	—	2	—	—
Average bushels stored by those storing Irish potatoes	12	6	7	3	114	†	†	13	9	10	—	—

† Average not computed for less than 10 cases.
[1] Grown in garden or truck patch.

Appendix Table 18.—Quantity of Home-Produced Eggs Consumed on Part-Time Farms, by Type of Farm, by Color of Operator, and by Subregion, 1934

Eggs consumed	Textile White Commercial	Textile White Noncommercial	Coal and Iron White	Coal and Iron Negro	Atlantic Coast White Commercial	Atlantic Coast White Noncommercial	Atlantic Coast Negro	Lumber White Commercial	Lumber White Noncommercial	Lumber Negro	Naval Stores White Commercial	Naval Stores White Noncommercial
Total	43	250	204	124	24	47	142	39	37	132	37	34
None	4	95	80	54	7	8	53	1	6	20	11	29
1 to 19 dozen	2	7	9	26	2	3	21	2	1	23	9	4
20 to 49 dozen	6	62	15	28	1	9	42	3	4	38	5	1
50 to 99 dozen	16	53	43	10	3	13	21	11	11	28	3	—
100 to 199 dozen	12	29	48	5	7	13	4	10	10	17	3	—
200 dozen or more	3	4	9	1	4	1	1	12	5	6	6	—
Average number of dozen of eggs consumed by those consuming home-produced eggs	92	73	113	38	152	84	47	160	117	69	124	†

† Average not computed for less than 10 cases.

Appendix Table 19.—Quantity of Home-Produced Poultry Consumed on Part-Time Farms, by Type of Farm, by Color of Operator, and by Subregion, 1934

Dressed poultry consumed	Textile		Coal and Iron		Atlantic Coast			Lumber			Naval Stores	
	White				White			White			White	
	Commercial	Noncommercial	White	Negro	Commercial	Noncommercial	Negro	Commercial	Noncommercial	Negro	Commercial	Noncommercial
Total	43	250	204	124	24	47	142	39	37	132	37	34
None	9	116	94	66	6	11	86	2	7	23	8	28
1 to 19 pounds	1	10	12	30	1	5	25	1	3	12	3	1
20 to 49 pounds	2	36	32	15	5	14	27	3	3	39	16	1
50 to 99 pounds	6	44	41	8	2	11	4	9	8	37	8	3
100 to 199 pounds	12	36	22	5	8	4	—	16	6	12	2	1
200 pounds or more	13	8	3	—	2	2	—	8	10	9	—	—
Average number of pounds of poultry consumed by those consuming poultry	173	85	70	35	117	67	26	156	153	75	44	†

† Average not computed for less than 10 cases.

Appendix Table 20.—Quantity of Milk Produced on Part-Time Farms, by Type of Farm, by Color of Operator, and by Subregion, 1934

Milk produced	Textile		Coal and Iron		Atlantic Coast			Lumber			Naval Stores	
	White				White			White			White	
	Commercial	Noncommercial	White	Negro	Commercial	Noncommercial	Negro	Commercial	Noncommercial	Negro	Commercial	Noncommercial
Total	43	250	204	124	24	47	142	39	37	132	37	34
None	3	43	92	110	11	23	116	8	14	87	5	25
1 to 499 quarts	—	2	—	1	—	3	—	3	1	5	4	—
500 to 999 quarts	—	4	6	—	—	—	11	4	3	16	2	1
1,000 to 1,499 quarts	2	21	11	2	—	2	11	8	8	9	5	3
1,500 to 1,999 quarts	3	14	6	2	1	—	1	—	—	7	5	—
2,000 to 2,499 quarts	6	40	6	2	3	6	2	5	2	4	5	3
2,500 to 2,999 quarts	6	42	21	4	—	1	1	3	4	2	2	1
3,000 to 3,499 quarts	7	39	8	—	2	8	—	2	2	—	2	1
3,500 to 3,999 quarts	3	12	21	1	—	—	—	3	1	1	3	—
4,000 to 4,999 quarts	7	17	24	1	—	3	—	1	2	—	2	—
5,000 quarts or more	6	16	9	1	7	1	—	2	—	1	2	—
Number of cows producing milk [1]	64	216	112	13	47	35	31	56	24	48	69	13
Average number of quarts per cow producing milk	2,440	2,650	3,069	2,709	2,440	1,770	920	1,375	1,941	1,265	1,081	1,283

[1] Exclusive of cows purchased after January 1, 1934.

Appendix Table 21.—Quantity of Home-Produced Butter Consumed on Part-Time Farms, by Color of Operator and by Subregion, 1934

Butter consumed	Textile	Coal and Iron		Atlantic Coast		Lumber		Naval Stores
	White	White	Negro	White	Negro	White	Negro	White
Total	293	204	124	71	142	76	132	71
None	48	93	110	46	134	29	93	36
1 to 49 pounds	7	4	1	—	2	6	19	7
50 to 99 pounds	33	11	4	7	4	14	9	7
100 to 199 pounds	106	37	5	12	—	20	8	12
200 to 299 pounds	69	21	1	4	2	4	2	1
300 pounds or more	29	37	3	2	—	3	1	8
Unknown	1	1	—	—	—	—	—	—
Average number of pounds of butter consumed by those consuming home-produced butter	190	234	176	151	100	124	73	167

Appendix Table 22.—Quantity of Home-Produced Pork Consumed or Stored on Part-Time Farms, by Type of Farm, by Color of Operator, and by Subregion, 1934

Dressed pork consumed or stored	Textile		Coal and Iron		Atlantic Coast			Lumber			Naval Stores	
	White		White	Negro	White		Negro	White		Negro	White	
	Commercial	Noncommercial	White	Negro	Commercial	Noncommercial	Negro	Commercial	Noncommercial	Negro	Commercial	Noncommercial
Total	43	250	204	124	24	47	142	39	37	132	37	34
None	10	117	136	84	16	26	119	1	14	44	4	32
1 to 99 pounds	—	—	—	5	—	1	8	—	2	14	—	—
100 to 199 pounds	2	17	17	18	—	7	4	2	6	27	2	1
200 to 299 pounds	6	29	13	9	1	4	5	5	5	17	1	—
300 to 399 pounds	8	34	13	3	1	1	1	6	6	10	1	1
400 to 499 pounds	4	23	8	3	2	3	2	4	3	6	1	—
500 to 599 pounds	5	12	4	2	1	2	3	6	1	6	3	—
600 to 999 pounds	5	15	12	—	2	3	—	7	—	6	7	—
1,000 pounds or more	3	3	1	—	1	—	—	8	—	2	18	—
Average number of pounds of pork consumed or stored by those consuming or storing home-produced pork	460	366	376	217	†	306	230	583	249	263	1,263	†

† Average not computed for less than 10 cases.

Appendix Table 23.—Quantity of Roughage Produced on Part-Time Farms, by Type of Farm, by Color of Operator, and by Subregion, 1934

Roughage produced	Textile		Coal and Iron		Atlantic Coast			Lumber			Naval Stores	
	White				White			White			White	
	Commercial	Noncommercial	White	Negro	Commercial	Noncommercial	Negro	Commercial	Noncommercial	Negro	Commercial	Noncommercial
Total	43	250	204	124	24	47	142	39	37	132	37	34
None	11	220	190	122	8	37	130	13	31	103	14	34
1 to 2 tons	17	27	9	2	2	7	10	6	5	18	5	—
3 to 4 tons	12	2	3	—	2	2	—	4	1	5	8	—
5 to 9 tons	2	—	1	—	6	1	1	10	—	6	4	—
10 to 14 tons	—	—	1	—	3	—	1	5	—	—	1	—
15 to 19 tons	—	—	—	—	2	—	—	1	—	—	—	—
20 tons or more	1	—	—	—	1	—	—	—	—	—	5	—
Unknown	—	1	—	—	—	—	—	—	—	—	—	—
Average number of tons of roughage produced by those producing roughage	3.4	1.4	2.9	†	11.0	3.0	3.4	6.5	†	2.8	13.1	—

† Average not computed for less than 10 cases.

Appendix Table 24.—Quantity of Field Corn Produced on Part-Time Farms, by Type of Farm, by Color of Operator, and by Subregion, 1934

Field corn produced	Textile		Coal and Iron		Atlantic Coast			Lumber			Naval Stores	
	White				White			White			White	
	Commercial	Noncommercial	White	Negro	Commercial	Noncommercial	Negro	Commercial	Noncommercial	Negro	Commercial	Noncommercial
Total	43	250	204	124	24	47	142	39	37	132	37	34
None	5	226	130	49	5	25	33	1	23	20	—	34
1 to 9 bushels	—	5	2	11	—	2	34	—	—	14	2	—
10 to 19 bushels	—	8	4	37	—	4	37	—	1	15	—	—
20 to 29 bushels	3	4	12	14	2	4	18	—	3	23	1	—
30 to 49 bushels	3	4	15	9	1	5	12	2	5	29	—	—
50 to 74 bushels	6	3	13	3	2	4	4	1	3	12	1	—
75 to 99 bushels	5	—	12	—	2	2	—	2	2	5	2	—
100 to 149 bushels	12	—	8	—	3	—	2	4	—	9	4	—
150 to 199 bushels	1	—	3	—	1	—	1	8	—	2	4	—
200 to 299 bushels	8	—	4	1	1	—	—	7	—	2	14	—
300 to 399 bushels	—	—	1	—	1	1	1	6	—	—	3	—
400 to 599 bushels	—	—	—	—	1	—	—	3	—	—	5	—
600 bushels or more	—	—	—	—	5	—	—	5	—	1	1	—
Average number of bushels of corn produced by those producing corn	101	21	68	21	310	48	21	281	41	49	228	—

Appendix Table 25.—Relation Between Cash Receipts From All Products Sold and Total Cash Farm Expenses[1] on White Noncommercial and Negro Part-Time Farms, by Subregion, 1934

Cash receipts from all products sold	Textile		Coal and Iron				Atlantic Coast				Lumber				Naval Stores	
	White noncommercial		White		Negro		White noncommercial		Negro		White noncommercial		Negro		White noncommercial	
	Number of cases	Average cash expenses	Number of cases	Average cash expenses	Number of cases	Average cash expenses	Number of cases	Average cash expenses	Number of cases	Average cash expenses	Number of cases	Average cash expenses	Number of cases	Average cash expenses	Number of cases	Average cash expenses
Total	250	[2] $92	204	$73	124	$15	47	$62	142	$26	37	$55	132	$38	34	$25
None	102	[2] 71	108	52	112	13	26	44	62	7	22	50	31	12	30	24
$1 to $49	75	83	55	68	8	†	13	69	54	21	10	52	26	24	3	†
$50 to $99	37	107	16	100	3	†	3	†	14	35	5	†	35	22	1	†
$100 to $199	28	132	21	147	1	†	3	†	7	†	—	—	24	54	—	—
$200 or more	8	†	3	†	—	—	2	†	5	†	—	—	16	120	—	—
Unknown	—	—	1	†	—	—	—	—	—	—	—	—	—	—	—	—
Average cash receipts		$45		$33		$4		$30		$38		$15		$96		†

† Average not computed for less than 10 cases.
[1] Exclusive of taxes and rent.
[2] Exclusive of 1 case for which expenses were not available.

Appendix Table 26.—Amount Paid for Hired Labor on Part-Time Farms, by Type of Farm, by Color of Operator, and by Subregion, 1934

Amount paid for hired labor	Textile White Commercial	Textile White Noncommercial	Coal and Iron White	Coal and Iron Negro	Atlantic Coast White Commercial	Atlantic Coast White Noncommercial	Atlantic Coast Negro	Lumber White Commercial	Lumber White Noncommercial	Lumber Negro	Naval Stores White Commercial	Naval Stores White Noncommercial
Total	43	250	204	124	24	47	142	39	37	132	37	34
None	12	146	61	43	3	19	110	5	9	90	7	22
$1 to $4	—	62	63	51	—	5	15	—	3	10	—	7
$5 to $14	9	27	55	29	—	7	14	1	13	16	4	5
$15 to $24	4	6	11	—	1	8	—	1	8	5	7	—
$25 to $49	4	5	8	1	1	4	1	2	3	4	4	—
$50 to $99	9	2	3	—	2	1	—	12	1	5	8	—
$100 to $199	1	2	1	—	3	1	—	7	—	2	5	—
$200 to $499	3	—	2	—	3	2	1	10	—	—	2	—
$500 or more	1	—	—	—	3	—	1	—	—	—	—	—
Unknown	—	—	—	—	8	—	—	1	—	—	—	—
Average amount paid for hired labor on farms having hired labor	$86	$11	$14	$5	$350	$34	$18	$151	$17	$25	$76	$5
Average amount paid for hired labor per crop acre on farms having hired labor	$4.00	$6.40	$5.50	$4.40	$11.50	$9.30	$4.70	$3.60	$5.10	$2.50	$1.80	$3.60

Appendix Table 27.—Number of Persons, Except Heads, 12 Years of Age or Over, Working on Part-Time Farms, by Color and by Subregion, 1934

Number of persons, except heads, 12 years of age or over, working on farms	Textile White	Coal and Iron White	Coal and Iron Negro	Atlantic Coast White	Atlantic Coast Negro	Lumber White	Lumber Negro	Naval Stores White
Total	293	204	124	71	142	76	132	71
No member except head	26	47	19	24	27	4	4	31
Wife only	132	50	42	27	54	30	56	20
Wife with 1 or more other members	94	65	40	11	42	33	59	12
1 other member	17	25	14	6	10	3	7	4
2 other members	15	15	2	3	4	2	4	2
3 other members	5	2	5	—	4	3	—	1
4 or more other members	4	—	2	—	1	1	2	1
Farms on which wife worked	226	115	82	38	96	63	115	32

Appendix Table 28.—Distance to Place of Employment of Heads of Part-Time Farm and Nonfarming Industrial Households, by Type of Farm, by Color, and by Subregion, 1934

| Distance to place of employment | Textile — White | | Coal and Iron | | Atlantic Coast | | | Lumber | | | Naval Stores — White | |
	Commercial	Noncommercial	White	Negro	White Commercial	White Noncommercial	Negro	White Commercial	White Noncommercial	Negro	Commercial	Noncommercial
PART-TIME FARMERS												
Total	43	250	204	124	24	47	142	39	37	132	37	34
None	2	5	—	—	4	5	3	1	2	3	—	—
Less than ½ mile	5	131	28	62	1	4	26	6	9	43	2	3
1 mile	10	54	42	30	6	8	51	4	13	43	17	13
2 miles	5	13	39	9	2	4	29	2	4	17	10	14
3 miles	8	20	31	5	4	2	14	4	4	8	5	3
4 to 5 miles	7	13	23	7	3	10	14	9	2	9	1	1
6 to 9 miles	3	11	30	10	3	8	4	7	1	7	1	—
10 miles or more	3	2	11	1	1	6	1	6	2	1	1	—
Unknown	—	1	—	—	—	—	—	—	—	1	—	—
Average number of miles to place of employment	3.2	1.4	3.3	1.6	3.0	4.3	1.8	[1] 4.5	[2] 1.9	1.6	2.1	1.6
NONFARMING INDUSTRIAL WORKERS												
Total	314		222	346	103		105	92		103	49	
None	2											
Less than ½ mile	181		113	43	49		40	37		38	11	
1 mile	94		50	92	27		42	38		40	11	
2 miles	21		23	56	15		13	12		23	6	
3 miles	11		20	22	2		3	1		1	5	
4 to 5 miles	3		7	101	3		3	—		—	9	
6 to 9 miles	1		6	28	3		2	1		—	5	
10 miles or more	1		3	4	3		—	3		1	2	
Unknown	—		—	—	1		2	—		—	—	
Average number of miles to place of employment	0.8		1.6	2.8	[3] 1.1		1.1	1.3		1.3	[4] 2.7	

[1] Exclusive of 1 case who traveled 40 miles weekly to work.
[2] Exclusive of 1 case who traveled 170 miles weekly to work.
[3] Exclusive of 3 cases who traveled 36 miles biweekly, 50 miles weekly, and 26 miles weekly, respectively, to work.
[4] Exclusive of 1 case who traveled 87 miles weekly to work.

Appendix Table 29.—Industry of Heads of Part-Time Farm and Nonfarming Industrial Households, by Color and by Subregion, 1934

Industry in 1934	Part-time farmers								Nonfarming industrial workers							
	Textile	Coal and Iron		Atlantic Coast		Lumber		Naval Stores	Textile	Coal and Iron		Atlantic Coast		Lumber		Naval Stores
	White	White	Negro	White	Negro	White	Negro	White	White	White	Negro	White	Negro	White	Negro	White
Total	293	204	124	71	142	76	132	71	314	222	346	103	105	92	103	49
Agriculture	3	—	—	9	94	8	63	—	—	—	—	—	—	—	—	—
Forestry	1	—	—	—	—	2	3	1	—	—	—	—	—	—	—	—
Fishing	—	—	—	—	1	—	—	—	—	—	—	—	—	—	—	—
Extraction of minerals:																
Coal mining	—	14	10	—	—	—	—	—	—	61	132	—	—	—	—	—
Iron mining	—	54	22	—	—	—	—	—	—	69	61	—	—	—	—	—
Other extraction of minerals	—	1	—	—	—	—	—	—	—	—	—	—	—	—	—	—
Manufacturing and mechanical industries:																
Building and construction	10	3	—	2	5	9	15	3	9	76	142	2	9	—	—	—
Food and allied	4	—	—	1	—	2	1	1	7	16	11	—	3	—	—	—
Iron, steel, machinery, and vehicles:																
Blast furnaces, steel rolling mills, and coke works	—	93	77	—	—	—	—	—	—	—	—	—	—	—	—	—
Car and railroad shops	2	1	—	1	—	—	—	—	—	—	—	7	1	—	—	—
Other iron, steel, machinery, and vehicles	5	7	1	—	—	1	—	—	—	—	—	—	—	—	—	—
Saw and planing mills	—	—	—	3	2	2	8	11	8	—	—	2	—	12	30	—
Furniture and other woodworking	—	—	—	3	1	4	17	1	—	—	—	—	—	80	73	—
Paper, printing, and allied	—	—	—	—	—	19	—	—	3	—	—	2	—	—	—	—
Cotton mills	113	—	—	—	—	—	—	—	165	—	—	—	—	—	—	—
Knitting mills	7	—	—	—	—	—	—	—	20	—	—	—	—	—	—	—
Other textile	73	—	—	1	—	—	—	—	24	—	—	—	—	—	—	—
Independent hand trades	1	1	—	1	—	1	—	—	—	—	—	1	3	—	—	—
Turpentine farms and distilleries	—	—	—	—	—	—	—	37	—	—	—	—	1	—	—	49
Fertilizer factories	1	—	—	3	14	—	1	—	—	—	—	1	17	—	—	—
Asbestos products	—	—	—	—	—	—	—	1	—	—	—	42	—	—	—	—
Other manufacturing and mechanical	10	6	5	7	3	2	6	1	9	—	—	11	10	—	—	—

Transportation and communication:																
Construction and maintenance of streets	1	1	—	3	4	2	2	2	—	—	—	—	1	—	—	—
Garages, greasing stations, etc.	6	—	—	—	—	1	—	—	1	—	—	—	—	—	—	—
Postal service	2	—	—	—	—	—	—	—	3	—	—	—	—	—	—	—
Steam and street railroads	5	9	6	9	10	3	5	2	12	—	—	5	2	—	—	—
Other transportation and communication	1	1	—	8	2	8	2	4	2	—	—	5	29	—	—	—
Trade:																	
Automobile agencies and filling stations	10	2	—	1	—	4	1	—	11	—	—	2	—	—	—	—
Wholesale and retail trade	25	8	2	16	1	5	1	6	22	—	—	9	11	—	—	—
Other trade	2	—	—	1	1	—	—	—	—	—	—	1	—	—	—	—
Public service (not elsewhere classified)	6	—	—	2	3	1	—	—	3	—	—	12	2	—	—	—
Professional service	4	1	—	—	—	—	1	—	—	—	—	—	2	—	—	—
Domestic and personal service	1	3	—	—	1	2	5	—	15	—	—	2	12	—	—	—
Industry not specified	—	—	1	—	—	—	1	—	—	—	—	—	2	—	—	—

Appendix Table 30.—Occupation of Heads of Part-Time Farm and Nonfarming Industrial Households, by Color and by Subregion, 1934

Occupation	Textile	Coal and Iron		Alantic Coast		Lumber		Naval Stores
	White	White	Negro	White	Negro	White	Negro	White
PART-TIME FARMERS								
Total	293	204	124	71	142	76	132	71
Proprietary	10	2	—	10	1	3	—	1
Clerical	36	17	—	4	1	8	2	4
Skilled	71	105	19	22	6	32	17	10
Semiskilled	160	47	32	24	6	22	14	16
Unskilled:								
Farm laborer	3	—	—	8	91	7	62	—
Servant	4	2	2	—	2	—	6	—
Other unskilled	9	31	71	3	35	4	31	40
NONFARMING INDUSTRIAL WORKERS								
Total	314	222	346	103	105	92	103	49
Proprietary	2	—	—	1	3	—	—	—
Clerical	42	11	6	13	1	2	—	1
Skilled	74	120	46	33	12	33	15	3
Semiskilled	185	23	53	49	23	49	36	14
Unskilled:								
Servant	2	—	4	—	13	—	2	—
Other unskilled	9	68	237	7	53	8	50	31

Appendix Table 31.—Industry of Heads of Part-Time Farm and Nonfarming Industrial Households, by Color and by Subregion, 1929

Industry in 1929	Part-time farmers								Nonfarming industrial workers							
	Textile	Coal and Iron		Atlantic Coast		Lumber		Naval Stores	Textile	Coal and Iron		Atlantic Coast		Lumber		Naval Stores
	White	White	Negro	White	Negro	White	Negro	White	White	White	Negro	White	Negro	White	Negro	White
Total	293	204	124	71	142	76	132	71	314	222	346	103	105	92	103	49
Agriculture	38			12	84	12	64	37	30	2	4	2	3	10	12	17
Forestry and fishing	1				1	3	2					1			4	
Extraction of minerals		70	30							119	185					
Manufacturing and mechanical industries:																
Building and construction	16	7		4	3	9	16	2	10	1		3	7	3	2	
Food and allied	4						1		7	2			4		2	
Iron, steel, machinery, and vehicles	7	98	77	3	2	4		12	11	90	139	8	1	1	1	
Saw and planing mills			1	3	1	9	10	1	2				2	14	28	
Furniture and other woodworking					1	16	15		1					50	38	
Paper, printing, and allied									3			2	2			
Cotton mills	76								132			1	1	1		
Knitting mills and other textile	68								24			1				
Independent hand trades	2				1	1								1		
Turpentine farms and distilleries		7	7	8	12		6	2	7	1				2		30
Other manufacturing and mechanical	4	11	6	18	19	1	10	1	24	2	6	41	22	4	2	2
Transportation and communication	20	3	2	16	4	8	2	4	28	2	6	8	26	4	7	
Trade	34	2		3	3	7	1	6	7	2	1	13	6		2	
Public service (not elsewhere classified)	7				2	1					1	10	3			
Professional service	4	3			1				11			3	3			
Domestic and personal service	2			1	3	3	1	1				1	9	2	2	
Industry not specified	1		1	3			2		17				3			
Unemployed	9	3			5	1	2	4		1	4	9	13		3	

Appendix Table 32.—Number of Days of Off-the-Farm Employment[1] of Heads of Part-Time Farm and Nonfarming Industrial Households, by Type of Farm, by Color, and by Subregion, 1934

Number of days employed	Textile		Coal and Iron		Atlantic Coast			Lumber			Naval Stores	
	White				White			White			White	
	Commercial	Noncommercial	White	Negro	Commercial	Noncommercial	Negro	Commercial	Noncommercial	Negro	Commercial	Noncommercial
PART-TIME FARMERS												
Total	43	250	204	124	24	47	142	39	37	132	37	34
1 to 49 days[2]	1	1	1	—	1	—	3	—	1	1	2	—
50 to 99 days	5	11	50	53	3	7	38	6	2	20	31	—
100 to 149 days	4	21	58	58	3	1	44	2	4	13	2	3
150 to 199 days	9	44	44	6	4	4	19	8	5	32	2	7
200 to 249 days	10	112	29	5	2	15	19	12	10	43	—	13
250 to 299 days	3	31	10	1	3	9	10	5	9	11	—	2
300 to 349 days	8	19	12	1	4	8	5	5	5	6	—	6
350 days or more	3	10	—	—	4	3	4	1	1	6	—	3
Unknown	—	1	—	—	—	—	—	—	—	—	—	—
Average number of days employed	214	218	156	112	219	229	155	211	221	191	83	241
NONFARMING INDUSTRIAL WORKERS												
Total	314		222	346	103		105	92		103	49	
1 to 49 days	—		—	—	—		1	—		—	—	
50 to 99 days	3		52	156	3		23	1		2	1	
100 to 149 days	24		74	133	3		19	4		11	6	
150 to 199 days	39		48	34	13		15	14		14	10	
200 to 249 days	113		32	20	11		14	23		35	16	
250 to 299 days	78		8	1	38		11	41		37	10	
300 to 349 days	47		7	2	27		14	6		2	6	
350 days or more	10		1	—	8		8	3		2		
Average number of days employed	233		151	114	261		189	240		221	221	

[1] At principal off-the-farm employment (job with the largest earnings).
[2] A few cases working off the farm less than 50 days were enumerated.

Appendix Table 33.—Number of Different Off-the-Farm Jobs Held by Heads of Part-Time Farm and Nonfarming Industrial Households, by Color and by Subregion, 1934

Number of off-the-farm jobs	Textile	Coal and Iron		Atlantic Coast		Lumber		Naval Stores
	White	White	Negro	White	Negro	White	Negro	White
PART-TIME FARMERS								
Total	293	204	124	71	142	76	132	71
1	276	199	123	66	129	73	124	68
2	15	5	1	5	13	3	7	3
3	2	—	—	—	—	—	1	—
NONFARMING INDUSTRIAL WORKERS								
Total	314	222	346	103	105	92	103	49
1	305	218	340	96	92	83	90	41
2	8	4	6	7	12	7	11	8
3	1	—	—	—	1	2	2	—

Appendix Table 34.—Earnings [1] From Industrial Employment of Heads of Part-Time Farm and Nonfarming Industrial Households, by Type of Farm, by Color, and by Subregion, 1934

Earnings from industrial employment	Textile		Coal and Iron		Atlantic Coast			Lumber			Naval Stores	
	White				White			White			White	
	Commercial	Noncommercial	White	Negro	Commercial	Noncommercial	Negro	Commercial	Noncommercial	Negro	Commercial	Noncommercial
PART-TIME FARMERS												
Total	43	250	204	124	24	47	142	39	37	132	37	34
$1 to $99	2	2	1	1	—	—	56	—	—	12	26	—
$100 to $249	5	16	12	38	2	11	53	—	—	77	11	6
$250 to $499	11	42	55	74	5	5	22	10	8	28	—	12
$500 to $749	4	96	59	9	3	6	4	11	7	12	—	8
$750 to $999	11	52	34	2	4	10	—	11	13	1	—	6
$1,000 to $1,249	5	22	22	—	4	2	3	4	4	1	—	2
$1,250 to $1,499	1	9	7	—	1	6	—	3	3	—	—	—
$1,500 to $1,999	4	7	10	—	3	6	—	—	1	1	—	—
$2,000 to $2,499	—	3	4	—	1	1	—	4	1	—	—	—
$2,500 or more	—	1	—	—	1	—	—	—	—	—	—	—
Unknown	—	—	—	—	—	—	4	—	—	—	—	—
Average earnings	$733	$722	$736	$337	$1,006	$820	$181	$650	$610	$258	$95	$536
NONFARMING INDUSTRIAL WORKERS												
Total	314		222	346	103		105	92		103	49	
$1 to $99	—		—	—	—		5	—		1	3	
$100 to $249	6		14	86	1		25	2		8	32	
$250 to $499	75		69	202	10		50	19		57	9	
$500 to $749	74		52	50	14		19	48		37	3	
$750 to $999	76		47	8	30		3	14		—	2	
$1,000 to $1,249	33		18	—	21		1	5		—	—	
$1,250 to $1,499	15		7	—	13		1	3		—	—	
$1,500 to $1,999	23		10	—	11		1	1		—	—	
$2,000 to $2,499	9		2	—	2		—	—		—	—	
$2,500 or more	3		3	—	1		—	—		—	—	
Average earnings	$853		$731	$372	$1,020		$388	$654		$430	$260	

[1] At principal off-the-farm employment (job with the largest earnings).

Appendix Table 35.—Employment of Members¹ in Addition to the Head of Part-Time Farm and Nonfarming Industrial Households, by Color and by Subregion, 1934

Number of members working in addition to the head	Textile		Coal and Iron				Atlantic Coast				Lumber				Naval Stores	
	White		White		Negro		White		Negro		White		Negro		White	
	Number	Per-cent	Number	Per-cent	Number	Per-cent	Number	Per-cent	Number	Per-cent	Number	Per-cent	Number	Per-cent	Number	Per-cent
PART-TIME FARM HOUSEHOLDS																
Total	293	100	204	100	124	100	71	100	142	100	76	100	132	100	71	100
No member except head	135	46	154	75	104	83	57	80	45	32	47	62	36	27	54	77
Wife only	53	18	2	1	6	5	2	3	42	30	6	8	48	36	3	4
Wife and 1 or more other members	17	6	1	1	2	2	1	1	36	25	5	7	29	22	2	3
1 other member	46	16	37	18	10	8	5	7	5	4	13	17	13	10	10	14
2 other members	31	10	9	4	2	2	4	6	9	6	3	4	4	3	1	1
3 other members	5	2	1	1	—	—	2	3	3	2	1	1	1	1	1	1
4 or more other members	6	2	—	—	—	—	—	—	2	1	1	1	1	1	—	—
NONFARMING INDUSTRIAL HOUSEHOLDS																
Total	314	100	222	100	346	100	103	100	105	100	92	100	103	100	49	100
No member except head	144	46	187	84	280	81	78	75	51	48	60	65	44	42	33	68
Wife only	105	34	1	*	16	5	4	4	33	31	7	8	42	41	7	14
Wife and 1 or more other members	15	5	1	*	4	1	1	1	9	9	5	5	9	9	4	8
1 other member	31	10	28	13	37	11	16	16	8	8	18	20	5	5	2	4
2 other members	14	4	4	2	8	2	3	3	2	2	1	1	2	2	3	6
3 other members	4	1	1	*	1	*	—	—	1	1	1	1	1	1	—	—
4 or more other members	1	*	—	—	—	—	1	1	1	1	—	—	—	—	—	—

* Less than 0.5 percent.

¹ 16-64 years of age.

Appendix Table 36.—Number of Years in Which Public or Private Relief Was Received by Part-Time Farm and Nonfarming Industrial Households, by Color and by Subregion, 1929–35

Number of years in which relief was received	Textile	Coal and Iron		Atlantic Coast		Lumber		Naval Stores
	White	White	Negro	White	Negro	White	Negro	White
PART-TIME FARM HOUSEHOLDS								
Total	293	204	124	71	142	76	132	71
None	254	123	22	52	93	69	109	64
1	27	57	64	7	38	4	10	1
2	10	18	31	9	7	3	10	1
3	2	5	5	3	4	—	—	5
4	—	1	1	—	—	—	—	—
5	—	—	1	—	—	—	2	—
6	—	—	—	—	—	—	1	—
Average number of years in which relief was received [1]	1.4	1.4	1.5	1.8	1.3	†	2.0	†
NONFARMING INDUSTRIAL HOUSEHOLDS								
Total	314	222	346	103	105	92	103	49
None	256	124	99	87	82	80	96	35
1	38	58	158	7	8	10	3	10
2	20	36	59	9	11	2	4	4
3	—	4	17	—	2	—	—	—
4	—	—	11	—	—	—	—	—
5	—	—	2	—	—	—	—	—
Unknown	—	—	—	—	2	—	—	—
Average number of years in which relief was received [1]	1.3	1.5	1.6	1.6	1.7	1.2	†	1.3

† Average not computed for less than 10 cases.
[1] By those receiving relief.

Appendix Table 37A.—Number of Rooms in Dwellings of Part-Time Farm Households, by Size of Household and by Color, 1934

Rooms in dwelling	Size of household											
	Total	1	2	3	4	5	6	7	8	9	10	11
WHITE												
Total	715	3	48	101	149	141	104	65	46	24	20	14
1 room	2	—	—	—	1	—	—	—	—	1	—	—
2 rooms	17	1	4	2	1	7	2	—	—	—	—	—
3 rooms	67	—	7	10	15	10	12	6	5	1	—	1
4 rooms	196	1	14	29	40	44	26	18	12	4	5	3
5 rooms	217	1	13	31	49	46	28	17	16	7	6	3
6 rooms	136	—	3	18	30	25	21	14	9	4	8	4
7 rooms	40	—	2	4	9	4	9	5	3	2	—	2
8 rooms	17	—	2	3	1	5	1	1	—	3	1	—
9 rooms	10	—	2	2	—	—	4	—	—	2	—	—
10 rooms or more	13	—	1	2	3	—	1	4	1	—	—	1
NEGRO												
Total	398	3	53	60	54	72	53	40	20	13	12	18
1 room	6	—	1	2	1	1	—	1	—	—	—	—
2 rooms	90	2	15	17	10	20	13	7	1	2	—	3
3 rooms	99	1	17	20	13	15	10	10	5	3	3	2
4 rooms	140	—	14	15	20	22	20	16	11	5	6	11
5 rooms	39	—	3	4	8	9	5	2	3	3	—	2
6 rooms	20	—	2	2	1	5	4	4	—	—	2	—
7 rooms	2	—	—	—	—	—	1	—	—	—	1	—
8 rooms	1	—	—	—	1	—	—	—	—	—	—	—
Unknown	1	—	1	—	—	—	—	—	—	—	—	—

Appendix Table 37B.—Number of Rooms in Dwellings of Nonfarming Industrial Households, by Size of Household and by Color, 1934

Rooms in dwelling	Size of household											
	Total	1	2	3	4	5	6	7	8	9	10	11
WHITE												
Total	780	2	118	185	158	122	91	51	28	17	7	1
1 room	6	—	4	1	1	—	—	—	—	—	—	—
2 rooms	92	—	30	31	10	11	4	3	2	1	—	—
3 rooms	112	1	16	30	28	16	8	7	3	—	1	—
4 rooms	240	—	32	55	55	39	26	19	6	6	2	—
5 rooms	190	—	18	46	37	36	28	13	6	3	2	1
6 rooms	103	—	15	18	22	14	15	5	6	7	1	—
7 rooms	29	1	2	3	5	4	7	3	4	—	—	—
8 rooms	4	—	1	1	—	—	1	1	—	—	—	—
9 rooms	3	—	—	—	—	2	1	—	—	—	—	—
10 rooms or more	3	—	—	—	—	—	1	—	1	—	1	—
NEGRO												
Total	554	2	117	143	115	70	46	28	13	8	4	8
1 room	29	—	13	14	—	—	1	1	—	—	—	—
2 rooms	116	1	29	37	27	13	3	4	2	—	—	—
3 rooms	216	1	53	50	49	25	18	16	2	1	—	1
4 rooms	121	—	15	27	27	21	14	3	5	4	4	1
5 rooms	41	—	5	8	8	7	5	1	3	2	—	2
6 rooms	21	—	2	5	4	2	2	2	1	1	—	2
7 rooms	2	—	—	—	—	—	—	1	—	—	—	1
8 rooms	4	—	—	1	—	1	1	—	—	—	—	1
9 rooms	1	—	—	—	—	—	1	—	—	—	—	—
Unknown	3	—	—	1	—	1	1	—	—	—	—	—

Appendix Table 38.—Average Number of Rooms in Dwellings of Part-Time Farm and Nonfarming Industrial Households, by Color and by Subregion, 1934

Size of household	Textile — Greenville White — Number of cases	Textile — Greenville White — Average number of rooms per dwelling	Textile — Carroll White — Number of cases	Textile — Carroll White — Average number of rooms per dwelling	Coal and Iron — White — Number of cases	Coal and Iron — White — Average number of rooms per dwelling	Coal and Iron — Negro — Number of cases	Coal and Iron — Negro — Average number of rooms per dwelling	Atlantic Coast — White — Number of cases	Atlantic Coast — White — Average number of rooms per dwelling	Atlantic Coast — Negro — Number of cases	Atlantic Coast — Negro — Average number of rooms per dwelling	Lumber — White — Number of cases	Lumber — White — Average number of rooms per dwelling	Lumber — Negro — Number of cases	Lumber — Negro — Average number of rooms per dwelling	Naval Stores — White — Number of cases	Naval Stores — White — Average number of rooms per dwelling
PART-TIME FARM HOUSEHOLDS																		
Total	190	5.1	103	4.7	204	5.2	124	3.5	[1]39	5.6	[2]141	3.2	76	4.5	132	3.7	71	4.9
1 to 3 persons	37	4.9	20	4.2	37	4.9	36	3.4	11	6.0	[2]45	2.9	18	4.1	34	3.2	19	4.9
4 to 5 persons	76	5.0	45	4.3	95	5.2	46	3.4	10	4.7	36	3.2	28	4.1	44	3.9	28	5.1
6 to 7 persons	45	5.5	22	5.0	49	5.4	28	3.6	9	4.9	37	3.4	16	4.8	28	3.9	17	4.9
8 persons or more	32	5.5	16	4.1	23	5.3	14	4.1	9	6.8	23	3.7	14	5.6	26	3.3	7	4.3
NONFARMING INDUSTRIAL HOUSEHOLDS																		
Total	216	4.8	98	2.9	222	4.5	346	3.5	103	4.8	105	2.8	92	3.7	[3]101	2.9	49	3.6
1 to 3 persons	100	4.6	48	2.4	71	4.3	154	3.2	30	3.9	54	2.2	34	3.1	[2]53	2.6	22	4.2
4 to 5 persons	70	4.9	30	3.0	89	4.5	121	3.4	40	4.7	32	3.4	32	3.8	32	3.2	19	3.6
6 to 7 persons	29	5.0	15	3.5	51	4.9	46	3.8	22	5.5	14	4.2	20	4.1	[2]13	3.2	5	3.8
8 persons or more	17	5.2	5	4.2	11	5.0	25	4.4	11	5.9	5		6	4.5	3	4.7	3	3.0

[1] Exclusive of all white commercial farmers and of white noncommercial farmers with off-the-farm employment in agriculture.
[2] Number of rooms unknown for 1 case.
[3] Number of rooms unknown for 2 cases.

Appendix Table 39.—Number of Persons per Room [1] in Part-Time Farm and Nonfarming Industrial Households, by Color and by Subregion, 1934

Subregion and color	Part-time farm households					Nonfarming industrial households				
	Total	1 person or less per room	2 persons or less but more than 1 per room	3 persons or less but more than 2 per room	More than 3 persons per room	Total	1 person or less per room	2 persons or less but more than 1 per room	3 persons or less but more than 2 per room	More than 3 persons per room
Textile:										
White	293	159	115	18	1	314	194	97	20	3
Coal and Iron:										
White	204	129	67	8	—	222	142	73	6	1
Negro	124	46	51	26	1	346	177	142	23	4
Atlantic Coast:										
White	71	44	24	3	—	103	69	32	1	1
Negro	142	41	55	31	15	105	30	55	17	3
Lumber:										
White	76	35	36	4	1	92	44	40	7	1
Negro	132	58	49	20	5	103	47	34	20	2
Naval Stores:										
White	71	44	23	3	1	49	26	20	1	2

[1] According to accepted housing standards, 1 person or less per room is considered adequate; 2 persons or ess, but more than 1 per room, crowded; 3 persons or less, but more than 2 per room, overcrowded; and more than 3 persons per room, greatly overcrowded.

Appendix Table 40.—Condition of Dwellings of Part-Time Farm and Nonfarming Industrial Households, by Color and by Subregion, 1934

Condition of dwelling	Textile	Coal and Iron		Atlantic Coast		Lumber		Naval Stores
	White	White	Negro	White	Negro	White	Negro	White
PART-TIME FARM HOUSEHOLDS								
Total dwellings	293	204	124	71	142	76	132	71
No repairs needed	95	91	23	19	8	28	26	8
Exterior or interior repairs needed	181	101	86	47	127	40	115	50
Roof repairs needed	51	42	33	16	94	24	66	21
General structural repairs needed	30	27	51	10	34	11	55	26
NONFARMING INDUSTRIAL HOUSEHOLDS								
Total dwellings	314	222	346	103	105	92	103	49
No repairs needed	89	82	98	42	22	23	15	2
Exterior or interior repairs needed	214	128	174	49	77	67	80	47
Roof repairs needed	44	42	133	18	15	21	44	1
General structural repairs needed	19	42	54	5	9	1	3	13

Appendix Table 41.—Conveniences in Dwellings of Part-Time Farm and Nonfarming Industrial Households, by Color and by Subregion, 1934

Convenience	Textile		Coal and Iron		Atlantic Coast		Lumber		Naval Stores
	Green-ville	Carroll	White	Negro	White	Negro	White	Negro	White
	White	White							
PART-TIME FARM HOUSEHOLDS									
Total dwellings	190	103	204	124	¹ 39	142	76	132	71
Number having:									
Electric lights	168	79	192	81	22	1	12	2	12
Running water	98	8	185	108	18	4	3	2	17
Bathroom	71	6	102	12	17	—	2	2	5
No conveniences	20	24	7	12	14	137	64	129	51
NONFARMING INDUSTRIAL HOUSEHOLDS									
Total dwellings	216	98	222	346	103	105	92	103	49
Number having:									
Electric lights	211	71	216	145	97	24	62	11	—
Running water	191	7	221	293	103	86	56	24	1
Bathroom	109	4	111	56	101	10	47	20	—
No conveniences	5	27	—	50	—	19	17	71	48

¹ Exclusive of all white commercial farmers and of white noncommercial farmers with off-the-farm employment in agriculture.

Appendix Table 42.—Communication and Transportation Facilities of Part-Time Farm and Nonfarming Industrial Households, by Color and by Subregion, 1934

Facility	Textile		Coal and Iron		Atlantic Coast		Lumber		Naval Stores
	Green-ville	Carroll	White	Negro	White	Negro	White	Negro	White
	White	White							
PART-TIME FARM HOUSEHOLDS									
Total households	190	103	204	124	¹ 39	142	76	132	71
Number having:									
Telephone	13	2	17	—	4	—	4	—	1
Radio	140	54	144	19	20	1	17	4	8
Automobile	133	52	93	5	31	18	49	23	11
No telephone, radio, or automobile	21	29	42	102	6	124	25	108	54
NONFARMING INDUSTRIAL HOUSEHOLDS									
Total households	216	98	222	346	103	105	92	103	49
Number having:									
Telephone	26	—	9	2	8	3	7	1	—
Radio	151	33	161	84	57	10	34	2	1
Automobile	103	27	85	17	49	2	30	17	10
No telephone, radio, or automobile	43	50	52	254	30	95	44	84	39

¹ Exclusive of all white commercial farmers and of white noncommercial farmers with off-the-farm employment in agriculture.

Appendix Table 43A.—Changes in Residence Since October 1, 1929, of Part-Time Farm Households, by Type of Farm, by Color, by Tenure, and by Subregion, 1934

Number of changes in residence since October 1, 1929	Textile				Coal and Iron				Atlantic Coast						Lumber						Naval Stores			
	White				White		Negro		White				Negro		White				Negro		White			
	Commercial		Noncommercial						Commercial		Noncommercial				Commercial		Noncommercial				Commercial		Noncommercial	
	Owner	Tenant	Owner	Tenant	Owner	Tenant	Owner	Tenant	Owner	Tenant	Owner	Tenant	Owner	Tenant	Owner	Tenant	Owner	Tenant	Owner	Tenant	Owner	Tenant	Owner	Tenant
Total	20	23	82	168	70	134	23	101	13	11	22	25	55	87	25	14	12	25	26	106	16	21	4	30
None	14	5	52	75	59	79	22	85	11	3	8	6	51	57	17	7	5	8	23	54	11	5	3	12
1	5	14	28	35	8	44	—	14	2	7	13	17	4	24	8	5	5	10	3	41	2	7	1	11
2	—	2	2	28	3	10	1	2	—	1	1	2	—	6	—	2	1	4	—	6	3	8	—	6
3	1	2	—	21	—	1	—	—	—	—	—	—	—	—	—	—	1	2	—	5	—	1	—	1
4 or more	—	—	—	9	—	—	—	—	—	—	—	—	—	—	—	—	—	1	—	—	—	—	—	—
Average for those changing their residence	†	1.3	1.1	2.2	1.3	1.2	†	1.1	†	†	1.1	1.1	†	1.2	†	†	†	1.7	†	1.3	†	1.6	†	1.4

† Average not computed for less than 10 cases.

Appendix Table 43B.—Changes in Residence Since October 1, 1929, of Nonfarming Industrial Households, by Color, by Tenure, and by Subregion, 1934

Number of changes in residence since October 1, 1929	Textile		Coal and Iron				Atlantic Coast				Lumber				Naval Stores	
	White		White		Negro		White		Negro		White		Negro		White	
	Owner	Tenant	Owner	Tenant	Owner	Tenant	Owner	Tenant	Owner	Tenant	Owner	Tenant	Owner	Tenant	Owner	Tenant
Total	29	285	40	182	70	276	16	87	7	98	2	90	11	92	—	49
None	26	144	35	117	65	212	16	64	7	82	2	49	8	58	—	11
1	3	90	2	36	5	39	—	20	—	14	—	24	3	25	—	24
2	—	27	1	17	—	21	—	3	—	1	—	14	—	3	—	5
3	—	18	1	9	—	3	—	—	—	—	—	2	—	5	—	7
4 or more	—	6	—	3	—	1	—	—	—	1	—	1	—	1	—	2
Unknown	—	—	—	—	—	—	—	—	—	—	—	—	—	—	—	—
Average for those changing their residence	†	1.6	†	1.7	†	1.5	—	1.1	—	1.1	—	1.5	†	1.5	—	1.8

† Average not computed for less than 10 cases.

Appendix Table 44.—Tenure Status in 1929 and 1934 of Part-Time Farmers Who Operated Farms in 1929, by Color and by Subregion

Subregion, color, and tenure status in 1929	Tenure status in 1934	
	Owner	Tenant
Textile:		
White	91	164
Owner	76	4
Tenant	15	160
Coal and Iron:		
White	65	61
Owner	61	5
Tenant	4	56
Negro	21	26
Owner	19	—
Tenant	2	26
Atlantic Coast:		
White	19	15
Owner	16	—
Tenant	3	15
Negro	53	64
Owner	51	1
Tenant	2	63
Lumber:		
White	30	28
Owner	18	—
Tenant	12	28
Negro	22	89
Owner	21	—
Tenant	1	89
Naval Stores:		
White	20	41
Owner	18	—
Tenant	2	41

Appendix Table 45.—Number of Days Heads of Part-Time Farm and Nonfarming Industrial Households Were Incapacitated, by Color and by Subregion, 1934

Number of days head was incapacitated	Textile	Coal and Iron		Atlantic Coast		Lumber		Naval Stores
	White	White	Negro	White	Negro	White	Negro	White
PART-TIME FARM HOUSEHOLDS								
Total	293	204	124	71	142	76	132	71
None	197	171	101	59	71	43	73	66
1 to 4 days	20	3	5	2	4	5	21	4
5 to 9 days	19	5	4	1	8	7	19	—
10 to 14 days	26	7	4	3	21	5	5	1
15 to 19 days	4	—	2	—	10	—	1	—
20 to 29 days	10	7	4	2	2	3	2	—
30 to 39 days	6	4	2	2	14	5	6	—
40 to 49 days	5	3	1	—	—	3	3	—
50 days or more	6	4	1	2	12	5	2	—
Average number of days incapacitated for those who were incapacitated	18	28	15	24	26	25	14	†
NONFARMING INDUSTRIAL HOUSEHOLDS								
Total	314	222	346	103	105	92	103	49
None	207	192	319	97	92	49	61	26
1 to 4 days	23	3	5	1	—	5	1	—
5 to 9 days	26	4	3	—	2	7	4	8
10 to 14 days	17	7	4	—	7	15	11	8
15 to 19 days	6	2	4	1	—	—	—	3
20 to 29 days	18	2	3	1	1	2	9	3
30 to 39 days	8	5	1	—	2	4	10	—
40 to 49 days	3	2	1	—	—	2	2	1
50 days or more	6	5	6	3	1	8	5	—
Average number of days incapacitated for those who were incapacitated	18	33	33	†	24	27	32	14

† Average not computed for less than 10 cases.

Appendix Table 46.—Education of Heads of Part-Time Farm and Nonfarming Industrial Households, by Color and by Subregion, 1934

Education of heads	Textile	Coal and Iron		Atlantic Coast		Lumber		Naval Stores
	White	White	Negro	White	Negro	White	Negro	White
PART-TIME FARM HOUSEHOLDS								
Total	293	204	124	[1] 39	142	76	132	71
None	9	7	20	2	49	3	20	4
1 to 4 grades completed	58	23	53	7	74	19	82	17
Grade school not completed [2]	78	83	25	10	17	22	16	17
Grade school completed	47	34	6	6	1	14	3	6
1 to 3 years high school	79	28	9	10	1	15	8	19
High school completed	11	18	1	2	—	3	2	3
1 to 3 years college	7	5	—	1	—	—	1	2
College completed	3	—	—	1	—	—	—	—
Unknown	1	6	10	—	—	—	—	3
Average grade completed	6. 4	7. 0	3. 8	6. 5	2. 1	5. 7	3. 2	6. 0
NONFARMING INDUSTRIAL HOUSEHOLDS								
Total	314	222	346	103	105	92	103	49
None	17	17	44	4	26	5	15	5
1 to 4 grades completed	66	33	137	15	32	13	49	19
Grade school not completed [2]	76	65	120	15	23	29	22	14
Grade school completed	42	45	16	31	11	15	7	7
1 to 3 years high school	79	41	17	25	9	27	6	4
High school completed	20	15	5	10	2	3	2	—
1 to 3 years college	12	3	5	—	1	—	1	—
College completed	2	2	—	1	1	—	—	—
Unknown	—	1	2	2	—	—	1	—
Average grade completed	6. 4	6. 8	4. 3	6. 8	4. 0	6. 2	3. 7	4. 3

[1] Exclusive of all white commercial farmers and of white noncommercial farmers with off-the-farm employment in agriculture.

[2] This category includes grades 5–7 for the Coal and Iron Subregion, and grades 5–6 for all other subregions.

Appendix Table 47.—School Attendance and Employment of Youth, 16–24 Years of Age, in Part-Time Farm and Nonfarming Industrial Households, by Color, by Sex, and by Subregion, 1934

School attendance and employment, by sex	Textile	Coal and Iron		Atlantic Coast		Lumber		Naval Stores
	White	White	Negro	White	Negro	White	Negro	White
YOUTH IN PART-TIME FARM HOUSEHOLDS								
Total	212	167	110	48	109	59	74	52
In school	51	77	51	18	31	20	20	28
Employed	115	33	10	12	52	19	38	9
Neither employed nor in school	46	57	49	18	26	20	16	15
Male	111	84	48	28	51	29	39	29
In school	21	37	26	11	16	9	8	16
Employed	69	26	6	7	31	9	25	6
Neither employed nor in school	21	21	16	10	4	11	6	7
Female	101	83	62	20	58	30	35	23
In school	30	40	25	7	15	11	12	12
Employed	46	7	4	5	21	10	13	3
Neither employed nor in school	25	36	33	8	22	9	10	8
YOUTH IN NONFARMING INDUSTRIAL HOUSEHOLDS								
Total	141	134	177	67	41	37	37	10
In school	38	53	52	25	6	8	11	2
Employed	78	25	28	22	24	18	15	7
Neither employed nor in school	25	56	97	20	11	11	11	1
Male	68	63	82	41	13	21	16	7
In school	18	21	22	15	2	4	4	1
Employed	40	21	18	16	9	13	10	6
Neither employed nor in school	10	21	42	10	2	4	2	—
Female	73	71	95	26	28	16	21	3
In school	20	32	30	10	4	4	7	1
Employed	38	4	10	6	15	5	5	1
Neither employed nor in school	15	35	55	10	9	7	9	1

Appendix Table 48A.—Availability of Specified Social Organizations and Participation of Part-Time Farm Households in These Organizations, by Color and by Subregion, 1934

Organization	Textile Greenville White Available[1]	Participating[2]	Textile Carroll White Available[1]	Participating[2]	Coal and Iron White Available[1]	Participating[2]	Coal and Iron Negro Available[1]	Participating[2]	Atlantic Coast White non-commercial Available[1]	Participating[2]	Atlantic Coast Negro Available[1]	Participating[2]	Lumber White Available[1]	Participating[2]	Lumber Negro Available[1]	Participating[2]	Naval Stores White Commercial Available[1]	Participating[2]	Naval Stores White Non-commercial Available[1]	Participating[2]
Total households	190		103		204		124		39[3]		142		68[3]		132		37		34	
Church	188	180	103	103	202	195	124	123	39	36	142	142	67	63	132	129	37	21	34	21
Adult church organization	187	91	93	24	198	56	123	30	33	10	71	48	66	22	119	53			28	2
Young people's organization	187	101	93	9	199	95	123	62	32	8	48	18	63	18	115	35			27	4
Sunday School	190	177	79	86	202	161	124	108	39	26	142	122	68	63	132	121	1	1	31	11
School club	111	41	79	7	112	27	57	7	1				21	2	31	5				
Athletic team	148	30	102	16	170	35	112	19					48	13	72	13			31	10
Fraternal order	142	49	93	27	130	19	110	11	25	8	36	21	33	11	42	16			28	3
Labor union	76	12			152	75	123	47	5	3			19	6	15	4			14	10
Parent-Teacher Association	140	75	93	7	196	79	122	22	35	13	24	4	58	5	33	14	9		34	2
Boy Scouts	66	3	55		191	13	7	1	12	1			32	1	6					
Girl Scouts	65	2			108	11	7	7	12	1			8		4					
Cooperatives	1	1											6		1					
Women's organization	64	12	71	4	44	6	82	1	1	1			28	12	33	22				
4-H Club	22	2	78	5				5					67	31	100	19				
Special interest group	50	4			16	5	7						16	1	1		1			
Other	63	40			17	2	62		3	3	10	9	6	3	5	4				

[1] "Available" means number of households to which specified organization was available.

[2] "Participating" means number of households with 1 or more members participating in specified organization.

[3] Does not include 8 agricultural cases.

Appendix Table 48B.—Availability of Specified Social Organizations and Participation of Nonfarming Industrial Households in These Organizations, by Color and by Subregion, 1934

Organization	Textile Greenville White Avail.[1]	Partic-ipat-ing[2]	Textile Carroll White Avail.[1]	Partic-ipat-ing[2]	Coal and Iron White Avail.[1]	Partic-ipat-ing[2]	Coal and Iron Negro Avail.[1]	Partic-ipat-ing[2]	Atlantic Coast White Avail.[1]	Partic-ipat-ing[2]	Atlantic Coast Negro Avail.[1]	Partic-ipat-ing[2]	Lumber White Avail.[1]	Partic-ipat-ing[2]	Lumber Negro Avail.[1]	Partic-ipat-ing[2]	Naval Stores White Avail.[1]	Partic-ipat-ing[2]
Total households	216		98		222		346		103		105		92		103		49	
Church	216	209	98	89	206	190	346	340	103	95	105	103	92	80	103	101	43	35
Adult church organization	216	112	49	9	213	67	346	134	101	23	96	24	92	18	103	23	3	3
Young people's organization	216	79	49	3	206	68	345	91	99	22	55	7	91	9	103	2	8	3
Sunday School	216	190	50	39	206	159	346	290	103	76	105	84	92	51	103	71	23	11
School club	152	29	49	4	205	66	323	40	18	1	2	—	83	—	95	—	—	—
Athletic team	209	39	97	7	187	44	340	59	80	10	2	6	90	2	103	—	7	1
Fraternal order	207	48	49	9	159	43	336	6	42	22	23	3	82	4	97	4	1	—
Labor union	94	16	—	—	206	83	333	134	103	13	30	11	66	24	77	20	—	—
Parent-Teacher Association	208	51	48	5	210	81	125	37	87	33	94	—	92	1	98	—	4	—
Boy Scouts	168	10	9	—	179	12	112	1	85	4	2	—	82	—	1	—	—	—
Girl Scouts	157	3	—	—	175	15	—	—	—	1	2	—	—	—	—	—	—	—
Cooperatives	2	—	—	—	17	—	148	15	—	—	—	—	60	—	92	—	—	—
Women's organization	67	10	—	—	127	11	233	28	2	2	5	3	82	4	93	2	2	—
4-H Club	9	—	10	—	3	—	2	—	—	—	—	—	67	2	97	—	—	—
Special interest group	27	2	10	—	82	16	103	2	3	3	1	1	82	—	93	—	—	—
Other	15	7	10	—	2	2	162	—	—	—	—	—	33	4	43	—	—	—

[1] "Available" means number of households to which the specified organization was available.

[2] "Participating" means number of households with 1 or more members participating in specified organization.

Appendix Table 49.—Number of Part-Time Farm and Nonfarming Industrial Households in Which One or More [1] Persons Held Office in One or More Social Organizations, 1934

| Organization | Part-time farm households | | | | | | | | | Nonfarming industrial households | | | | | | | | |
	Textile Greenville (White)	Textile Carroll (White)	Coal and Iron (White)	Coal and Iron (Negro)	Atlantic Coast (White)	Atlantic Coast (Negro)	Lumber (White)	Lumber (Negro)	Naval Stores (White)	Textile Greenville (White)	Textile Carroll (White)	Coal and Iron (White)	Coal and Iron (Negro)	Atlantic Coast (White)	Atlantic Coast (Negro)	Lumber (White)	Lumber (Negro)	Naval Stores (White)
Total households	190	103	204	124	³62	142	³68	132	71	216	98	222	346	103	105	92	103	49
Total offices held [2]	107	4	76	26	7	48	6	27	3	36	1	54	102	8	27	1	11	5
Church	11	—	13	15	3	36	—	14	1	4	—	14	56	1	17	—	4	2
Adult church organization	13	1	13	1	—	—	2	4	—	5	—	4	14	—	2	—	—	—
Young people's organization	23	—	18	2	1	—	—	2	1	5	1	4	9	3	1	1	4	1
Sunday School	36	1	23	7	3	11	4	5	—	14	—	15	17	—	7	—	—	2
School club	8	1	3	—	—	—	—	—	—	1	—	3	2	—	—	—	—	—
Athletic team	2	—	3	—	—	—	—	—	—	1	—	3	4	—	—	—	—	—
Fraternal order	2	1	—	1	—	—	—	1	1	1	—	3	—	1	—	—	1	—
Labor union	1	—	—	—	—	—	—	1	—	—	—	1	—	1	—	—	—	—
Parent-Teacher Association	7	—	2	—	—	—	—	—	—	—	—	3	—	2	—	—	—	—
Boy Scouts	—	—	—	—	—	—	—	—	—	2	—	3	—	—	—	—	2	2
Women's organization	2	—	—	—	—	—	—	—	—	1	—	1	—	—	—	—	—	—
Other	2	—	1	—	—	1	—	—	—	1	—	—	—	—	—	—	—	—

[1] In practically all households, only 1 member held office in any given organization.
[2] Assuming 1 member per household per organization.
[3] Nonagricultural cases.

Appendix C

METHODOLOGICAL NOTE

THE METHODS of studying combined farming-industrial employment must be evaluated with reference to the questions which the survey was designed to answer [1] as well as with reference to the procedures employed. A sample representative of all types of part-time farming enterprises was not desired but rather a sample of specific types of farming-industrial combinations. The present study differs from most part-time farming studies in that it was based on a selected rather than an unselected sample of part-time farms and in that it compares specific farming-industrial employment combinations with full-time industrial employment.

SELECTION OF COUNTIES

After the subregions were roughly delimited on the basis of pre-aominating manufacturing or extractive industry (figure A), the next problem was to select counties for special field studies. Criteria for selecting the counties were as follows:

That the county have as its predominant manufacturing or extractive industry the industry which characterized its subregion.

That the county be representative of a major type of agriculture in the subregion.

That the county contain a reasonable number of part-time farmers as indicated by 1930 Census data.

On the basis of these criteria, and as a result of preliminary field investigation, the following counties were chosen for survey:

    I. Cotton Textile Subregion:
        Greenville County, South Carolina.
        Carroll County, South Carolina.
   II. Coal and Iron Subregion:
        Jefferson County, Alabama.

---

[1] See Introduction, p. XIX.

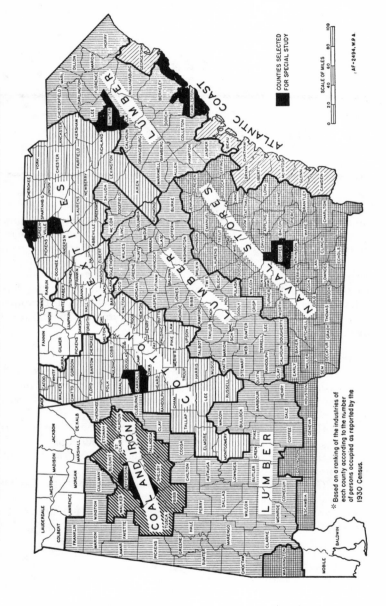

FIG. A – INDUSTRIAL SUBREGIONS* OF ALABAMA, GEORGIA, AND SOUTH CAROLINA

* Based on a ranking of the industries of each county according to the number of persons occupied as reported by the 1930 Census.

COUNTIES SELECTED FOR SPECIAL STUDY

SCALE OF MILES
0 20 40 60 80 100

AF-2494, W.P.A.

III. Atlantic Coast Subregion:
    Charleston County, South Carolina.
IV. Lumber Subregion:
    Sumter County, South Carolina.
V. Naval Stores Subregion:
    Coffee County, Georgia.

For the location of the counties, see figure A.

REPRESENTATIVENESS OF COUNTIES

Since the objective of the survey was to learn how persons who combined farming with specific types of industrial employment fared economically and socially as compared with full-time industrial workers in the same industry in the same locality, the validity of the conclusions of the study does not hinge entirely on the representativeness of the selected counties, however desirable it may be that each county be reliably representative of its subregion.

One basis for the selection of counties, as pointed out above, was the presence of certain industries employing a proportionally larger number of persons than other industries. To that extent the selected counties represent the subregions. Moreover, they represent the major types of agricultural conditions within each subregion. However, they are not representative in some other economic and social aspects (tables A–E). Furthermore, some counties are fairly closely representative of their subregions on many points while others deviate sharply on most of the items listed.

Table A.—Medians of Specified Economic and Social Indices for the Cotton Textile Subregion and for Greenville County, South Carolina, and Carroll County, Georgia

	Medians		
Specified indices	Cotton Textile Subregion (73 counties)	Greenville County, South Carolina	Carroll County, Georgia
Percent Negro 1930	31. 7	23. 8	22. 2
Percent illiteracy 1930	8. 7	8. 1	5. 5
Percent increase in population 1910–1920	[1] 7. 2	29. 4	12. 6
Percent increase in population 1920–1930	[2] 1. 1	32. 2	−1. 4
Percent tenancy 1930	68. 1	62. 7	67. 5
Value land and buildings per farm 1929	$2, 111	$3, 285	$1, 961
Value land and buildings per acre 1929	$30	$69	$39
Per capita retail trade 1929	$150	$265	$185
Inhabitants per telephone 1930	[3] 44. 8	26. 4	40. 6
Inhabitants per passenger car 1930	[4] 10. 5	6. 8	9. 9
Inhabitants per income tax return 1930	[5] 257. 5	69	346
Percent population under 20 years 1930	49. 1	47. 0	49. 1
Per capita value of manufactured products 1929	[6] $192	$495	$159

[1] Following 12 counties not included due to change in boundaries or organization of new county during the 1910–1920 period: Barrow, Campbell, Fulton, Gwinnett, Jackson, Lamar, and Walton, Ga.; Abbeville, Fairfield, Greenwood, Lexington, and Richland, S. C.
[2] Following 12 counties not included due to change in boundaries or organization of new county during the 1920–1930 period: Campbell, Fulton, Lamar, and Pike, Ga.; Cherokee, Kershaw, Lexington, Newberry, Richland, and York, S. C.; Elmore and Montgomery, Ala.
[3] Following 4 counties not included due to lack of census information: Haralson, Heard, and Paulding, Ga.; Randolph, Ala.
[4] Following 3 counties not included due to lack of census information: Haralson and Paulding, Ga.; Randolph, Ala.
[5] No report on income tax returns for Heard, Ga.
[6] Exclusive of 8 counties with less than 10 manufacturing employees.

Table B.—Medians of Specified Economic and Social Indices for the Coal and Iron Subregion and for Jefferson County, Alabama

	Medians	
Specified indices	Coal and Iron Subregion (10 counties)	Jefferson County, Alabama
Percent Negro 1930	23. 9	38. 9
Percent illiteracy 1930	8. 6	7. 5
Percent increase in population 1910–1920	16. 0	36. 9
Percent increase in population 1920–1930	[1] 10. 0	39. 2
Percent tenancy 1930	55. 9	42. 9
Value land and buildings per farm 1929	$1, 990	$4, 775
Value land and buildings per acre 1929	$26	$89
Per capita retail trade 1929	$171	$357
Inhabitants per telephone 1930	56. 4	15. 1
Inhabitants per passenger car 1930	11. 8	8. 5
Inhabitants per income tax return 1930	184. 5	34. 0
Percent population under 20 years 1930	47. 4	39. 4
Per capita value of manufactured products 1929	$193	$559

[1] Following 2 counties not included due to change in boundaries: Calhoun and Etowah, Ala.

Table C.—Medians of Specified Economic and Social Indices for the Atlantic Coast Subregion and for Charleston County, South Carolina

	Medians	
Specified indices	Atlantic Coast Subregion (9 counties)	Charleston County, South Carolina
Percent Negro 1930	59. 1	54. 2
Percent illiteracy 1930	13. 4	17. 0
Percent increase in population 1910–1920	[1] 2. 5	([1])
Percent increase in population 1920–1930	[2] 0. 1	([2])
Percent tenancy 1930	20. 8	31. 8
Value land and buildings per farm 1929	$2, 469	$4, 621
Value land and buildings per acre 1929	$20	$58
Per capita retail trade 1929	$105	$267
Inhabitants per telephone 1930	92. 9	19. 1
Inhabitants per passenger car 1930	13. 1	9. 1
Inhabitants per income tax return 1930	169	40
Percent population under 20 years 1930	46. 7	42. 9
Per capita value of manufactured products 1929	$124	$322

[1] Following 2 counties not included due to change in boundaries: Beaufort and Charleston, S. C.
[2] Following 2 counties not included due to change in boundaries: Liberty, Ga., and Charleston, S. C.

Table D.—Medians of Specified Economic and Social Indices for the Lumber Subregion and for Sumter County, South Carolina

Specified indices	Medians	
	Lumber Subregion (104 counties)	Sumter County, South Carolina
Percent Negro 1930	57. 5	67. 5
Percent illiteracy 1930	15. 5	18. 9
Percent increase in population 1910–1920	[1] 1.8	(¹)
Percent increase in population 1920–1930	[2] −3.4	(²)
Percent tenancy 1930	72. 3	73. 8
Value land and buildings per farm 1929	$1,868	$2,397
Value land and buildings per acre 1929	$23	$43
Per capita retail trade 1929	$113	$192
Inhabitants per telephone 1930	[3] 52. 5	35. 2
Inhabitants per passenger car 1930	[4] 14. 4	10. 7
Inhabitants per income tax return 1930	397	126
Percent population under 20 years 1930	50. 4	53. 1
Per capita value of manufactured products 1929	[5] $58	$117

[1] Following 20 counties not included due to change in boundaries or organization of new county during the 1910–1920 period: Bleckley, Houston, Macon, Peach, and Pulaski, Ga.; Allendale, Bamberg, Barnwell, Berkeley, Clarendon, Colleton, Edgefield, Florence, Hampton, Jasper, Lee, McCormick, Orangeburg, Sumter, and Williamsburg, S. C.
[2] Following 14 counties not included due to change in boundaries or organization of new county during the 1920–1930 period: Houston, Macon, Monroe, and Peach, Ga.; Bamberg, Berkeley, Clarendon, Colleton, Edgefield, Florence, Lee, McCormick, Sumter, and Williamsburg, S. C.
[3] Following 5 counties not included due to lack of census information: Choctaw and Cleburne, Ala.; Chattahoochee, Glascock, and Quitman, Ga.
[4] Cleburne, Ala., not included due to lack of census information.
[5] Exclusive of 6 counties with less than 10 manufacturing employees.

Table E.—Medians of Specified Economic and Social Indices for the Naval Stores Subregion and for Coffee County, Georgia

Specified indices	Medians	
	Naval Stores Subregion (54 counties)	Coffee County, Georgia
Percent Negro 1930	34. 5	26. 6
Percent illiteracy 1930	11. 4	8. 8
Percent increase in population 1910–1920	[1] 15. 1	(¹)
Percent increase in population 1920–1930	[2] 2. 6	5. 8
Percent tenancy 1930	65. 4	63. 9
Value of land and buildings per farm 1929	$2,361	$2,634
Value of land and buildings per acre 1929	$25	$20
Per capita retail trade 1929	$119	$139
Inhabitants per telephone 1930	[3] 54. 3	39. 7
Inhabitants per passenger car 1930	14. 8	14. 7
Inhabitants per income tax return 1930	462	267
Percent population under 20 years 1930	51. 5	52. 6
Per capita value of manufactured products 1929	[4] $66	$59

[1] Following 22 counties not included due to change in boundaries or organization of new county during the 1910–1920 period: Appling, Atkinson, Bacon, Berrien, Bulloch, Brantley, Candler, Cook, Coffee, Clinch, Emanuel, Evans, Lanier, Long, Lowndes, Montgomery, Pierce, Tittnall, Trentlen, Seminole, Wate, and Wheeler, Ga.
[2] Following 11 counties not included due to change in boundaries or organization of new county during the 1920–1930 period: Berrien, Brantley, Charlton, Clinch, Decatur, Lanier, Long, Lowndes, Pierce, Seminole, and Wayne, Ga.
[3] Echols, Ga., not included due to lack of census information.
[4] Exclusive of 1 county with less than 10 manufacturing employees.

SELECTION OF CASES FOR ENUMERATION

After sufficiently typical counties were selected, the next problem was that of determining how cases should be selected for enumeration in the field.

Since the survey dealt with combined farming and industrial employment, the part-time farmers were to be found in the vicinity of centers of employment. Hence, for each selected county a center, or centers, of the leading manufacturing or extractive industry was designated. Thus, the textile mill areas of the city of Greenville were the centers of enumeration for Greenville County. Carrollton and two small neighboring mill towns were the centers of enumeration for Carroll County.

As both time and field staff were limited, and as it was desired to limit the sample to homogeneous and specific industrial and occupational groups, the types of cases to be enumerated in each county were definitely specified.

In view of the primary interest of this study in problems connected with low income groups, the occupational classifications to be enumerated were limited to clerical and kindred occupations, and skilled, semiskilled, and unskilled occupations as classified by Dr. Alba M. Edwards of the Bureau of the Census.[2] Certain groups within these classifications were also omitted to give a sample within a fairly limited income and status range (table G).

For each center of enumeration, the industries within which to enumerate the full-time workers were specified. The only limitation put on the comparable sample of part-time farmers was that they be in the same general locality (same or contiguous townships) and that their nonfarm occupations fall in the groups indicated above. The assumption was that in most cases part-time farmers would be enumerated who were in the same industrial and occupational classifications as the full-time workers.

Since industries differed as to the employment opportunities they offered Negroes and whites, a policy was adopted of taking white samples only in industries that employed whites chiefly (i. e., textile mills); Negroes only in industries that employed Negroes chiefly (i. e., lumbering and sawmilling); and a divided sample in those industries that offered considerable employment opportunity for both racial groups (i. e., iron and steel mills or mining). In each case, the same restrictions as to race were applied to full-time workers and to part-time farmers. Table F indicates the number sought in each category and the actual sample enumerated.

Further criteria for the selection of the cases to be enumerated in the part-time farm and nonfarming industrial groups, as specified in

---

[2] See *Journal of American Statistical Association*, December 1933, pp. 377–387.

the instructions accompanying the household schedules, were as follows:

Selection of Full-Time Industrial Families

1. Include only households which had male heads who were physically capable of working at a full-time job during 1934.

2. Include only households whose heads were employed for at least 50 days each in 1933 and in 1934 in clerical and kindred occupations, and skilled, semiskilled, and unskilled occupations, with the exceptions indicated on the list of occupations (table G).

3. Do not include families operating (whether owning or renting) as much as three-fourths of an acre of tillable land in either 1933 or 1934 or who produced farm products valued at $50 or more in 1933 or 1934.

Table F.—Size of Sample Sought in Each County, by Industry [1] and by Color, and Actual Sample Enumerated

County	Part-time farmers				Nonfarming industrial workers			
	White		Negro		White		Negro	
	Sample sought	Sample enumerated	Sample sought	Sample enumerated	Sample sought	Sample enumerated	Sample sought	Sample enumerated
Total	775	715	335	398	750	780	450	554
Greenville, S. C.	200	190			200	216		
Industries to be sampled: Textile Manufacturing other than textile Service								
Carroll, Ga.	100	103			100	98		
Industry to be sampled: Textile								
Jefferson, Ala.	200	204	100	124	200	222	250	346
Industries to be sampled: Coal mining Iron mining Iron and steel milling								
Charleston, S. C.	75	71	135	142	100	103	100	105
Industries to be sampled: Any manufacturing or allied industry except forestry, sawmill, woodworking, iron and steel, or textile								
Sumter, S. C.	100	76	100	132	100	92	100	103
Industries to be sampled: Forestry, sawmill, woodworking								
Coffee, Ga.	100	71			50	49		
Industry to be sampled: Turpentine and rosin								

[1] Industrial restrictions were not applied to part-time farmers.

Selection of Part-Time Farm Families

1. Include only heads of households supplementarily engaged off the farm in 1934 in clerical and kindred occupations, and skilled, semiskilled, and unskilled occupations, with the exceptions indicated on the list of occupations (table G).

2. Do not include families operating (whether owning or renting) less than three-fourths of an acre of tillable land in 1934 unless they produced farm products valued at $50 or more in 1934.

3. Include only families that have been operating the same farm at least since January 1, 1933. They may have been full-time farmers in 1933 or before, in which case they are eligible for enumeration provided that they were part-time farmers in 1934.

4. The total number of days of "off this farm" employment for the head of the household must have been at least 50 in 1934.

5. Include only households which had a male head who was physically capable of working at a full-time job in 1934.

In each case the oldest able-bodied male (physically capable of holding a full-time job) between the ages of 18 and 64 inclusive in 1934 was considered the head of the household. Households which did not have an able-bodied male between the ages of 18 and 64 in 1934 were not enumerated.

METHOD OF ENUMERATION

In enumerating full-time industrial workers, the field man went from house to house along the streets previously selected as representing the industry to be sampled until he had secured the prescribed number of cases that met the conditions of eligibility for enumeration.

In enumerating part-time farmers, the main and auxiliary highways of the townships contiguous to the enumeration center were mapped out. The enumerator assigned to the part-time farm sample was instructed to cover the roads in one township and to enumerate all part-time farmers who met the conditions of eligibility. When one township was thus covered, he proceeded to do the same for the adjacent one; and so on until the required number of qualified cases had been enumerated.

The cases enumerated were spotted on a map. In each section of this report dealing with the individual counties, these maps are exhibited, and it will be seen that the cases are fairly well distributed.

STUDY OF INDUSTRIES

The chief manufacturing and extractive industries of each subregion were carefully studied. Special tabulations by counties were made from the original schedules of the Census of Manufactures for 1929, 1931, and 1933. Special tabulations of the 1930 Census, reports of the Bureau of Labor Statistics, and Federal Emergency Relief Administration studies of the usual occupations of relief clients were used. Other principal sources of data were the following: the Bureau of Mines, Department of Agriculture, Department of Labor, Department of Commerce, Federal Trade Commission, N. R. A. reports, and trade publications. The material was analyzed by expert industrial engineers.

In addition to this material, field inspection of the selected industries in each of the six counties was made by the engineers.

Table G.—Gainful Workers in the United States Classified Into Social-Economic Groups,[1]
by Occupation: 1930

GROUPS AND OCCUPATION

CLERKS AND KINDRED WORKERS:

       Inspectors, scalers, and surveyors—log and timber camps.[2]
       Baggagemen and freight agents—railroad.
       Ticket and station agents—railroad agents—express companies.[2]
       Express messengers and railway mail clerks.
       Mail carriers.
       Radio operators.
       Telegraph messengers.
       Telegraph operators.
       Telephone operators.
       Advertising agents.[2]
       "Clerks" in stores.
       Commercial travelers.[2]
       Decorators, drapers, and window dressers.[2]
       Inspectors, gaugers, and samplers—trade.
       Insurance agents.[2]
       Newsboys.
       Real-estate agents.[2]
       Salesmen and saleswomen.
       Abstracters, notaries, and justices of peace.[2]
       Architects, designers, and draftsmen's apprentices.[2]
       Apprentices to other professional persons.
       Officials of lodges, societies.[2]
       Technicians and laboratory assistants.
       Dentists' assistants and attendants.
       Librarians' assistants and attendants.
       Physicians' and surgeons' attendants.
       Agents, collectors, and credit men.
       Bookkeepers, cashiers, and accountants.
       Clerks (except "clerks" in stores).
       Messenger, errand, and office boys and girls.
       Stenographers and typists.

SKILLED WORKERS AND FOREMEN:

       Farm managers and foremen.
       Foremen—log and timber camps.
       Foremen, overseers, and inspectors—extraction of minerals.
       Blacksmiths, forgemen, and hammermen.
       Boilermakers.
       Brick and stone masons and tile layers.
       Cabinetmakers.
       Carpenters.
       Compositors, linotypers, and typesetters.
       Coopers.
       Electricians.

---

[1] Exclusive of *Professional Persons* and of *Proprietors, Managers, and Officials.*
[2] Excluded from enumeration.

SKILLED WORKERS AND FOREMEN—Continued.

    Electrotypers, stereotypers, and lithographers.
    Engineers (stationary), cranemen, hoistmen, etc.
    Engravers.
    Foremen and overseers—manufacturing.
    Puddlers.
    Glass blowers.
    Jewelers, watchmakers, goldsmiths, and silversmiths.
    Loom fixers.
    Machinists, millwrights, and toolmakers.
    Mechanics.[3]
    Millers (grain, flour, feed, etc.).
    Molders, founders, and casters (metal).
    Painters, glaziers, and varnishers (building).
    Paper hangers.
    Pattern and model makers.
    Piano and organ tuners.
    Plasterers and cement finishers.
    Plumbers and gas and steam fitters.
    Pressmen and plate printers (printing).
    Rollers and roll hands (metal).
    Roofers and slaters.
    Sawyers.
    Shoemakers and cobblers (not in factory).
    Skilled occupations (not elsewhere classified).
    Stonecutters.
    Structural ironworkers (building).
    Tailors and tailoresses.
    Tinsmiths and coppersmiths.
    Upholsterers.
    Bus conductors.
    Conductors—street railroad.
    Foremen and overseers—steam and street railroads.
    Locomotive engineers.
    Locomotive firemen.
    Aviators.
    Foremen and overseers [3]—transportation.
    Inspectors—transportation.
    Floorwalkers, foremen, and overseers—trade.
    Firemen—fire department.
    Marshals, sheriffs, detectives, etc.
    Policemen.
    Foremen and overseers—cleaning, dyeing, and pressing shops.
    Foremen and overseers—laundries.

SEMISKILLED WORKERS:

    Semiskilled Workers in Manufacturing:
        Apprentices to building and hand trades.
        Apprentices (except to building and hand trades)—manufacturing.
        Bakers.
        Dressmakers and seamstresses.
        Dyers.
        Filers, grinders, buffers, and polishers (metal).

---

[3] Not otherwise specified.

SEMISKILLED WORKERS—Continued.

　Semiskilled Workers in Manufacturing—Continued.

　　Milliners and millinery dealers.
　　Oilers of machinery.
　　Enamelers, lacquerers, and japanners.
　　Painters, glaziers, and varnishers (factory).
　　Operatives [3]—manufacturing.

　Other Semiskilled Workers:

　　Boatmen, canal men, and lock keepers.
　　Sailors and deck hands.
　　Chauffeurs and truck and tractor drivers.
　　Boiler washers and engine hostlers.
　　Brakemen—steam railroad.
　　Motormen—steam and street railroads.
　　Switchmen, flagmen, and yardmen—steam and street railroads.
　　Telegraph and telephone linemen.
　　Apprentices—transportation.
　　Other occupations—transportation.
　　Apprentices—wholesale and retail trade.
　　Deliverymen—bakeries and stores.
　　Other pursuits in trade.
　　Guards, watchmen, and doorkeepers.
　　Soldiers, sailors, and marines.
　　Other public service pursuits.
　　Other occupations—professional service.
　　Attendants—pool rooms, bowling alleys, golf clubs, etc.
　　Helpers—motion picture production.
　　Theater ushers.
　　Other attendants and helpers—professional service.
　　Barbers, hairdressers, and manicurists.
　　Boarding and lodging house keepers.
　　Other operatives—cleaning, dyeing, and pressing shops.
　　Housekeepers and stewards.
　　Deliverymen—laundries.
　　Other operatives—laundries.
　　Midwives and nurses (not trained).
　　Other pursuits—domestic and personal service.

UNSKILLED WORKERS:

　Farm Laborers.

　Factory and Building Construction Laborers:

　　Firemen (except locomotive and fire department).
　　Furnacemen, smelter men, and pourers.
　　Heaters (metal).
　　Laborers [3]—manufacturing.

　Other Laborers:

　　Fishermen and oystermen.
　　Teamsters and haulers—log and timber camps.
　　Other lumbermen, raftsmen, and woodchoppers.
　　Coal mine operatives.
　　Other operatives in extraction of minerals.
　　Longshoremen and stevedores.
　　Draymen, teamsters, and carriage drivers.

---

[3] Not otherwise specified.

UNSKILLED WORKERS—Continued.
    Other Laborers—Continued.
        Garage laborers.
        Hostlers and stablehands.
        Laborers—truck, transfer, and cab companies.
        Laborers—road and street.
        Laborers, including construction laborers—steam and street railroads.
        Laborers [3]—transportation.
        Laborers in coal and lumber yards, warehouses, etc.
        Laborers, porters, and helpers in stores.
        Laborers—public service.
        Laborers—professional service.
        Laborers—recreation and amusement.
        Stagehands and circus helpers.
        Laborers—cleaning, dyeing, and pressing shops.
        Laborers—domestic and personal service.
        Laborers—laundries.
    Servant Class:
        Bootblacks.
        Charwomen and cleaners.
        Elevator tenders.
        Janitors and sextons.
        Launderers and laundresses (not in laundry).
        Porters (except in stores).
        Servants.
        Waiters.

---

[3] Not otherwise specified.

Source: Edwards, Alba M., "A Social-Economic Grouping of the Gainful Workers of the United States," *Journal of the American Statistical Association*, December 1933, pp. 377–387.

Appendix D

COUNTIES IN INDUSTRIAL SUBREGIONS

I. Textile

Alabama:
  Chambers
  Elmore
  Lee
  Montgomery
  Randolph
  Russell
  Tallapoosa
Georgia:
  Banks
  Barrow
  Bartow
  Butts
  Campbell
  Carroll
  Catoosa
  Chattooga
  Cherokee
  Clarke
  Clayton
  Cobb
  Coweta
  De Kalb
  Douglas
  Elbert
  Fayette

Georgia—Continued.
  Floyd
  Franklin
  Fulton
  Gordon
  Gwinnett
  Habersham
  Hall
  Haralson
  Harris
  Hart
  Heard
  Henry
  Jackson
  Lamar
  Madison
  Meriwether
  Muscogee
  Newton
  Paulding
  Pike
  Polk
  Richmond
  Rockdale
  Spalding
  Stephens

Georgia—Continued.
  Troup
  Upson
  Walker
  Walton
  Whitfield
South Carolina:
  Abbeville
  Aiken
  Anderson
  Cherokee
  Chester
  Fairfield
  Greenville
  Greenwood
  Kershaw
  Lancaster
  Laurens
  Lexington
  Newberry
  Oconee
  Pickens
  Richland
  Spartanburg
  Union
  York

II. Coal and Iron

Alabama:
  Bibb
  Blount
  Calhoun
  Etowah

Alabama—Continued.
  Jefferson
  St. Clair
  Shelby
  Talladega

Alabama—Continued.
  Tuscaloosa
  Walker

III. Atlantic Coast

Georgia:
  Bryan
  Camden
  Chatham

Georgia—Continued.
  Glynn
  Liberty
  McIntosh

South Carolina:
  Beaufort
  Charleston
  Georgetown

IV. Lumber

Alabama:
  Autauga
  Barbour
  Bullock
  Butler
  Cherokee
  Chilton
  Choctaw
  Clarke
  Clay
  Cleburne
  Coffee
  Conecuh
  Coosa
  Crenshaw
  Cullman
  Dale
  Dallas
  Fayette
  Franklin
  Greene
  Hale
  Henry
  Lamar
  Lowndes
  Macon
  Marengo
  Marion
  Monroe
  Perry
  Pickens
  Pike
  Sumter
  Wilcox
  Winston
Georgia:
  Baldwin

Georgia—Continued.
  Bibb
  Bleckley
  Burke
  Calhoun
  Chattahoochee
  Clay
  Columbia
  Crawford
  Crisp
  Dooly
  Dougherty
  Glascock
  Greene
  Hancock
  Houston
  Jasper
  Jefferson
  Jones
  Lee
  Lincoln
  McDuffie
  Macon
  Marion
  Monroe
  Morgan
  Oconee
  Oglethorpe
  Peach
  Pulaski
  Putnam
  Quitman
  Randolph
  Schley
  Stewart
  Sumter
  Talbot

Georgia—Continued,
  Taliaferro
  Taylor
  Terrell
  Twiggs
  Warren
  Washington
  Webster
  Wilkes
  Wilkinson
South Carolina:
  Allendale
  Bamberg
  Barnwell
  Berkeley
  Calhoun
  Chesterfield
  Clarendon
  Colleton
  Darlington
  Dillon
  Dorchester
  Edgefield
  Florence
  Hampton
  Horry
  Jasper
  Lee
  McCormick
  Marion
  Marlboro
  Orangeburg
  Saluda
  Sumter
  Williamsburg

V. Naval Stores

Alabama:
  Covington
  Escambia
  Geneva
  Houston
  Washington

Georgia:
  Appling
  Atkinson
  Bacon
  Baker
  Ben Hill

Georgia—Continued.
  Berrien
  Brantley
  Brooks
  Bulloch
  Candler

Georgia—Continued.
  Charlton
  Clinch
  Coffee
  Colquitt
  Cook
  Decatur
  Dodge
  Early
  Echols
  Effingham
  Emanuel
  Evans
  Grady

Georgia—Continued.
  Irwin
  Jeff Davis
  Jenkins
  Johnson
  Lanier
  Laurens
  Long
  Lowndes
  Miller
  Mitchell
  Montgomery
  Pierce
  Screven

Georgia—Continued.
  Seminole
  Tattnall
  Telfair
  Thomas
  Tift
  Toombs
  Treutlen
  Turner
  Ware
  Wayne
  Wheeler
  Wilcox
  Worth

Appendix E

SCHEDULES

F.E.R.A. DRS-138

STATE_____

COUNTY_____ .

TOWNSHIP OR DISTRICT_____ .

FEDERAL EMERGENCY RELIEF ADMINISTRATION
HARRY L. HOPKINS, ADMINISTRATOR
DIVISION OF RESEARCH, STATISTICS, AND FINANCE
CORRINGTON GILL, DIRECTOR

PART-TIME FARM SCHEDULE

ENUMERATORS RECORD NO._____

DATE TAKEN_____

ENUMERATOR_____

LINE NUMBER	NAME OF EACH MEMBER OF HOUSEHOLD	RELATION TO HEAD	AGE	LAST GRADE IN SCHOOL COMPLETED	IN SCHOOL DURING LAST SCHOOL YEAR	STATE OF BIRTH (COUNTRY IF OTHER THAN U.S.)	COLOR OR RACE	AVERAGE NUMBER OF HOURS PER DAY WORKED ON THE FARM IN EACH MONTH IN 1934 (EXCLUDE HOUSEWORK) J F M A M J J A S O N D	NUMBER OF DAYS INCAPACITATED FOR WORK IN 1934	ANY PERMANENT PHYSICAL HANDICAP SPECIFY	MILES TO PLACE OF USUAL EMPLOYMENT	MEANS OF TRANSPORTATION	TIME REQUIRED FOR ROUND TRIP	FREQUENCY OF MAKING TRIP
A	1	2	3	4	5	6	7	8	9	10	11	12	13	14
1														
2														
3														
4														
5														
6														
7														
8														
9														
10														
11														
12														
13														
14														
15														

B EMPLOYMENT OF HEAD OF HOUSEHOLD OFF THIS FARM 1934:

	NAME OF FIRM AND/OR PLACE WHERE WORK IS USUALLY DONE	SPECIFIC OCCUPATION	TYPE OF BUSINESS OR INDUSTRY	NUMBER OF FULL DAYS EMPLOYED IN: J F M A M J J A S O N D	TOTAL	AVERAGE HOURS PER DAY WORKED	AVERAGE HOURLY RATE OF PAY	TOTAL EARNED FROM THIS EMPLOYMENT 1934
	1	2	3	4	5	6	7	8
1								
2								
3								
4								

C PRINCIPAL EMPLOYMENT OF HEAD OF HOUSE OFF THE FARM IN 1929: OCCUPATION_____ ;
TYPE OF BUSINESS OR INDUSTRY_____ ; AMOUNT EARNED IN 1929 FROM THIS EMPLOYMENT_____

D EMPLOYMENT OF OTHER MEMBERS OF THE HOUSEHOLD OFF THIS FARM IN 1934:

"A" SECTION LINE NUMBER OF THE PERSON	SPECIFIC OCCUPATION	TYPE OF BUSINESS OR INDUSTRY	TOTAL EARNED IN THIS EMPLOYMENT 1934
1	2	3	4
1			
2			
3			
4			
5			
6			

E INCOME FROM ANY SOURCE OTHER THAN FARM OR EMPLOYMENT INDICATED IN B AND D 1934:

"A" SECTION LINE NUMBER OF THE PERSON	SOURCE	AMOUNT IN 1934
1	2	3
1		
2		
3		
4		
5		
6		

F.

LINE NO.	CROPS AND LIVESTOCK PRODUCTS 1934	PRODUCTIVE UNITS	CROPS HARVESTED AND LIVESTOCK PRODUCTS	J	F	M	A	M	J	J	A	S	O	N	D	QUARTS CANNED	QUANTITY STORED, DRIED OR CURED	QUANTITY SOLD	RECEIPTS
		1	2							3						4	5	6	7
1	A. GARDEN	A.	X	X	X	X	X	X	X	X	X	X	X	X	X	X			
2	IRISH POTATOES		X													X			
3	SWEET POTATOES		X													X			
4	TOMATOES		X														X		
5	OKRA		X																
6	PEAS		X																
7	SNAP BEANS		X														X		
8	LIMA BEANS		X																
9	CABBAGE		X													X	X		
10	LETTUCE		X													X	X		
11	PEPPERS		X													X			
12	SQUASH		X																
13	CUCUMBERS		X														X		
14	ASPARAGUS		X														X		
15	RHUBARB		X														X		
16	BEETS		X																
17	CARROTS		X																
18	ONIONS		X																
19	RADISHES		X													X	X		
20	TURNIPS		X													X			
21	COLLARDS		X														X		
22	WATERMELONS		X													X	X		
23	CANTALOUPES		X													X	X		
24	OTHER		X																
25																			
26																			
27	B. FRUITS	X NO TRS.	X BU.	X	X	X	X	X	X	X	X	X	X	X	X		X		
28	APPLES	NO TRS.	BU.																
29	PEACHES																		
30	BERRIES	NO BSH.	QT.																
31																			
32	OTHER																		
33																			
34	C. DAIRY PRODUCTS	X	X	X	X	X	X	X	X	X	X	X	X	X	X	X	X		
35	MILK	X	QT.													X	X		
36	BUTTER	X	LB.													X			
37	CHEESE	X	LB.													X			
38	OTHER	X														X			
39		X														X			
40	D. POULTRY	X	X	X	X	X	X	X	X	X	X	X	X	X	X	X	X		
41	MEAT	X	B.														X		
42	EGGS	X	DZ.													X			
43	E. LIVESTOCK PROD.	X	X	X	X	X	X	X	X	X	X	X	X	X	X	X	X		
44	PORK	X	LB.																
45	VEAL	X	LB.																
46	OTHER	X																	
47		X																	
48	F. FIELD CROPS	X	X	FED												X	X	X	X
49	CORN	A.	BU.													X			
50	COTTON		BALES		X											X	X		
51	TOBACCO		LB.		X											X	X		
52	PEANUTS		LB.													X			
53	OTHER ANN. LEGUMES		LB.													X			
54	HAY		TON													X			
55	SORGHUM		GAL.													X			
56	SUGARCANE		GAL.													X			
57	OTHER																		
58																			
59																			
60																			
61	G. FUEL	X	CDS. OR TONS	X												X	X		
62		X		X															
63	H. MISCELLANEOUS	X	X	X															
64	HONEY	X	LB.	X															
65	OTHER	X																	
66																			
67																			
68																			
69																			

G.

1 WAS GROCERY BILL LESS MAY–OCTOBER THAN DURING WINTER MONTHS? _____
    IF SO HOW MUCH PER MONTH? _____
2 APPARENT STANDARD OF LIVING: 1   2   3   4   5

H.

	FARM LAND OPERATED	1934	1929
		1	2
1	CROP LAND	A	A
2	PASTURE		
3	WOOD LAND		
4	OTHER		
5	TOTAL		

I.

	TENURE	1934	1929
		1	2
1	ACRES OWNED		
2	ACRES RENTED		
3	IF PLACE IS OWNED WHAT WOULD IT RENT FOR NOW _____		

J.

	LIVESTOCK: JAN. 1	1934	1929
		1	2
1	HORSES AND MULES		
2	MILK CATTLE		
3	OTHER CATTLE		
4	SWINE		
5	POULTRY		
6	OTHER (SPECIFY)		

K.

	FARM EXPENSES	1934
1	HIRED LABOR	
2	FEED	
3	FERTILIZER	
4	LIVESTOCK PURCHASED	
5	SUPPLIES	
6	MACHINERY REPAIRS	
7	INSURANCE	
8	TAXES	
9	RENT	
10	OTHER	
11	TOTAL	

L. DESCRIPTION OF WAY DAY, WEEK, MONTH OR YEAR IS DIVIDED BETWEEN FARM WORK AND OTHER EMPLOYMENT

_____
_____
_____
_____
_____
_____
_____
_____

M. IMPORTANT IMPLEMENTS OR MACHINERY 1934

	KIND OF MACH. OR IMPL.	SIZE	AGE	COST NEW
1				
2				
3				
4				
5				
6				
7				

N.

1 NUMBER OF YEARS HEAD OF HOUSE HAS BEEN ON THIS FARM_____

2 NUMBER YEARS HEAD HAS BEEN A PART-TIME FARMER SINCE 1929_____

3 CHECK RESIDENCE OF HEAD OF HOUSE ON OCT. 1ST, 1929:
OPEN COUNTRY____; VILLAGE____; TOWN____; CITY____

4 NUMBER OF CHANGES IN RESIDENCE MADE BY HEAD OF HOUSE SINCE
OCT. 1ST, 1929_____.

5 NUMBER OF YEARS HEAD OF HOUSE HAS LIVED ON A FARM SINCE HE WAS
SIXTEEN YEARS OF AGE_____.

O.

1 KINDS OF WORK PERFORMED ON FARM IN 1934 (EXCLUSIVE OF HOUSEWORK): BY WIFE_____
BY OLDER CHILDREN_____; BY YOUNGER CHILDREN_____

2 KINDS OF WORK PERFORMED ON FARM IN 1929 (EXCLUSIVE OF HOUSEWORK): BY WIFE_____.
BY OLDER CHILDREN_____; BY YOUNGER CHILDREN_____

3 NUMBER OF ACRES IN GARDEN IN 1929_____

P.

1 DWELLING: TYPE OF CONSTRUCTION_____; DIMENSIONS_____; NUMBER OF STORIES____; YEAR CONSTRUCTED_____.
NUMBER OF ROOMS_____; RUNNING WATER_____; BATHROOM WITH RUNNING WATER_____; ELECTRIC LIGHTS_____;
CONDITION OF DWELLING_____

2 OTHER CONVENIENCES: TELEPHONE_____; RADIO_____; AUTOMOBILE (YEAR AND MAKE)_____

3 OTHER BUILDINGS (CHECK THOSE PRESENT): BARN____; GARAGE____; POULTRY HOUSE____; OTHER (SPECIFY)_____

4 TYPE OF ROAD ON WHICH THIS FARM IS LOCATED: CONCRETE____; HARD SURFACED____; GRADED____; DIRT____

5 HOW FAR IS THIS FARM FROM A HARD SURFACED ROAD_____

Q. INDICATE BY "A" SECTION LINE NUMBER THE FREQUENCY OF ATTENDANCE OF EACH PERSON IN THE HOUSEHOLD AT THOSE ORGANIZATIONS LISTED
BELOW WHICH EXIST IN THE COMMUNITY (INFORMATION AS OF 1934):

	SOCIAL ORGANIZATION	DID ORGANIZATION EXIST IN COMMUNITY IN 1934	NUMBER MONTHS ACTIVE IN 1934	TIMES PER MONTH MEETS WHEN ACTIVE	NO ATTENDANCE	LESS THAN ONCE PER MONTH	ONCE PER MONTH	TWICE PER MONTH	THREE TIMES PER MONTH	FOUR OR MORE TIMES PER MONTH	HELD OFFICE IN 1934
							ATTENDANCE IN 1934				
		1	2	3	4	5	6	7	8	9	10
1	CHURCH										
2	ADULT CHURCH ORGANIZATION										
3	YOUNG PEOPLES ORGANIZATION										
4	SUNDAY SCHOOL										
5	SCHOOL CLUB										
6	ATHLETIC TEAM										
7	FRATERNAL ORDER										
8	LABOR UNION										
9	TRADE OR BUSINESS ASSOCIATION										
10	LIBRARY										
11	P.T.A.										
12	BOY SCOUTS										
13	GIRL SCOUTS										
14	COOPERATIVES										
15	OTHER WOMENS ORGANIZATIONS										
16	4-H CLUB										
17	SPECIAL INTEREST GROUP										
18	OTHER										

R.

1 AMOUNT OF INDEBTEDNESS JAN. 1ST, 1935: REAL ESTATE MORTGAGE_____; CHATTEL MORTGAGE_____.

2 AMOUNT OF INDEBTEDNESS JAN. 1ST, 1930: REAL ESTATE MORTGAGE_____; CHATTEL MORTGAGE_____.

S. AMOUNT IN DOLLARS OF RELIEF AND AID RECEIVED BY THIS HOUSEHOLD:

		1929	1930	1931	1932	1933	1934	1935
		1	2	3	4	5	6	7
1	PUBLIC (GOVERNMENTAL) RELIEF							
2	PRIVATE (EXCLUSIVE OF HELP FROM RELATIVES) RELIEF							
3	HELP FROM RELATIVES							

F.E.R.A. FORM DRS-139

STATE _____

COUNTY _____

TOWNSHIP OR DISTRICT _____

STREET AND HOUSE NUMBER _____

FEDERAL EMERGENCY RELIEF ADMINISTRATION

HARRY L. HOPKINS, ADMINISTRATOR

DIVISION OF RESEARCH, STATISTICS AND FINANCE

CORRINGTON GILL, DIRECTOR

FULL-TIME INDUSTRIAL SCHEDULE

ENUMERATOR'S RECORD NO. _____

DATE TAKEN _____

ENUMERATOR _____

LINE NUMBER	NAME OF EACH MEMBER OF THE HOUSEHOLD	RELATION TO THE HEAD	AGE	LAST GRADE IN SCHOOL COMPLETED	IN SCHOOL DURING LAST SCHOOL YEAR	STATE OF BIRTH (COUNTRY IF OTHER THAN U. S.)	COLOR OR RACE	NUMBER OF DAYS IN-CAPACITATED FOR WORK IN 1934	ANY PERMANENT PHYSICAL HANDICAP (SPECIFY)	MILES TO PLACE OF USUAL EMPLOYMENT	MEANS OF TRANSPORTATION	TIME REQUIRED FOR ROUND TRIP	FREQUENCY OF MAKING TRIP
A	1	2	3	4	5	6	7	8	9	10	11	12	13
1													
2													
3													
4													
5													
6													
7													
8													
9													
10													
11													
12													
13													
14													
15													

B. EMPLOYMENT OF HEAD OF HOUSEHOLD IN 1934

	NAME OF FIRM AND/OR PLACE WHERE WORK IS DONE	SPECIFIC OCCUPATION	TYPE OF BUSINESS OR INDUSTRY	NUMBER FULL DAYS EMPLOYED IN: J F M A M J J A S O N D	TOTAL	AVERAGE HOURS PER DAY WORKED	AVERAGE HOURLY RATE OF PAY	TOTAL EARNED FROM THIS EMPLOYMENT IN 1934
	1	2	3	4	5	6	7	8
1								
2								
3								
4								

C. PRINCIPAL EMPLOYMENT OF HEAD OF HOUSE IN 1929: OCCUPATION _____ . TYPE OF BUSINESS OR INDUSTRY _____
AMOUNT EARNED IN 1929 FROM THIS EMPLOYMENT _____ . TOTAL CASH INCOME OF HEAD FROM ALL SOURCES IN 1929 _____
TOTAL CASH INCOME OF ALL OTHERS IN HOUSEHOLD FROM ALL SOURCES IN 1929 _____ .

D. EMPLOYMENT OF OTHER MEMBERS OF THE HOUSEHOLD IN 1934

"A" SECTION LINE NUMBER OF THE PERSON	SPECIFIC OCCUPATION	TYPE OF BUSINESS OR INDUSTRY	TOTAL EARNED IN THIS EMPLOYMENT IN 1934
1	2	3	4
1			
2			
3			
4			
5			
6			

E. INCOME FROM ANY SOURCE OTHER THAN EMPLOY-MENT INDICATED IN B AND D IN 1934

"A" SECTION LINE NUMBER OF THE PERSON	SOURCE	AMOUNT IN 1934
1	2	3
1		
2		
3		
4		
5		
6		

F.

1 DID THE HEAD OF THIS HOUSEHOLD DO ANY GARDENING OR FARMING IN 1934 _____ ; 1929 _____

2 NUMBER OF YEARS HEAD OF HOUSE HAS LIVED ON A FARM SINCE HE WAS SIXTEEN YEARS OF AGE _____

1 HOW LONG HAS HEAD OF HOUSE LIVED IN THIS COMMUNITY_____
2 NUMBER OF DIFFERENT COMMUNITIES HEAD HAS LIVED IN SINCE OCT. 1ST, 1929_____
3 CHECK RESIDENCE OF HEAD OF HOUSE ON OCT. 1ST, 1929: OPEN COUNTRY____; VILLAGE____; TOWN____ CITY____
4 CHECK TENURE OF THIS HOME: OWNED____; RENTED____; OWNED BY EMPLOYER____
5 IF HOME IS RENTED, WHAT IS ANNUAL RENTAL_____
6 IF HOME IS OWNED, WHAT WOULD IT RENT FOR (ANNUAL RENT)_____
7 DESCRIPTION OF DWELLING: TYPE_____; TYPE OF CONSTRUCTION_____; NUMBER STORIES____; NUMBER ROOMS____;
    RUNNING WATER____; BATHROOM WITH RUNNING WATER____; ELECTRIC LIGHTS____; CONDITION_____
8 OTHER CONVENIENCES: TELEPHONE____; RADIO____; AUTOMOBILE (YEAR AND MAKE)_____
9 TYPE OF STREET OR ROAD ON WHICH DWELLING IS LOCATED: CONCRETE____; OTHER HARD SURFACE____ GRADED____; DIRT____

H.   INDICATE BY "A" SECTION LINE NUMBER THE FREQUENCY OF ATTENDANCE OF EACH PERSON IN THIS HOUSEHOLD AT THOSE ORGANIZATIONS
     LISTED BELOW WHICH EXIST IN THE COMMUNITY (INFORMATION AS OF 1934)

	SOCIAL ORGANIZATION	DID ORGANIZATION EXIST IN THE COMMUNITY IN 1934	NUMBER MONTHS ACTIVE IN 1934	TIMES PER MONTH MEETS WHEN ACTIVE	ATTENDANCE IN 1934						HELD OFFICE IN 1934
					NO ATTEND-ANCE	LESS THAN ONCE PER MONTH	ONCE PER MONTH	TWICE PER MONTH	THREE TIMES PER MONTH	FOUR TIMES PER MONTH	
		1	2	3	4	5	6	7	8	9	10
1	CHURCH										
2	ADULT CHURCH ORGANIZATION										
3	YOUNG PEOPLES ORGANIZATION										
4	SUNDAY SCHOOL										
5	SCHOOL CLUBS										
6	ATHLETIC TEAMS										
7	FRATERNAL ORDERS										
8	LABOR UNIONS										
9	TRADE OR BUSINESS ASSOC.										
10	LIBRARY										
11	P.T.A.										
12	BOY SCOUTS										
13	GIRL SCOUTS										
14	4-H CLUB										
15	COOPERATIVES										
16	OTHER WOMEN'S ORGANIZ.										
17	SPECIAL INTEREST GROUPS										
18	OTHER										

I.

1 AMOUNT OF INDEBTEDNESS, JAN. 1ST, 1935: REAL ESTATE MORTGAGE_____; CHATTEL MORTGAGE_____
2 AMOUNT OF INDEBTEDNESS, JAN. 1ST, 1930: REAL ESTATE MORTGAGE_____; CHATTEL MORTGAGE_____

J.   AMOUNT IN DOLLARS OF RELIEF AND AID RECEIVED BY THIS HOUSEHOLD

		1929	1930	1931	1932	1933	1934	1935
		1	2	3	4	5	6	7
1	PUBLIC RELIEF (GOVERNMENTAL)							
2	PRIVATE RELIEF (EXCLUSIVE OF HELP FROM RELATIVES)							
3	HELP FROM RELATIVES							

K.   APPARENT STANDARD OF LIVING: 1, 2, 3.

Index

INDEX

○